Endless Horizons

100 Years of the Prettejohn Family in Kenya

Michael Prettejohn

Michael Prettejohn

ISBN# 978-9966-7570-3-6

Cover Painting: Mike Ghaui

Published by Old Africa Books

A division of Kifaru Educational and Editorial Consultants LTD

PO Box 65, Kijabe, 00220, Kenya

Printed by English Press, Nairobi

Dedication

This book is dedicated to my first grandson, Howard Henley, who lost his life at the early age of 18 to a hippopotamus. With his love of wildlife and the wide open spaces, he was following in the footsteps of his father and both grandfathers in professional hunting. Both grandfathers survived mauling by lion and other life killing incidents over many years, so it was particularly sad that Howard was taken from us at such a tender age.

Michael Prettejohn

Acknowledgements

My thanks to Sarah Seth-Smith for her excellent research and editing of the early chapters of this book. In addition, the other people who have supported in the final editing and story contributions to this book are: Tony Archer, Juliette Shears - Fundraiser for the Bongo Project - Barney Gaston and Martin Anderson.

Forward

By Tony Archer

Kenya is a unique country. Of all of Britain's former African colonies, Kenya alone has the most varied of habitats ranging from a seaboard to 17,040 foot Mount Kenya, heavily forested mountains, semi desert in the north and touching on Lake Victoria, the world's second largest lake, and all this divided by the Great Rift Valley with both its saline and fresh water lakes. To complement these features Kenya. has among the very best National Parks and Game Reserves in Africa.

Mike Prettejohn and I have known each other for over seventy years. I was his best man at his wedding to Gill, chief witness when he married Jane, and I knew Diane before Mike met her, she and I being Godparents to the same Becker family in Botswana. Mike's son Giles is also my Godson.

At Kenya's Independence in 1963 the African population stood at around 7,000.000 with 58,000 Europeans and some 250,000 Asians. Due to the Soldier Settlement Schemes following both the First and Second World Wars, an element with similar farming and education backgrounds was attracted to Kenya. The Asian community, many of whom came originally to help construct the Kenya & Uganda railway construction at the beginning of the century, stayed mostly in the towns and centred their lives around commerce and skilled practical operations. At that time Asians were not permitted to purchase or develop agricultural land.

During the Second World War when the majority of European young born in the early 1930s had reached education age, only six schools – three junior and three secondary – existed for primary and secondary schooling. Because of the strict fuel rationing during the war, the three-monthly up-country terms were mostly catered for by train transport. This meant that children from all over Kenya and some from Uganda and Tanganyika were confined to either boys' or girls' primary or secondary schools. Hence this very small community got to know one another very well over a four to five year period.

Mike and I fell directly into this category, both at Pembroke House, Gilgil, and the Prince of Wales School in Nairobi. While at these schools Mike and I used to periodically visit each other's parents and on several occasions I stayed with Mike at his grandparents, the Harries, with Jock, better known as 'Black Harries'. On one such occasion I will always remember during a sumptuous breakfast attended by many begging dogs, Jock putting a large blob of butter on his knife then wiping it off on a hound's nose before continuing to spread butter on his own toast!

We were fortunate enough to spend many holidays together exposed to Kenya's vast wildlife resources enjoying not only its magnitude, but also legally being allowed to hunt. Where else could a pair of teenagers shoot their first rhino together, followed later by an elephant a piece shot on license?

In this book, written with great modesty, Mike relates of his escapes from encounters of life threatening episodes with a rhino, a buffalo – finally killed by a bullet that ended up in Mike's backside – mauled by a cattle killing lion, and finally harmfully stabbed in his own home by a marauding gang, one member of whom used a family sword snatched off the sitting room wall to pierce Mike's abdomen. I do not know of any other Professional Hunter having survived so many injuries.

It is important that much of the history of the Prettejohn family's early involvement in Kenya and Southwest Africa is taken from written records by Joe, Mike's father. Mike's own crossing of the Sahara, both by land and air, is also substantiated by records and dates from diaries. Likewise his records of flying to many parts of Africa, and in particular his scientific involvement with Steve Collins collecting butterflies, is also accurately reported.

Not many people who have been involved in so much of the

above can also have been deeply implicated in serious farming and the development of the 1.5 million acre Galana Game & Ranching Scheme. This would not have been possible without the support of one of Mike's first safari clients, Martin Anderson. Marty and Mike did a great deal together. Marty recently wrote the history of the Galana Company and revisited Kenya at the age of 89 for a short stay in 2012.

In conclusion, many of us Kenya-born citizens, together with others, are very pleased that Old Africa has decided to publish this book in keeping with its vision of collecting 'Stories from East Africa's past.'

Mike's current work on the mountain bongo, at 80 years of age, is of extreme importance to the survival of this 'Critically Endangered' species, and must receive all possible support, both locally and internationally.

This book is a must to read for all interested in the early to recent development of Kenya, together with the numerous other events during the Prettejohn family's over 100 years of involvement in Kenya.

Introduction

As Churchill once wrote, "Luckily life is not so easy as all that; otherwise we should get to the end too quickly…" As you will read from the chapters that follow, life was not easy for the original settlers in Kenya. It required much determination, often long periods of solitude, and discomfort with tropical diseases and language barriers. But, for most Kenyans, they would not dream of exchanging this for an 'easy' life in suburbia! It was indeed the challenges and diversity of what one could do, in such an exciting, beautiful and extreme environment. For many this would be a dream (or nightmare, full of perils and danger) but for me it has been my inspiration, my passion and my life. I would not have exchanged this opportunity for the world. It has been a privilege to lead this life, and to share friendships with many such dedicated people. Many of these are now gone – my mentor Eric Rundgren, who almost an animal himself in many ways, taught me to hunt, to survive in the bush and the ways and habits of different animals. We spent many days together in the wilds, laughed long and loud, and sometimes almost cried with his bullying tactics, but as his apprentice, lessons were learnt and never to be forgotten. There were Bunny Allen, George Adamson, Raymond Hook, Pat Ayre as well as others of my own generation – Tony Archer, Tony Seth-Smith and many others. I spent time with all of them, laughing and listening to hunting tales of yore. As you will discover there have been numerous challenges and hardships at times, but as Churchill reflected these experiences are 'lucky' – and I agree completely with his sentiment.

As Elspeth Huxley reflected, if you live long enough you find, much to your surprise, that you have lived through a part of history; people and events that you recall as if they had lived yesterday vanish into a seamless past and turn into legends. This has especially been so in the case of British Colonial History in Africa, which ended over 40 years ago. Elderly colonials have become period pieces in their own lifetime; and now that they are obsolete and therefore harmless, a certain indulgence has crept into the general attitude towards them, softening the disdain in which they were previously held.

I hope our families will continue to enjoy this splendid country. With advancing technology, our lives will differ but hopefully the very essence of pure nature and adventure will remain.

M.G. Prettejohn, Mweiga 2012

Contents

Book One 1900 to 1952
Black Harries – The Story of Jock Harries
1	Black Harries	17
2	A Colony in the Making	20
3	Early Settlement	26
4	Lands & Cattle	30
5	The Great War	40
6	Acquisition and Jail	47
7	A new Beginning	51
8	Masailand	55
9	Zanzibar and South West	62
10	Otjihavera	68
11	Diamonds & Disappointment	72
12	Otjihavera revisited	77
13	Larmudiac	83

Book Two 1921 – 1963
The Story of Joe Prettejohn (my father) and his brother Dick
14	Dick Prettejohn	92
15	Early Days	97
16	Crossroads	109
17	A Falling Out	116
18	Coles Plain	133
19	The War	150
20	The Emergency	162

Book Three   1932 – now
M.G. Prettejohn – My Story
21	My Early days & School	186
22	School & Holidays - Breaking Bounds & Safaris	200
23	Leaving school, safaris & departure to England	217

24	The long way home	234
25	To ranching & professional hunting	261
26	A Hunting Synopsis & other Stories	288
27	Hunting Companions & African friends	317
28	Flying Safaris-Flights & Frights	328
29	Extending Ranching- The Galana & Taita Stories	360
30	Back to Conservation	401

Book One
1900 to 1952

Chapter One

BLACK HARRIES
THE STORY OF JOCK HARRIES

As I ran to escape a charging rhino, I realised I was losing ground. I turned and shot it in the head firing from the hip using a hefty old .600 double rifle, a German-made Robert Schuler that weighted 18 pounds. I had inherited the rifle from Jock Harries, the man I regarded as my grandfather because he had married my grandmother.

Generations of Kenya family relationships have evolved into tangled webs of interconnecting threads through marriage, divorce and re-marriage. Confusing to the outsider, and often painful and even tragic, these convolutions unravel in time without rancour because Kenya's white society is too small to allow it. Divorce in England in the early 1900s was rare, but the Prettejohn family's Kenya involvement began through separation and re-marriage. It could never be said, however, that the Prettejohn family was ever part of the rich Happy Valley set, whose reputation for decadent hedonism inspired the oft-repeated quip: "Are you married or do you live in Kenya?"

My grandmother Gwendoline Gwynne Howell and 'Jock' Herbert Michael Harries lived as children barely ten miles apart in Pembrokeshire. They grew up together as constant, inseparable companions. Their childhood love continued into adulthood, but as first cousins, children of two sisters, marriage would be denied them by law. At the age of twenty my grandmother married Richard Buckley Prettejohn. They had four children: Uncle Dick, my father

Howel, or Joe as he was known, and twins, Aunts Bertha and Gwenydd. Bertha died young from peritonitis. Four years after my grandmother's marriage to Richard Prettejohn, her childhood friend Jock left Pembrokeshire to make his life in Kenya in 1904.

Even with my grandmother's affections focused on Jock, my grandparent's marriage would probably have been workable but loveless. Over the years, though, with my Grandfather Prettejohn spending much time on plantations in India, the two simply grew apart. Inevitably my grandmother and Jock, despite the social constraints and the years they had been separated, finally chose to live together.

Kenya, where the less restrictive Indian colonial law prevailed, particularly with regards to marriage, provided the solution. My grandmother separated from Richard Prettejohn and went to Kenya to marry Jock Harries. My father, then at school at Wellington, first learned of all this aged seventeen.

Perhaps due to the stigma of divorce at the time and the moral dilemma caused by my grandmother's remarriage to Jock, there is a void surrounding my grandfather Prettejohn, which incuriosity on my part until now, and a lack of correspondence, has not entirely filled. I never knew my grandfather Prettejohn. My memories are of Jock Harries, who married my grandmother and usurped that role.

Just short of six feet tall, Jock was immensely strong with a broad chest matched by muscled arms and shoulders. He wore a prominent bushy moustache that offset his swarthy complexion. Although I only remember him from his late fifties, when he had grown somewhat stouter, he never lost that confident military bearing and became in many ways better looking with a raffish air and winning smile. The quality most people remember was his voice: melodious and clear, an actor's voice that belied his brigand-like appearance. Headstrong and physically imposing, he could be described as a bull of a man in the admired African sense of *dume*, but there was something of the bully in him too. He could be difficult over money matters although the trappings of money meant nothing to him. He was unconventional – a character they said – who disdained the rules by which society normally lives, and did pretty much as he pleased. That's not to say he was discourteous. On the contrary, he had great charm. However, he was known to be cantankerous and quick to lose his temper, and relentlessly unforgiving when slighted. Neither a party nor a club man, he had no time for small talk, nor did he feel the need to keep up appearances. He tended to quarrel with his neighbours – particularly those of a liberal persuasion – and had a reputation for being hard on his labour. However, he reserved a particular animosity for authority, in particular civil servants, who Jock felt deliberately set out to be as obstructive and pettily obtuse as possible.

Due to the debilitating effects early on of the malarial-related blackwater fever, an often fatal condition, Jock lost his hair and grew a beard, black like his eyes, which earned him the nickname 'Black' Harries. The Africans dubbed him Karasi, meaning 'bent neck,' because Jock always walked with his head tilted to one side, due I suspect from a fall from a horse.

Jock 'Black' Harries at the Nakuru Agricultural Show in the 1940s.

Chapter Two

KENYA: A COLONY IN THE MAKING

The rapid increase of population, the closing of the hitherto available outlets for emigration and for industrial expansion, as well as markets for our goods, and the sources of supply of our needs, indicate the time is not far distant when the teeming population of Europe will turn to the fertile highlands of Africa to seek new fields of expansion. It is possible therefore, that British Central and East Africa may be the embryo empires of an epoch already dawning- empires which, in the zenith of their growth and development, may rival those dependencies which are now the pride of the Anglo-Saxon race.

Captain Lugard,
Officer of the Imperial British East Africa Company
in charge of administering Uganda 1890

I now include a potted background to Kenya's early colonial history and settlement in this and the following chapter, to provide the framework, the chrysalis from which successive Prettejohns emerged. In light of anti-colonial sentiment and the denigration of the colonial ideal, I hope the facts presented in these two chapters will help set the record straight.

Britain, ever the reluctant player in the 'scramble for Africa,' refused to become involved in its citizens' imperialistic ambitions. Even as far back as 1823 when the Arab rulers of Mombasa, threatened by the Imam of Muscat, pleaded with the Captain of a British survey vessel to take the town under British protection, the Government refused to intervene. Later, in 1877, Sultan Barghash of Zanzibar offered Sir William Mackinnon, founder of the British India Steam Navigation Company, a seventy years' lease of Zanzibar, Pemba, and the mainland colony from Kismayu (now Somalia) to the Rovuma River (now the boundary between Tanzania and Mozambique). His request for Government backing to the Sultan's proposal was flatly denied. However, by the 1880s German imperialistic designs forced Britain to play a more direct role when she granted a royal charter to McKinnon's Imperial British East Africa Company in 1888. The charter conferred upon it the rights to administer and trade between Uganda and the coast.

This did not stop Germany from meddling; the German agent, Dr Carl Peters, was busy securing treaties well within the East African Protectorate along the Tana River with inducements of protection against the warring Maasai. He intercepted letters at Kavirondo (now Luo country on the eastern shores of Lake Victoria) from Uganda's ruler to the Company's agent, Frederick Jackson, appealing for help against the Mohammedans under the Kabaka's nominal rule. Britain was finally shaken out of her complacency when Peters planted the German flag on Ugandan soil. The outcome of this national territorial game was the Anglo-German agreement drawn up at the Brussels Conference of 1890 that accorded that 'sphere of influence' to the British.

With the Germans out of the equation, Mackinnon's problems were only just beginning as he now had to contend with the French. The French Government had no interest in Uganda's natural wealth, but since the country contained the sources of the White Nile, the French saw Uganda as the door to their eastward advance into the Upper Nile basin. The Company thus found it impossible to continue administering Uganda, and could no longer afford a costly war either with the Kabaka, who had taken the French side, or with the Mohammedans, or both at once. Mackinnon's Company again appealed to the British Government to intervene. The British would willingly have washed their hands of the problem had it not been for public opinion influenced by the Christian Missionary Society – more against the Catholic French, it seems than interested in converting the heathen – and the persuasive voice of Captain Lugard. Lugard was seconded to the Imperial British East Africa Company where he commanded a small force of Sudanese troops recruited from Egypt – plus a few remnants of Emin Pasha's force, the German explorer who governed Equatoria Province in the Sudan – to defend the Company's interests.

In 1893 the British Government declared a provisional protectorate over Uganda, whose border then ran down the centre of Lake Rudolph in the north in an almost straight line east of Lake Baringo and Lake Naivasha and on to German East Africa in the south. The German East Africa border skimmed Lake Natron's northern shore and took in half of Lake Jipe. The East Africa Protectorate, later to be called Kenya, only just encompassed Nairobi for the borders between Uganda and Kenya ran through Fort Smith, near today's Kikuyu town. The Union Jack replaced the Company flag, and two years later the British Government bought out the Company for £250,000. This sum was half as much as it had cost the BEAC to administer the lands over which it had been granted its 1888 charter. Many of its officers, including Frederick Jackson, a renowned ornithologist (later knighted), joined the service of the Government. Under the protectorate, Britain administered vast swathes with only a handful of men, mostly in their early twenties. These men, serving as Provincial and District officers, aided by a small team of Goan clerks, had the Herculean task of preventing tribal warfare, introducing a system of governance and order and generally seeing to the welfare of the peoples within their bailiwick. They were men of principal and integrity, dedicated to mould the primitive society into their European ideal.

At the 1890 Brussels Conference the various international players had agreed to put an end to the slave trade by linking central Africa with the 'civilized' world by rail and telegraph. For her part, Britain promised to build a railway from the coast to the interior.

Later dubbed the Lunatic Express, this rail line was a most extravagant, and at the time ludicrously unjustifiable, venture costing the British taxpayer £5.5 million pounds, or £9,500 a mile, from the seaport of Mombasa to Kisumu on Lake Victoria. Overseen by a handful of British engineers, construction started in 1897 using around 35,000 indentured labourers from India and was completed four years later in 1901.

At this time Kenya, whose borders then stretched from just east of Naivasha to the coast, did not enter the political equation; it was merely a large tract of land over which the railway had to pass to get to the lake. Like French thinking before them, the British Government now justified the railway – there was as yet no economic justification - as a tool to administer Uganda, which contained the source of the Nile, a strategic link to controlling Egypt and the Suez Canal, and thereby solidifying its grip on trade with India.

While Whitehall deliberated on the wider picture, Lugard initiated the possibility of European settlement – advocating the Mau Escarpment as a good place to start –as early as 1893 in *The Rise of our East African Empire*:

"The area is uninhabited and of great extent; it consequently offers unlimited room for the location of agricultural settlements or stock-raising farms. Here, if anywhere in Central Africa, in my opinion, would be the site upon which to attempt the experiment of European settlements.

"The soil is extremely rich, and covered with an excellent and luxuriant pasture throughout the year with which is mixed white clover and trefoil. I think it not impossible that a fruit export, such as has been so successfully developed in New Zealand and California, might prove one of the industries of future settlers...The speciality of this district would, I think, be the establishment of ranches and cattle-runs on the rolling savannahs of rich pasture. Stock rearing and sheep-farming would be suitable employment for European settlers."

Also struck by Kenya's potential as an ideal area for new settlement was Hugh Cholmondeley, the third Baron Delamere, who visited the country for the first time in 1897, the same year the first rails were laid. He set off from Berbera in Somaliland with a large caravan of horses, mules and camels and a retinue of Somali porters and gun bearers swelled by disparate tribal camp followers picked up en route. A truly remarkable undertaking, the expedition crossed unknown territory, hostile, dry and waterless with only the vaguest of maps sketched by a handful of recent explorers to guide it.

Through Somalia and down Abyssinia's eastern flank, the expedition headed for Lake Rudolph passing first through the areas of the nomadic Boran and Galla tribes. This territory remained as yet unclaimed by any European Power – though not immune to Ethiopian expansion and bloody skirmishes under her despotic ruler, the Emperor Menelik, who claimed that all the country "all the way south to Mombasa" was his. Menelik's ambitions included a Greater Somalia including the Ogaden and Eritrea in Ethiopia and "all land in Kenya where there's an anthill and a thorn tree."

Delamere's caravan arrived in August 1897 at Marsabit, a forested mountain overlooking vast stretches of acacia bushland, home to the Rendille and Samburu nomads. Their wilderness home and that of the Boran and Galla tribes later formed part of Kenya's Northern Frontier District. The expedition then wound its way west through Laisamis to Lake Rudolph, skirting around the lake's southern point westwards, and down the Turkwel River, before crossing overland again to Lake Baringo and the Laikipia Plateau. On reaching the Laikipia high land in early 1898, the first thing that struck Delamere was the luxuriant vegetation, climate, and the sheer uninhabited emptiness he encountered.

At the time of his arrival, the Laikipiak Maasai, who inhabited these Laikipia plains, had been seriously depleted by the recent depredations of their southern brothers, the Purko clan. Furthermore, their stock had been decimated by rinderpest, a cattle disease that had swept through the entire county in the mid-1890s. The population would be further reduced through the ravages of smallpox throughout the years of 1898 to 1902.

Kenya's population stood at approximately seven million at independence in 1963 and has grown to about 40 million in 2011. So it's hard for anyone who has only known Kenya since independence to think the land could ever have seemed empty of people. But the best estimate is that Kenya's entire population in 1898 was only about one million. The Maasai, numbering at the time only about 45,000, controlled almost two-thirds of the country. Because other tribes feared them, the Maasai aggressively contained the others in vastly smaller tribal boundaries. This fear extended to western explorers and it was only five years before Delamere's first visit that the Scottish explorer Joseph Thomson had dared pass through Maasailand. Pastoralists, the Maasai wandered with their herds over huge stretches of land. If disease broke out somewhere, they simply quarantined the area by moving on with their herds to someplace else.

Chapter Three

EARLY SETTLEMENT

"As a European colony in equatorial Africa it will have in virtue of its position a more than national importance; its development will mean the opening of a new world and its destinies will influence a whole continent."

Sir Charles Eliot

The Foreign Office did not at first wish to embark on land issues – indeed were completely at sea over it – until the completion of the railway. Nevertheless in 1897 regulations were drafted empowering the Commissioner for Uganda to make grants, unlimited in size, on 21-year leases. These limited leases, saddled with as many pre-conditions as strings in an orchestra, were totally impractical and did little to encourage settlement.

Sir Charles Eliot, appointed as Commissioner of Uganda in 1900, was a brilliant diplomat, intellect and linguist. He realized the costly railway could not be borne forever by the British taxpayer and would have to be financed from within. Despite a two-rupee hut tax imposed upon the natives, revenue amounted to less than one-third of expenditures. Eliot didn't feel the relatively small African population could produce enough raw materials to trade. Eliot felt the only way to make the railway pay was to fill the empty spaces along it with crops that could be carried out by rail and traded for machinery carried in. His proposal met with approval.

Eliot also saw that administering the East African Protectorate

4th KAR Uganda c. 1907.

(Kenya) from Entebbe in the Kabaka's kingdom beyond Lake Victoria was unwieldy and impractical.

He incorporated the area east of Lake Victoria into the East African Protectorate in 1902. In the same year, from his ramshackle headquarters amidst Mombasa's railway yards and tin-roofed warehouses, Eliot instigated a Lands Department whose officials drafted the Land Ordinance Act of 1902, which followed the Canadian homestead principle, allowing the applicant to take up 160 acres to start with, and a further 160 acres provided he fulfilled stringent development clauses. The process could be repeated in order to acquire up to one square mile, or 640 acres. The ordinance also allowed the purchase of freehold land in lots of up to 1000 acres.

The new ordinance, actually drafted by Eliot's deputy, Frederick Jackson, was barely less restrictive than the previous one and remained conditional on Government red tape. The rules governing timber stipulated: "All standing timber is the property of the Crown. The tenant may not sell any except with the permission of the forest officer and may not clear except for cultivation…Tenants must be prepared to import their fencing, as the Government will not ordinarily supply timber from the forest for the purpose." Prevented the right to cut timber, the tenant was also handicapped by the illegality of stocking goats, constructing roads, shooting game, and had no rights to divert natural water sources – all of which belonged to the Crown. Such requests not only had to pass by the various local departments, but were also forwarded on to Whitehall for sanction.

Delamere, meanwhile, had returned to England and married Florence Cole, daughter of the Irish peer, the Earl of Enniskillen, who accompanied him on a second visit to the Protectorate late that year when he called on Eliot. At the time of their meeting, Delamere had not considered taking up land himself but hoped to realise his dream of opening up the country to settlement. He told Eliot that "such rules as these make the taking up of land by men of a free race almost an impossibility…When it is recognised that the pioneer's chief object in going to a new country is to make money, only then will it be possible to get him to come."

The experiment had not attracted new settlement, and Eliot had to agree with Delamere's view. Eliot changed the regulations to allow freeholds at two rupees (one penny) an acre. This more lenient approach had immediate effect and settlers began to arrive in 1903 from England, Scotland and Ireland, America, South Africa, Australia, Canada, New Zealand, Germany and Rumania.

Until then only a handful had taken up small leaseholds on the edge of the Kikuyu tribal lands near Nairobi on which they successfully grew a variety of vegetables, particularly potatoes. One of these included Dr Atkinson who had accompanied Delamere on his first expedition from Berbera, and to whom Delamere later sent the first pedigree Shorthorn bull as a gift. The White Fathers' mission introduced coffee seed from Arabia in 1896 and started a plantation at their St Austin's mission outside of present day Nairobi in 1900. Rich forest loam, good rainfall and sunshine provided the ideal conditions for fruit and vegetables: cotton, tobacco, castor oil, sunflowers, aloes, sisal, ground nuts, hemp, wheat, oats, barley, sugar and maize were all tried and flourished.

When Delamere decided to settle in Kenya, he was interested in stock. He recognised many similarities between Kenya and

Australia and New Zealand, where he had spent time in his early twenties. Delamere knew it was not enough for a new settler to take up land without capital to develop it. He was the first to attempt large-scale projects. The Government turned down his request for land at Laikipia to raise sheep, reasoning it was too far from the administrative centre and the railway. Delamere's second request for a 100,000-acre concession that ran from below the foothills of the Aberdares to Lake Naivasha was also turned down because Eliot felt it would cause hardship to the Maasai. Delamere was finally granted an area totally unoccupied further northwest between Njoro and the Molo river. Along with an order for duck, geese, chickens, and some pheasant, he imported rams to cross breed with native ewes. This concession was granted on a 99-year lease at an annual rent of £200, and conditional on an additional investment of £5000 to develop the land over five years. Delamere brought in sheep from Australia as well as wheat, ploughs and harvesters.

Although land could be cheaply acquired in Kenya, pioneers took great financial risk: stock thefts, unknown diseases, suitability and bureaucratic impediments all took their toll. While Delamere paid the equivalent of one penny an acre, a native ewe cost him thirty times as much and sheep soon proved a failure in the Njoro area.

Delamere mortgaged his English estate and borrowed heavily, as would Jock Harries and other early settler pioneers who followed.

Chapter Four

LANDS AND CATTLE

He packed his spears and went; went to the scented mornings, to the nights of the satin moon, that can lap the heart in solace, that can settle the soul in tune. Ye who have travelled the Wilderness, ye who have followed the chase, whom the voice of the forest comforts, and the touch of the lonely place; ye who are sib to the jungle and know it and hold it good-praise ye the name of Nimrod, a fellow who understood.

Nimrod

Jock Harries was born in Pembrokeshire, South Wales, that 'Little England beyond Wales,' where his family had an estate, Hilton. He was schooled at Cheltenham College followed by a spell at the Royal Military Academy at Woolwich and the Royal Garrison

4th KAR Uganda c. 1907, Jock Harries centre right, Catchpole centre left.

Artillery in which he served in the forts around Milford Haven and later at Gibraltar and in India. When asked in his passing out papers to describe the mechanism of the breach of a howitzer, he had no idea so he wrote, "The breach mechanism of the howitzer is like the Peace of God, it passeth all understanding."

Jock moved to Kenya in 1904 to pursue his military career, and he was transferred to the 4th Battalion of the King's African Rifles. This regiment was formed in 1902 amalgamating the Uganda Rifles, the East African Rifles operating from Fort Jesus in Mombasa, and the Central African Regiment that operated in Ashanti, Gambia, Mauritius and Somaliland.

The Fourth Battalion took part in several punitive expeditions and armed patrols in Uganda and neighbouring territory. The best

4th KAR Uganda Askari. Raw material and finished product.

documented among these were against the Lumbwa and other peoples of western Kenya between 1902 and 1906, a mission to Lake Kivu, southwest of Uganda, in 1909, and in British Somaliland in a campaign against Sheikh Muhammad Abdullah Hassan – the Mad Mullah – in 1909 and 1910.

Unfortunately no records survive of Jock's involvement, if any, in these campaigns. He certainly used the time to explore and hunt, mainly for ivory. The 4th K.A.R. was involved with the administration of the whole of Uganda and much of the Southern Sudan, and Jock hunted in that 'no man's land' between Kenya, the Sudan, Uganda and Ethiopia known as the Lado Enclave, an area leased by Belgian's King Leopold who personally benefited from the sale of elephant licences to approved individuals for twenty pounds. A licence allowed the holder unlimited elephant over a five-month period within a year.

Hunting elephant in tall grass.

Karamoja Bell best describes hunting the Lado in his classic account *The Wanderings of an Elephant Hunter.* With grass taller than a man's head for most of the year, Bell hunted elephant from a portable stand or sat on his gun bearer's shoulders in order to see to shoot. Consequently he needed to get up as close to the elephant as possible using a light, accurate

Jock with ivory trophies.

Carrying the ivory.

rifle with little recoil. Other than a few photographs, Jock's hunting episodes remain untold. We do know that one consignment of ivory shipped abroad fetched around three thousand pounds, the future down payment on land Jock purchased at Njoro on the Mau Escarpment.

Jock hunted mainly with a Rigby 7mm, but also carried a German made Robert Schuler .600 double rifle as back up. (After Jock's death, both of these rifles were left to me. The Rigby 7mm rifle handled

Camping scene, 4th KAR Uganda

beautifully and I used it until the barrel wore out. The .600 weighed some 18 pounds. I lugged it around the bush for a couple of years until my gun bearer observed that better use could be made of it as a *rungu* (club). I agreed and sold it to buy a Rigby .450, together with a set of .458 barrels, a far more practical and easier rifle to handle. I only used the .600 twice: the first time on a buffalo when the gun not only bowled over the animal but the recoil flattened me as well; on the second occasion I was escaping a charging rhino and realised I was losing ground. I shot it in the head firing from the hip just as it was about to impale me on its horn. I tell more about the rhino story in chapter 25).

Once Jock found himself camped in the same area as Sir Frederick Jackson, now knighted and appointed Governor of Uganda. Jock was pleased to accept an invitation to dine and arrived that evening accompanied by his African batman. The following morning he was surprised on breaking camp by the arrival of a runner demanding the

Jock Harries seated, overseeing the set up of camp.

return of the Governor's silver. Much embarrassed by the accusation, Jock confronted his batman, who told him since his bwana's standard of tableware fell far short of that of the Governor's, he had simply wished to put the matter right.

Jock resigned his commission with the 4th K.A.R. in 1910, a move which so angered his father that he threatened to "cut him off without a penny." Regardless, Jock bought eight hundred acres in Njoro from Berkeley Cole, Delamere's brother-in-law, with the proceeds amassed from ivory taken out of the Lado Enclave. The farm was named Larmudiac after the Maasai name *Olari lo Lamutin* – the water of the bulrushes. In 1911 a mutually agreed treaty between the Government and the Maasai reunited the clans by moving the northern Laikipia Maasai to join up with their southern brethren in the Narok area. The treaty exchanged 4500 square miles of Laikipia for 6500 square miles in the south.

The Laikipia Maasai were very few in numbers after inter clan clashes and further reduced by smallpox, after which they lost most of their cattle and goats to rinderpest. Following the small pox outbreak, Maasai from the central Rift Valley areas were first moved up north to Laikipia in 1904. The idea behind this move was to free the land on either side of the railway and open it up to new immigrants who would make commercial use of the land, and contribute to financing the railway. However, a few years later it was felt it would be more practical to contain the whole of the Maasai tribe within a single area, which resulted in the treaty of 1911.

In 1911 as the Maasai trekked southwards, Jock permitted them to stopover on Larmudiac to water their cattle at the springs. In return they agreed to pay him two cows for every one hundred and eighty animals that passed through. These animals, of Zebu stock, formed Jock's initial stock herd. Maasai cattle were then a sturdy breed due to crossbreeding.

Subsequently, by mortgaging part of his Welsh Estate, Jock purchased a further 3000 acres adjoining Larmudiac from another settler, Algey Cartwright. At this time the Government was offering two 4000-acre blocks of open bush country in the Lake Nakuru forest between Larmudiac and the lake. Jock acquired both for 6-pence an acre to be paid over 20 years. By the close of 1912 he owned 11,800 acres of ranching land. As his acquisitions surrounded the Nishi Forest, accessible only through his private holding, he managed to get the grazing rights on a further 10,000 acres.

To stock Larmudiac, Jock bought cattle in Ankole in Northern Uganda. He had first come to know the Acholi people whilst serving there with his regiment, and had observed that their cattle would make excellent beef animals. He also believed them to be free of tuberculosis and possibly immune to tsetse fly, which the Maasai cattle were not. (When my father travelled there in the 1950s, cattle movement was restricted due to an outbreak of tuberculosis with which the cattle were riddled.)

Ankole cattle from Northern Uganda,
known for their large horns and resistance to disease

35

An Acholi dance in Northern Uganda.

In early 1913, two years after purchasing Larmudiac, Jock returned to the Mbarara District of Uganda with a fellow farmer, Frank Hobson, best remembered for importing his whisky in casks direct from Scotland. The pale-skinned Ankole cattle are distinguished by their long and elegant horns that can measure almost as much in length as the height of the animal itself. At that time the only way forward was to stock native cattle and to upgrade these with imported bulls. With the Ankole tribal region well off the beaten track, Jock counted on acquiring cheap stock. Unfortunately, neither man documented their epic safari, but we do know it took many months travelling entirely on foot and swimming across rivers driving ahead of them, on the return journey, several hundred head of stock of which 400 survived. Hobson originally came up to Kenya from South Africa. He was a frequent guest on Larmudiac where he'd spend a night on his way from his farm at Molo to buy supplies in Nakuru, a lengthy journey then undertaken by ox-wagon or on horseback. Hobson later died in the early 1930s from massive bee stings.

Much of the land in Eastern Uganda and Western Kenya through which they passed was heavily populated. Although there would not have been much game meat, there was plenty of millet and maize. I remember Jock telling me how they did little shooting on the way

Jock Harries on the right while having breakfast in the bush, c. 1908.

On safari crossing Njoro plains enroute to the Mara, c.1908.

back since they were too busy herding cattle and mindful also that firing shots could cause the herd to panic and stampede. Conversely, he and Hobson did wonder how the *mpishi* (cook) provided them with so much fresh meat, and were horrified to learn the man came from the Manyema tribe, purported to be cannibals. Suspecting the worst, they summarily dismissed the cook and the party decamped immediately.

During the First World War the Belgians employed Manyema men as *askaris* (watchmen). Judging from captured German documents of the time that listed missing soldiers "believed eaten by Manyema," these eaters of men posed a greater threat than the bullet. A Belgian Officer, wary of the way his *askari* looked him over with conceived ill intent, took to sleeping outside his tent facing them with a machine gun.

On his return to Larmudiac, Jock set about crossing the Ankole cattle with selected cows originally acquired from the Maasai. He then crossed the progeny with Hereford and Shorthorns, and later still with Red Poll imported from England and South Africa. Although superior breeds such as the Boran succeeded the Ankole, my son Giles has recently been approached by South African ranchers, whose interest in Ankole cattle results from a need today to reintroduce the hardier qualities of a purely African breed lost through years of cross-breeding.

With the onset of the First World War, Jock was asked by Ewart Grogan, a fellow pioneer and early settler, in his capacity then as Intelligence Liaison Officer between the British and the Belgians, to train up and supply the Belgian Army with the hardier Ankole cattle to pull the supply carts.

Despite the varied crossbreeding from that time, I remember seeing cattle with the distinctive Ankole horns even as late as the 1950s. When in 1923 my father took over the running of the cattle, numbering some 1800 head, he set aside a small herd of pure Ankole from which to crossbreed. He crossed straight-backed cattle with the humped Zebu to produce the Boran, a particular line first developed in Kenya by ranchers, including the Australian Harold White, Brian Currey, Myles Fletcher and Gilbert Colvile. The Boran was specifically bred for its hardiness, a natural immunity to disease, and its ability to walk long distances to water. Since there was ample water on Larmudiac, more exotic breeds were introduced to give a heavier and quicker-maturing animal whilst maintaining the Boran's hardier qualities. (When the breed almost died out after Kenya's independence, my son Giles and the Kenyons once again instigated a Boran breeding program in the 1980s, giving the breed world recognition by starting the process of selection, registration and recording with artificial insemination, and embryo production. The Boran is today a much sought-after breed whose embryos are implanted into cattle from Australia to South Africa.)

Chapter Five

THE GREAT WAR

At the outbreak of war in 1914 Jock signed up again with the 4th KAR. The country was unprepared for hostilities. Neither the British nor the Germans in East Africa wanted war; they particularly did not want the Africans to see the white men slugging it out among themselves. Furthermore, they believed Europe should sort out its quarrel without involving East Africa. Unfortunately, in a bid to flex British muscle, two cruisers bombarded German-occupied Dar es Salaam in Tanganyika, which only exacerbated hostilities. The Germans retaliated by invading the strategically vital border area around Taveta followed by an attack on the railway, the colony's lifeline. Settler volunteers responded. Armed with a pocketful of ammunition and weapons ranging from double-barrelled elephant guns to light carbines, volunteers converged on Nairobi by train or mule forming themselves into mini regiments: Bowker's Horse, The Plateau South Africans,

Jock Harries, 4th KAR, during the Great War guarding the railroad near Voi.

Arnoldi's, Ross's and Cole's Scouts, among others. The latter incorporated eight hundred Somalis who marched down to Nairobi to offer their services, and were organised into a troop of mounted scouts under Berkeley Cole. Though ill equipped and untrained, these disparate groups were amalgamated into a fighting force known as The East African Mounted Rifles (EAMR) to defend the border and railway which ran just fifty miles from it.

Setting off with great enthusiasm and hope, this mixed bag of elephant poachers, store-keepers, white hunters, transporters, and settler farmers embraced every nationality, including a Turk who was promptly incarcerated when someone realised Turkey was aligned with the enemy. Fighting with them were African volunteers: Nubians, Somalis, Maasai and others. All were quite unprepared for the hardships of the waterless *nyika* bush of Tsavo and the diseases – malaria, dysentery, sunstroke, blackwater, gangrene, sleeping sickness – to which many a man or animal would succumb. Bowker's Horse was jokingly referred to as Bowker's Foot after the Germans stole the remnants of its horses and mules that had survived the ravages of tsetse fly. The force proved utterly inadequate for the job. There was no organised transport, no medical or field hospitals in place and no food. The men were forced to live off game they shot until even this became scarce.

An intelligence unit was hastily formed with the remnants of the Game Department, which already had a staff of native spies (one of whom was normally attached to each safari to see that the game laws were not infringed) and a corps of informers to detect ivory poaching. This was headed by the Chief Game Warden, Captain Woosnam. One of its officers was Colonel Richard Meinertzhagen, a ruthless administrator best known for his part in the Nandi rebellion. Working behind enemy lines, Meinertzhagen boasted that he surprised an unsuspecting German officer on Christmas Eve tucking into his Christmas pudding. The Colonel shot the hapless officer and finished off his festive meal before retreating undetected.

With the arrival of Indian troops in early 1915 the role of the East African Mounted Rifles largely disappeared, and many returned to their farms. They had held the border at a critical time without help save for one battalion of the King's African Rifles. One embittered soldier wrote: "These Generals, these Colonels, in their spick and span uniforms, with the confined brain pans of a set of strutting poultry, how could one feel any confidence in such people?"

Later in 1915 with a change of government and a shift in the command structure, Ewart Grogan, as settler spokesman, rallied the remnants of the EAMR into an efficient force under General Smuts from South Africa, who arrived early in 1916 to take over supreme command.

By the end of 1916 the EAMR was disbanded. It left no records nor appeared in any army lists. It received little official recognition save General Smuts' tribute:

"In the history of human endurance this campaign deserves a very special place and the heroes, who went through it uncomplainingly, doggedly, are entitled to all recognition and reverence. Their Commander-in-Chief will remain eternally proud of them."

Although later strengthened by Indian, South African and Rhodesian battalions, and Belgian troops, the courage and cussedness of this rag-tag army of individuals had played an important role in repelling General Von Lettow-Vorbeck, the much-feared Commander-in-Chief of German East Africa.

We know little of Jock's personal involvement during this war period, but Jock did spend time with a battalion of the 4th KAR stationed in the Voi area around Maktau, at Maungu, and on Pika Pika Hill, a rocky *kopje*, from which the soldiers guarded the railway line between Mombasa and Nairobi. I am involved today in a ranch in the same area where Pika Pika Hill is situated. You can still see remnants

Near Voi during the Great War. Jock on left and Catchpole on right.

Capture of a German machine gun, Taita c. 1914.

of stone fortifications facing out in all directions on the summits of these rocky outcrops – on Pika Pika and the Karissa Hills some five miles to the south – where the 4th KAR had been billeted with their machine guns.

By August 1914 arrangements had been made to patrol the entire length of the railway line and the Anglo-German border. Most of this was done by volunteers and railway employees. It was not until early September of that year that the 4th KAR, together with a few men from the 1st and 3rd and 2nd Companies of the 29 Punjabis, were sent to take over. It is on record at this time that the patrols were hampered less by the enemy than by lion and rhino. One Company lost every carrier on patrol when the men, faced with a charging rhino, threw off their loads and ran off, eventually finding their way back to base at Mzima. After this a pack of lion-hunting dogs was sent down from a privately owned kennel in Nairobi; the hounds fared no better.

The stations were manned by Indian stationmasters fondly referred to as *babus*. The literal translation of some of their telegraphed messages generally caused much amusement when received: "Dear Sahib," went one sent from the stationmaster at Sultan Hamud, "my humble self just has had arrival of runner with bad news. 100 Germans about to descend to take over my station. Please send 1 rifle and 100 rounds of ammunition." We don't know whether his confident marksmanship was rewarded, but help must have reached him in one form or another for a few months later the same *babu* tapped out another coded message referring to the inadequacy of his tented accommodation: "Dear Sahib. I have by extreme good luck a beautiful damsel who has consented to be my wife, but the problem is my dear Sahib about my abode. I am therefore requesting that you may see your way to be giving me even one single erection."

The first successful action against the German raiders by the 4th King's African Rifles occurred in January of 1915 when a detachment under Lieutenant Oldfield of the 4th KAR battled it out with half as many machine guns as were deployed by the German force. Although Oldfield died in the battle, the Germans were forced back to base with no damage incurred to the railway line or the locomotives. Up to this point the Germans had been mining the railway at night, at times blowing up as many as five different sections of line. There were 35 locomotives awaiting repair from these raids.

During the night of this battle, on hearing German voices, a contingent of the 4th KAR crept up in the dark and opened fire. When, at dawn, the carnage revealed a German surgeon treating wounded men, the British Commanding Officer asked for a volunteer officer to visit the German camp under the protection of a white flag to apologise. His mission naturally required him to report back on enemy positions. Jock, a lieutenant, volunteered. Apart from observing native spies ill-concealed in the desiccated *commiphora* bush, and none too silent either, he reported back that the Germans appeared demoralised, recognising they were up against superior forces.

'Black' Harries centre, Catchpole right, Effendi left.

By late September the 4th KAR under the command of Lieutenant Foster, together with a company of Punjabis, led a series of counter attacks against the Germans that successfully pushed them back to the border. Foster sustained a serious injury and died soon after making it back to base. For many Punjabis this was their first taste of battle, in a war zone environment of flat, featureless and waterless thorn bush in which a man could easily lose his way and, maddened by thirst, die there in his tracks. They fought bravely, but many reported sick having sustained self-inflicted wounds to a hand or foot.

Today much of the Voi area is watered by a pipeline from Mzima Springs, but in 1915 there would have been no water at all throughout the dry season. This fact caused the Germans to confine themselves on their way in to the railway from the border with Tanganyika through Mount Kasigau, where there were springs, or down following the Tsavo River. Some of the larger waterholes retain water for a time after the rains in April and May and again in October and November. This enabled the enemy to attack on a much wider front. As a deterrent, the 4th KAR put notices around the pans to the effect that the water had been poisoned. To sustain the lie they replaced freshly killed birds around the source. This ploy worked for a time - soldiers elected to die naturally of thirst rather than be poisoned – until the German High Command lodged an official complaint to the effect that poisoning water went against the rules of engagement.

In December, with a force of six hundred men, the Germans claimed Kasigau in British held territory. The majority of British soldiers garrisoned there had been forewarned, and managed to get away. It was not until the end of January 1916 that General Smuts, with reinforcements of Rhodesian and South African troops, retook Kasigau, forcing the Germans back to the border. It was a hard-fought battle. The Germans had the advantage of the hilltops from which they could fire onto the opposing forces below. Many on both sides died simply from thirst, lack of food, and malaria. Animals, too, died from thirst and tsetse fly-related disease.

This is the last recorded episode we have of Jock's

Somali hanging in 1915 after a mutiny.

involvement with the 4th KAR. Some contingents remained in the area, others returned to Uganda and the Lake Victoria area to repel perceived German attacks into Uganda. This never happened. From 1916 on the Germans were steadily pushed further south.

A photograph found among Jock's personal belongings shows he knew about the 5th KAR's operations in Somalia in 1917, though it's not certain he was actually there himself. The caption in Jock's handwriting reads:

"In Sept 1915 the Aulihan Somali of Jubaland, British East Africa, having first lulled the D.C. Post at Serenli into a sense of security by their protestations of loyalty and desire to help the British against the Germans in German East Africa, treacherously rushed the garrison by setting fire to their own houses, and when the garrison turned out to assist getting the fire under control, making an organised attack on them. Everyone within the garrison was murdered including the white officer J.E.Elliot. They then took off with all the rifles and ammunition of some 160 men. It was not until 1917 that they were well hammered by the 5th K.A.R. when some 26000 camels were confiscated, the tribe disarmed, and many of the leaders hanged. They were hanged in public 6 at a time at all the principal places throughout Jubaland and their bodies refused burial. After which there was no more trouble!"

Chapter Six

ACQUISITIONS AND JAIL

Soon after hostilities ended, Jock returned to England in 1919 for the first time in fifteen years. After a day ashore in Aden, he hired a boat to take him back to the ship. Half way there the boatmen refused to go any further until Jock had handed over an additional extortionate sum of money. His first thought was to jump into the sea and swim. However, good sense prevailed: he simply pushed the three men into the sea and rowed back. Letting the rented boat drift free, he boarded the ship to a cheering ovation from the watching passengers.

Gwen Harries ex-Prettejohn, Author's grandmother.

How matters were settled between Jock and my grandfather Prettejohn remain unknown, but Gwen willingly left England to return with Jock and live with him on Larmudiac.

I never met my grandfather. The only photograph I have shows him as a young man, possibly at the time of his marriage in 1900. He is formally dressed in black, his starched white collar stranding proud. There's not a hair out of place. A strong, square jaw gives him a look of imposing

Rickshaw transport, Nairobi.

sternness. He stares out through the frame, his expression implacable, unreadable, his body half facing away from the camera as though he finds the whole business of being photographed tedious, and is steeling himself for it to be over as quickly as possible.

By the time Jock returned to England my grandmother Gwen had led a relatively independent life. Not only was she financially independent, but also she had brought up her children and managed her Welsh properties almost single-handedly. For much of the first part of their marriage grandfather stayed away in Ceylon managing his tea interests there. This was followed by a spell soldiering in Egypt with the Gloucester Hussars. In Egypt my Grandfather Prettejohn received severe burns from an x-ray administered for a back injury sustained earlier in Ceylon as a result of a motorcycle accident. The x-ray so badly affected a nerve in his leg that he was left with a jerky Saint Vitus Dance tic. Invalided out, he returned home, but almost as soon as he had recovered, he left England again to fight in France with the Scot's Guards, miraculously escaping that war's terrible trench massacre, followed by a spell in Ireland policing with the Black & Tans.

Jock's parents joined him and Gwen on their voyage out to Africa.

Jock's earlier misdemeanour now forgiven, Jock's father agreed to finance and expand the farm. That same year the British Government implemented a soldier-settlement scheme to simultaneously develop the Colony and offer a new life to those who had fought in the War. Fifteen hundred new settlers arrived. Jock and his father each drew land in Laikipia, which they then exchanged for two smaller farms adjoining Larmudiac in a better rainfall area, Olbwan and Naishi.

In late 1920 an incident occurred that threatened to alter Jock's life. Besides the cattle, Jock farmed pigs and had imported a number of 'Large Whites.' He employed a young Kikuyu boy to herd the pigs and graze them in the day on the fresher grasses around the dam. One evening the Kikuyu boy, in a hurry to get home, beat to death a sow about to farrow. Livid, Jock punished the boy by thrashing him with a *kiboko* (hippo-hide whip). The boy disappeared. Nothing was heard of him until his parents arrived a fortnight later to demand compensation, saying the boy had died from the beating. Jock firmly believed the caning could not possibly have been severe enough to cause death. He thought it more likely the boy had received a further beating at the hands of his father for the shame brought upon the family.

Jock and Gwen at Larmudiac Farm in Njoro.

The Government, however, perceiving the settlers to be taking the law too much into their own hands, sought to crack down on such incidents. It was also unfortunate that Jock had recently come to the notice of the judge at a court hearing involving a similar case. Jasper Abraham had been charged with the death of a *syce* (groom), who, detailed to fetch the post, had severely beaten and galloped to exhaustion an imported mare in foal, resulting in her aborting. The *syce*, on instructions from Abraham, was given a severe hiding and locked up for the night. The following morning he was found dead. As the son of a Bishop, Abrahams got off lightly with a nine-month sentence. However, Jock, in protest, walked out of the courtroom and deliberately pushed past the Judge's bench knocking ink over his notes. Jock feared the worst when he in turn was summoned to court. Jock was sentenced to six months in prison.

The European prison was then housed in Mombasa's historic Fort Jesus overlooking the Indian Ocean. A spell there was not too onerous, little different from staying at the Mombasa Club across the road from which His Majesty's guests could order meals and invite a member to make up a four for bridge. Africans referred to prison as *Hoteli ya Kingi George* (King George's Hotel) for although it was meant to be a place of punishment, inexplicably, it provided its inmates with comfortable accommodation and a square meal.

Jock joined Abrahams and two others in prison – Batchelor was in for debt and Hawkins, a contractor by trade living at Njoro, had been sentenced for extorting a confession of theft from a servant by tightening his thumb in a vice after returning home to find all his clothes missing. When Hawkins reported the theft and his actions in getting the man to confess, the police rightly considered the methods Hawkins had used constituted a worse crime than the theft itself.

Chapter Seven

A NEW BEGINNING

After her remarriage to Jock and while Jock was serving his prison sentence, my grandmother Gwen returned to England in early 1921 to collect my father, Joe, and Aunt Gwenydd, recently returned from Switzerland where she had been packed off to stay with her former governess. My uncle Dick was then at Sandhurst. Father hoped on leaving Wellington to go up to Cambridge to study modern languages after which he was destined to follow an uncle in the Chinese Customs Service.

He was already aware after my grandfather Prettejohn's return from War in 1919 that all was not well between his parents; when Gwen wrote to him at school from Cairo in the summer term of 1920 to say she was leaving grandfather and was on her way out to Kenya with Jock, he was not surprised.

By the time grandfather visited Wellington to see my father and explain the separation, my father must have weighed up the situation in his mother's favour for he later wrote: "Undoubtedly my mother meant more to me than my father who I had seldom seen from 1911 to 1919."

Father joined his mother and sister Gwenyhdd in Southampton directly from school where they stayed in a run-down boarding house for fear that grandfather might have a last-minute change of heart and claim custody of his children. The following day the family boarded the SS *Walmer Castle*, a two-funnelled ship of some seventeen thousand tons. They stopped briefly at Funchal in Madeira where they visited the market, father experiencing his first taste of exotic fruits - loquats and custard apple – before reaching Cape Town. After three nights on shore and a visit to the flower market, they steamed on around the coast to Port Elizabeth where a shore landing had them slung over the side, six to a basket, and deposited onto a tug which took them to the wharf. There they visited the snake park – a large round tank-like structure over which the viewer peered onto a seething coil of slithering reptiles. Finally they reached East London and Durban, waiting a fortnight there for the British India Company ship, the *Korea*, to take them on to Mombasa.

Non-whites - Indians, Malays and Africans- slept on the main deck wherever they could find a space and cooked their own food over spirit lamps and braziers. "Those are the sort of passengers I like", said the *Korea's* captain. "No grumbling about food or accommodation." The captain, father recalled, was a tough character with small eyes set close together in a face that resembled a Large White pig. On a previous trip to Mozambique he had thrown a Portuguese pilot overboard for some perceived slight, steering the ship into port himself. Fortunately the crew of the pilot boat hauled him aboard before the sharks got to him.

Father particularly enjoyed Lourenço Marques (now Maputo, the capital of Mozambique) where he made a good deal of money at the roulette table. The South African curator of the zoo told them how he'd chosen to put down some wild dog that would not settle and pined continually, rather than allow them be torn to pieces in a Roman-style bout with lion that the local Portuguese officials suggested would make excellent entertainment for the Governor. Visiting a 16th century fort on the island town of Maçambique, then used as a prison for local miscreants as well as political prisoners from Portugal, father watched with horror the pathetic way the prisoners reached out through the bars begging for food.

He found the river port of Beira, then without deep water berths, sordid with "streets of sand lined with corrugated iron warehouses and brothels."

At Dar es Salaam the *Korea* arrived too late to take advantage of the high tide thus delaying entrance to the harbour until the following day. The hull of a German warship deliberately sunk to block the harbour entrance had only partially been removed, forcing larger vessels to enter it on a high tide. Father's first impressions were favourable: "Dar es Salaam is the most picturesque place. The entrance is no more than two hundred yards wide for perhaps half a mile leading into a serene, inland lake, almost round about five miles in diameter, and fringed with coconut palms and mango trees."

He merited the Germans with its fine buildings, tree-lined avenues and open squares, and noted: "the Governor's Palace standing on a narrow promontory facing the open sea now lies in ruins from Royal Navy shelling."

Despite the town's former glory, father was not sorry to leave for the war had destroyed its infrastructure and there was nothing of note to see or do there. Most of the town's German residents had been repatriated, leaving the fate of their beautiful residential stone houses to the bureaucratic whims of the British.

The next day the *Korea* reached Kilindini harbour on Mombasa Island through a narrow half-mile gap in the coral reef. "As we steamed up the narrow channel we could see the northern passage leading to the old Arab port of Mombasa still used by dhows from Arabia as it has been for now countless years, and Fort Jesus, the fort built by the Portuguese in 1593." Having seen the state of the prisoners on the island of Maçambique, father no doubt wondered how Jock was faring in his six-month's of incarceration in Fort Jesus.

Colonel Grogan's company had recently embarked on an ambitious project to build deep water berths on a concession granted him three years earlier, and later bought back by the British Government for £350,000 as a coaling berth. Father recalls 'hundreds of Africans' carrying *kerais* of excavated earth on their heads that they dumped in piles 'like termite mounds' on the pier. Seeing for the first time the squat and bulbous trunks of baobab trees outlined behind Grogan's Mbaraki concession, father later wrote: "…my first view of that lovely country that was to be my home for the next forty-two years."

With the help of an Arab agent they cleared immigration and customs formalities and boarded the evening train bound for Nairobi. The coaches were private, without common corridor. They dined on the platform at Voi, a hundred miles up the track, which they reached at nine in the evening, nearly five hours after departure, and later breakfasted at first light at Makindu.

The train reached the Kapiti and Athi plains just as the sun rose. Such wealth of game freely roaming the plains stirred father's senses. University and a future career in the Chinese Customs services began to pall. Excitement and renewed expectation determined him "never to return to England."

The arrival of the Mombasa train would have been a scene of great excitement. Ali Khan's mule-drawn Victorias provided transport for the luggage while rickshaw drivers vied with one another to take on passengers. There were no taxis and a dearth of cars. The few stone buildings on Nairobi's main street, Government Road, stood out from corrugated iron and timber shops.

There were then only three hotels in Nairobi of any consequence: close to the station stood the original Stanley, a double-storey building somewhat run down with wooden balconies overhanging a large veranda at street level; the New Stanley which had just opened (not comparable to the present New Stanley Hotel on Standard Street); and, further out, the Norfolk, started in 1904 by Major C.G.R. Ringer. Accommodation was basic: bathing consisted of a tin bath filled from *debes* – four gallon petrol cans – carried up on a servant's head, and a jug of hot water brought in with the morning tea for shaving. The family headed to the Norfolk, the preferred settler residence-in-town, to await Jock's imminent arrival directly from prison.

Father witnessed some wild behaviour at the bar at the Norfolk on his first night there. A South African, much the worse for wear from an evening's drinking elsewhere, stumbled in brandishing two loaded six-shooters. When he refused to hand them over, an off-duty policeman at the bar thought he'd call his bluff by betting him he couldn't shoot six bottles straight off the shelf. The policeman lost his bet, for the South African not only shattered six bottles with the one pistol but downed six more with the other. The diminutive policeman did then have the satisfaction of handcuffing the drunk, now his guns were unloaded, and hauled him off to the clink to sober up.

Chapter Eight

MAASAILAND

Embittered by his imprisonment, and deeply antagonistic at what he perceived to be Government intransigency in its dealings with the settler, Jock had already decided to sell up and leave Kenya altogether for South Africa. He also felt at the time his case came up that his fellow settlers had not rallied round, and said as much to Powys Cobb at the bar. Powys Cobb was one of Kenya's largest landowners with 6000 acres in Molo, another 3000 on the Mau escarpment, a sheep farm at Naivasha, as well as a sisal plantation at Kilifi on the coast.

Others tried to dissuade Jock from leaving, but he remained adamant. Finding a buyer for his large tract of land in Kenya was not easy, although a deal was shortly made with Ben Birkbeck, who bought Larmudiac with a down payment of £10,000 at eleven percent interest by way of a mortgage, agreeing to pay the balance as soon as money from his Trust was settled.

Jock saw no problem with this arrangement as Birkbeck was connected to the Birkbecks, co-founders with the Buxton and Barclay families of Barclays Bank. In fact, it was well known that Birkbeck was a financial lightweight, but Jock couldn't wait to turn his back on Kenya.

While negotiations with Birkbeck were in progress, Jock arranged for the outfitter Boyce Aggett, who lived at Kijabe, to equip a safari by ox wagon to southern Maasailand, and took along his old prison mate, Hawkins, as camp manager. This was to be Jock's definitive Kenya safari before he left the country for good.

As they waited for preparations to be made ready, Jock took off for a few days to hunt bongo in the forest above the Kijabe escarpment. (Finding a bongo in that area, even in those early days, would have been rare, a fact which led father to believe Jock had 'found' the trophy head he brought back. Nevertheless, Jock did collect one later in the Mau Forest, above Larmudiac. Both bongo heads hang on my veranda at Mweiga.)

Jock's cousin, Bertie Warren Davis, who had been working for Jock on Larmudiac, joined the party for the safari knowing he would shortly be headed for the Lupa Goldfields in Tanganyika. Aggett set up the first base camp close to the main road below the Kijabe escarpment.

Intent on recording the scenic arrival of the weekly mail cart pulled by a team of ten mules, father ran to the front of the mule train to take photographs. This unaccustomed activity caused the mules to panic and become entangled in their traces. It took the better part of an hour to coax them back into line. Only ten miles from the camp lay the extinct, ridged volcano of Longonot which father and Aunt Gwenydd climbed accompanied by an old Swahili guide. They found climbing its steep ridges fairly exhausting and were glad to take a break at the top where, in places, the crater lip is so narrow they could sit astride and look down to its green bottom and to the large flat-topped thorn trees growing there. Father and Gwenydd returned the way they'd come, reaching camp well after dark. They came across lion and buffalo spoor, but thankfully didn't encounter either animal as father was not yet experienced with a rifle on big game.

On another day they walked beyond Longonot to Lake Naivasha stopping under the fever trees below the town to picnic, and on around the lake to overnight in an abandoned house on its northern shore. Father notes how high the water was then (May 1921) "lapping right into the belt of thorn trees that surround the lake."

A team of sixteen oxen pulled the wagon packed with tents, beds, chairs, food and medical boxes. Two handlers drove the team and a young boy, known as *shika kamba* or 'pull-rope,' led the oxen by a *rheim*, the South African term for the harness made from cow or buffalo-hide. In addition there were four riding mules with two *syces*. The camp staff included two tent boys, a cook, his assistant – the all-important kitchen *toto* – and a dozen porters.

An outbreak of bovine pleuro-pneumonia among the Maasai cattle meant that the oxen they set out with were not permitted to cross the district border boundary. This necessitated manhandling the wagon some distance across a quarantined stretch to meet with a fresh team on the other side.

The men walked or rode the mules while the women travelled most of the way in the wagons covering about 25 miles a day. If the hunting was promising, the party would stay put for a few days. Leaving the dusty floor of the Rift Valley and climbing over the tail end of the forested Mau Escarpment, they dropped down to Narok and crossed over the Southern Uaso Nyiro River onto the Loita Plains. Despite seeing a great variety of game in the areas through which they passed, nothing had prepared father for the sheer numbers he saw there. The party – only the third group in the area since the war – camped on the Loita Plains for several days to hunt, and collected many fine trophies including four magnificent lion.

They had great sport hunting lion, a risky business that entailed confronting them on mule-back. Since they were only after black-maned lion, the hunt at times took on a reverse mode when an obstreperous female with cubs or a young, non-trophy male, rushed at them. One mule, slow to change direction, got his backside mauled but lived.

The Buganda cook, grown fat on kitchen perks, considered himself a cut above the rest, too superior to help carry the porters' forty-pound loads. A kettle and umbrella were as much as he was prepared to burden himself with. One particularly hot afternoon he lay down to rest under an Ol-Amalogi tree (*Maerua*) whose dense parasol canopy is shaped as high as the tallest animal can reach to feed off its nutritious leaves and seed pods. On the point of closing his eyes for a long afternoon's siesta, what he thought was a large pod fell into his lap. It took him a few seconds to realise it was very much alive.

Fortunately for the cook, the green mamba and he took fright in equal measure and fled simultaneously in opposite directions. His narrow escape delighted the rest of the team and cured him ever after of lazing about under trees.

Father took pity on a six-foot python he befriended after he and Bertie rescued it from a pack of camp dogs that had it bayed up a tree. He fed it on the march with any small animal – rat, mouse or bird – they could catch. Slow to withdraw his hand on one occasion, he was left with a deep triangular bite that healed into a jagged scar I remember well. He and the python parted company on their return to Nairobi for thirty rupees.

From the Loita Plains upstream of the Uaso Nyiro the party made for Ngorongore where the Government had recently put in dams for the Maasai. Here they shot duck, which made a welcome change from game meat.

On the way to the Mara River they camped for a few days in the Lemek Valley where they shot buffalo, crawling sometimes on hands and knees for the bush was exceedingly thick then, and the buffalo wary. They looked over hundreds of elephant but never found the big ivory they were hoping for. As Jock had shot his fill in the Lado Enclave, he was not prepared to shoot anything less than ninety

Joe Prettejohn, Michael Prettejohn's father, camping in Maasailand.

pounds. They fished for tilapia in the river, which was full of crocodile and hippo, neither of which they shot. Nor did they shoot waterbuck for no one, including the porters, would eat the meat.

About twenty miles on the other side of the Mara River is Lolgorien where gold had recently been discovered. Jock and Gwen took the opportunity to spend a couple of days to look at a mine there and left the Mara camp with some porters. The mine manager, an Australian mining engineer called Tobay, had come to Kenya from South Africa on his retirement after working on the Premier Diamond Fields outside Pretoria during the mining boom. He now worked for the American millionaire and philanthropist, Sir Northrup McMillan, who owned Juja Estate and a mountain called Ol Donyo Sabuk (Big or Fat Mountain in Maasai) near Thika.

Perhaps as an inducement to pave the way for Jock to cough up some money for Tobay's future mining plans, Tobay gave Gwen a fine aquamarine stone he had collected on Ol Donyo Sabuk. He believed the possibility of finding gemstones along the Athi to be very real and told them the story of the Dutchman who had turned up in 1910 at the Blue Posts hotel in Thika with a tobacco pouch filled with diamonds he claimed to have mined "somewhere near the Athi River." The truth of his claim was never confirmed for he never returned from South Africa where he was headed.

Geologically, explained Tobay, the area is made up of volcanic ash, mostly degenerated into black-cotton soil, through which intrude two granite formations, Ol Donyo Sabuk and Deacon's Hill. The latter hill took its name from the man who bought the land, including the hill, with the £700 proceeds from the sale of his Magadi Soda Company. Without bothering to terrace it, he simply ploughed from the bottom to the top in ever decreasing circles to plant maize and coffee.

About the time of the Dutchman's discovery, crystalline minerals – aquamarine, tourmaline, zircon and garnet – had been found where the two hills meet in an area of volcanic ash that had merely been compressed and not yet degenerated into soil. This discovery, backed by the Dutchman's claim, formed the basis for the Ndarugu diamond rush of 1911 that temporarily emptied Nairobi of would-be fortune makers. However, the pretty gems proved worthless; though diamond-shaped, zircons are brittle and many of those picked up were marred by red or blue discolouration.

Tobay, however, was not to be so easily put off and had done some prospecting on his own account. He had found signs of diamondiferous ground in the shape of garnet, olivine serpentine, and pieces of 'blue ground' kimberlitic while panning streambeds in the area, and believed there might be some truth in the Dutchman's find. He intended, as soon as his Lolgorien contract was up, to go back to South Africa to raise the capital necessary and return to the Athi to prospect for himself.

After this visit, my Grandmother Gwen and my Aunt Gwenydd were inspired to look for gold-bearing quartz – or other precious stones – along the Mara River. Grandmother did come across a likely source, but unfortunately she could not retrace her steps and the potential discovery remained undisclosed.

Still camped on the Mara River, and shortly before heading back, a Maasai *morani* came in to ask for help in ridding his *manyatta* of a leopard that had been eating the goats. Father, who saw his chance to bag a first, accompanied the man back to assess the situation. They chose an abandoned hut to use as a blind and made a decent-sized hole in one wall through which he would shoot when the leopard came. Before dark he took up position with a couple of motherless kid goats. He hoped their bleating would attract the leopard. He selected a 12-bore shotgun with a paradox barrel, loading the one with a slug the other with buckshot. Under the barrels he strapped a three-cell torch. To sustain his vigil, the *morani* had given him a gourd of sour milk. Knowing the gourd had been washed out with urine that has the dual purpose of acting as a natural sterilizer and souring the milk, he viewed the offering with suspicion at first. To his surprise, however, he found the drink refreshing and would later carry a supply on his daily cattle rounds.

Father had been led to believe the leopard would not come much before midnight, so he tried to take an early nap despite the noise and chatter outside that vied with the racket set up by the plaintive goats. Semi dozing, he was brought fully awake a few hours later by a commotion and the sharp drum of hooves by his panicked bait. He grabbed the gun and switched on the torch. The beam revealed the leopard already half way through the hole in the wall! Before he could loose off a shot, the leopard fled. By this time the whole camp was awake and although father sat up for the rest of that night, now fully alert, and over the following two nights, the leopard never came back. The party left the area and father missed his chance.

Awakened on another occasion by a camp dog that ran howling into his tent to take refuge under the bed, father suspected a leopard to be the cause. He shone the torch around outside, gun at the ready, but saw nothing and went back to bed. Soon he and the dog drifted off to sleep. In the morning, however, the dog was nowhere to be seen. Finding tracks of a leopard nearby, father could only surmise the leopard had snatched the dog.

On the homeward leg father remembered particularly the camp on the Siyapei River and the nearby hot springs from which water gushed out at boiling point.

The safari concluded with their return to Nairobi by train from Kijabe. It was the last time father travelled to the Mara by ox-wagon. Motor vehicles soon took over. The Mara became the hunting ground for anyone bent on filling contracts for zebra skins then on offer as a result of a world shortage for leather after the War. Now much of the area is a Game Reserve and has become the country's principal tourist attraction.

Chapter Nine

ZANZIBAR AND SOUTH WEST AFRICA

With negotiations to sell Larmudiac seemingly concluded, the family set sail from Mombasa in early September 1921 on a small coastal steamer bound for the island of Zanzibar.

Zanzibar is an historical Arab town dominated then by the Sultan's beautiful palace on the waterfront. Whitewashed stone houses with latticed windows lean towards each other across narrow streets. At the first docking you are assailed by the pungent scent of cloves mixed with that of drying copra. Like many ports along the coast, Zanzibar shares an Arab heritage through the ivory trade and slaving. At the time of father's visit it was predominantly Arab with a smattering of races from the Indian subcontinent.

The only hotel catering to Europeans went under the all-encompassing name, Africa Hotel. Situated in the middle of the town near the mosque, the noise from the general hubbub on the street kept them awake at night, and the call of the muezzin to prayer woke them too early in the morning. "It was pretty grim," father recalled. "We were served tinned fish for dinner despite the fact the island is surrounded by sea."

Always on the look out to make a deal, a Goan jeweller by the name of de Souza visited the travellers to show them his tempting selection of gems: sapphires, rubies, aquamarines and pearls. Buyer and seller bartered furiously ending up the best of friends, each with the impression that a bargain had been won.

When de Souza learned Jock was on his way south to look for

land, he introduced him to Arab and Indian plantation owners. Gwen was most taken with the island, which reminded her of Ceylon, and nearly persuaded Jock to buy a 700-acre coconut plantation. The island had high rainfall and good soil, but father feared he would be left behind to run things, and dissuaded Jock and his mother from buying land in Zanzibar.

For the sake of a quiet night the family moved out of the Africa Hotel. De Souza found them camping equipment that they set up on a bay to the south of the island where they collected oysters at low tide. The shell, known locally as *panga-jembe,* is L-shaped, the long end like a machete (*panga*), the short end like a hoe (*jembe*), and the tiny pearl lies between the two.

De Souza told them pearls were plentiful on the island and he had bought some of good quality from local fishermen, including a three-pound bag in weight from a Mozambique fisherman. Father told him he too had been offered pearls at Moçambique on his way up from Durban earlier that year, but had turned them down as being too small.

"Why not start with a pearl industry here?" suggested de Souza enthusiastically. "I could arrange it through the Sultan so that you'd have a monopoly." Father feared yet another enterprise which he would be left to deal with, and they declined the offer.

Father found Zanzibar a depressing place despite its lush and verdant beauty. The Arabs had lost their *raison d'être* with the end of the slave trade. The clove industry had slumped and many, former Arab grandees, found themselves in debt to Indian merchants to whom they were forced to sell their land and possessions. The humid climate did not appeal to him and he was relieved when they set sail for Durban on the *Korea*, the same ship they earlier sailed in to Kenya.

No sooner had the *Korea* set sail when the captain received a distress signal from a Portuguese passenger ship, the *Quilemane*, that had run aground on a reef a couple of hundred miles to the south of Zanzibar. The Captain scented salvage money and ordered, "All steam ahead." The *Quilemane*, a former Deutsche Ost Afrika mail steamer, had been harboured in a Portuguese port at the outbreak of the War and been commandeered and renamed. The *Korea* caught up with the beleaguered vessel late-morning on the second day. It was quickly rumoured aboard that its captain, a young twenty something, had been distracted from his duties by partying the evening before along with his crew and passengers, and had allowed his ship to run aground in dead calm seas.

Positioning himself hard astern, the *Korea's* captain lost no time in sending a cable across. This soon broke, as did a second. He then suggested the *Quilemane* jettison some of its cargo. Groundnuts floated to the surface, and passengers amused themselves by salvaging bobbing booty in buckets on the end of ropes. Finally, just before dark and in a still calm sea, the *Quilemane* was floated off using the last of the cables and left heading north with a bad list to starboard. The *Korea's* captain and crew gleefully added up their share of the salvage money which, father later learned, the Portuguese government reneged on.

Father had hoped to see the ship's purser, who he had gotten on so well with on his voyage out. His enquiries met with amusement as his co-officers explained with a tinge of admiration how the purser had absconded to Australia with a fortune entrusted to him by South African Indians for whom he had regularly smuggled out gold to Bombay. First gaining their confidence as a man of integrity, he finally cashed in, safe in the knowledge that their illegal machinations prevented them from coming after him.

Also on board was the mining engineer Tobay, who Jock and Gwen had met at Lolgorien. Tobay was on his way to South Africa to visit his brother for Christmas and raise the necessary capital to start prospecting for diamonds on the Athi River. Never one for letting a potential business opportunity slip by, Jock arranged that father would join Tobay on his return at the beginning of 1922. To finance this arrangement, Jock pledged five hundred pounds.

Mid voyage Jock changed his plans declaring they would head immediately for South West Africa (now Namibia). Land there was advantageously cheaper than in South Africa where the Dutch were already long established. Also South West Africa's German settlers were pulling out as a result of the dramatic post-war devaluation of the German mark that bankrupted the country.

From the port of Durban the family embarked on a five-day train journey northwards through Natal's rolling green country and the foothills of the Maluti Drakensberg Mountains climbing steeply to Johannesburg, and on south again through Orange Free State and Cape Province. Father described the oddity of the second-class coaches – which level of travel the parsimonious Jock chose – in having an open veranda at the back of the carriage with chairs and a table from which to enjoy sundowners and view the scenery. The carriage housed three bunks on the same side, sparing little room between the top bunk and the luggage rack. To father's dismay, he was always consigned the latter.

The train reached the Windhoek and Cape Town junction of De Aar in Cape Province. "A more desolate and windy stretch would be hard to imagine," father wrote. They waited two hours for a train to Windhoek. Travelling north again, just short of half way between De Aar and Windhoek, the train stopped at Upington on the Orange River. To relieve the cramped conditions of the train, Jock broke their journey there to await the arrival of the Windhoek train three days later. "The river was very low," noted father. "You could walk across it easily." A ferry lay idle waiting for the river to swell. Irrigated lucerne and fruit groves were in evidence, whose splash of green made a welcome change from the wind-shorn scrub and the ubiquitous pepper trees that adorned every station.

Despite travelling such vast distances through the northern edge of the Karroo and the south western part of the Kalahari Desert, an almost dead level inland sea of sand, up to the high Namibian plateau, father was disappointed to see so little game apart from the odd springbok, the occasional flock of sheep and virtually no cattle. He wondered why they had left Kenya on this harebrained mission to find pastures green in this bleak landscape. He was relieved to reach Windhoek, the end of their journey for the time being.

Windhoek is about a hundred and forty miles inland from the

Atlantic and lies in hillier, though still sandy, terrain. Patches of vines grew on the slopes interspersed with large thorn trees and scrub. Since the streets were unpaved and the roads not tarred, father was amazed to see a number of stone buildings – and gardens! Father made no mention at first of Windhoek's indigenous population; he simply stated: "Everything was German. German was the lingua franca of the country, for both whites and blacks." He was surprised the Germans had not been repatriated after the war as they had been in Tanganyika. In South West Africa they still farmed the land they owned and ran the businesses. Father was glad of the tutorship of his former German language master at Wellington, 'the Hun', as he was now able to communicate and act as translator for the others.

They stayed at the Thuringer Hof Hotel where father recalled the black waiter at breakfast: "He lounged by the door to the kitchen waiting for us to finish our porridge when he'd shout, 'Stek mit ei.'" The order was immediately followed by a plate half hidden under an enormous slab of steak topped with a couple of fried eggs.

The economy had fallen through the roof starting with the post-war slump that brought the price of commodities to an all time low: an ox or cow fetched five pounds and sheep around a pound a head. When the German mark dropped from fifty to a hundred thousand everyone thought it had bottomed out. People began to sell stock and mortgage farms to buy up marks. It then further slumped to four hundred thousand bankrupting many, and left a trail of despondency and despair to the point that conversation inevitably turned to so-and-so's recent suicide.

Conversely, one luckier investor father met owned properties in Hamburg on which he had raised a ten thousand pound mortgage on a single building – worth at the time about two hundred thousand marks – which he was able to repay in full with a postage stamp!

Barter became the norm. German farmers, the majority from Bavaria and Saxony, drove pony carts into Windhoek once or twice a month loaded with home-made sausages, smoked meats, sauerkraut, pickles and jams in exchange for sugar, tea, coffee and flour. Half the farms were for sale – no doubt Jock was comfortably aware he had not come all this way for nothing – but most were in hock to the bank.

Jock looked at various places with a land agent. Getting around was not easy; there were few cars and fewer roads, the latter often impassable either through deep sand *luggas* or swollen rivers. They soon learned the trick to get the car through sand was to switch off the engine, put the car in top gear and wind the starting handle while simultaneously walking backwards apace with the turning wheels – a laborious but sure method.

About this time father developed severe appendicitis, a condition that had first manifested itself in Durban where they docked earlier in the year on their way out from England. Father was sent to the convent in Windhoek where it was removed. "Nine inches long like a German sausage," noted father proudly. Worse than the operation was his humiliation, as a result of a linguistic misunderstanding, when the nuns asked him to shave.

"But I've just done so."

"Nein, Nein!" said the nuns as they undid his pyjamas; there was no escaping their meaning.

He obviously enjoyed his stay in the convent. The nuns were marvellous, the food good. Father, who later developed a cheese enterprise in Kenya, remarked on a particularly good cheese the nuns made that "smelled of dogs' turd." On a more tragic note the patient next door attempted to put an end to his insolvent miseries and father wrote: "The rest of my stay was uneventful except for a Prussian blowing his brains out in the room next to mine. Unfortunately he made a bad job of it and merely made a beastly mess and lived, groaning most of the time."

Chapter Ten

OTJIHAVERA

Out of hospital ten days later father found Jock negotiating to purchase Otjihavera Ranch, a 9,000-hectare (about 22,000 acres) spread 25 miles north of Windhoek with an annual rainfall of 12 inches. The price at a pound an acre included a thousand head of cattle and some poor-quality grade Karakul sheep. There were neither fences nor roads. Other than natural waterholes in the rains, the only permanent good water came from a spring on the flat lands to the west of the railway that ran through the middle of the ranch, and from a few smaller springs in the hills.

Heavily bushed flat lands, dominated by red-barked camel thorn, extended over two-thirds of the total. Winter grass provided hay over summer. The remainder was steep and rocky hill country, only negotiable on foot or on horseback, and heavily grassed with a sweet and palatable tufted variety the locals called silver grass.

The main house and stores looked across the railway to the ganger-cum-stationmaster's house. It was roomy and had a good quantity of crockery left over from the days when the trains had no dining car and passengers stopped over for a meal. Spacious cool cellars offered respite from the summer's ferocious heat, "a heat we were little used to even in Kenya." Nights could be cold, in winter particularly when the water in the jug would freeze over.

Of the stock that came with the sale of Otjihavera, the cattle comprised eleven different breeds of bull including Simmenthal, Pinagauer, red and white Friesian, Danish Red, Brown Swiss and even a Jersey. It was usual then, as in Kenya, to import thoroughbred bulls from Europe to upgrade the native cow. Later Hereford, Shorthorn and Sussex were imported. The Liebig family, Otjihavera's nearest neighbours, whose ranch measured a hundred square miles, had imported a herd of Sussex from England that did well.

To tide Jock over until the money from the sale of Larmudiac had come through, he took out a loan to develop the farm. He put down boreholes and fenced the flat country into 100-acre paddocks, using camel thorn fence posts and 10x13g oval steel wire. A borehole sunk at the foot of the hills provided water piped to the house and labour camp that up until then had had to rely on the station water tank filled sporadically by railway tanker.

The hills were too steep and rocky to fence. Cattle roamed free so long as the springs and waterholes lasted. Building dams was not practical as there were no suitable sites on the flat. Excavations at the base of the hills would have soon become silted up or broken through by the force of water that ran down the gullies and streambeds in the rains.

Jock immediately limited the bull stock to a few of the best beef breeds, particularly the Simmental as these were readily available locally. His initial policy to buy in and breed up would later change in favour of sheep, which would prove the best economic option. Steers were sold off as two-year olds at around ten pounds a head to the Imperial Cold Storage, or to agents who would either trek large mobs across the Kalahari to the Johannesburg market during the rainy season, or rail them south to Cape Town. There was not much money to be made in cattle, and no local market for them. Cattle would be rounded up every three months for branding, weaning or castrating. Handling these tasks turned into a riotous, rodeo-style affair as the animals were in good condition and really wild.

There were virtually no cattle diseases negating frequent dipping. The only dead animal, father remembered, was a cow that died in the middle of the labour camp. Jock suspected it had died by having a stick thrust up its anus, which kills without leaving any telltale sign. The men were denied their prize, however, for they were instructed to leave the cow pending post mortem. The vet never arrived and the meat rotted.

The mainstay of the ranch was the sale of Karakul pelts, better known in the fur trade as Persian lamb. The broad or fat-tailed Karakul originated in Uzbekistan and is probably one of the oldest breeds of domestic sheep. Archaeologists have found evidence of Karakul pelts from 1400 BC, and the breed is represented in carvings found in ancient Babylonian temples. Bred to survive on marginal lands and able to withstand temperature extremes, the German Government instigated a Karakul Breeding Station in Windhoek with a nucleus sent out from Halle, the progeny of an earlier gift from a Russian Tsar to the German Emperor. With too few ewes as yet to go around, the Station held a yearly sale of rams to upgrade the native sheep. Newly born lambs have tightly curled silky black fur. Theirs is a short life for they are skinned before they are three days old to provide the commercial lambskin which, according to the quality and tightness of the curl, is classified as Persian lamb, Karakul, broadtail, krimmer or astrakhan. The finest pelts come from unborn lambs. Before the Breeders' Sale, buyers would be committed to the deal on the basis of a photograph showing the quality and tightness of curl.

At the time Jock bought Otjihavera, the breed had also been established in South Africa at Grootfontein by Alex Holme, who later became Director of Agriculture in Kenya. On behalf of the South African Government, Holme sent five rams to Kenya, to its Government Stock Farm, with the purpose of upgrading the Maasai sheep – also fat-tailed – and by way of a thank-you to the Maasai for the animals they had given South African troops during the War.

Jock's requests for pure-bred ewes from the Windhoek station denied, he wrote off to South Africa but there, too, his request was turned down. Much later when demand in South Africa dropped – Karakuls fared less well in the damper climate further south – Jock negotiated to buy the station's entire pure-bred stock for a ridiculously low price, which he brought back by train to Otjihavera. Thus Jock became the largest private breeder of Karakul in South West Africa and did well out of them.

In February 1922 father received word from Tobay to say he was ready to start prospecting. Jock made arrangements for the release of the promised five hundred pounds and sent father on his way. Father had so far enjoyed the Otjihavera venture, but was glad of the six-month break for it was a lonely, secluded life for an eighteen-year old.

Chapter Eleven

DIAMONDS AND DISAPPOINTMENT

Father met up with Tobay in Johannesburg to catch a train as far as Durban where they boarded the British India ship, the *Taroba*, bound for Mombasa, and long due for the knackers' yard.

A fellow passenger, Lord Wilton, a member of the Grosvenor family, was on his way to Kenya to stay with his sister, Lady Mary Boyd. (Mary Boyd's son, Robin was my fellow pupil at Pembroke House School. The family is merited with being the oldest settler family in the Nanyuki district through her two daughters Jane Tatham-Water and Peggy Barkas. Peggy has never lived elsewhere.) A big spender, Wilton was reputed to have inherited a million pounds, which he managed to get through before the age of 21. The Boyds, on the other hand, never had a penny. Throughout the *Taroba*'s short voyage, Wilton and his party liberally quaffed champagne and partied, barely registering the enforced delay whilst divers from Laurenco Marques were brought in to cut through a heavy steel cable that had broken loose and become snagged in the propellers. The remaining passengers took to their bunks as the ship wallowed, too sick to stay up on deck.

On arrival in Kenya the two prospectors lost no time in acquiring equipment to prepare for a safari in the field. They were some of the last people to stay at The Stanley, the original, for it would soon be obliterated by an explosion, fortunately when empty, but undeniably engineered to collect on insurance.

As in South West Africa and the rest of the world, the Kenya economy had been affected by the Post War slump, further exacerbated by currency changes: the 1920 rupee changed to the florin, and two years later to the shilling, devaluing each time. Diamonds, it would seem, would solve all.

Father and Tobay took the train as far as Thika and the Blue Posts Hotel where the story of the Dutchman's diamond find had first come to light. The hotel was managed by Sidney Horne and his wife who Tobay had got to know whilst managing for McMillan at Ol Donyo Sabuk. Horne helped them to acquire porters and labour, most of whom came from western Kenya around Lake Victoria, and who were immune to malaria, particularly bad in the area to which they were headed. Horne agreed, for a share in the potential profits if any, to send stores and medicines down as required and, more importantly, promised to keep quiet about the venture. Thus manned, they set out east to the Athi River on foot.

Father was detailed to establish a semi-permanent camp and labour lines, which he built using *Makindu* palms for poles and grass thatch. He also made good use of the palm's straight rib to make furniture and ladders. On clearing the land, they immediately found signs of previous diggings, the remains, Tobay felt assured, of the Dutchman's excavations. Tobay immediately pegged the area into prospecting claims, and gravitated and concentrated gravels looking for indicators – olivine, garnet and zircon.

Work started at 7:30 am and went through to 4:30 pm. Father supervised while Tobay concentrated on washing and testing gravel samples from the streambeds. Father also provided the camp with meat. The north bank of the Athi had been designated Crown Land and provided plenty of game and game birds: impala, bushbuck, buffalo, waterbuck, kongoni, and guinea fowl and yellow-necked spurfowl. There were also hippo and crocodile in the river. Jock had loaned him a 12-bore paradox shot gun and a Manlicher .256 rifle he had left stored with the Nairobi armourers Shaw & Hunter, now Kenya Bunduki. He had trouble with the .256, which he concluded was as a result of Shaw & Hunter, its custodians, repeatedly hiring it out. When shooting for the pot failed, they bought sheep or lamb off the local Wakamba.

Traditionally a tribe of hunters, the Wakamba are excellent trackers and taught father a lot.

Father also attended to the sick at roll call assisted by the Buganda cook, a young man who had previously worked in a dispensary. This multi-talented Bugandan not only cooked, cared for the sick, washed, ironed and patched the clothes, but also was made responsible for paying out the wages.

Syphilis was rife among the Wakamba. When the Governor informed Churchill that venereal diseases were far too common throughout the country, Churchill replied: "Ah! *Pox Britannica!*" Father and Tobay were often laid low by malaria despite dosing themselves with quinine, and everyone was plagued by pepper ticks and the jigger flea. Pinhead sized pepper ticks cluster by the thousands on the end of a grass shoot and lie doggo until brushed off. A rubbing-down with liberal doses of paraffin works miracles but the itching persists for weeks afterwards. As for the excruciatingly itchy jigger flea who lays its eggs in a toe, only the African is experienced with needle or knife tip at removing the egg-sac whole.

The many rivers and streams in the area come down in spate during the rains and could only be forded by a precarious balancing act across fallen tree trunks. So the two prospectors had few visitors. The Hornes visited intermittently to bring in supplies and check on progress. On one visit they brought a fellow prospector, Cullinan, whose brother was reputed to have found the famous Cullinan diamond. Cullinan showed great enthusiasm and his encouragement added weight to their continuing efforts.

Other than hyena that ransacked the camp at night, and hippo that soon acquired a taste for the thatched walls, there were few distractions. Tobay opened up the first shaft by blasting through basalt rock to about ten feet where he found garnet and olivine, both associated with diamonds. These he subjected to the hydrofluoric acid test that dissolves all but the hardest corundum, without result. He blasted again to forty feet without finding anything, and then sank a second shaft that went down to sixty feet where he did at last hit on gravels that showed promise. Now full of hope, he sent samples to a mining friend working as a sorter for De Beers in Pretoria. Along with the good news that the tested samples had proved conclusive, and the specific gravity correct for diamonds, the bad news reported the samples to be too small to be of any value other than for industrial use.

By this time Tobay and father had been digging, drilling and blasting for six months, the money had come to an end and Jock was not about to finance further such a speculative venture. Hiding the evidence of their workings with thorn scrub, they packed up and returned to Nairobi. The mining lease still had a further six months to run, and Tobay, undaunted, counted on returning. He was not put off by the report from Pretoria, and would ascertain the validity of the find once he himself returned to South Africa.

Tobay had packed the samples in his brief case for the trek back, but at the last minute he transferred them to a pocket, a prescient inkling as his briefcase was stolen on the train from Thika.

Coincidentally, a well-respected geologist, Dr Hans Merenski, also working for De Beers, and who was to have a Platinum Reef named after him, happened to be travelling on the same steamer on which father and Tobay embarked as far as Durban. He and Tobay discussed the project at length, and Merenski offered to take the samples and get them re-tested. According to those tests the stones were demoted to zircons, and deemed utterly worthless. That was the last father saw of the 'diamonds' they'd worked so hard to collect. Nor did he ever work with Tobay again for the prospector soon sank his life and dreams into alcoholic oblivion.

It was not until thirty years later, in the early 1950s, that father would be tempted once more to take an interest in searching for diamonds on the Athi when idle talk kindled the excitement of an amateur mining friend, Mike Barrett, who quickly succeeded in getting his hands on some spare capital, and engaged the ready services of an Australian mining engineer. To father's dismay the area, once teeming with game, had since been turned into uniform rows of sisal following the post war boom in that commodity, with the remainder settled on by Wakamba squatters. Once the flooded shafts had been located and pumped out, the original pickaxe marks were still clearly visible. However, the timing of their venture was ill suited for it was 1952, the year the State of Emergency was declared. Father returned to the farm and the mining engineer, left alone at the mine, soon lost his nerve on hearing reports of sightings of armed terrorists passing close to camp – the Wakamba tribe had many Mau-Mau sympathisers – and the workings were once again abandoned.

Later the wooden building that served the Mines Department in Nairobi burned down with the loss of many of its early records, including the register of Tobay's mine. To build up destroyed departmental records, the Secretary for Mines contacted father to see if he'd be willing to show the site to a young consultant South African geologist, Jolyon Halse, holding out the carrot that father would be party to any share should the workings prove viable.

Halse's impression on arrival was not hopeful. He dismissed the area saying the formation would be highly unlikely to produce diamonds. Not insensitive to father's dashed hopes, Halse promised to return when he had more time to complete a thorough investigation. He never did, and father immigrated to South Africa in 1963.

Chapter Twelve

OTJIHAVERA REVISITED

On his way back to Otjihavera father stayed a week with Tobay in Boksburg where his brother owned a pub. It was mid-winter when he arrived, with heavy night frosts and cold mornings. He and Tobay spent a relaxed week rising late and visiting Boksburg's many pubs. The much older Tobay was a heavy drinker, but father, not yet nineteen, made the mistake of trying to match him. They visited the defunct Cinderella gold mine where Tobay set in motion a tipper bucket that hung suspended at one end of high cable. It careened down the line and collided with father, knocking him out cold; he woke up hours later spread-eagled on the conveyor belt.

Before father left Otjihavera for Kenya at the beginning of that year, Jock had asked him to report back on the Larmudiac situation, as all requests and demands for money had so far been met with silence. Birkbeck, he learned, was literally drinking himself to death, and had run up debts with the local Indian *duka wallah* – without whose generous lines of credit many a settler would have gone to the wall – who had commandeered some of Jock's best beef animals in recompense. Birkbeck had specifically been instructed not to sell any stock until he had paid for Larmudiac in full. It was evident Birkbeck's Trustees had no intention of ever paying. Jock and Gwen found themselves with no option but to return to Kenya to repossess Larmudiac, and pay off the £10,000-pound mortgage plus the interest. They left father behind with Ludwig, the German manager, to run Otjihavera in their absence.

When Jock returned to Kenya he took with him a record kudu head, which he had shot on the ranch in South West Africa. Jock's kudu head now hangs with his bongo trophy on my veranda at Sangare, near Mweiga.

During father's six months absence prospecting with Tobay, the developments Jock had instigated on Otjihavera were now almost complete, and Ludwig was becoming a dab hand at skinning Karakul and marketing pelts through a co-operative society in Leipzig in Germany.

Soon after his return, father found himself a good horse choosing two fillies out of a stampeding mob running wild on an adjoining ranch, the products of Arab mares and an imported English thoroughbred stallion called Monty, the son of a Derby winner. He gave up with one that would never accept being saddled up, let alone ridden; the other proved its worth and was his willing and loyal companion carrying him the length and breadth of the ranch on his daily rounds.

Father concentrated on the cattle. When there was a good moon in the hot season, he would ride out at night to check on the stock or look for breaks in the fencing. He dreaded the task of weaning, branding and castrating the cattle, which came round every three months. Infrequently handled, and roaming within such large enclosures, the cattle proved difficult to muster and handle. Cows with calves at foot consequently behaved with the instincts of a wild animal and could turn on you without provocation. The exercise seldom succeeded without a couple of the men sustaining broken bones and bruised ribs. As to the breaking of fences, kudu were not a problem as they could jump them. Ostrich, on the other hand, frequently broke through becoming ensnared, with the result that Ludwig determined to rid the place of them altogether. Killing the game we so value today seems extraordinarily shortsighted. But in those days game was considered competition to domestic livestock, carriers of disease, a nuisance, a pest, vermin and summarily exterminated.

Riding a light Cape cart pulled by two sturdy Basotho ponies – "game little animals, hardy as anything and rather reminded me of the Welsh cobs" – Ludwig and father either drove the ostriches onto unfenced land or into a corner where they shot them with rifles. They fed the meat to the pigs. Father added an exclamation mark in his diary, supposedly at the incongruity of feeding ostrich meat to pigs.

On one bright moonlight night ride father came across a porcupine making for its earth a hundred yards off. Curious to see how it behaved and if a porcupine could really shoot quills, he galloped ahead, dismounted and waited, armed with a bayonet. The porcupine arrived and turned round as if to go down the earth backwards, when suddenly father felt a sharp pain in his ankles. Looking down he saw a quiver of quills scattered at his feet and three deeply embedded. The attack surprised him and before he could think of retaliation the porcupine had disappeared.

They kraaled the sheep at night to protect them from leopard. Leopard there lacked the temerity of Kenya's leopards, seldom jumping into a pen. Rarely, too, did they lose a calf as the cattle defended their young. If they did lose sheep it was more likely due to a toxic bulb that sprouted soon after the rains rather than from predators.

Together with cattle and sheep, there were a number of pigs for which there was a good market in Windhoek. They fed the pigs on the remains of old cows, slaughtered lamb and donkey. They bought donkeys from the pound in Windhoek for practically nothing. The job of killing a donkey was fortunately Ludwig's. His method was quick: a single blow to the head with a sledgehammer. On one occasion he brought down the sledgehammer with his usual aplomb only to have the head of the hammer come loose and strike the unfortunate Ovambo who held the halter. The Ovambo dropped like a stone, while the donkey, still blindfolded, ran off braying to freedom. Fortunately for the Ovambo helper, his concussion was brief.

Domestic arrangements at Otjihavera were bachelor-run at best. Perishables stayed fresh stored in a Heath-Robinson cold room built with walls of charcoal sandwiched between two layers of wire mesh over which they ran water from a perforated pipe along the top; the whole apparatus was wind-ventilated. The floor and shelves were made of concrete. An Ovambo woman came in to wash up and clean, but Ludwig did all the cooking. He made bread, and dried pasta to add to soups. He pickled seasonal vegetables, gherkins mainly, that he stored in three-gallon earthenware jars. Ludwig also concocted a type of smooth cottage cheese – the same stink cheese father had so admired after losing his appendix in Windhoek – with skimmed milk to which he added a half measure of butter. On Sundays he and father would take it in turns to bake a cake from a recipe out of their single German cookbook. "Another blitzkucken!" teased Ludwig.

As they lived day in day out off roasted goat or sheep, hot first time round and thereafter cold, father was surprised when Ludwig invited two visiting policeman to lunch for he knew how much Ludwig disliked them. The meat dish, father later learned to his disgust, had been made from a chunk of the sheep-killing leopard whose carcass father had passed on the rubbish dump earlier that day.

The majority of the labour force was made up of Ovambo. Father likened the Ovambo to Kenya's hard-working Kikuyu. Like them, Ovambo society is a matriarchal one. Part of the Bantu family, it is generally thought the Ovambo migrated southwards from the great lakes in East Africa. Conversely, father found the Herero to be sullen, surly and unreliable. This was hardly surprising in view of recent history. Herders with close links to their land, the Herero rose up against the Germans in 1904 but were brutally crushed as a result of the infamous 'Extermination Order' during which 75 percent of the population perished and the survivors were scattered all over the country. The suppression of the Herero revolt was one of the bloodiest in European colonial history. But it is generally acknowledged that whilst the Hereros were fighting for their survival against land-hungry Germans, the German troops' brutal measures were at least partly the result of alleged atrocities committed by the Herero.

After the German defeat in the Great War, the Governor General of South Africa, Lord Buxton, visited Windhoek and told the Herero Chieftains that the English recognised Herero sovereignty and their interests would be paramount. This caused great anxiety among the German settlers who felt the Herero, who had guns, needed little encouragement to rise up again. Warned of just such a threat, father and Ludwig spent Christmas of 1922 barricaded in the Station House where there was a telephone, taking it in turns to do sentry duty throughout the nights.

1922 was one of the worst drought years. As a result, the birth rate among the cattle dropped and many farms let their cattle roam unchecked making easier the job of cattle rustling. Thefts were wholesale: syndicates operating out of Windhoek fenced the stolen cattle, which were immediately trained down to the Union (South Africa). The sheep suffered less from the drought, although three-quarters of the lambs had to be slaughtered to save the ewes. Otjihavera ran about 3000 head of sheep and maintained a policy to up-grade the sheep and increase the size of the flock. Persian lamb coats are exceedingly expensive as the hair on a Karakul pelt is not uniform. It takes many pelts from which a quantity of matched pieces of the same quality and pattern is cut to make up a coat. A short coat at that time would have cost upwards of six hundred pounds. Add a nought and you have some idea of what the price would be today.

Ludwig and father's social life on Otjihavera was dismal. The only neighbour father felt any kinship with was a Bavarian, Herr Goesinde, who he rode over to see from time to time. Goesinde and his wife and their young children fulfilled for him the role of family he obviously missed. His nearest neighbour, a hick South African by the name of Proudfoot, was the ganger/stationmaster who lived in the house opposite on the other side of the railway line. They had little in common and their meetings were infrequent unless unavoidable when Mrs Proudfoot visited to "borrow something – food, saucepan or spanner."

To relieve the tedium of life on Otjihavera father rode the 25 miles into Windhoek leaving early in the morning and getting back late evening. Sometimes, if there were stores to be brought back, he would take the Cape Cart with the Basotho ponies. There was little to tempt father into staying in Windhoek. There was no cinema or theatre, only a zoo with very few animals and a botanical garden. "If

I stayed the night there was nothing to do but drink." The Germans drank copious amounts – around thirty-eight glasses boasted the barman of the Turnhalle, the town's sole social focal point.

Father's Namibian interlude came to an end in June 1923 after eighteen months. Besides frequently falling ill to recurring malaria, a relic from his time on the Athi River, Jock needed him back in Kenya to help get Larmudiac back on its feet. He took a train to Swakopmund which, father recalled, "had been a thriving resort in its German heyday with a yacht club, but was now absolutely dead and in the depths of despondency." His last views of Namibia from aboard the ship bound for Mombasa were of unending sand, interspersed with the emerald-green oases of sweet surface water pumped up by windmills that lined the shore between Swakopmund and Walvis Bay.

Chapter Thirteen

LARMUDIAC

Although nearly two years had elapsed since father first arrived in Kenya, he had not yet got as far as Njoro, nor seen the much-talked-about ranch, Larmudiac. Anxious to get there at last, he wasted no time in Nairobi, but headed directly by train for Njoro. Exhausted by days of continual travel, the last few miles to Sabugo house by ox-cart seemed to take forever.

Larmudiac stands at 7000 feet with its back to the Mau Escarpment, whose forested slopes, at that time still covered in the grey green of the African olive and the deeper hues of feathery podo and cedar, rise to over 10,000 feet. The forests echoed with the sounds of birds and colobus and Sykes monkeys. Larmudiac looked northward across wheat-coloured plains of tall grass that comprised two farms recently purchased by Jock, Olbwan and Naishi, and beyond to Lake Nakuru's flamingo-fringed shores and the distant Aberdare Mountains. It was an ever-changing landscape of depth and colour according to the weather and the time of day, from cool grey to blue and indigo and deep purple in the shadows of billowing and scudding clouds unique to African skies. In the rains

Grandmother Harries' ox-drawn buggy

these mass overhead: titan sculptures simultaneously scored at the base with the jagged charcoal strokes of rain-filled vapour as their tops retain the sun's reflected glow. The nights and early mornings are cold, the days pleasantly cool. Father simply could not believe Jock could

Naishi house and dam on Larmudiac.

have contemplated turning his back on this God-given lush beauty for the arid wastes of Namibia.

The Harries were unconventional to say the least, and ran their setup in a haphazard and bohemian manner. In Nellie Grant's published letters she writes to her daughter, the author Elspeth Huxley, describing the Harries' setup (father thought the description unfair):

"They lived like the pigs they grew, only didn't house themselves as they did the pigs. But inside an awful house – if you were bold enough to go to lunch there – you found an enormous, genuine refectory table, about sixteen really good Chippendale chairs, Black Harries carving a colossal hunk of meat at one end of the table and Ma Harries dismembering innumerable fowls at the other.

"Black Harries was immensely strong and once pulled a wounded leopard backwards by the tail out of a bush saying: 'It's a cat, so it will pull away from me.' Then he finished it off by a blow to the head. One day, I was having trouble putting some of my young stock through the cattle dip. Harries happened to come by: he picked up a three-quarters grown steer which got back to front in the dip, lifted it right off its legs, swung it round to face the right way and pushed it into the dip.

"The savagery they lived in! Such a mixture. Fierce dogs

biting guests on arrival, the lovely Chippendale chairs, and dirt everywhere. Worse was to come when they moved from Larmudiac to another vast holding in Solai. You walked up to the house, or hut, deep in animal bones. When you sat down to a meal you had to push Muscovy ducks off the Chippendale chairs. A hatch was opened between kitchen and living room and an indescribable, utterly horrible stench belched forth, followed by the food. The Harries' bedroom, a large rondavel, was shared between the marital bed and a large, probably 500-egg, incubator. The roof above was lined with a tarpaulin to keep the incubator, not the Harries, dry."

Joe Prettejohn and his mother Gwen at Larmudiac, 1920s.

Perhaps when Nellie wrote this she'd just had a set to with Jock, as was often the case. In one of Elspeth's last books written before she died – ***Out in the Midday Sun - My Kenya*** – Elspeth describes the contrasting nature of two of Nellie's Njoro neighbours and the acrimony that existed between Nellie and Jock:

"At the other extreme from the Lindstroms in their attitude to life and labour was the Harries family, headed by Black Harries, so called because of his swarthy countenance and bushy black beard. His attitude towards his labour was the reverse of permissive, and he was on bad terms with some of his neighbours, including Ingrid (Lindstrom) and Nellie; he conducted against them a war of chits which would arrive at all hours with messages such as 'Your squatters' cattle have broken into my maize' or 'I have reason to believe that you

are sheltering one of my boys who has run away and is hiding on your land.' No one paid much attention to these missives. Nellie said that the Harries lived like the pigs they kept, in a sort of gypsy encampment surrounded by discarded bones, but she was prejudiced against them, as she was the first to admit."

Sabugo is a Maasai term for cold and wet high country. Sabugo house had originally been built by Berkeley Cole from whom Jock bought the ranch. Later additions and homely touches had long since evaporated following Ben and Ginger Birkbeck's departure. The house was well described a pigsty: its walls were made of uneven, bark-covered cedar off-cuts haphazardly wired together. Sunlight shafted through the cracks to mingle with dust from packed earth floors. The whole was topped by an untidy mop of thinning thatch through which the rain poured in. At the front of the house, in a stretch of scum-green water, swam ducks and geese, wild birds, too, who shat on the lawn – or what might have been a lawn if it were not for the fowls' scratching and pecking. Their feathers, indistinguishable from dogs' half-chewed and sun-bleached bones, littered the ground. Gwen limited her household organisation to keeping everything 'walkable'

Naishi dam on Larmudiac.

under lock and key safe from pilfering servants – a common enough belief at the time. She had little concern for the English antiques brought out from various Welsh properties, so long as these were utilitarian.

The neighbours might have frowned on the way they lived, but such eccentricities and chaos appealed to children for they, like the domestic animals, ran wild or galloped the ponies without censure. Tobina Cole, who lived for a few years with Nellie Grant after her mother died, remembers joyous rides chasing rhino with Jock. She also remembers him seeing a water bailiff off the farm, shouting after his retreating back that if he dared return with his superior, they'd have to bring an ambulance.

Jock's super human strength was legendary. David Hopcraft, who now ranches not far from Nairobi, remembers a visit as a child shortly after his parents had moved to Njoro from Naivasha in the 1930s. Jock invited the family over, as he did with all newcomers to the district. On the way over, Hopcraft told the small boy that the man he was about to meet was one of only two men in the country to have passed the South African test of supreme strength by lifting a 44-gallon drum filled with water onto the back of an ox-wagon. In awe, David shyly put out a hand and was surprised by the warmth of Jock's greeting in return; his firm handshake and obvious pleasure made David feel he was an accepted member of that normally distant adult world as Jock banished the dogs and led him chatting to his seat at the tea table.

The Hopcrafts would become one of the district's largest pig producers. David also recalls the story of a new manager, a young man fresh off the boat from England. Hopcraft had ordered him to oversee the loading of pigs onto a railway wagon. Desperately trying to gain the upper hand, for the situation was quite beyond his control with squealing pigs divided in all directions, Jock turned up. By way of example, and to the young man's surprise, Jock grabbed a brace taking a hind leg in each hand, and heaved the pigs onto the truck, exhorting him meanwhile: "Now that's how it's done my boy. Get on with it!"

In the late 1930s Kathleen Fielden and her first husband Robin Ball, an agricultural officer in charge of the Plant Breeding Station at Njoro, visited Larmudiac to buy pigs. One of the herd boys received a gash while loading the pigs onto the lorry. Kathleen, newly arrived in the country, reached into her handbag and produced a piece of plaster, which she administered to the bleeding cut. She and Robin then went into the house for a drink. "A man servant appeared," Kathleen recalls, "bearing a large netted cage, its floor lined with straw, which he carefully laid upon the table. Gwen rose taking a key from a bunch tied around her ample waist to unlock the door. We all sat spellbound thinking this must be some prize cockerel the Harries were nurturing. Imagine our surprise then when instead an alarm clock was brought out. Gwen wound it up, replaced it on its straw bed with the due reverence of a priest administering Holy Communion, and said as she locked the door again: 'These fellers will break anything!'"

On the point of driving home, Robin was surprised to see nine pigs rather than the eight they had bought. "He'll never know!" said the African pig boy.

During the lean years of the depression, the staple diet, maize, fell from twelve shillings a bag to three. Milk and beef prices were at an all time low, and the market for pigs ceased to exist. Jock let his loose to forage for themselves.

Pig farming, as with all commodities, tends to follow the maxim: 'When you're in, the price goes down, and up when out.' At a time when pigs were in short supply, Jock received a telegram from the Uplands Bacon factory near Nairobi asking him to supply 50 pigs. Jock organised the labour into driving the swamp around Larmudiac dam to round up as many pigs as they could. This produced a net of about 60, which they herded to

Stockyard on Larmudiac.

Njoro and loaded onto the train. As the wagon doors were opened on arrival, the pigs dashed out in a bid to regain their wild and carefree existence. It took some mustering to herd the small band of hardy but skinny pigs back into order. Jock soon received another telegram from Uplands stating that the condition of the pigs delivered was of unacceptable quality. In reply Jock told them bluntly it was pigs they'd asked for and pigs they'd got. They didn't argue and paid up.

Michael Prettejohn

Book Two

1921 - 1963

The Story of Joe Prettejohn (my father)
and his brother Dick

Chapter Fourteen

DICK PRETTEJOHN - MY UNCLE

Jock had led father to believe that in return for his help in running Larmudiac, Otjihavera would in time be his, together with a one-third share of Larmudiac. While his immediate and most basic needs were taken care of, and his social life confined to the occasional picnic with close neighbours, he was not paid a salary, a situation he accepted on the grounds that his labour and dedication equated to ownership.

Jock also lured father's elder brother, Dick Prettejohn to Kenya with promises that never materialised. Dick was born in Ceylon at the turn of the century but returned to England for good at the age of three with Grandmother in time for father's birth. Dick's Kenya chapter coincides with his younger brother's return from South West Africa, the two coming together at their mother's behest to help Jock repossess Larmudiac. Dick relinquished his commission with the Skinner's Horse in India and arrived four months later in October 1923 with his wife Vivienne.

Uncle Dick Prettejohn.

After Sandhurst, Dick served with the Welsh Regiment in India for a year before joining the Skinner's Horse. In England he had become engaged to Joan Festing-Smith, a granddaughter of Lord Kimsales. But on his first leave he met Vivienne Le Suear Green and her brother Jack on the boat home. He fell madly for Vivienne, and broke off his engagement with Joan the minute they got ashore in England. Vivienne was ten years Dick's senior and a fraction of his imposing height. No one understood the attraction for she was short, square and slightly bow-legged, traits that age only accentuated. The daughter of the Postmaster General in Mauritius, she had been staying in India with an Aunt who, father claimed, was the "keeper of a Bombay boarding house." Although Vivienne purported to share French and English parentage, she was never socially accepted in Kenya where her provenance was viewed with suspicion. Likewise, Jock took against her and their relationship got off to a bad start, a state of affairs that went a long way to souring Jock and Dick's friendship.

Dick and Vivienne soon found they were strapped for cash. Vivienne and the Harries were barely on speaking terms. Sadly, there were no children. But despite all, Dick never ceased loving her. In testimony, when Dick died in the early 1970s, I found Vivienne's room untouched, enshrined since her death many years before, her dressing table neatly laid with half-filled scent bottles and powder boxes covered in cobwebs and dust, and her dresses, which exuded a musty smell of old scent, hung in the cupboard exactly as she had left them.

He never married again – although the family hoped he might avoid loneliness in later life by teaming up with Fish Lindstrom's widow, Ingrid. Dick spent his last years on Larmudiac a virtual recluse.

Aunt Vivienne with dogs and a friend on Larmudiac.

Tony Seth-Smith, a great friend and professional hunter, farmed nearby to Uncle Dick in the 1960s. Tony knew that the Quelea birds, extremely damaging to wheat and not dissimilar in their raiding antics from locust, were roosting in the extensive reed beds around the dams. He suggested to Dick that he and some friends come over with their shotguns one evening to encourage the Quelea to move on elsewhere. Dick joined them in a line strung out along the water's edge. Tony first fired a couple of rounds of buckshot into the thick reeds to get the birds up. After a time he heard to his dismay the distinct bovine bellow of an animal in distress. How was he to explain to Dick that one of his purebred Red Polls had become the victim of Quelea control?

"Damn it," said Dick, "that bull's bin missing a couple days – couldn't think what had happened to it." Fortunately, and to Tony's relief, the animal had merely become mired in the mud and was hauled out unscathed.

Dick was the sort of man younger men automatically addressed as 'Sir.' From the standpoint of height he certainly had the advantage, and when spoken to would stare his interlocutor down before clearing his throat, an action which emitted a low growl. You were never quite sure that he had in fact heard you and you should repeat the question or greeting, or whether you had said something to offend. Like Jock he was never without a hat. In his latter years he drove a 1960s Holden which I still use as my Nairobi car and leave at Wilson Airport. On his rare visits into Nakuru Dick would invariably be accompanied by two or three Maasai, all sitting bolt upright. Driving behind him, Tony recalls an image of Dick's flat-topped sola topi at the

Aunt Vivienne with baby waterbuck.

wheel and behind it a row of bald, black heads with elongated ears punctured and adorned with beads that bobbed and swayed in unison over the bumps.

Aunt Vivienne with colobus monkey.

In the early days, however, life was indeed dull; Dick and Vivienne had few friends. Vivienne's social status apart, there were few neighbours, and Dick, who had played polo in India, found he could not now afford it. It was not until Vivienne's brother Jack Green – he had dropped the Suear – came out that Vivienne and Dick regained their independence by joining Jack and others in an enterprise farming essential oils from geraniums into which Dick invested his army gratuity.

Jack Green had a wild story to tell about a man named Deeming, the perpetrator of a gold heist and subsequent murder. Deeming purportedly raided a gold train on its way from the Transvaal to Lourenço Marques in Mozambique, shot the guards, and got away with gold bars worth £15,000, an absolute fortune in today's terms. He escaped through Delagoa Bay where he boarded an Arab dhow, eventually reaching Lamu on Kenya's north coast where he disembarked. His stay on the island was short lived; enquiries were being made forcing Deeming to move on. Hiding the bulk of the bullion, he hurriedly boarded another dhow for Aden from whence he shipped out to Australia where he bought land and took up farming.

He later murdered a woman and her children, burying the bodies under a cement floor, and was sentenced to the gallows. On the night before his execution, Deeming confessed to the governor of the jail how, before being forced to flee from Lamu, he had hidden the bulk of the gold by burying it in a grave. He had first noticed the grave, one of five cut out of the side of a sand dune, and enclosed by a low coral rag wall on the ocean side of Shela Village on Lamu's south eastern corner. His confession pinpointed the grave as that of Boatswain William Searle who had fallen to his death from the mast of a British Man O'War. The concrete slab covering the grave, he had noticed, was fissured with a sapling growing through it. He had hidden the gold beneath the slab.

Deeming had asked the prison Governor to send a full account of his confession to a South African relative. It was thought that the South African did visit Lamu but was unable, even with help from the authorities, to locate the grave and returned empty handed.

Jack Green told this story to a friend of his in Mombasa who published it in the local newspaper. At the time, 1938, he and Jack made plans to go to Lamu to look for the grave with a map that Green claimed to have. Green's journalist friend couldn't go and the shared trip never materialised. However, when Green, who never had a penny, (the essential oils business had been underwritten by friends and in the final analysis produced little profit) died in the Seychelles twenty years later, he left his sister, Dick's wife Vivienne, £30,000. This legacy came as such a surprise that father and Dick could only speculate that a successful outcome to unearthing Deeming's buried treasure was the only way Green could have come by such a tidy sum.

After the Second World War a group from Kenya visited Lamu to look for the treasure. They found the gravesite and the concrete slab described buried under sand, but further probing concluded nil result, an empty hole, the gold long gone. I visited the site in Lamu many years later. The graves and the sand disturbances are still there but few today know of this story told to us by Uncle Dick's brother-in-law Jack Green.

Chapter Fifteen

EARLY DAYS - 1920s

At the time of the brothers' arrival, Jock had a total holding of about 15,000 acres. In addition he had grazing rights over 10,000 acres leased from the Forest Department at a paltry annual rent of one cent an acre. Magnificent tall cedars grew on the reserve's upper reaches giving way lower down to flat-topped acacia and *euphorbia candelabra* forest.

As herd numbers increased, Jock bought a further 4,000 acres in 1925 on the Mau Escarpment above Lake Elmenteita off the Block family paying a pound an acre for their Kitungwen farm, a marked increase from the 6d an acre he paid for Larmudiac in 1911. "Thank goodness I now have no land and no overdraft," said a relieved Block after the sale.

To give Jock access to the Makalia River that flows into Lake Nakuru, and as a holding ground for cattle moving between Njoro and Elmenteita, Jock acquired a further 500 acres from 'Dirty' Douglas whose nickname reflected a manner of living similar to that of the Harries. Douglas had extensive land holdings around the country. Such are the ramifications of Kenya families that Douglas's wife, Elizabeth, would marry Will Powys the second time round. Their children, Charles, Gilfrid and Rose were my contemporaries and very much a part of my life from the time we were all children growing up around Mount Kenya. Later, Gilfrid Powys and I would become partners in the million-acre Galana Development Scheme in Kenya's arid coastal hinterland. The Douglas' first marriage produced a daughter, Delia, who married David Craig. The Powys and Craig families are today, two and three generations later, Kenya's largest white land owners ranching and game ranching extensive acres north of Mount Kenya.

By the end of the 1920s Kenya settlers had steadily gained a measure of independence from London regarding land regulations, labour laws, and fiscal matters through the dogged efforts of their spokesmen such as Delamere and Grogan. 1927 was a boom year and land prices soared. Exports exceeded imports for the first time in 1928. The railway had been extended with a network of branch lines and was in profit.

In the late 1920s taking advantage of a wheat farm adjoining Kitungwen that had gone into receivership, Jock relieved its owner, Owen, of 1,000 acres. 1930 saw Jock's final expansionist purchase for the area negotiated by swapping 1,500 head of mixed cattle for 1,500 acres adjoining the Douglas land, bringing his entire holding, excluding the rented forest grazing, to 22,000 acres. Its owner, Barrett, had felled 75 percent of this once-forested holding, resulting in subsequent Kikuyu grass coverage that now afforded excellent grazing.

Initially, the two brothers shared the tasks of overseeing clearing, planting and stock-rearing, but this would soon divide between the two: father becoming solely responsible for stock whilst Dick, by preference and ability, took on the building, dam-making and fencing, and the mechanical side which went hand in hand with arable management. Father began with a herd of about 1,800 head. Seven years later, at the time of the Barrett purchase, the stock had swelled to 5,500.

In a bid to weed out earlier Hereford stock, whose pale eyes were prone to sunburn, Jock had gone over to Shorthorns. By 1925, imported Red Poll bulls superseded the Shorthorns and were used almost exclusively, except on the heifers. These were put to the hardier, humpback Boran bulls.

The dairy herd comprised some 600-head milked between six moveable dairies. The milking ritual, morning and evening, never

Red polls, imported stock from the UK, on Larmudiac.

failed to delight father. Allotted a quota, each milker calls in turn a cow by name, whistling her into place on a rising or descending note *who-whuo, whow-hit, who-weeo, u* whereupon the animal nuzzles her nose deep into a *kerai* filled with bran or cattle-cake and pushes the food around while finches and sparrows dart in to pick up the spillage. Thus occupied, the milker greases her udders before squatting down on his haunches in that easy fluid way that Africans do, to begin his task with a gentle downward massage. The first splash of milk hits the bucket with a metallic echo, the sound becoming ever subdued as his rhythmic milking fills it. Timed to finish just as the cow licks up the last of the grain, he slaps her rump and sends her clattering on her way. He then hands the bucket to another for weighing and recording. The milk is poured into the separator, the empty bucket handed back. The milker whistles up the next and bends to his task once more.

The cream, separated out every other day, was sent by train to Lumbwa to the Co-operative Creamery where Jock sat on the board. Labour had first call on the skim milk, whilst the remainder was fed to the pigs. These consisted mainly of the Large White variety with Tanworths introduced later to give the baconers extra length.

As cattle numbers rose, water development became essential.

In addition to the main Larmudiac dam and surrounding swamp, Jock had put in two non-permanent dams on the Olbwan and Naishi farms lower down. Together with the slender Naishi River, which ran for about six to eight months of the year, there were also two good springs: one central to his entire holding, the other on its southern boundary. The Makalia, then a permanent stream, fed the Forest Reserve grazing. Shortly after Dick's arrival, Jock put in a second dam at Sabugo and laid in piping from the central spring, via troughs, to Olbwan, four miles away. Boundary fencing was first erected followed by field delineation.

Gwen met the development costs from funds derived from her English estates. She also funded her own projects that included importing poultry – geese, chickens, turkeys and duck - and the paraphernalia that went with them. Gwen later embarked on a market-gardening enterprise, in which she was assisted by assorted young men and women from England, eventually retailing the produce through her own shop in Nakuru, the Farmers' Mart.

Dick built himself and Vivienne a small house a few miles distant from Sabugo on the same ridge, while father put up a simple wattle and daub bachelor pad at Naishi, where he could more easily supervise an 800-acre section of newly cleared land planted with maize.

Two interchanging teams of sixteen oxen, pulling three-furrow disc ploughs, worked approximately four acres a day. The first team in-spanned at first light, and worked through until midday when the second team took over until evening. It was a wonderful sight to watch these great bull eunuchs, guided by a single man and the crack of his whip, as they lumbered and toiled uncomplaining. An occasional swish of tail and twitching ear were the only signs of irritation at the incessant probing and pecking from tickbirds.

Father and Dick spent weekends hunting buffalo in the Forest Reserve to deter them from raiding the maize, none too successfully father noted, for the paltry yield of five bags to the acre was testament to nightly forays by herds of up to a hundred buffalo.

Dick's hands were full with fencing and dam building, and father was increasingly occupied with the cattle, so Jock later took on a one-legged South African to supervise the cultivation. Unfortunately named Van de Merwe, a name so associated with anti-Boer jokes, the mere mention of his name on introduction would tickle the memory of past jokes.

In those early days farm labour was difficult to come by. The country's indigenous population was only a tenth of what it is today and the concept of working for cash was alien to its culture. As land was a greater inducement than cash, the system of squatters came into being with the dual purpose of clearing the land cheaply and of providing a way of life for the labourer, particularly for the agricultural-based tribes – the Kikuyu and the Kipsigis. In this way squatters cleared about 2,000 acres of bush on Olbwan. Squatters were under three-year contracts, with a month's notice either side, to work 180 days a year and in addition produce two sons to work on the farm on a salaried basis with rations. Surplus produce grown by the squatter was sold to the farm at an agreed, fixed rate. The women were similarly employed in the less arduous roles of grass cutting for thatching or cleaning and picking maize. In addition to growing food, each family kept up to 50 sheep or goats. The pastoralist Maasai, assisted by men of the Kipsigis tribe, herded. The Kipsigis made excellent grooms but had

Pay day on Larmudiac.

Michael Prettejohn

a tendency to drink the highly potent, and sometimes fatal, alcohol made from honey and grain.

Stock losses ran up to about five percent a year. Theft then was negligible. Disease took its toll, particularly diseases carried by tick, fly and mosquito. However, the greatest losses were incurred through predators: wild dog, leopard and hyena.

Marauding leopard killed on Larmudiac.

As in South West Africa, Kenya farmers and ranchers in those early days – and a few even today – had little sentiment where wildlife competed for grazing or preyed upon domestic stock. Of the predators, wild dog was the easiest to exterminate being on the whole fearless of man and at the same time curious. They and hyenas were also easy prey to poisoned meat. (In recent years with the loss of game, and the loss in particular since independence of large tracts of land and wildlife habitat, people have been made more aware of the necessity, though not without some loss obviously, to combine the two. Some of the larger ranches, such as the Craig family's Lewa Ranch, turned entirely to game ranching in the early 1980s, a move which has brought in more revenue from tourism than from cattle. My small ranch at Mweiga successfully combines the two.)

Lions were a menace to the cattle and were considered vermin

Father rode an average of 15 miles a day, seven days a week, to check on or count the various herds, usually accompanied by one of his Maasai headmen, Kikori or Barteli.

His horse had been named Fisi, the Swahili word for hyena, after surviving a savage attack as a foal that left the jugular exposed. Understandably difficult to break, and prone to bolt for no good reason, she was high-spirited with a sense of humour, if a horse can be said to have one, as though

Joe Prettejohn lived on horseback checking on the stock.

determined to live life to the full in defiance of early adversity.

On one occasion in 1926, armed with a rifle and accompanied by Barteli, father rode out along the eastern Forest Reserve boundary that bordered Boy Long's Nderit Estate, on the trail of a pack of wild dogs particularly numerous and troublesome at that time. Barteli had been telling father the story of how the Maasai Laikipiak clan, who traditionally inhabited the northern Laikipia plains, succeeded in merging with the much larger Purko clan from the south.

The Purko chiefs, Barteli related, stipulated that a merger would only be possible if the Laikipiak were to overcome the Herculean conundrum of producing six pairs of sandals with hair on both sides, and a gourd filled with fleas. The meeting was to take place at Eburru, north of Lake Naivasha, where water gushes out of the ground in a series of hot steam jets. In due course the Laikipiak met as agreed with the six pairs of sandals made out of donkeys' ears and a gourd filled with the small, chopped pieces of a wildebeest's tail. As soon as they opened the gourd over a steam jet, the hairs flew out in the manner of fleas. The astounded Purko were forced to concede. Now merger made them the most powerful of the clans and enabled them, after a three-day scrap, to banish the Uasin Gishu Maasai living on the Elmenteita plains back to the Uasin Gishu Plateau around Eldoret.

Engrossed in listening to the story, and with the reins hanging slack over Fisi's saddle, father was totally unprepared when his horse bolted. Mindful of not being swept off by a protruding branch as he

103

Maasai warriors at a ceremony.

galloped towards a patch of forest ahead, he threw his gun away to snatch at the reins with both hands. Fisi stumbled and father fell. He landed heavily, the breath knocked out of him. He realised immediately he had dislocated his elbow and the pain in his back was acute. Barteli administered to him in the best way he knew how by placing a foot on father's stomach and yanking the protruding elbow bone painfully back into place. He then helped father up, found the discarded rifle, and they set off for home. Fisi, meanwhile, trotted on ahead just out of reach.

On the way back they passed by a milking bail supervised by Kikori, who was well known for his natural healing abilities. He had cured a cow with a dislocated spine by keeping her suspended above a wooden platform. To everyone's amazement, as soon as she was lowered back onto her feet sometime later, she simply walked off mended. They stopped by and asked Kikori to have a look at father's elbow and he gave it his healing touch. Although well after dark by the time father and Barteli reached home, Gwen insisted he go immediately to Nakuru to see the doctor and get an x-ray done. Tired and in some discomfort, the ride to town, only twenty miles or so as the crow flies, took the rest of the night and seemed eternal.

Other than diagnosing a hairline fracture, Doctor Tennant could only express his admiration for Kikori's adroit manipulation.

Returning from a year's visit to England in 1924, Jock and Gwen stopped off to see how Ludwig was getting on at Otjihavera. After this visit Jock took a renewed interest in Karakul sheep. Knowing that rams were available from the nucleus sent up earlier from Namibia by Holme for crossbreeding with Maasai sheep, he sent father off to buy red-tailed ewes.

Father left the farm with a small band of Maasai stockmen and pack-mules headed by Barteli, with donkeys and grade bulls to exchange, walking and riding over the Mau Escarpment to the Loita plains on the other side.

Since his first safari to the Mara in 1921, when the Maasai had appeared to father as a rather exotic and colourful race, he had come to know them as equals learning their language, Maa, and gaining their respect and trust. During the three-week stay on the Loita plains father became one of the very few white men at that time to be invited to a circumcision ceremony. As these were held only once every three or five years, his timing was fortunate.

The initiation of a boy or girl into adulthood is a mental and physical test of endurance, a test of his or her ability to cope with life's harsh realities as an adult. Father heard the deep sound of men's voices as he, Barteli and the others from Larmudiac made their way to the *manyatta* in the dark early hours just before dawn. Approaching the main cattle gate, the noise subsided as all eyes turned on father, curious. He felt slightly uneasy. The men were still wrapped warm in red blankets; their breath mingled in the cold morning air with the dust thrown up by stamping feet. An older man came forward followed closely by the initiate's father to welcome them into the manyatta.

Introductions over, father and his small band were invited to stand in the circle of elders. A single low hum was soon taken up in chorus and the singing began again. The traditional song, explained Barteli, encouraged the boy to withstand pain, or at times even to goad him into anger for the same purpose. Into the circle of excited onlookers walked the boy, naked, staring ahead of him as if in a trance. As a prelude to circumcision the boy was washed down with the water the Maasai call *engare entolu*, meaning axe-water. The water is left out over night with an axe head placed in the container to make it colder. The washing is both symbolic, a washing away of youthful transgressions and, in more practical terms, a means to numb the penis. The boy made his way to the centre of the circle where an ox hide had been spread out. He sat down, stretching his legs wide open before him.

A young man, probably a close relative, stood behind him and supported his back. A hushed silence followed. All eyes were fixed on the small figure as the circumciser came forward. With dexterous speed, he splashed the boy's face with a white chalky mixture – a blessing – and shouted, "One cut!" as he deftly removed the foreskin. The silence was maintained while the circumciser called for the ceremonial calabash of milk from an unblemished cow, one whose calves are still living, and washed the boy and his knife with it. At his final words, "Wake up, you are now a man," all tension broke; relatives and friends rushed forward to congratulate the youth on his courage and bravery. Had the boy cried out or flinched, the entire family would have been disgraced, his mother and father spat upon, and the family cattle in the kraal beaten until they broke loose. Guests would not have been able to partake of the feast, and all the months of preparation beforehand would have been for nothing.

Privileged to have shared this esoteric ceremony, father earned many new friends among the Maasai. Consequently, he returned to Larmudiac with the best part of a hundred selected red-tail ewes and hoggets, yearlings, either exchanged or for which he paid ten shillings a head. Thus Larmudiac's own Karakul experiment was born. Although Larmudiac's climate was little suited to this desert breed, Jock was ever determined to acquire more rams. He made enquiries in Germany, and even Russia, without result. Finally Ludwig smuggled six rams and 12 ewes out of South West Africa, which he brought up on a visit in 1926. How he boarded a ship with a small herd of goats without raising suspicion, history does not tell us.

From the point of view of yielding fine pelts, the project failed, but the resulting hybrid produced an excellent mutton sheep. On that occasion Ludwig, recently married, brought his wife. The visit ended in tragedy when she contracted a virus and died in Nakuru hospital, leaving Ludwig to return south alone.

Larmudiac Stock & Dairy Farm, then one of the country's largest, was considered a show farm, and one which government dignitaries or new settlers visited. Sir Edward Grigg, who had succeeded General Northey as Governor in 1925, drove up for the day in a splendid 1921, dark green Tourer Rolls. Jock later bought the car in the early 1940s, when he removed the body and replaced it with a Ford V8 pick-up body and cab. The bonnet alone remained in the original green, the rest he painted pink. Although my brother Richard expressed an interest in it, Uncle Dick, who had been left it by Jock, sold it off cheaply to a car buff in Nakuru. The latter restored it and its garish paintwork, and even entered the car in a local vintage car race, later selling it at a profit to a collector abroad.

The Prince of Wales visited Larmudiac in 1928 with the Duke of Gloucester. They were staying with Lord Francis Scott, who farmed in nearby Rongai at Deloraine, and whose niece, Alice, would later become the Duchess of Gloucester. They attended a lunch party arranged so the Prince could meet settlers from the area. "What a magnificent view," remarked the royal guest. "As far as I can see, the whole of Kenya survives on wonderful views and immense overdrafts?"

The Prince of Wales, who owned a ranch in Canada, had expressed an interest in seeing the progeny of cattle upgraded from native stock. Father was detailed to take the royal party around after lunch, and was keen to impress them. However, when shown the new milking machine, which father had taken the trouble to start up earlier, it spluttered and died, as was its wont, the moment they walked into the dairy. Father was not spared further embarrassment when they all stopped by the house again for a drink. On sipping a whisky, the Prince immediately asked for a soda water and was then noticed pouring the whole lot into a flowerbed. Somewhat taken aback, father hurried to the drinks table to re-examine the bottle, whose contents he had perceived to be rather too dark for Haig. He took a sip and immediately recognised the unpalatable taste of cough mixture. The medicine would have been bought in bulk and decanted into any available bottle. On hearing of the mix-up, the Prince laughed it off good-naturedly and accepted a re-fill of his preferred tipple.

When everyone had gone and the day's events were being mulled over, Jock said cough mixture was preferable to pee. He told father a story, against himself, of how he had ended up drinking sherry laced with his own pee. Suspecting the cook of drinking the sherry, he had first marked the bottle by way of entrapment. On noting further diminishment, and as a final deterrent, he had peed in it. Yet the contents of the bottle continued to disappear. He roared into the kitchen to have it out with the cook when the man explained: "Yes, Bwana, I poured it into last night's soup."

The following year Jock offered father a salary. Until then he had been content to work solely for his keep and pipe tobacco, which went down on the farm accounts. After eight cashless years, £15 a month seemed a lot of money until Jock proposed him for membership in the Rift Valley Sports Club in Nakuru when his first month's salary went on paying the entrance fee. The annual fee came to £5 and father soon realised he could not afford it and let his membership lapse along with any hopes for a social life outside his immediate neighbours.

The Lindstroms had a son and three daughters, all very much younger than father. Although much later he and Elspeth Grant, who married the scientist Gervais Huxley, would become great friends, the age difference at that time precluded any valid relationship. Elspeth's father, Jos Grant, spoke several languages and busied himself writing detective novels that were never published. Nellie, her mother, was full of fun and it fell to her to devise new schemes to make money, all of which soon succumbed to the vagaries of pest, weather and the slump.

Chapter Sixteen

CROSSROADS

Fearing that a dearth of suitable female company might limit father's existence to eternal bachelorhood, Gwen took matters in hand by arranging a visit to England with the dual purpose of visiting her mother in Wales while father would look over Red Poll cattle with a view to importing new blood stock for Jock.

Through Mervyn Ridley, a Red Poll breeder who farmed at Moiben close to Uganda's border, father had an introduction to visit Ridley's brother-in-law, Lord Cranworth. Lord Cranworth had been one of Kenya's earliest settlers, and had chronicled their pioneering efforts in his book, *A Colony in the Making*. Now Chairman of the Red Poll Society of Great Britain, Lord Cranworth invited father to stay on his estate, Grundisburgh, in Suffolk. A further introduction to the Cotswolds estate of the former wife of the Chairman of the Bank of England, Montague Norman, came his way after her visit to Larmudiac earlier.

Nine years had lapsed since father had left England and fashions in Kenya had not kept pace with those in England. He intended to put the matter straight by kitting himself out in suitable clothing at Simon Artz, the gentlemen's outfitters in Port Said, their first stopover on a journey by ship bound for the Mediterranean as far as Marseilles. From Marseilles he and Gwen would go overland to Calais and then across to Dover and to London. The ship arrived in Port Said early on a Sunday. Simon Artz was closed dashing father's hopes for new outfits. Father spent part of what little money he had on two boxes of one hundred Egyptian cigarettes. Customs in Marseilles relieved him of the rest, drawn to the contraband sticking out of his coat pocket. Practically penniless and now delayed, father only just managed to rejoin his mother and catch the Paris Express in time.

On arrival in Paddington he and Gwen were unable to find enough money between them to buy their onward tickets to Haverfordwest. Father had written ahead to his old prep school friend, Donagh O'Brien, who lived across the river, and now suggested to Gwen he should go there immediately and borrow the money from O'Brien.

The author's father, Joe Prettejohn.

As the taxi drew up to the Albany Mansions on the Albert Bridge Road, father noticed a pretty girl staring through the window of an upstairs flat, and suddenly became aware of his unsuitable garb and incongruous solar topi. Learning from the porter that O'Brien was away, he re-boarded the waiting taxi back to Paddington.

At the station Gwen borrowed money from a fellow passenger from the Union Liner that had brought them as far as Marseilles so they could continue their onward journey to Wales and to my great grandmother's house, 'The Bungalow,' on the sea at Musselwick, near St. Ishmaels, on the south coast of Pembrokeshire.

As the train steamed out of Paddington, the comforting and soporific chuntering of wheels took Gwen back to her early married life in England before the family moved to the Pembrokeshire farm near Haverfordwest, Heathfield, and when they still lived at the Grange, a pretty Georgian house at Winterbourne, near Bristol. In the summer holidays, while my grandfather was away on tea business in Ceylon, she and the children, with their nannies, travelled to Milford on the Great Western Railway. Arriving at Milford late evening, they would be met by a horse and carriage to take them the eight remaining miles in the dark to her mother's house. It was during one of these summer visits, in 1907, that Aunt Gwenydd and her twin sister Bertha were born.

On this trip my grandmother Gwen and may father were headed for the Bungalow, one of many family properties. (See appendix for a more detailed review of the various family properties).

At The Bungalow Gwen and my father received a wonderful welcome from family and old friends.

After a few days in Wales my Aunt Gwenydd, father's sister, joined him on a trip to the Royal Agricultural show held that year, 1929, in Harrogate in Yorkshire.

After spending a few days looking over Red Poll breeds at the Royal Show, father went to London and stayed with O'Brien while Aunt Gwenydd stayed elsewhere in town with friends.

That evening O'Brien arranged for father to join a dinner party in Chelsea at his fiancée's flat; an intimate dinner for four. At first father assumed the prettier of the two girls, a brunette, was O'Brien's fiancée. His hopes soared when he learned that she was not O'Brien's intended. Her name was Constance Trevor and she was the girl from the Albany Mansions who had been staring out of her window.

Constance Trevor lived with her widowed mother and her old nanny Jones. O'Brien suggested that as Constance was on holiday from her teaching job at a local kindergarten, she would have time to show father around London and help him buy the right clothes. Constance then invited him home to dinner to meet her mother, who told him of the tragedy she faced when her husband, manager of a nitrates mine in Chile, had been killed in a riding accident. Pregnant with Constance at the time, and desperate to have the child in England, she had ridden over the Andes on a mule as far as Buenos Aires where she caught a boat sailing for England. However, she did not quite make it; Constance was born at sea off Cape Ushant.

Father was completely smitten by Constance. For his last evening in London, father arranged an evening of theatre followed by a supper party for Constance and her mother Trevvie, together with Donogh O'Brien, his fiancée and Ronnie Nicholson. (Ronnie, another school friend from his prep school Jumpers, would later be one of my godfathers). Little used to evening dress, it took father a good half hour to untangle the mystery of tying a bow tie. It had never occurred to me that father was in any way sentimental but on that evening he remembered exactly what Constance wore, and how during the performance he pulled a green ostrich feather from the voluminous floating collar of feathers that adorned her simple silk dress of the same colour, which he later lovingly placed in his stud box.

Father and Aunt Gwenydd returned to the Bungalow and found their mother in a fury at having been charged 35 guineas by her own uncle, Jack Warren Davis, who had been called down from London to treat her for a bout of rheumatic fever. Davis, having once treated King George V for the flu-like symptoms of psittacosis (parrot's disease) was known to charge his patients three guineas a mile, so Gwen had gotten off lightly. Davis was mad on cars and drove a Bugatti with a broad leather strap holding the bonnet together.

The next day father set off in Aunt Gwenydd's Morris Cowley to the Cotswolds to look at Mrs Fitzgerald's herd of Red Polls. Her agent, Arnold Foster, took him round pointing out history and pedigree, while a manservant had washed and polished his car and re-filled it for his onward journey to Suffolk.

Father arrived at the Cranworths in time for tea. Lord Cranworth discussed Kenya and its economic future with him as they walked around the garden. Cranworth was somewhat put out when father suggested that stock and sisal would be Kenya's future, rather than wheat and maize, in which Cranworth had heavily invested. Father would prove his argument over the coming slump years of the Depression, which neither realised would soon be upon them.

After a last Red Poll exploratory tour to the Roes in Essex, father motored directly to London and the Albany Mansions to see as much of Constance as possible. Gwen and Aunt Gwenydd were already in London staying at a hotel and Aunt Gwenydd suggested the obvious: "Invite Constance to stay at the Bungalow."

In the taxi on the way to the station that evening, father proposed. Walking along the cliffs overlooking Milford Haven and Dale the following day, Constance agreed to marry him. They hastened back to the Bungalow to break the news to father's grandmother, and then to St. Ishmaels to send a telegram to Constance's mother, Trevvie. Before they returned together to London, father talked of family and showed her round the various family properties. They visited Trewarren House and the site of Llanelwedd Hall, which had burned down not long after the death of Howel Gwynne.

He told her of the tale that lay behind the 'ghost room' where he was born in Llanelwedd and the woman in the full length portrait that hung in the Bungalow – a woman holding up a key with which she appeared to beckon. This was the wife, the story goes, of a Gwynne, a staunch Royalist, whose botched attempt to poison Cromwell by drugging the wine, forced him to flee to France where he died in a paupers' prison. It was said that he had amassed a great collection of emeralds but his impoverished end concluded that he must have hidden them somewhere within the walls of the hall before his escape.

Such was the legend that family members made subsequent excavations of the cellars and an old underground passage that led from the hall to Builth Castle but found no treasure except in my great grandmother's day, for a bricked in cupboard containing a porcelain dinner service. She and my grandmother Gwen used the china to the last piece. Today, of Llanelwydd Hall and Builth Castle outside the town of Builth Wells, only a grassy mound remains.

Father also showed Constance around the Trewarren House built in 1840. It stood at the head of a then deeply forested valley running down from the village of St. Ishmaels to the family's private beach, Monk Haven. Beyond, seen from the towers along Trewarren's walled enclosure, lay Milford Haven and Angel and Dale forts standing sentinel either side of its harbour. According to old records, the sandstone wall, which enclosed a 120-acre deer park, had taken three years to build at a cost of three pence a yard. The house and its contents would be sold in the 1950s to a potato farmer. I attended the sale and remember, regretfully, the wonderful collections of stuffed birds, guns and other treasures going under the hammer for a pittance.

All the timber used in the building of Trewarren was of teak from the Pembroke shipbuilding yards. A cast iron staircase led upstairs to seventeen bedrooms on the second floor, and maize of servants' quarters on the floor above it. Rare for its day, the ballroom had been constructed with a suspended dance floor.

Another feature of note that father showed off was a small round tower on the clifftop above Milford Haven known as The Malakof that had been built by a great uncle of great grandmother Anne Jane Gwynne Howell. Sir Michael Biddulph had the tower constructed along the lines of the defensive Malakof tower at Sebastopol on his return from the Crimea in 1855. The Trewarren boys used it as their summer house camping out there when fishing in the harbour and up the Cleddau estuary, or setting nets and lobster pots around the islands outside the harbour. Biddulph was a good water colourist and several of his landscapes hung in the Bungalow, which would be the last repository for family memorabilia from a fast-declining landed breed. Both my given name and that of Jock were passed down from him. On his retirement from military service, Biddulph was made Keeper of the Tower of London.

Life in Kenya, father warned Constance after these visits, would be a very poor imitation indeed. On the other hand, the privileged life, which he and Dick had been brought up to, would be relegated to history. Rampant inflation after the Great War, from which emerged twenty-one million wounded, and the loss of eight and-a-half million lives, had ended an era.

In London once more, father stayed at Mrs Trevor's flat where the three discussed the formalities of marriage and a future, concluding they should wait while father returned to Kenya to build a house. It would also give Constance time to reconsider his proposal. He worried how a London girl, not even one used to the

English country, would take to living in the African bush twenty miles from her nearest neighbour. The wedding would be set for May the following year.

My grandmother Gwen's planning had borne fruit; father returned to Kenya in October with the promise of a wife and newly acquired knowledge on breeding Red Poll cattle.

Chapter Seventeen

A FALLING OUT

Just as the Colony's agricultural endeavours began to take shape, swarms of locust invaded from the north devouring whole crops and grassland. The collapse of the New York stock market and the ensuing depression, which had a worldwide knock-on effect causing a downward spiral in commodity prices, were as keenly felt in Kenya as elsewhere.

Despite the Depression, local district associations continued to advertise for new settlers. Each vied with the other, publishing pamphlets praising the merits of its particular bailiwick. I have dated 1933 entitled *Come to Kenya and Visit Njoro*. In the foreword the President of the Njoro Settlers' Association wrote:

> "...If each seems to lay special emphasis on the merits
> of its own district, the reader will appreciate the fact that
> local pride runs high in Kenya and that, in a Colony whose
> Highlands are good throughout, inter-district rivalry is
> a healthy feature of that proper pride in Kenya which, in
> its natural riches, beauty and charm, is second to no other
> Colony."

The pamphlet is full of helpful hints to the newcomer as to the means of travel, its cost, his expectations, the climate, building and land costs, household requirements and clothing, the engagement of servants and their requirements, to the prospective settler's general entertainment: racing, polo, golf, tennis and bridge. A house could be built for as little as eighty pounds or six hundred pounds for something grander. A note of hope is reflected in *Farming Notes*:

> *Although at the present time (October 1933) the slump in world commodity prices makes it impossible to say that any crop can be farmed at a profit, it can definitely be claimed for Kenya that with the recovery of world conditions she will be able to compete favourably with any other country in quality of produce and production costs.*

The notes on household servants comprised a guide to wages in ascending order of ability according to race – native (unskilled), Somali (tried and tested), and Goan or Seychellois (skilled), and advised on rations commensurate with his custom. "The engagement of a household staff," continues the advice, "is a matter of the greatest importance... Practically no female natives are as yet trained to domestic service (except ayahs); therefore the staff will consist of 'Boys.'" (At the time of Kenya's independence this term of address was considered demeaning and dropped. The custom of ringing for a servant was similarly viewed and outlawed by decree.)

The Larmudiac Stock and Dairy Farm was listed in the pamphlet as a farming enterprise worthy of a visit. Other farms listed included the Plant-breeders Experimental Station, the Lolchorai and Clutterbuck stud farms, Ngata Farm which specialised in cereals using the most up-to-date methods, and Nyanza Ltd., the world's largest scented geranium plantation.

It is doubtful that either father or

Joe and Constance on their wedding day in London

On the way to Kenya aboard the Usaramo.

Constance gave the Depression much thought. My parents' wedding reception in Piccadilly had been a modest affair attended mainly by friends and family on my mother's side.

They were married at a small chapel opposite the Army & Navy Stores, since destroyed by German air raids. On father's side only the best man, cousin Michael Warren Davis, and Uncle Jack lent support. Jack produced a magnum of champagne and a dry biscuit to sustain father before the service in the manner of a sailor condemned to walk the plank. My parents spent their honeymoon in Italy waiting to board the Deutsche Ost Afrika Line ship, *Usaramo*, at Genoa.

They carried on board crated boxes of assorted household goods bought with £500 borrowed against a yearly allowance of £150. Gwen had arranged for her Welsh agent, Sydney Thomas, to pay this sum into father's account with Barclays in Builth Wells - an account he maintained for life – in quarterly instalments. Added to this, Jock would double father's monthly Kenya salary to £30, and provide the newly married couple with a car, a box-body Durant.

On board they met James Charles, another of my godfathers, who farmed at Sotik and would become a lifelong friend of my parents. They also met Ted and Juliana Kerrison, a couple like them travelling out for the first time on honeymoon. The four teamed up to play bridge and took full advantage of organised shipboard partying, a final fling before the sobering reality of Larmudiac under Jock's stern paternalism and the financial constraints of the slump. The two women attended Swahili lessons in the afternoon. Ted Kerrison, already farming at Lumbwa, lost his sense of humour when his wife pushed him into the pool drenching his new Burberry dinner jacket in seawater – a hint, no doubt, of things to come for they would soon part company.

(Juliana was a first cousin of Lady Mary Boyd. Juliana later married Gerald Burton and moved to a retirement plot in Naro Moru not far from where we lived. Not long after, Lady Mary Grosvenor, a great sportswomen, came to stay. She was soon persuaded to purchase a nearby farm on the forest edge called "Waraza" and it was decided Juliana would look after it for her. When Lady Mary Grosvenor came out on several holiday visits I took her out buffalo hunting. She in turn invited me to stay at Kylestrom Lodge in Scotland where I hunted deer in the Reay forest, and had some great salmon fishing with her on the Laxford. The Burtons had no children, so after Gerald died, Juliana gave the house to my brother Richard and his wife Alix. Juliana stayed on with them until Waraza was sold and she moved back to England just before Kenya's independence. Juliana was a

Travelling on the Uganda Railway.

Nairobi scene c. 1930s.

gutsy woman being the first woman entrant in the East African Safari Rally, a test of both participant and vehicle.)

When they arrived in Mombasa, the Fords, whose acquaintance father had made on a previous boat trip, entertained the four for the day and saw them onto the overnight train for Nairobi that evening.

Early the following morning, Ted Kerrison's cousin Commander Kerrison Kiddle met them with the unexpected and sad news of his imminent departure for England. The slump had broken him and with no buyer coming forward, he had little alternative but to abandon his Rongai maize farm.

At Njoro the four parted company; the Kerrisons went on to Lumbwa by train, while father and Constance travelled the remaining ten miles to Larmudiac by ox-wagon. Jock viewed their mountain of luggage and sundry boxes with a critical eye, weighing up the cost and expressing his views on the profligacy of youth. He had little faith that father's new London bride would last the course.

While the Naishi house was being finished, my parents stayed with Jock and Gwen at Sabugo in a guest annexe that had fortunately retained some of Ginger Birkbeck's civilizing influence, and was a good deal more attractive than the rest of the house. There were never less than seven for meals that included Miss Forward, the young housekeeper from England, and Mr Steward, who ran Gwen's

Prettejohn house Naishi c. 1932.

growing poultry enterprise. Apart from Aunt Gwenydd, who was also staying then at Sabugo, Constance had little in common with any of them: she didn't ride, knew nothing of poultry farming or growing vegetables, and was not welcomed to help out in either the running of the house or Gwen's Nakuru grocery.

Father and Constance were relieved to move into their own mud and wattle house overlooking the new dam at Naishi. Father had attempted to turn what had been his bachelor pad into something grander for Constance by adding on three thatched rondavels linked by passageways, and consisting of two bedrooms, a sitting room and dining area. The bathroom, then without plumbing or door, stood detached. In the evening barefooted servants padded in with *debes* of hot water heated on an open fire to fill the tin bath. To afford some privacy, father had tacked onto the bathroom, at an angle, a narrow Z-shaped walkway. An outside 'long drop' lavatory and kitchen completed the white-washed complex. When their first visitor, James Charles, came to stay, he was confronted on his way into the bathroom by the back end of a cow. In search of something to drink, she had become lodged in the entrance, unable to go either forwards or backwards. The Naishi house, though basic, was at least removed from Sabugo and parental interference by a good twenty miles.

Newly independent, their days took on a gentle rhythm with father riding out at first light to attend to cattle business, while Constance did what most women of her day did: make a home. They would come together in the evenings over a Martini – a small luxury afforded by his increase in salary – and dine in full evening dress so as not to let 'standards' drop. In time such formality at home would give way to pyjamas and dressing gown with the added flourish of a cravat for the man and house-coat for the women.

At weekends they drove out somewhere new for a picnic or met friends living in Nakuru such as Katie and Carl Jungblut, the agent for Deutsche Ost-Afrika Line for western Kenya.

Micky Wheeler, the Nakuru vet, knew all the farmers around. Like most Irishmen he was fond of a drink, and enjoyed practical jokes. He lived in a row of houses built for railway personnel just outside the town. Returning with friends from the cinema late one evening, Micky noticed a pram left out in one of the adjoining gardens and thought it would be fun to get wheeled home. The next morning the police called on him over a matter of theft and did not share the joke.

The road out of the farm where father and Dick lived led past the Sabugo house. After Jock had grumbled for the 'nth time about how much these little outings were costing, father opened up a new road that led directly to town so he and Dick could use it unseen.

When Constance developed appendicitis, father spared no expense in travelling with her to Nairobi for the operation. This was their first visit there in a year. Such extravagance confirmed Jock's suspicion that Constance was as capricious and spoiled as only a city girl could be. Doctor Tennant from Nakuru also voiced his disapproval for having his medical expertise usurped by another.

After Constance recovered, father sent her back to England to

Family picnic using the Rugby car

spend time with her family. Her mother Trevvie returned with her to stay with them at Naishi for a couple of months. Jock's dislike of Constance was nothing to what he felt for her mother, who he described as a troublemaker.

For a change of pace father and Constance, now a few months pregnant, left the farm for a few days' break with the Kerrisons at Lumbwa. On the point of leaving, a milker approached the car, an argument ensued and father, already frustrated by the late start, lost his temper and struck the man. This episode shocked Constance. She remained unnaturally silent for the remainder of the journey. That evening she miscarried.

To make up for her loss, Constance lavished her affections on a caracal kitten (also called the African lynx) she called Sally. Sally grew into a beautifully spotted, deep chestnut feline with pointed black-tufted ears, who shadowed Constance wherever she went. The lynx was great fun; she teased the Alsatians mercilessly by ambushing and jumping on them when they least expected it. In time Constance became pregnant again. Unable to leave the farm for any length of time, father arranged for her to stay with Mrs Gain, who lived close to the hospital and took in expectant mothers. The Gain's young son, who was detailed to drive Constance into hospital when her time came, vowed never to repeat the experience because someone asked if he were the father.

At last, on 8th September 1932, the long-awaited news arrived by

telephone. Father had a son. It was I, christened Michael Gwynne Prettejohn.

Gwen arranged for a trained nurse from England to help mother. Miss Crickmer was no beauty but proved highly competent and unflappable. My arrival did not suit Sally who became

Young Michael Prettejohn with his father Joe. increasingly jealous. After an incident when a leopard cub a neighbour brought over to 'play' received a vicious mauling, mother realised that a crying baby might attract a similar bout of aggressive behaviour. From then on the lynx was put in a cage and fed with moles brought in off the farm. Mother took Sally for walks with the dogs in the evening, but someone always had to remain behind to see that she did not run back on her own and harm me. Sadly, as so often happens with wild animals kept as pets, Sally escaped her cage one morning and did not return. When, months later, they found her emaciated skeleton not far from the house, mother was distraught.

Michael Prettejohn at Naishi.

In that same year, a murder in Nakuru caused great excitement as only such exceptional happenings within a small community can. A half-American Indian youth by the name of Ross invited Mrs Gain's niece, the beautiful Winnie Wilksinson, to the cinema. Mindful of tongue-wagging gossip, Winnie said she would only go if she could bring a friend who worked in the chemist's. Ross drove the two girls, not to the cinema as planned, but to the top of Menengai crater. There he ordered them out of the car. To Winnie's horror, Ross shot her girlfriend dead. He grabbed Winnie, now extremely frightened and beside herself with shock, and told her he could not live without her, that if she did not run away with him he would turn the gun on himself. She broke free and ran down the hill screaming. Ross soon caught up with her. At first he tried to calm her by agreeing to drive her home, but ended by stilling her hysterics with a bullet.

He then drove back to his mother, who naturally asked him what had become of the two girls. Ross confessed, admitting that he had killed a girl but had left Winnie alive. She, poor woman, had little option but to call the police who arrived immediately.

The police soon found the body of the chemist's girl the following morning, but there was no sign of Winnie. All members of the local Defence Force, including father who was still recovering from a bout of flu, were called out with orders to bring labour for a systematic search of the area. Over a thousand men gathered at the assembly point. Mostyn, a pilot based at Wilson Airport, made an aerial search of the crater. Hours later when Winnie had still not been found, Harry Featherstone-Haugh and Jimmy Beaston, leaders of the local Defence Force, angrily threatened the police that if they did not bring Ross back from Nairobi to tell them where Winnie's body was, they'd take matters into their own hands.

It was well after midnight when a manacled, but still defiant Ross, stepped out of a police car at the top of the crater. Despite facing an angry mob ready to lynch him, he held out until four in the morning when he finally revealed the scene of his crime, worn down by repetitive questioning in the glare of the cars' headlights. He was later tried by a Nairobi court, found guilty and hanged by Hoppie Marshall, the hangman who smoked a pipe through a hole in his cheek.

Climbing about Menengai's steep slopes for six hours while still recovering from flu had not improved father's condition. Doctor Tennant advised some leave and suggested a restorative holiday at sea level.

Father, mother, Trevvie, with Miss Crickmer in charge of me, travelled on the overnight train to stay at Mombasa's Tudor Hotel in town. The Stanway family was also staying there. Like many farm managers at that time, Jack Stanway had just lost his job. They were waiting to board a ship for South Africa where Stanway would be employed working on an emerald mine in the Transvaal. The two families kept in touch, and two years on father found Stanway a job as cattle manager on Nderit, a 5,000-acre ranch at Elmenteita owned by Boy and Genessie Long. Some years later the two families' cosy friendship would be abruptly severed due, I only learned much later, to Jack Stanway threatening to run off with mother.

Concerned for my health after a go of malaria, the family cut short the holiday and returned to Naishi. There they learned that my Uncle Dick had been given the sack; Jock blamed the slump. Cereal growers took the brunt with maize down to three shillings a 200-pound bag. Cattle breeders fared as badly. The pick of in-calf heifers could be bought for a fiver, and butterfat dropped to below fifty cents a pound. However, the more likely reason for Dick's dismissal was Jock's intense dislike of Vivienne. Jock soon employed another in Dick's place, an old stock inspector who had taken a young Kipsigis girl as his wife. Jock also gave him overall responsibility for the cattle, a move which incensed father.

Kenya's 1930s Gold Rush attracted many intent on recouping their losses after finding themselves out of a job or facing bankruptcy. Traces of gold found in the Yala River, and later a nugget weighing 9.5 ounces collected from the Wacheeshe River, led to a source at Kakamega, an area in the west of Kenya. You could pitch a tent for a rental of three shillings a month, or build a thatched hut of mud and wattle for thirty shillings. Dick, now unemployed, teamed up with Vivienne, Harry Featherstone-Haugh and Jack Green to stake their claim. They floated a company into which Trevvie, who intended to sell up in London and settle in Kenya for good, put some of her savings.

Dick and Vivienne made a popular couple with Vivienne's gallic culinary skills earning them many new friends among the hopefuls whose poor billeting fell short of a homely one. For Vivienne this Kakamega episode was a happy one as everyone was penniless and there was little scope for social pretentiousness. A former gold digger described the camp kitchen as little more than a lean-to shelter in which a discarded petrol tin, balanced on hot coals on an open fire, served as oven. In deference to the torrid climate and overheated kitchen, the cook wore little save a simple kikoi wrapped round his middle. Sweat poured off his body as he patted and rolled the pastry into shape across the gleaming expanse of his anatomy.

Father was hurt and angered by Dick's dismissal and the fact that his own responsibilities for cattle had been overridden, so he and Dick got together to dream up a plan to break free from Jock's control and buy their own farm. Had not Howel Gwynne, their great-uncle, left his properties and shares in trust for Gwen and her children? They consulted a lawyer and showed him a copy of the Gwynne will. Russell, the lawyer, led them to believe they could borrow against what he termed 'reversionary interests.'

Naively buoyed by this possibility, they went to see Chettle, the auctioneer, who told them that Gray's widow was selling up at Lanet, just outside Nakuru. Gwen knew of their plan, but kept it secret from Jock. In fact, she was all for it, but needed to get a second opinion from Sydney Thomas and a lawyer there. In the meantime father and Uncle Dick made Mrs Gray an offer. Unfortunately, Jock later met the widow out shopping and she asked why Jock had sent father to negotiate the sale and not come himself. Jock was livid to think father had been negotiating on his behalf. He called father up to Sabugo. "What the bloody hell do you think you're doing? What right do you think you have to buy up land without my permission?"

"Actually," father replied smugly, "Dick and I were negotiating to buy it ourselves."

Fortunately for father and Dick the plan never materialised; weakening commodity prices would soon have sucked them dry. Sydney Thomas advised Gwen that the trust could not be broken, and her children would only inherit on her death. Dick returned to Kakamega and father went back to an uncomfortable proximity with Jock on Larmudiac.

In late 1933 Jock was called to England following the death of his mother. When Gwen's own mother died some eleven months later, she too left to sort out family affairs. Before she got there Jock visited The Bungalow ostensibly to start the process of winding down. A collection of gold sovereigns that Gwen's mother had showed father on his visit three years earlier never again surfaced, nor did the family record on which father had added his marriage in 1930. Jock left father in charge of the cattle on Larmudiac and employed George Tyler to assist him. Father and George came from similar backgrounds and got on well. George's wife Eileen, a niece of Barbara Cartland, had a private income, which always made George feel inadequate. He once asked father's advice on the delicate question of love-making. "Give her a drink or two before you go to bed," father advised. The next day George confided lugubriously, "I gave her a glass of port and she just fell asleep."

Before leaving for Pembrokeshire, Jock hired a young butcher from Haverfordwest named Thomas, the nephew of a close family friend we knew as Aisy. Mary Rogers from Haverfordwest had accompanied my great grandmother to India for the birth of Gwen in 1880. In her role there as nanny. Mary had been dubbed Aisy, a mispronunciation of the Indian word for nursemaid, *ayah*. Aisy's nephew Thomas came out to Kenya in 1930 to manage the butchery, an enterprise run in conjunction with Gwen's grocery, after a succession of butchers proved dishonest. While father and Tyler were given the day-to-day responsibility of running the farm, Jock left Thomas in charge of the financial side of things, the farm accounts and the Nakuru businesses.

Thomas ran things well for a while, but soon fell prey to his new managerial status, leaving the day to day business of butchering to his staff and to White, his new assistant, whilst he took off mid morning on some pretext or other - usually a pint or two – and seldom returned for the day. White had a reputation for playing around with native women, a habit that cost him his life when he was hacked to death on the farm six months later. The butchery nearly cost Thomas his when he found himself involuntary locked into the cold room. Had a late shopper not caused the door to be opened, poor Thomas might have found himself as rigidly frozen as the carcasses he had been throwing about to keep warm.

Thomas signed the cheques but when father asked for money, Thomas always fobbed him off with some lame excuse. Finally, in exasperation, father appealed to Gwen telling her that the situation was becoming impossible, and that the Maasai herdsmen had not been paid for nearly six months. She simply opened the safe and revealed a stash of £800 in cash.

In total Jock and Gwen had been gone for nearly fifteen months when father made plans to go to England in May of the following year to see a specialist for his back. He was in constant pain from the injury sustained when he fell from his horse out hunting wild dog. Manipulation and repeated visits to local doctors had not eased it. Father wrote off to Jock to ask if he and Gwen would be back before May as they were expecting a second child due late January, and planned on taking the baby and me, aged two-and-a-half, back with them.

Michael Prettejohn, standing, while his mother Constance holds baby Richard.

Jock replied that they should go ahead with their plans. He and Gwen would either be back by May or on their way back. Father booked a passage for Southampton through his friend Carl Jungblut who arranged for the four of us to travel "Kenya Settler Class" on a German ship for £62 return fare. George Tyler and his family moved into the Naishi house and so George could manage the farm while father was away.

Now with two children at foot – my brother Richard was born on the first day of February 1935 – their shipboard circle of friends widened once again. These included the Lanes from the Kinangop, the chain-smoking Mu Bullock, Ibbie Mitchell, and the Lees. The Lees had two children the same age as us. Mother received plenty of advice and help from the old ladies on board who clucked over Richard and took turns carrying him about. I had been given a tricycle with no pedals. To the consternation of the same old ladies, who thought I would fall overboard, I happily pushed my way to speed up and down the deck.

Mother's idea to present Richard as an organ grinder's monkey at the children's fancy dress party met with dismay; instead she presented him as a pin cushion. Curly-headed, I went as 'Bubbles' from the famous Victorian soap advertisement. When the grown ups' turn came, father said it was far too hot to dress up, keeping secret the fact that he had already organised his disguise the day before. The ship's barber glued on bits of hair collected up off the floor, the barman provided straw bottle wrappings to make a grass skirt, and the ship's carpenter a wooden club. Thus attired, he surprised everyone that evening walking off with first prize, a camera. Wincing with pain as mother yanked off glued bits of hair in their cabin later that night, he wondered if it had all been worth it.

On Jubilee Night the ship was docked at Marseilles and the bar closed. Secreted flagons of Chianti bought earlier in Genoa were produced to celebrate the 25th anniversary of King George V's accession to the throne. The band played 'God Save the King' and many retired to bed quite tipsy. Father maintained that my natural powers of observation started at an early age when I asked him if the sea was rough as he swayed about so much.

The ship arrived in Southampton at the end of May when late snows made news headlines. Aunt Gwenydd, then acting as companion to Mrs Mansell Pleydell, met them in the old lady's car and drove them to Dorset. Mrs Mansell Pleydell was Charlotte Warren Davis's sister married to father's great-uncle Gilbert. Unlike her sober suffragette sister, the old lady liked a drink or two and extended

Author's brother Richard at Stanways in Elementaita.

130

her hospitality to lending my parents her London house in Foulis Terrace.

Richard was to be christened at Shoreham-by-Sea where his godmother, Dot Echlin, lived. Dot Echlin had spent most of her married life in the Falkland Islands where her husband had been Governor. She was very badly off and could not put us all up in the small house she and her daughter lived in, so she had arranged for us to stay in a pub close by. Aunt Gwenydd then drove father on to London where he picked up a car – a Ford 9 – he had bought through Hughes & Co. in Nakuru on hire-purchase to be shipped back with them on their return journey. Father visited his uncle Dr Jack Warren Davis there who diagnosed rheumatoid arthritis in the spine, but the treatment had no effect so Davis put him in touch with an osteopath, an ex-butcher. Temporarily relieved of pain, father motored to Pembrokeshire to discuss with his mother and Jock the worsening state of affairs at Larmudiac under Thomas. To add weight to his argument, he brought with him letters George Tyler had sent.

Jock retaliated angrily by blaming father, not Thomas, for Larmudiac's financial mess. "Couldn't you have waited until I got back?" Stifling a frustrated riposte, father meekly offered to return immediately, which offer Jock brushed aside saying, "I'll deal with Thomas when I get back."

In the end father's treatment, now in the hands of an American-trained doctor in Park Street introduced by his school friend O'Brien, took five months. While our parents stayed in London, we were boarded out with mother's old nanny Jones who lived outside Worcester. From time to time they would gather us up for a spell at the Bungalow.

In the meantime, Jock and Gwen had returned to Kenya. Jock sacked Thomas and sold the butchery. George Tyler also left to run a small farm Eileen had bought. Relations between Jock and father never improved, and it would appear that Gwen was no support either. Though Jock continued to berate father for Larmudiac's financial troubles, his real resentment resulted from his two step-sons' attempts to meddle with Gwen's will and buy their own place.

After father's treatment, my parents returned with us to Kenya. My grandmother Trevvie had made arrangements to sell her flat. She bought an annuity with money from the sale of shares, and made plans to sail out to Kenya at the beginning of 1937. To Jock, this move was the last straw. He sent a note down to Naishi, received while mother was cutting father's hair, stating his objection to Trevvie coming on a permanent basis to live on Larmudiac.

Father was beside himself with anger. He leaped out of the chair, his hair half cut, and drove up to Sabugo. He flung open the door to the drawing room and, without preamble, told Jock what he thought of him, adding, "Either Trevvie stays with us or I'm leaving." Jock reminded him that he was on contract and required to give six month's notice.

"You'll get my notice alright," father said, "and then we're gone!"

Chapter Eighteen

COLE'S PLAIN

O nce tempers had simmered, father wondered if, with a young family and no job to go to, his outburst had not been too hasty. On a conciliatory note Jock offered to raise his salary and promised more managerial control. Father replied that he would only stay if Jock formed a company and gave him a one-third stake. Jock refused. This left father with no alternative but to work out his six-month notice and look for another job.

Micky Wheeler suggested he see Eric Pardoe, the General Manager of Cole Estates. Father had met Pardoe on previous occasions when he used to drive Jock, a fellow Director of Lumbwa Creameries, to Board meetings. At the time Pardoe worked for the Standard Bank as General Manager of Powyslands Ltd., a conglomerate of agricultural businesses initiated by Powys Cobb that included Keringet, a 30,000-acre ranch at Molo, and 10,000 acres on the Indian Ocean at Kilifi. Obviously a man of vision and probably ahead of his time, Powys Cobb extended his empire to the Sudan with a large tract bordering the Juba River where he funded an irrigation scheme for growing bananas. How he forfeited his Kenyan properties to the bank I do not know. He lost out in the Sudan when the British Government bought him out in order to hand over that part of Jubaland to Italy as a slice of Italian Somaliland.

Father's timing was fortunate for Lady Eleanor Cole happened to be looking for a good cattleman to develop a dairy farm at Naro Moru on Mount Kenya's southwestern slopes. Her brother-in-law Berkeley

Cole had bought the farm, some 4,000 acres, subsequent to selling his original 800 Njoro acres with the Sabugo House to Jock. Berkeley Cole called his Naro Moru Property Home Farm and he lived there, a bachelor, until he died at 43 from black-water fever in 1927.

As a child Pam Scott described in her diary a visit with her parents to Berkely Cole's farm:

> *"We have got a rather dirty little room with a very suspicious looking bed which I sprinkled freely with Keating's* (insecticide powder) *and a glorious big bath. I was inches deep in red dust and it was a great luxury to lie and soak as long as I liked. It is the fashion in this country to dine in pyjamas and dressing gown which takes a little getting used to. I can't describe how curious Mr Cole appeared as he slouched into the drawing room in a very old pair of slippers and what looked like shrunken crepe drawers and an old bed jacket. It certainly was not long enough to make any pretence of hiding his naked legs. I was startled and Francis* (her father) *thought I would have hysterics. However Mr Cole was quite unmoved and made no allusion to his strange attire. During dinner a large cat wandered all over the table and a huge Russian boarhound, a magnificent animal, ate off our plates at will."*

Berkeley and Galbraith Cole were sons of the Irish peer the Earl of Enniskillen. Berkeley had subsequently acquired crown land and bought other farms in the Mount Kenya foothills, amounting to some 67,000 acres over what is still referred to today as Cole's Plains. Stretching from Naro Moru in the north to Mweiga in the south, it is a cold and windswept expanse dotted with whistling thorn, a stunted acacia with stiff thorns and swollen black galls. When the wind blows, it whistles through the holes at the base of the galls made by ants who share a symbiotic relationship with the tree that houses them in return for protecting it from browsers. The Cole Estates thus comprised the larger Solio Ranch and the detached Home Farm run in conjunction with Galbraith's Kikopey cattle ranch at Elmenteita under Pardoe's management. Kikopey bordered Soysambu Ranch, owned by their sister and her husband Lord Delamere. Soysambu is one of the very few properties still owned and run by direct Delamere descendants, Hugh Delamere and his son Tom Cholmondeley.

Andrew Enniskillen, Galbraith and Eleanor Cole's grandson, recently came with his wife Sarah to stay with us at Mweiga, to look for his great uncle Berkely Cole's grave on the banks of the Naro Moru River. Toothless Kikuyu elders showed us the site. A few remembered my father having either worked for him or grown up on the Home Farm. The area has been split up into Kikuyu smallholdings since Kenya's independence, and its magnificent podo and cedar trees cut down for charcoal and firewood. Beside the grave that Berkely shares with his inseparable and loyal Somali servant there remains a desiccated rose bush struggling to survive; the marble gravestone is inscribed with a line from Shakespeare's 'Julius Caesar':

> *"And whether we shall meet again, I know not.*
> *Therefore our everlasting farewell will take forever and*
> *forever,*
> *Farewell Cassius.*
> *If we do meet again why we shall smile,*
> *If not, then this parting was well made."*

Andrew Enniskillen did not inherit Solio: his filial due was squandered by his American stepmother who sold the ranch to a fellow countryman, Court Parfet, whose son runs it today combining ranching and tourism. Although this quirk of fate must rankle, Andrew has successfully made his way first running his own charter company, Sunbird. He was then appointed Managing Director of Air Kenya, followed by a stint with a financial institution, and latterly Africa Air Rescue. He and Sarah now live close by on our Sangare Conservancy.

Galbraith had died by the time father met Eleanor Cole. In the very early days of the colony Galbraith was tried and deported for shooting a Maasai stealing sheep. In fact he never left Kenya, but stayed disguised as a Somali. He met his death by his own hand putting an end to a long illness and unforgiving pain.

Eleanor Cole was the niece of Arthur J. Balfour, British Prime Minister in 1902. She and Galbraith had two sons, David and Arthur, both still at Eton when father approached her for a job. Lady Cole offered father a

Author's mother at Naro Moru House Farm

salary of twenty pounds a month, a third less than that Jock had given him. However, the prospects were good and Eric Pardoe told him that providing funds were available, father would have a free hand to get the dairy on its feet. Pardoe also agreed to father taking the necessary time off to fulfil his duties with the Kenya Regiment, which he had recently joined.

Mother packed up the Naishi house and railed the contents ahead to Naro Moru, after which father left us and the Alsatians with the Stanways at Elmenteita until he had got things organised there. His journey, one that takes only a couple of hours today, took him the entire day then in 1937. He arrived late evening on a cold and bitter September day. Gerald Southey, who managed the sheep on Solio and been installed there as temporary manager, had little to offer in the way of home comforts other than a bed and a couple of horse blankets. Fortunately, all their household goods had arrived the day before, and father unpacked some bedding.

Southey showed father round the farm. It soon became apparent that its nascent dairy was in a mess. Southey was foremost a sheep man, little interested in cattle, particularly dairy animals. The dairy sustained a 75% loss among its hand-reared calves from bacillary necrosis and scouring due to the unsanitary conditions in which they were kept. Father improved the latter ailment considerably by feeding the calves a cupful of pomegranate jelly in their milk; the Maasai concoct a similar treatment from acacia bark. Many of the cows aborted, a condition later diagnosed as 'contagious abortion.' Added to this, the two pedigree bulls that ran with the herd had epivag, an incurable type of bovine venereal disease that renders both sexes sterile. Despite the relatively short distance to the creameries in Nanyuki, milking started at the ungodly hour of 4 am by the poor light of kerosene lamps. The cows were too cold to let down their milk, and the milkers' fingers too frozen to work the udders. Immediately on taking over, father made changes: milking started at sunrise; he instigated cleaner working conditions; he re-designed the calf pens and milking bale into mobile units, and inspected and treated the calves for any sign of bacillary infection. Later on, once a vaccine for contagious abortion became available, he inoculated the calving cows against it. At the outset the herd was too small as an economic unit, so father drove down to Solio once a month where he and Tom Rawson Shaw, the cattle manager there, chose from the in-calf heifers any animal they thought would make a suitable dairy cow.

The nearest neighbour was an eccentric and irascible Irishman by the name of Pat Kenealy reputed to mark his clothes and sign cheques simply 'Pat.' He owned the land between the Home Farm and Solio, and had never forgiven Berkeley Cole for usurping his territory, believing as the second oldest settler (arriving in 1911) that only he had the right of use over land extending beyond his borders. Before Berkeley Cole's arrival, Kenealy had had an extensive irrigation channel dug from the upper reaches of the river across what became Solio to his farm. Relying largely on this source of water for irrigation, he was furious when Berkeley acquired Solio, and never missed an opportunity to get back at him. Berkeley had never denied him the water that ran through it, but Kenealy persisted in his vendetta by digging an impassable ditch one day across Berkeley's driveway, and shot a dog he said was trespassing.

With the herd numbers building up well, East Coast Fever, a

tick-borne disease, broke out without warning on Solio resulting in a potential 18-month quarantine period in which no stock could be moved in or out. Just prior to the outbreak father had brought up a number of new heifers. With no fencing as yet on the Home Farm, he engaged night herders to contain the cattle and protect them from predators. Arriving early one morning as usual to inspect the new recruits and oversee the milking, he received a report that the new intake had returned to Solio in the night taking with them the rest of the herd. This was a serious setback as the calves needed feeding and not one cow remained. There was only one thing to do: get them back immediately before either Kenealy got wind of it or the veterinary office in Nanyuki. He bundled as many herders and milkers as he could get in the car and sped off to Solio. They quickly found the herd there, fortunately intact, and father instructed the men to drive the mob back the intervening three miles as fast as possible while he drove slowly back behind them. Kenealy had somehow learned of the fiasco and was waiting for them. "Get those damned cattle off my place or I'll call Beaumont in." Father could only think that anything the District Veterinary Officer might hand out would be preferable to losing the entire herd for the stipulated quarantine. Ignoring

Naro Moru House. The author's mother called it the 'Cigar Box.'

Kenealy's bluster, he urged the men and cattle on. As good as his threat, Keanealy reported the incident. Beaumont the vet arrived later in the day but was surprisingly sympathetic to the circumstances. That evening my parents called on Kenealy to apologise, explain and to reassure him that all necessary anti-tick precautions had been taken that very morning. Kenealy greeted them, invited them in for a drink and supper and the usual evening's hand of bridge as though nothing had happened.

Once father had settled in, Gerald Southey returned to Solio, and father collected us up from Elmenteita. The manager's house was built of cedar planks overlaid at the joints on the inside by 1" x 2" strips of wood that barely kept out the winds that swept down from the mountain across the plains. Kenealy's irrigation furrow ran above the house and on occasion flooded over sending rivulets of muddy water through it. This became a constant source of irritation. It was useless complaining to Kenealy, and only served to exacerbate neighbourly relations. Besides, father found it useful to draw water from it for his own purposes in return for which he helped with maintenance. Mother dubbed the house 'the cigar box' for its rectangular shape and overall wooden structure complete with cedar-shingle roof.

Not long after we had joined him, Lady Eleanor Cole paid a visit on a day of torrential rain. She was quite horrified on our behalf to see how much the roof leaked and offered to pay for repairs. My mother suggested that it would be better, in view of Kenealy's flooding furrow, to move the entire 'box' to the site of Berkeley Cole's old house. Eleanor Cole agreed for since Berkeley's death his house had fallen into disrepair hastened by a tenant who kept pigs in the panelled dining room. Duly dismantled, the manager's house was moved down to the last nail, for these were in short supply, and reassembled to incorporate the old dining room with its mullioned windows and panelled interior, and a storeroom that would be my bedroom.

Before the war there were few neighbours. Kenealy's fist wife, Gypsy, had left Kenealy by the time my parents arrived, and had taken their two daughters Pam and Billy with her. Whenever he and Gyspy had a domestic set-to before she eventually left him for good,

Kenealy would threaten to shoot himself. His usual ploy was to sound off the gun within hearing distance of the house and then not return until late at night, hoping that Gypsy would repent and rush out to look for him. Kenealy soon replaced the void left by Gypsy by canoodling with the district vicar's wife, Frances, who he got pregnant. They lived in a pretty stone house with corrugated iron roof surrounded by an irrigated garden and orchard. Despite Kenealy's unpredictable behaviour, we all loved him. As children we sat spellbound whilst he told us stories, embellished no doubt, but we believed every word. He claimed Elspeth Huxley had used his character in one of her detective stories *Murder at Government House*. When much later father had cause to introduce the two he said, "Elspeth, you know Pat of course."

"No," replied Elspeth, "I don't believe we've met."

Frances was seldom out of the saddle or riding clothes and always looked as though she could do with a good wash. She tended to ride over unannounced to see her neighbours at inconvenient times. "Just popping in Darling," she'd call out. She did her best to enlist me in the local pony club but I never managed to get the stubborn little pony to move forward and Frances thankfully wrote me off as a 'non- starter.' If anyone were in trouble, she would be the first to help. She felt sorry for an old bachelor who had been in the Kings African Rifles with Kenealy sharing action in the First War. His adherence to the gin bottle had since overshadowed any ability to look after himself, so Frances took Captain Gerrie Wilson under her motherly, buxom wing, a kindness that did not auger well with Kenealy who was under the impression that Frances was 'straying.'

Herbert Rayner, father's assistant, happened to be tinkering with a tractor in the workshops when he noticed Kenealy striding past with holstered pistol heading upstream towards Gerrie Wilson's house. He called out some interrogative greeting that went unheeded. A few minutes later Frances arrived having lost a shoe and out of breath. "Quick Herbert! You've got to stop Pat. He's on his way to shoot Gerrie." Rayner jumped on the tractor and tore off. He had to go the long way round to avoid the furrow but got there just ahead of the Kenealys. He found Wilson in his usual inebriated state and little concerned by the warning Rayner gave. Kenealy arrived shortly, puffing and red in the face followed by a barefoot Frances; both collapsed on the veranda done in by the effort of walking there. Wilson offered them all a drink and thus revived Rayner returned on the tractor, and the good Captain drove Kenealy and Frances home.

These dramas became a habit and it was not long before father received a note at breakfast time asking him to take Frances and 'Ponk,' Frances and Pat Kenealy's daughter, to Nanyuki station. They needed to get away, she had scribbled, before Kenealy did them in. Father recognised yet another groundless drama and threw the note into the wastepaper basket and sent the messenger home. Another note followed which he also ignored, but when a third missive arrived mother became anxious and said, "Joe, if you don't do something and Pat carries out his threat, you'll never forgive yourself." Thus urged, he drove off but decided to go to Chico Basto first for further advice and moral support. Chico Basto told him to leave well alone. "Don't do anything of the sort. You'll get nothing but trouble for your pains." As usual nothing happened.

The earliest European settler, Arnold Paice, arrived in the district a year ahead of Kenealy, in 1910. Paice traded in cattle before joining up with Tom Chillingworth in 1905 when they bred ostrich in Naivasha. On his own at Naro Moru 'Paicey,' as he was fondly referred to by everyone, bred shorthorn cattle and kept pigs. He built his house with bricks from a homemade kiln and thereafter would send a cartload of bricks to every newly arrived married couple. In the very early days he delivered his baconers to the Uplands factory by driving them the seventy miles over the Aberdare Mountains at 10,000 feet to Naivasha Station on the other side, a trip that took the best part of three weeks. Latterly he lived with an army friend, Captain Browne of 'Sam Browne belt' fame, who was very deaf. Browne died tragically when Paicey ran him down accelerating out of the garage unaware that Browne was behind him; Browne failed to hear the car start up.

As a young man Paicey had fought in the Boer War. Father took

Elspeth Huxley to see him in the 1950s as she, ever the writer, was keen to hear of his experiences first hand. He showed her his diary and photographic record as he recounted his personal experiences of the War in South Africa from the time he shipped out with his regiment to East London, the long march to Queenstown and the camp there, and promised to leave her all his memorabilia on his death.

Nearer to father's age than either Kenealy or Paice was Chico Basto. Chico had been brought up in Madeira and come to Kenya through an unusual turn of events. Two nephews by marriage, Francis and Robert Hamilton-Gordon, farmed coffee near Nyeri. The land was a disastrous choice for coffee and never made any money. Fortunately, Francis Hamilton-Gordon had a very rich mother-in-law, Mrs Turner, who bought a farm near them at Mweiga not far from where I now live. When her son-in-law proved incapable of running that farm and eventually committed suicide, old Mrs Turner called for Chico. Chico ran the farm and looked after Mrs. Turner who lived in a grand house in the garden, until her death when her daughter, Dot Hamilton-Gordon, made the farm over to Chico.

Chico always used to say of his German wife, Lola, that he married her as she spoke no Portuguese and he no German and little English. Married before to an Englishman she had an only child, a daughter, but disliked children and refused to have any more with Chico; a pity as Chico would have made a wonderful father. He gave me my first rifle, an old .22. Lola had a fiery temper and a jealous nature. She kept a framed photograph of Chico on the bedside table, and on the dressing table one of her departed husband. Whenever Chico got on the wrong side of her, he would return home to find his photograph placed on the lavatory seat and that of her former husband upgraded to the bedside table. When really out of favour, she locked him out for the night. She and Chico were very popular, and Lola and my mother were great friends, but we children hated her. She made us take off our shoes, if we happened to be wearing any, before coming into the house and talk in whispers. And she always yelled at the servants. Soon after Chico gave me my rifle I got to feel the brunt of Lola's wrath when I aimed at and missed a bird sitting on the wire that ran from the generator house to the main house, severing the wire. I remember being so angry at the time that I sulked about the garden beheading all Lola's flowers.

A brief separation, the couple thought, would do them good and Lola suggested Chico take a holiday on the coast. This proved to be Lola's undoing. Chico fell madly for the receptionist at the hotel in Malindi and a short time later had moved Beryl and her children in with him. This was most awkward for my parents who knew Beryl when they all lived at Njoro. She had come out to Kenya after answering an advertisement as a dentist's receptionist. Within a few days of her arrival in Kenya, to everyone's surprise, she and the dentist returned to Nakuru as husband and wife. The couple had a small farm just outside Nakuru. When there happened to be something of note going on there, a party or dance, Beryl would invite mother to stay in order to give her a break and a chance to get away from the farm and from small babies. They had rather lost touch after Beryl's husband died and Beryl and later my parents moved away from Nakuru. Now that she had come back into their lives, my parents were reluctant to acknowledge Beryl until father had established that Chico had seen Lola right. In the intervening period between Lola moving out and Beryl moving in, my parents had to steer a diplomatic course between the warring parties. Lola would arrive one day with furnishings only for Chico to take them back the next.

In time Lola moved to Nairobi and subsequently returned to Germany. Beryl made a wonderful wife, and Chico welcomed Beryl's children. He was now a lot better off as Beryl brought with her some capital and the Nakuru farm, which they later sold. Once Chico came into the Turner property after the war, he indulged in fast cars and an aeroplane.

Chico was exceptionally generous and would often fly father around the country. On their first outing together, soupy skies forced Chico to fly well east of his destination, but the weather continued to close in. Chico flew into cloud and re-emerged partially upside down giving them both a few moments of heart-stopping panic before Chico managed to right the plane. On another occasion flying to Nairobi,

Chico stopped off in Nakuru. "A little business I have to attend to," said Chico, and then flew on explaining to father on the way that the parcel secreted under the seat contained £8,000 collected from the sale of Beryl's farm, cash bounty on which he did not intend to pay tax.

As they approached Wilson Airport, Chico circled round and told father to look out for a light from the direction of the control tower. "I can see a red light," said father.

"That'll do," replied Chico and flew straight in, landed, and immediately steered a course off the runway onto the adjoining grass verge. Father was on the point of asking what the hell he thought he was doing when he heard the roar of throttling engines as a Dakota swept in behind them.

Chico's flying skills improved and even mother in time agreed to go up with Richard and me. After the war the two families shared many bird shooting trips, flying to Garbatula and camping out on Benane Springs hunting for sand grouse. Father and Chico flew while mother and Beryl drove us children, once we had attained a more manageable age, with all the camping equipment. We might go as far as the Lorian Swamp for goose and duck or for olive pigeon near Meru Forest, or on the odd weekend father sent the lorry ahead to a favoured spot on the Ewaso Nyiro River near Archer's Post, where we swam in the crystal clear waters of Buffalo Springs, a vast pool that had been blasted out of the limestone by South African Air Force personnel during the war.

Some Samburu warriors happened by the springs one day and stopped to stare at the incongruous sight of half-naked *mzungus* (whites) floating about in the water. They burst into howls of laughter and everyone wanted to know what was so funny. Father spoke Maa, a language the Samburu share with the Masaai, and realised Chico's tubby girth was at the root of their mirth. "Just look at that man," they said. "He's got breasts like a woman!" Thinking Chico might be offended, father waited until the red *shukas* had moved on before translating. Chico thought it all a huge joke.

Chico was great with children and would entertain them at parties 'sitting' on a window ledge telling them jokes in his guise as a dwarf, an impression he devised standing at the window with the help of another hidden crouched below the sill with his arms encased in gum boots encircled around Chico's waist, which he waved about mimicking the dwarf's legs. Chico also sang beautifully and was easily persuaded to do so at parties when he'd sing a rather ribald version of 'Sweet Violets.'

Unlike the poor immigrant populations of the Americas searching for a better life, Kenya's settler community at the outset was made up largely of people from the British Isles from privileged backgrounds and landed county families. The English of that ilk, as opposed to the Irish on the whole, are a breed that only feels comfortable if they can place you in the English scheme of social hierarchy – school, regiment, university, accent, turn of phrase – assessing and weighing you up by tuning into every subtle nuance. Usually the lower down the scale they are, the more judgemental they become. Such were the Lucases, Alan and Paddy, who lived on the edge of Mount Kenya's Forest Reserve in the gracious manner of the gentleman farmer. They enquired of Gladys Gooch, "Do you know the Prettejohns? What sort of people are they?" Reassured that father's antecedents were military men and 'our kind of people,' the Major invited my parents to dinner. There was a long pause between the soup and the main course in which Paddy attempted to maintain her dignity when the order of serving did not go to plan. An elephant, it transpired, had blocked the open passage dividing kitchen and dining room, delaying dinner until the great pachyderm moved on.

Others living nearby were Major Geoffrey and Edith Baines and Gladys Gooch. Gladys ran a highly efficient racing stable and stud farm and welcomed the Prettejohn family as newcomers sending down fruit and vegetables on a regular basis. Born at the turn of the twentieth century, Gladys had been considered a great beauty when she came out to Kenya at the age of nineteen with her first husband, an ex-cavalryman. She soon left Pollock for Eric Gooch who farmed in the area with his brother Kenneth. Before our arrival Eric Gooch had broken his neck and died riding out after warthog, a fatal weekend's entertainment based on the Indian cavalry sport of 'pig sticking.' (No one ever warned Piers Mostyn, another neighbour, when he took on a horse that had a habit of crossing its legs at the gallop, leading to Mostyn's demise from a broken neck as well).

Widowhood did not suit Gladys, the 'Rose of Nyeri,' for long. She soon took up with Nigel Graham, also a former Njoro neighbour, who had gone bankrupt there and taken on the job as Club Secretary of the Muthaiga Country Club in Nairobi where Gladys often stayed for race meetings.

My mother was gregarious in contrast to my father's retired, more serious nature. She was completely happy at Naro Moru where she made many friends, played the piano in church, played bridge and entertained friends and friends' children. My parents both loved young people and throughout their lives in Kenya, and later in South Africa, opened their house to anyone in need of a home away from home. When father was not spending allotted training weekends with the Kenya Regiment, they often spent weekends away including visits to Eric and Priscilla Pardoe on Kikopey. Pardoe suggested, in view of the ongoing Epivag and contagious abortion problems, that father attend the artificial insemination course on the Government farm at Naivasha run by Dr Jim Anderson, a pioneer in the field. The course revolutionised breeding practices. On completion, father bought the necessary equipment, built crushes, and collected sperm from unaffected bulls with which he inseminated the cows. Later, towards the end of the war, he was able to engage the services of an Italian prisoner of war captured in Abyssinia and held in the Kitale Civilian Detention Camp. The man happened to be an expert in the field of sterility among cattle, having worked on it his entire life in Italy and Austria. Father went with Albert Keyser, who had been having the same problems with his cattle, to meet the Italian. When he enquired about the possibility of a transfer to Nanyuki, the authorities were only too happy to see the man go as the wife of a senior official in Kitale had fallen in love with him. He showed father his methods of pregnancy testing, the key, he said, to efficient breeding. Father passed the method on to us.

It was usual before the war for the larger landowners to employ young men from England as 'pupils' rather in the manner of today's gap-year students. The young men came on recommendation, or were children of friends, were paid next to nothing but usually had a private income. Father had put in about a year's work for Cole Estates when he was told to expect a young Scot, James McKillop, as his pupil. McKillop and his sister lost their mother at a very young age and had been brought up by their maternal grandparents, the Nasmiths, joint owners of Fife Coal Mines and Nasmith Steel. On the grandparents' death, even before he had left school, McKillop inherited a third share of the coal and steel empire from which he derived a considerable income.

When the young 20-year old failed to show up, father was little surprised on receiving a note from the Indian storekeeper at Naro Moru to say a young man had broken down about five miles short of the farm. "Typical," thought father as he drove off to collect him, wondering whether his new pupil would not turn out to be a liability. The first thing father saw as he approached a brand new Ford pick-up stopped in the middle of the road was a pair of boots sticking out through the passenger window. McKillop was not in the least put out by having caused any delay, which he had sensibly sat out with a book, and was oblivious to the fact that he had run out of petrol, "Can't think what's wrong," he intoned breezily. " The damned car just stopped."

From then on McKillop was put to work supervising fencing and planting fast-growing eucalyptus along the fence lines as a windbreak. He learned to inseminate and vaccinate against the tick diseases of anaplasmosis and red water fever proving him less of a dilettante than his first impression implied. He had a good sense of humour and was wont to decorate the milk records with cartoon sketches of curly-tailed pigs or of father receiving a kick in the backside from a frisky calf he was attempting to inoculate. When Gladys Gooch complained that the new fence line ran straight across her road of access, McKillop replied that it would have been a pity to make a break in such a perfect line of fencing.

The newly acquired science of artificial insemination continued apace both with the dairy cattle and those on Solio where father would take over for Tom Rawson-Shaw if he were away, leaving McKillop in charge of the dairy. Insemination was then taken a step further and used on the sheep both on Solio and on Kikopey, taking sperm from a nucleus of Merino sheep smuggled in from Australia.

That year, 1938, changed all our lives: I was sent, age six, as a weekly border to Mrs Steptoe's Kindergarten in Nanyuki, innocent of the rumblings of an impending European war. Jock and Gwen called Dick back from the Kakamega Gold Fields to take over Larmudiac following their decision to move to a farm near Lake Solai. The most significant change for the immediate family, however, was McKillop's offer to give father a ten percent shareholding in his own farm and the management of it. The farm in question was none other than the detached Home Farm that had come up for sale as a result of a managerial decision between Eleanor Cole and Eric Pardoe to consolidate the Naro Moru side of the business to Solio.

Later Elspeth Huxley wrote the following nostalgic piece about our Naro Moru farm. "Below the forest's edge, open pastures roll away to meet the plain. Before the sun rises behind Mt Kenya, the

Naro Moru house Farm after the house was moved nail by nail and board by board and added on to the remains of Barclay Cole's house.

western horizon reddens beyond the Aberdares and throws into relief the crest of Kinangop, cut off from the plain below by a sea of mist as iridescent as a dove's breast. Bands of colour lie across this western horizon - red and black, grey and pink, peach and lavender; the plain takes the light reluctantly, as if holding on to the night's coolness. Behind you the snows of Kenya, suddenly close, are sketched against a hardening sky, startling in their ivory whiteness. The sun comes up and the plain lies open, the mists ascend to shroud the Aberdares, and slowly the great peak of Kenya hides an icy nakedness in the day's cloudy garment. Against such majestic scenery, cows tethered to stakes stand to be milked in the open, and a tractor chuffs its way to a field of barley. Two partners, James Mc Killop and Joe Prettejohn, own this 4,000-acre farm. One puts up the money, the other the skill and work, and all these elements are needed in good measure to turn this stretch of sour, windswept mountain-side into a productive concern…"

Just as McKillop & Prettejohn was born, Germany declared war. Father's call up papers arrived, and James McKillop left to join up with him in Nairobi.

Chapter Nineteen

THE WAR

E ngland was little prepared for war, its colonies less so. Although the Italians were still neutral at the outbreak of war, there was no doubt where their allegiance lay and they were reputed to have 150,000 well-armed troops stationed in Abyssinia, just a two day journey north from Nanyuki, with tanks, armoured cars, field guns and a small air force. Our side was so ill prepared that a single Bren gun per battalion used for training purposes was about as much as the country could muster. Father felt it safer to bring the family to Nairobi where he left us with friends while he joined the Nairobi-based 3rd battalion under the command of Colonel Hugh Mitchell. He would have preferred to stay closer to home with the 5th stationed in Nanyuki, but Mitchell had asked for him and arranged to give him a Commission as Full Corporal. The regiment headquarters were housed in the Nairobi Primary School until a flood of recruits and volunteers made it necessary to move to the Nairobi Agricultural Show Ground, then at Kabete. Many of the older members of the regiment, who had had training, were drafted as non-commissioned officers (NCO's) to the King's African Rifles battalions, while those with Commissions like father were kept back to train new recruits as they arrived.

General Dickinson, nicknamed 'Choitram' after the Indian proprietor of Nairobi's largest haberdashery on account of his round face and swarthy complexion, ran the OCTU (Officers Cadet Training Unit) and held three-month training courses on the showground. Two other recruits from the Nanyuki area, David Street and Peter Pillbrow, were also called to Nairobi. The three Nanyuki families rented a house in Muthaiga downhill from Kabete, a free wheel advantage from the showground all the way to the Club, of which membership as military members was affordable at ten shillings a month. Trevvie was with us and looked after us when our parents went out. For my parents the whole exercise was a little taxing but socially great fun. Sheila Yeatman, Gerry Alexander's mother, a good fun girl and prankster, thought the military top brass spent too much time clubbing rather than fighting, a point of view she demonstrated by removing their military headgear from the Club cloakroom and replacing it with bowler hats.

James McKillop would invariably be there at weekends. He usually took a single room with an outside shared bathroom. In the early hours one morning and rather the worse for wear, James got ready for bed forgetting he'd run a bath. Darting out without bothering to put on a dressing gown, the bedroom door slammed shut behind locking him out. Fortunately there was a narrow gap between the top of the door and the ceiling, which he, still youthful and slim, was able to reach by standing on a chair and squirming his way through.

"Oi knows whose tha' is," came a shrill voice from down the corridor. Loder, the housekeeper, woken by the commotion, had just caught sight of James' bare bottom disappearing through the gap. Cockney Loder was a dreadful snob. She had been in service in many of the grand English houses from the age of seventeen and, in Kenya, worked for the Scotts at Molo where she met the Duke and Duchess of York. She could always tell who was who by their "air brushes." Years later when the Duke visited Kenya and stayed at Muthaiga, Loder was invited to take tea with him. Crowing with one-upmanship, she boasted to Nigel Hendricks, "Oi 'ad tea wiv the Duke."

"No," said Nigel. "And you left him alone with the silver?"

General Dickinson later removed the entire regiment to a low-lying swampy area outside Kampala on the pretext that Kampala would be safer than Nairobi from enemy action. Fortunately, the officers were housed on high ground, but the health of the enlisted men was seriously at risk from malaria endangering them to a far greater degree than Italian bombardment. A fortnight later father returned to Kenya where the OCTU had moved to the Nakuru showground. We gave up the Muthaiga house to stay with the Stanway family at Elmenteita.

Father knew the commanding officer, General Lewin. Colonel Butt, the Chief Instructor, was a neighbour from Naro Moru and Nigel Graham, later Gladys Gooch's third husband, was the adjutant. Weekly field exercises were held outside the town. To father's acute embarrassment army bicycles were issued for the purpose and father, brought up in hilly Welsh country where children rode ponies, had never learned to ride a bicycle. Initially he was allowed to use his car until Lewin changed the venue to the upper slopes of Menengai Crater and simultaneously decreed that henceforth all would cycle due to the fuel shortages. The men were told to assemble on the parade ground in order to set off together. Nigel Graham knew of father's predicament and waited by the exit to the parade ground to see how father would cope. Unsteady and uncoordinated, father turned his head and raised his right hand to salute the Adjutant, whereupon the bicycle wobbled alarmingly. He and the machine toppled into Nigel Graham and upset the entire formation. Father hated the bicycle, spending each outing either pushing it up hill or connecting his forehead with the handlebars as he tried to brake downhill. The whole effort of cycling affected his health and strained an already weak heart. He had applied for a transfer to the 5th KAR for which he had to undergo a medical. Dr Jex Blake, a heart specialist, saw him in Nairobi and pronounced him unfit for military service recommending a discharge due to high blood pressure and a weak heart.

This came as a disappointment as father had hoped to take up the Agricultural Department's offer to take over the running of five farms in the Naro Moru area, including his own, but still remain attached to the army. Naturally, the Commanding Officer felt he had engineered his medical to suit himself. When called in, he assured the disapproving Lewin that he had not applied for the job, rather the Department had asked for his release, and that he really would have preferred to stay in the army. Mollified, the General offered him a choice of unit. He chose the 5th KAR stationed in Nanyuki. The Postings Board in Nairobi made a complete cock-up in posting personnel from Nyasaland, who spoke Chinyanja, to Swahili-speaking battalions. Conversely, they allotted Swahili-speaking Kenya and Tanganyika personnel to Nyasaland battalions. This caused a ruckus when a Nyasaland battalion, who had been assigned Swahili-speaking officers, mutinied at the point of sail from Mombasa to Somalia where they were to engage in action in defence of British Somaliland.

Despite the various Commissions awarded people at the outset of the war in September 1938, these were not gazetted until January 1940, which meant that for the intervening months everyone had to live on and provide for their families on a private's pay of three shillings a day. A full corporal received six shillings. The Nyasaland men were paid weekly which was a sore point with the Kenya contingent who blamed Dickinson.

Waiting in Nairobi for his discharge – in the end he would return home – father sold the brown Hudson Terraplane, for which Eleanor Cole had advanced him £60, replacing it with a second-hand Hudson with pre-selective gear change for £150. He was delighted to have made a profit on the deal, and the car did him well for years.

Though father's war role was short-lived, he went on to contribute in no small measure to the country's agricultural sector providing essential foodstuffs for British and Commonwealth troops as far as the Egyptian and Western deserts.

Jack Stanway, who had been declared unfit for military service after shooting his foot while testing a gun trap for leopard, had been left to look after the farm for the duration of the war. Now he would have to look for another job. Soon after father's return in early 1941, my grandmother Trevvie died aged 80 never knowing of the birth of her third grandchild, Timothy, born in December of that year. Trevvie, who had been instrumental in our move to Naro Moru, died peacefully and was buried in the Nyeri churchyard.

Timothy was born at the Nakuru Hospital where our mother could be close to me and Richard as Eileen Steptoe's kindergarten, which we attended, had temporarily relocated to Njoro for safety. Mrs

Steptoe and the school soon returned to Nanyuki, this time without Mr Steptoe, who had been replaced by an army man, Colonel Delaforce, an old Wellingtonian and contemporary of Uncle Dick. There was a dearth of teaching staff and my mother, a trained teacher, volunteered to help out. She could keep Tim with her there, coming home with us all at weekends. In turn we all went to Pembroke House Preparatory School where I won the Victor Ludorum in a tie in my last year. I was due to go to either Wellington or Harrow, and was down for both. The former was my father's school, and the latter a possibility due to my godfather James Charles being an old Harrovian. However, with the war on I was sent instead to the Prince of Wales School, at Kabete.

James McKillop, meanwhile, a non-Swahili speaker and deemed far too laid back for regular duties, had been posted to the ASC to serve his time in the sweltering heat of the arid Northern Frontier District. James could consume enormous quantities of beer at the best of times, but there his requirements for the beverage multiplied. Sending out one of his lorries to the only European-run shop with orders to bring back three crates of beer, he was astounded to receive in its place a crate of Bibles. The owner of the shop, a member of the Moral Rearmament group, naturally disapproved of alcohol. In camp James had installed a large armchair, not for his comfort as you might think, but in order to teach his dog not to sit on it. He was very friendly with one of his Sergeants, a Greek. (After the war James met the Greek while holidaying on the coast. The Greek was looking for a job and told James he would really like a job running a hotel. James looked for a place to buy and found a small run-down hotel – Shelly Beach – near Likoni. He installed the Greek as a manager and agreed to ante up for all the improvements, which were quite considerable. Soon after the hotel opened for business, a family, the Jollys came to stay. Mr Jolly who died a few months later in residence, claimed to have been an explorer in South America. After his death, Mrs Jolly and her two children continued to make Shelly Beach their new home. The Greek persuaded James to part with more money in order to restock the hotel with new crockery and cutlery saying he could buy it all more cheaply in Cairo. That was the last James saw of either his money or the Greek. Mrs Jolly then stepped in as manager. The hotel prospered and was popular. It is doubtful whether James saw any return on his capital, and when he died the hotel and all its contents were found to be in Mrs Jolly's name.)

Father ran his and James's farm, while also overseeing several other farms in the area whose owners had joined up. As he had been through the army training process, he was also selected to train Kenya Defence Force recruits for the Karatina, Nyeri and Nanyuki area. Its purpose was to provide personnel to guard strategic points against sabotage, to assist the police force in the event of native uprising and to guard against possibility of landings by Italian troops with the idea of holding up the enemy until combat troops arrived. Paul Clarke suggested at one of the endless security meetings that since Cole's Plains would make an ideal landing spot, it should be planted up with spiky sisal plants. "Let the I-ties land on that!"

Manpower being scarce, an Auxiliary Defence Force came into being to train Africans. Initially father was expected to pay the men for each parade out of his own pocket, only later being refunded by the Army Paymaster. Luckily, he had an understanding bank manager. To minimise travelling and training time, it became necessary, due to fuel shortages, to split the various companies into section and platoons. Father enlisted handpicked Kikuyu men, some of whom would become leaders of the Mau Mau rebellion, particularly those who were sent overseas, many of whom would serve in India where nationalism was at its height. These men – and those who fought in the 1914-1918 war – saw a very different side to the white man and white woman, experiencing for the first time a very different class and shade of individual, including white prostitutes. They were exposed to uncivilised behaviour and the cruelty that manifests itself particularly in times of war.

Early in 1940 South African troops arrived in Kenya and brought with them an assortment of old war and transport planes. Vickers Valencias were used to transport foodstuffs to troops in the Northern Frontier. At home one afternoon, we heard the sound of a large aeroplane approaching followed shortly by the noise of bombs and machine gun strafing. Father watched the plane through binoculars until he lost sight of it over the southern end of Cole's Plains. Thinking it must have landed, he bundled us into the car and drove over to Pat Kenealy's place, where he suggested to Frances that she take us and her children to the river for safety. Pat Kenealy was adamant that he could not appear until Frances had sewn his 1914-1918 war Military Cross onto his uniform, saying he would follow later. I was most reluctant to be left behind finding the situation hugely exciting, which a picnic on the river was not.

Chico Basto and Major Geoffrey Baines were already at the railway station when father arrived. The Goan stationmaster, visibly shaken, confirmed that a plane had indeed fired on them. Chico was not convinced and thought the plane had British markings. With a rifle apiece and Geoffrey Baines hobbling on two sticks, the three went off to investigate. The reason for the 'bombing' soon became apparent with the discovery of dead and wounded zebra and antelope. They spent the remainder of the day finishing off wounded game and returned in the early evening, the car filled with zebra haunches to feed the farm labour and the ten Alsatian dogs we had then.

At the station they were confronted by an irate OC from Nanyuki Head Quarters who took father to task, for his misleading telegram.

"What telegram?" father asked.

"Enemy plane bombing Naro Moru station and railway line" – signed OC KDF. Pat Kenealy, convinced by the gibbering stationmaster that the enemy had landed, had been the one who wired it off. The South African crew of the plane, it transpired, bored by lack of action on their weekly missions, thought they'd have some fun targeting the unfortunate animals grazing below.

Some weeks later the very same Vickers Valencia and crew made plans to knock out Fort Wilkinson, a mud and wattle fort on the Abyssinian-Kenya border abandoned by the British at the start of the war. On weekend leave with the Kenealys the crew related how they had resolved to relieve the tedium once again by bombarding the fort by dropping a 44-gallon petrol drum filled with scrap metal and explosives. When they realised that they could not get the drum through the door of the plane, they tied it to a wing. The idea was that a crewmember would sit beside it chain smoking until the moment arrived to light the fuse. As they circled the fort, the unsuspecting Italians came out to see what all the noise was about. The pilot went into a nosedive, the fuse was lit and the drum released. It first hit the ground harmlessly but bounced on towards the fort. The Italians fled. When the plane righted itself and the dust settled, the fort was gone. This mystery action soon came to light after one of the crew members had to be treated for a gunshot wound in the foot.

According to father, the South African Forces, and West African troops under Brigadier 'Piggy' Richards, who fought well gaining ground right through to Eritrea, bore the brunt of the whole East African campaign against the Italians in Abyssinia.

Italian prisoners of war were sent to various camps around the country and many were 'loaned out' to help on the farms where their building, engineering and artisan skills were highly appreciated. Felice Benuzzi and two other prisoners escaped from the Nanyuki prisoner-of-war camp with the sole purpose of planting the Italian flags on Mt Kenya's summit returning after reaching Point Lenana to a huge welcome from their fellow prisoners and a grudging respect from the British officers and men of the camp. It was a tremendous feat, considering they had little food to sustain them and inadequate warm clothing. Benuzzi wrote a charming book on the episode, *No Picnic On Mount Kenya*, and was appointed the Italian Vice Consul to Australia after the war.

An early arrival in the war had been an Indian Mountain Battery under the command of Major John d'Arcy, later GOC in Palestine. On retirement he bought Waraza Estate near us at Naro Moru. He and his wife Noel became great friends sharing many bird shooting expeditions to the Northern Frontier and a salmon fishing holiday in Scotland. Many of the Naro Moru farmers participated in these regular shoots – guinea fowl, yellow-necks, sand grouse – which were well organised with beaters and lines in the manner of European pheasant shoots. No bird ever went to waste and if there happened to be an excess, for there was no refrigeration then, Chico Basto flew the birds back to Nanyuki for friends or for the hospital for immediate consumption. As a young boy I took little interest in shotgun sport, preferring to hunt with a rifle, and would usually leave the line of guns to stalk something nearby, which did not make me popular when I happened to spook an animal that ran through the line. There were occasions when the line was broken involuntarily by a surprise lion, a charging buffalo or rhino. There'd be a sudden flurry of activity as the guns ran for cover.

As the war progressed and commonwealth forces moved the front line further north, Kenya's role was concentrated in supplying food for the war effort. The now important agricultural sector was re-organised under Cavendish Bentick – CB the future Duke of Portland.

Agricultural sub-committees were formed for each area. The District Agricultural Officer appointed the committee members, all farmers within his area, and subsequently the farmers themselves elected their own committee members and chairman. The chairmen of the sub-committees were automatically made members of the committees and members of the Board of Agriculture. They and other appointees representing the financial sector or agricultural bodies such as the Kenya Co-operative Creameries and the Uplands Bacon Factory took their cue under the overall chairmanship of C B. It all sounds rather bureaucratic but it worked extremely well. These committees were empowered to determine which crop a farmer grew and the acreage ploughed. In turn the farmer was guaranteed a minimum return paid by the Treasury for any pre-requisite crop. Again, with the approval of his sub-committee, a farmer could borrow money for the development of the crop over and above the guaranteed minimum return to be repaid at the end of the season at 5%. Once the farmer had harvested and stored his crop, he could realise 80% of the value paid to him though the Kenya Farmers' Association. Over the whole period of the war £67,000 was all the British Government had been required to ante up in guaranteed minimum returns.

At Karatina in the Kikuyu Reserve, where high rainfall suited market gardening, a dried vegetable factory using imported American machinery was established to help process vegetables for the army and help the small holder maximise his produce. The yields were good and many tons of dried vegetables were produced. The Kikuyu in the area profited. When the war ended, a British canning concern offered to take over the enterprise under a mixed Board of African and British members. In *Forks and Hope*, Elspeth Huxley wrote this about the dried vegetable plant. "The land on which the factory and its labour quarters stand had been leased to the Gov by the Local Native Council, with the consent of the owners, for the duration of the war and one year there-after. Now the end of the lease was approaching and the owners began to demand the return of their land. At the same time thousands of demobilized soldiers were returning: familiar sights in their slouch hats and dangling cigarettes, clustering at every teashop and duka, they cast about for profitable outlets for their gratuities, and where two or three ex-soldiers gathered together a 'company' was born. Soon the 'companies' had sprung up everywhere like lilies after rain - but quite often giving out the rank odour of unorthodoxy - and some of the leaders had organized a loose association called the United Companies of Mumbi...The United Companies of Mumbi then offered to buy the dried vegetable factory from Gov for £30,000. But thereafter it never worked again, and the onset of the Mau Mau rebellion put a stop to any new ideas."

A local engineer named 'Daddy' Barnes built a similar factory at Kerugoya, also in the Kikuyu Reserve. Barnes's simple engineering concepts could usually be mended with a bit of wire or string. My father was one of the first members of the Naro Moru sub-committee and subsequently, as the need to train for a KDF became redundant with the shift of war well beyond Kenya's northern borders, he was elected Chairman of both the local Sub-Committee and the District Committee, and made a member of the Board of Agriculture.

Towards the end of the war, when it was felt that Germany was on the run and the Italians had capitulated, the Board felt a new wave of soldier-settlers would be beneficial. CB's original Board of Agriculture became the Agricultural Settlement Board, under the Chairmanship of FOB Wilson, a rancher from Ulu east of Nairobi, whose two sons, Richard and Denis, were serving in the Navy. Father was appointed a member of the new Board. The British Government granted the Board a loan of three million pounds at 3-1/2 % and allotted it all Crown Land in the White Highlands not yet taken up. Two schemes were devised. The first, the Tenant Farm Scheme, was aimed at people with capital as little as £1500. The Board supplied the land and advanced money for its development at 4% - the half per cent difference took care of Board expenses. The Board also appointed among the farming community established farmers and ranchers as Land Valuers whose job it was to evaluate the tenant should he wish to buy his land. Once the Board was satisfied the tenant had sufficient knowledge and cash to make a go of it, he could pay off his loan over forty years. The second scheme, the Assisted Owner's Scheme, was designed for newcomers with sufficient capital to buy the land. The Board would then advance 80% of the value of the farm for improvements, or the purchase of stock and machinery, on which the farmer paid 4% again over forty years.

Egerton College, an agricultural college at Njoro, was expanded to take in any soldier-settler who had no farming experience. He would attend a six-month course there until the Board was satisfied he could go it alone. There were married quarters and wives were encouraged. Gerald Burton, a Senior Agricultural officer and later Julian Kerrison's second husband, was appointed to re-organise the college. He later joined the settlement Board as Executive Officer to advice on land purchase and agricultural matters.

Father was heavily involved with the Board and later with the European Agricultural Settlement Trust, which he felt did more than any other body to settle the 'White Highlands.' Despite Elspeth Huxley's prediction in the early 1950s that Kenya would gain its independence come what may – she was better politically informed than father who took little interest in politics – father refused to acknowledge it. I think he felt his life's work had come to nothing when independence was finally declared in 1963. However, for the moment his work with the Board is only beginning. The years between the end of the war and the beginning of the Emergency in 1952 were ones of huge development in Kenya. Land prices soared and farming was profitable.

James McKillop invested in a passion fruit farm in the Sotik area in western Kenya and financed father's enterprise canning cream. Father felt the excess milk could be more profitably used in the processed dairy products. He sought the advice of Mike Barrett, an instructor at Egerton and product of Reading University, with the result that he and James formed a new company, M.P. Products, in which James gave father a 25% stake. Father lost no time in building the factory with farm labour. He imported machinery, and was soon selling canned cream. This expanded to canned milk and cheese when M.P. Products bought out the Cains of Lamuria Processed Cheddar. When his competitor across the valley produced dried whole milk powder, father imported a roller-drying plant from Australia to concentrate on the production of skim powder. The factory would eventually employ a number of European personnel in finance, managing and marketing.

In the year after the end of the war most people in Kenya were too preoccupied with the minutiae of getting on with the day-to-day running of their businesses and farms to notice sporadic incidents, particularly in the Nyeri area, that marked the imminent danger of the Kikuyu uprising that would become known as the Mau Mau Rebellion.

Princess Elizabeth and Prince Philip being greeted at the Naro Moru church by Joe Prettejohn (left) and Geoffrey Baines (right).

Chapter Twenty

THE EMERGENCY

The Mau Mau, as it came to be officially recognised in 1949, was the latest of a long line of Kikuyu political societies that preached against European – and Indian – presence in Africa. Only the Mau Mau were more violent.

African nationalism really began after the first war, in 1920, with the Kikuyu Association, or Young Kikuyu Association, whose prime mover was Harry Thuku. Members were bound by oath not to sell any land to strangers. During this earlier period, oath-taking was a normal tribal practice. It had none of the sinister implications and degrading practices that would later be foisted by the Mau Mau on willing and unwilling members, contrary to native law and custom.

Harry Thuku was arrested two years later after a period of unrest sparked by the introduction of the *kipande* (employment ID card), combined with an increase in the poll tax and a decrease in agricultural wages as a result of falling commodity prices. At his trial it was deduced that the main theme of the movement was: "to stimulate enmity between black and white and to get people to consider that they are in a state of slavery which has been imposed upon them by Europeans." This theme and that of 'stolen lands' formed the cornerstone of African nationalism.

The year that Thuku was put under wraps, Johnstone Kamau (who later took the name 'Jomo' Kenyatta), an employee of the Nairobi Town Council, joined the movement, which now called itself the Kikuyu Central Association (KCA.) Its theme – "to get back the land" – mainly appealed to the town and city-based landless element. In 1928 Kenyatta was appointed General Secretary of the Association and its media editor of the *Mwigwithanaia* journal. At about the same time there was a breakaway movement from the Christian mission teachings, it being felt these were too removed from local Kikuyu custom, particularly in regard to polygamy and circumcision. When in 1929 the Church of Scotland Mission and other mission groups took a firm stand against female circumcision demanding the teachers renounce the practice or lose their jobs, there was a wave of resentment culminating in the murder of Hulda Stumpf, a missionary lady at Kijabe. Despite the death, the KCA felt the Europeans, through the church, intended to destroy Kikuyu customs, the foundations of the tribe. Thus was born The Kikuyu Independent Schools Association and The Kikuyu Karinga Education Association and numerous church congregations pulled away from the mission-run churches and formed their own independent churches. These associations and churches formed the framework on which Jomo Kenyatta organised the spread of Kikuyu nationalism. Kenyatta would later add to his portfolio, among other societies, Githunguri Teachers Training College. From 1929 on the Kikuyu would be a divided people. The traditionalists, the Kikuyu Karinga, were anti-Government and preached against the Europeans and the missions, while the Kikuyu Kirore believed their future lay in peaceful cooperation. The outcome of the rebellion might have been very different had this division between insurgents and loyalists not existed.

Over the heads of the Kenya Government, Kenyatta took a delegation of KCA members to London with a demand for *inter alia*, direct election by Africans to the Legislative Council adding, "Ultimately the number of Africans in Legislative Council should predominate." When his petition fell on deaf ears, Kenyatta went to Russia for three months. He joined the Communist party in 1930 and returned to Kenya, determined to make his mark and become the undisputed leader of the Kikuyu tribe. However, he only spent a few months in Kenya, hiding in Mombasa, where he consulted with KCA leaders and organised fund raising drives, before leaving for England where he would spend the next fifteen years.

At this point Harry Thuku, released at the end of 1930, had the greatest following among the tribe. On his release he gave the Government an undertaking to only oppose it constitutionally, an understanding that he kept to, although it would later cost him his life. In 1932 he was elected president of the KCA ousting the incumbent, Joseph Kangethe. However, this was short-lived and he in turn was ousted by Kangethe and the more extreme Jesse Kariuki, founder members of the movement, for "misappropriation of Association funds." When Thuku realised that his order ran contrary to methods of the extremists, he founded the Kikuyu Provincial Association (KPA) whose constitution stated: "Every member of the organisation will pledge to be loyal to His Majesty the King of Great Britain and the established Government and will be bound to do nothing which is not constitutional according to British traditions or do anything which is calculated to disturb the peace, good order and government."

The struggle between the two factions continued. The KCA stepped up its tactics to oust colonial rule. They formed an intelligence network through Kikuyu clerks in Government offices and infiltrated members into the Laikipia district. It formed cells in Thika, Fort Hall and Nyeri and increasingly inserted itself in the growing Trade Union movements, and took on board disaffected Kamba, Taita and Embu members – tribes that shared the same Bantu lineage with Kikuyu.

When it surfaced at the beginning of the war that the KCA was making overtures to the Italian Consulate and was in touch with Italian agents, the Government declared it an illegal society. Its headquarters in Badru House were closed and all documents confiscated. Investigations into the Association's affairs revealed that no accounts had been kept and no assets existed. What had become of member donations or those solicited for the upkeep of the Githunguri Teacher's Training College?

In 1944 a moderate, Eliud Mathu, was nominated as the first African Member of the Legislative Council. Mathu formed the Kenya African Union (KAU) with Harry Thuku as its chairman. Over the next few years, the moderate executive of the KAU would be infiltrated by former KCA members culminating in Jomo Kenyatta's election as its president in 1947. Since British law relied on the written word and eye-witness accounts, Kenyatta told his followers never to commit anything to writing, and only to commit illegal acts with, or in front of, those that could be trusted. He also knew that if he inserted the word "democracy" into his speeches, he would court sympathy for the cause. He was a brilliant speaker, a man of charisma, and he appealed to Kikuyu tribal identity.

Jomo Kenyatta had returned to Kenya from his self-imposed exile in England a year earlier, leaving behind an English wife. In one of his first private speeches, he announced that he disliked Europeans and Indians and that in the course of time they would all be removed from Africa.

On Jomo Kenyatta's return, he led the Kikuyu in the struggle for independence. By 1952 after several prominent loyal Kikuyu chiefs were shot or brutally murdered, and open violence was publicly preached, a state of emergency was declared on 20th October 1952 and Jomo was interned. (It was said that he never actually intended the movement known as "Mau Mau" to turn into such a violent organisation.)

Farmers barricaded themselves in and sent servants to be locked into their quarters as dusk fell, with a curfew being imposed. No African, other than a home guard or policeman, could be out after dark. Many settlers rejoined the KAR, Kenya Regiment or became Police Reserve Officers. Father became the leader of the Police Reserve in the Naro Moru area, from the main Nanyuki road to the base of Mt Kenya, while The Earl Enniskillen, then David Cole, was in charge of all the rest of the Naro Moru farms west of the road to the base of the Aberdares.

Father was issued with an automatic Beretta and led nightly patrols around the farms. Naro Moru House Farm, as our farm was called, became the centre of operations and contingents of the Regular Forces were stationed here to help in the patrols, and follow the gangs into the forest. It was a particularly hard time for the wives who were left alone for hours or days. Communications were not the best in those days. Radios, both stationary and hand-held, crackled away and were difficult to read or transmit. All the isolated farms were issued with Vary pistols to send a signal light into the sky if they were being attacked. As it was often difficult in the pitch dark nights to ascertain where the light was being fired from, father set up a sign post pointing to all the farms under his jurisdiction, to see where the light was being fired from and who was in trouble.

The Mau Mau gangs got larger and bolder and many soon became armed with stolen guns and pistols. They killed stock and took the meat away to the forest while they left many animals maimed and hamstrung. A farmer would go out in the morning to find all his dairy cattle standing on stumps unable to move and having to be putdown. A number of farmers and their families were brutally murdered around the country. One of these was in father's area of patrolling. A retired naval officer and his wife, the Morices, were attacked one night but instead of firing his Vary pistol into the air, he fired it into the gang. This deterred the gang but they went on to break into their manager's house a mile or so away. In the morning he was found savagely butchered and cut to pieces.

My mother often had to rise in the middle of the night or early hours of the morning to feed a patrol team returning from a sortie. Father one night led a patrol into the forest after a notorious gangster they called 'Big Foot' because of his huge footprints. Big Foot's gang ambushed father's patrol at point blank range from thick cover, but hit no one. The patrol returned fire and killed one, but I don't remember hearing if it was Big Foot.

A screening camp was set up on the farm under an FIO (Field Intelligence Officer) and slowly the anti-Mau Mau were sorted out and trained and put to work with the forces or as Home Guards. Much intelligence was gathered on gang movements, and ambushes were set with growing success until the large gangs broke up and retired to the forest where they were pursued by the military and cloak-and-dagger pseudo-gang teams. Through this intelligence the women groups taking food into the forest were also stopped and the gangs had to break up further, even into ones and twos, to survive on berries and animals they trapped. Many of these animals were eaten raw for fear of making fires from which the smoke could be spotted from the air by police wing air recces. It was not till 1956 that the emergency came to an end and father once again was able to return in earnest to developing the farm. Little did he know, or want to know, that although the battle was won, the 'wind of change' was blowing and Britain would soon dissolve all her colonies in spite of promises to the new settlers after the war that they and their land in Kenya would be protected for eternity.

In 1963 Independence was declared and our farm was engulfed in one of the earliest settlement schemes, organised by my father as chairman of the Naro Moru District Farmer's Committee. Elspeth Huxley, the great writer on Kenya, had always told him this would happen, but his reply was, "This will never happen. We will follow Southern Rhodesia and declare independence."

"How come?" she would ask. "There are only 60,000 white farmers and there are 6,000,000 blacks." Father didn't want to face up to the obvious facts for the future of the country.

In 1952 when the Emergency was declared, I had barely completed one year of a three-year course at an Agricultural College, Shuttleworth, in Bedfordshire, England. I wrote home that I wanted to return, but father insisted I finish the course. "This is going to be a long war and there will be plenty for you to do on completion of your course," he wrote. Against his will, I set about organising a way to get home. The story of my overland trip back to Kenya is told in detail later in the chapter 'A long way home.'

Reaching home in 1953 I applied to return to the Kenya Regiment, which I had joined when it started up again after the war, attending fortnightly camps and training. I was told to go for an interview with Colonel Morcolm. This I did. There were a number of us and I was in line behind a certain acquaintance named Bond. We were being interviewed to become a District Officer Kikuyu Guard (DOKG).

The door was ajar as Bond was being interviewed. "So you think you will make a better officer than remaining in the Regiment?" asked the Colonel.

Bond replied, "I don't know about that, but I will do better than someone interviewing behind a desk." Bond was out by his ear, and I was next to be interviewed by the then-enraged Colonel. I explained that from my hunting days in lower Embu, I knew that district well and wanted to be placed in this district. Also, I said I knew many of the officers working there. The Colonel said nothing, but gave me a note to immediately make my way to join Arnold Hoff who was a DOKG at the 'sharp end' in Fort Hall (now Murang'a) on the forest edge of the Southern Aberdares.

When I got there, Arnold's first words to me were, "Have you ever killed anybody?"

"No" I replied meekly.

"Well, you may tonight," he replied. "We have information of an oath ceremony to be held at midnight, and we are to make an ambush. Here is your Patchett, an automatic like a sten gun. Get familiar with it and with your team of Home Guards."

Taking a hand-drawn map, he explained, "I and my team will go in from here. You and your team will attack from here. Our password will be 'Jim' so be careful you don't shoot any of our own men." I went off to confer with my team with whom I was most impressed. They had been well trained, and knew exactly what to do. It was all new to me, but I was determined to learn fast, relying entirely on their judgement. The corporal in charge worked out the plan and I went to rest in my allotted hut until Arnold called me for a cup of tea and to further explain tactics. I was high with anticipation without the thought that came later, that I may be killed myself! Jimmy Candler, the previous DO, had been recently ambushed and brutally killed, so I was aware of the possibility.

At 11 o'clock in the evening, the rendezvous came round. I got ready to go. We all motored for a while together, then silently disembarked and prepared ourselves to walk the rest of the way to the oath site, a distance of some two kilometres. Arnold and his group set off in one direction while we took another path. We walked in single file, the Corporal leading the way followed by myself. It was very dark and extremely quiet. A torch could only be used to glimpse at the ground in order to make sure we were on the right track. An occasional hoot from an owl or the distant barking of a dog made me clutch the Patchett ready to fire. My eyes got used to the dark but I kept imagining things that weren't there. We started at a fair pace. The Corporal knew the way and he confidently marched forward giving me confidence. Soon we got near, and tip-toeing through the maize and banana plantation we could dimly make out the village huts. We knew the chosen hut and quietly fanned out around one side each taking our planned position. I lay down the Patchett at the ready. We heard voices and the corporal made a dash at the door kicking it open. Then all hell broke loose. The hut erupted and people came rushing out firing at random. We kept low so their bullets went high. The corporal opened up, shouting, "Jim," so we'd know who he was. He also ordered, "*Mikono juu*, Hands Up," but no one surrendered. They were off into the darkness like lightening.

We all opened up at the disappearing figures. The other team fired at them, too, and then we made a rush to the hut. We heard screams, but no one was left inside. All the oathing paraphernalia was there, beside a smoking fire. The shooting stopped and we joined up with Arnold's team and carefully took stock. There must have been at least 15 people in the hut with at least two weapons. We waited awhile in case of an ambush but they were all gone. Some five bodies were dead on the ground, including a member of my team. Had he been killed by one of us or by one of the Mau Mau? We never knew. His body was carried back to the waiting truck while at dawn the police and our full time District Officer, Don Clay, arrived to take fingerprints of the dead, collect the bodies, and arrange the burial of our man. Don Clay, who spoke Kikuyu fluently, was very consoling. He kept a 'goat bag' for such events to make sure our dead man's family were well compensated.

Such events were commonplace, and at the tender age of twenty one, I soon got used to seeing dead bodies. Most of our patrols and sorties came to nothing. Our main job was to protect Senior Chief

Njiiri and his family. He was a very distinguished old man and defiantly opposed Mau Mau preaching. Wherever he went he flew the Union Jack, and in the centre of his encampment flew a large edition, all the time. He was the number one target in the whole of Fort Hall for the Mau Mau, but I am glad to say he survived to the end.

I was with Arnold for some six months, before Don Clay gave me my own locations, 6 and 17, under Chiefs Philip and Erastus. Chief Philip was shot in the head while following up a gang and although he survived he became totally blind, but he bravely carried on his duties with plenty of support. Location 6 had a big population, but Location 17 was in the lower dry country going down to the Tana River on one side with the settled area of Makuyu on the other. It had a much sparser population. Although today the main Nairobi to Nanyuki road runs through the middle of this area, at that time there were few tracks and lots of wildlife.

My job in both these locations was to build Home Guard Posts, move the populace into protected villages, train the guards and accompany them on patrols to root out the smaller gangs.

The Home Guard posts had a bulletproof wall all around with two turrets at opposite ends so that they could shoot anyone outside the

Building a Home Guard Post, Location 17, Fort Hall district.

walls trying to enter. Outside this was a surrounding moat full of 'panjis,' sharpened stakes, and a draw bridge that could be pulled up during an attack and at night. An FIO officer and screening camp was also built for these locations to which we took suspects and prisoners caught on patrols for interrogations.

Manning a Home Guard Post.

In the early days, and especially for Location 17, there were not sufficient arms for all the Home Guards so I armed them with bows and arrows. There was a Catholic Mission nearby and the Father Rosano used to supply me with a very potent poison made from the Acokanthera tree to put on the arrows. On an attack one night at one of the Location 17 posts my men hit one of the Mau Mau terrorists (now called Freedom Fighters) in the thigh with a poison arrow and he did not go more than a few hundred yards before he died. If the Mau Mau had used poison arrows to ambush us instead of homemade guns, they would have been better off. Location 17 had large areas of lantana bush which was ideal for hiding. On one patrol into this area a man suddenly jumped out in front of me before I or any of my Guards could get a shot off. He fired directly at me from a very short distance, disappearing at the same time. I thought I must be wounded. I realised I wasn't dead, and I could not feel or find any wound! After letting off a magazine into the bush, we moved gingerly forward. There he was, dead on the ground with a hole in his forehead the size of an egg. His homemade gun was made from a piece of piping with a 12-bore cartridge jammed into the breech and a sharpened door bolt set with a rubber band to pierce the detonator when loosened by the trigger. Unfortunately for him and

Author and his dog Simba at the house in Kamahuha, Fort Hall.

very fortunately for me, the bolt blew backwards on detonation and went into his head, killing him instantly.

On moving to these new locations I first lived in a discarded *duka* (shop) built of stone with a corrugated iron roof. The smell of bat droppings was appalling and no matter what I did to clear it, the smell never subsided. After a few months I could stand it no longer. Our senior DOKG, or right hand man to the DC, was a Jock Rutherfurd. Jock had a reasonable house in Fort Hall Town. He suggested I move in with him as he had several spare rooms.

The town was more or less in the middle of my two locations so it was still easy to get around. I moved in with my *mpishi* (cook) Mungai whom I had taken on at the duka. Mungai stayed and moved with me wherever I went and was with me till he died some 50 years later. Now his son still works for my daughter and her husband.

Jock Rutherfurd had amazing stamina; he was at it all day and up all night swilling beer! He introduced me to his sister Gillian who later became my wife and mother of my three children.

172

Besides a shortage of arms, we had a shortage of vehicles so I opted to use my own. The old Dodge Power Wagon in which I crossed the Sahara was too cumbersome on those narrow and twisting roads so I sold it to Chief Erastus. I went to Mulji, the Indian garage proprietor in town, who sold me a Model A Ford Box Body, which I kept and used for many years.

He had completely rebuilt it so it was in excellent condition and could go anywhere. With a set of chains it would chug through the black cotton soil in the rains and because of its high clearance we seldom got bogged down. My two bodyguards sat in the back with their legs over the box on either side, rifles at the ready in case of an ambush. The only trouble I had was in heavy rain when occasionally the water off the roof would get into the petrol tank which was situated behind the dashboard with the filler cap on the top. On such occasions I would wait until the rain stopped, drain the water from the fuel cock on the line, drain the carburettor from a screw plug and off we would go. This happened once when I was driving home to Naro Moru. I had a companion District Officer with me, Mike Whittal, smoking his pipe while waiting for the downpour to subside. We heard a fast car approaching from behind.

It skidded violently in the wet mud and drove straight into our backside. We shot up the hill, Mike's pipe flying and bouncing off the windscreen. There was not even a dent at the back of the Box Body, but on looking back we saw a large black Humber saloon with the grill and radiator pushed against the fan with water gushing out everywhere. The poor lad had borrowed his father's Humber to report

A Model Ford Box Body used by author when he was District Officer, Kikuyu guard.

to the Police Training School in Kiganjo, some 50 miles on. He was already late and driving far too fast, but we managed to get him there eventually by towing the car behind us.

After a year or so, the gangs in the Reserve had either moved into the forest of the Aberdare Mountains, or had been captured, and the women now in villages had little chance to take them food. So my job became more of an administrative one. Cloak and dagger teams were then instigated to follow the gangs into the forest and volunteers were asked to join. I elected to participate under Ian Pritchard. We moved into the forest for a week or two at a time, a gang of two or three Europeans and half a dozen men captured from the forest gangs who had elected to 'turn' and guide us to the known hideouts. We wore wigs or large drooping monkey skin hats and blackened faces

Pseudo-gang, southern Aberdare forest.

and arms with 'stevo boot polish.' Women carried the rations as was the gang's way, following a short distance behind. At night we built a rough shelter of bamboo using the dried leaves as a bed.

We chose this area because it was difficult to approach without being detected. We took it in turns to guard the four corners, having to completely trust in our gang members. There was never an incident in which this trust failed. We gave ourselves a Gang name and as we were always after a specific gang, we'd leave a note for them in a piece of hollow

Pseudo-gang members, author on left.

bamboo, saying we would like to make contact giving a certain time and place, usually around midnight. The note would then be left in a known 'post office,' a fork in a particular tree. There would be a known password used to pass a guard who would then, in a successful encounter, have us wait in a certain spot while he went to inform his leader. If he panicked and tried to run away, he had to be caught and gagged. Sometimes he could be persuaded to lead us directly to their hideout, but on such occasions the gang would be gone by the time we got there, or

One of the team members, Johnny Vaas.

there had to be a shootout. On a successful meet we would capture the gang leader and have him make his mates surrender, explaining that they would not be killed, but trained as counter gangs if they so wished.

Waiting in the dark of night in utter silence was terrifying beyond belief, and it took great courage for our gang leaders to make contact without showing any fear and to give a plausible story before we could make a move. We, the '*mzungus*' (whites), had to remain in the background. However well we were disguised in boot polish, on close quarters we could easily be detected.

So we waited, fingers on the trigger of a weapon hidden under our coats, waiting for a signal to act. Only Kikuyu could be spoken, and in a known dialect. Sometimes it had to end in a shoot-out, but if successful we could retreat without a shot being fired and make it out of the forest and back to base as quickly as we could, with a bunch of prisoners to hand over for interrogation and the forming of new counter gangs. We could not sustain more than a week or ten days at a time at this game before nerves would break and we got what we called 'Bamboo Fever.'

It was such a relief to find a stream on the forest edge in which to wash off the stove polish and return to a good hot meal! Some of the prisoners felt a huge relief as well as they received a good meal and medical care, if required, for veldt sores, lice and malnutrition. Many of these men were in a very poor state after months or even years in the forest having been tortured and treated roughly by their own leaders.

Nights out in the bamboo.

A significant outcome of this work was in breaking up the larger gangs. The smaller groups then dared not make contact with others, and so lost touch with the outside world. Here's an example. In 1957 after the Emergency had been declared over, I went on a hunting safari

Cleaning off the Zebu Stove Polish at the end of a pseudo-gang sortie.

after bongo in the bamboo forest of eastern Mount Kenya. Unknown to us, a lone man watched our every movement. When he realised he was not being hunted himself, he surrendered to me. He was dressed in a bushbuck skin shirt and shorts with a large brimmed hat made of buffalo skin. He had not seen any other person in a year and did not realise the war was over. We handed him over to the police in Embu, the district HQ, and he was later given a sawmill.

As an interesting postscript, over 30 years later, a Belgian mountain climber named Luc Poppe strayed from his group and could not find his way out of the forest, eventually dying of exposure. The Park Warden was on leave, and Sarah Seth-Smith, who worked in the Belgian Embassy at the time, asked if I could help in looking for the lost climber. I immediately thought of this ex-terrorist who had lived in that area by himself for over a year. I located him, gave him a blanket and some rations and asked him if he could help. He set out, found the Belgian's tracks and located the body by a river in a very inaccessible gorge a week or so later. With the help of others, he retrieved the body and met me at a planned spot on the nearest road, where we delivered it on to the Police.

At my location in the Reserve after the forest sorties, I continued with the mundane work of road building and assorted administration chores. As Location 17 bordered the settled farms, and at the time had abundant wildlife, I was made an Honorary Game Warden to deal with marauding animals destroying the crops, or crocodiles on the Tana River, when they started killing people. Buffalo were the main problem in the settled area, and I enjoyed hunting them in the thick bush. Once three elephant strayed into a populated area and became very aggressive after stones were thrown at them with much shouting and beating of tins. I had to deal with the elephants before someone got killed.

Surrender of a Mau Mau in 1957 dressed entirely in wild animal skins. He hadn't seen anyone in a year and did not know the war was over

The only flat ground in Fort Hall

was in Location 17 so I was delegated to build the District Airfield. We did this by hand clearing and then levelling using a large tree dragged up and down behind my old Model A Ford. Soon after we completed the airstrip, I was informed that Colonel Morcolm was to fly in with my good friend 'Punch' Bearcroft, Head of the Police Airwing. He was to land at 11 am and I was to take him around the Home Guard Posts and then take him to lunch with the District Commissioner. A new Land Rover would be sent as the DC said it would be inappropriate for the Colonel to be taken around in a Model A Ford! When the plane roared in at 9.30 am, no new vehicle had arrived. I had a dog, a cross between a bull terrier, ridge-back and bull dog, who travelled with me everywhere. My dog rode in the back with my two askaris who sat on either side with their legs out, ready to fire and jump out if we ran into an ambush.

I had no option but to drive out to the strip and meet the Colonel in the Ford. We arrived at the strip just as the plane taxied up. My dog jumped out and ran after the plane. Punch came to a sharp stop as the dog approached. Punch hopped out with a big smile and a wink and as he came round to let out the Colonel and whispered, "Boy, you will be in trouble!"

And so I was. The Colonel reluctantly jumped into the Ford but

The author visiting a Home Guard Post with his dog Simba.

had a second fit when the dog boarded too. "Do we have to take the dog?" he asked.

"He comes with me everywhere and can sense a possible ambush," I explained. The Colonel said no more, other than utterances about having to discuss all this with the DC.

I took him to one of my further posts first, hoping to give the askaris time to be prepared, but on arrival they were still polishing their gear. The Colonel started to inspect and noticed one of the askaris had two bullets missing. "What did you use these for?" he asked.

"Oh Sir, the Bwana DO asked me to help him shoot a crocodile that had been eating goats and even one young girl was taken." The Colonel turned to me with a look of horror saying there was a war on and these men should not participate in this sort of thing. I gave him vivid accounts of the ambushes and patrols we had done together, how many terrorists had been killed or taken as prisoners, and the guns that had been captured. I then explained my role as an Honorary Game Warden too.

By the time we reached the second and third posts all was in order and inspections completed. But by then the Colonel had seen enough and was anxious to get on to lunch with John Pinney, the DC. John welcomed us to lunch and before the Colonel could present his accusations, John apologised profusely about the transport and the shortage of vehicles. He explained the stress he was under to cover all the activity that was going on in his District, which was probably the most war active district of all, in the country, followed by Kiambu, then Nyeri.

After a pre-lunch pink gin the Colonel mellowed while John said how active all his Kenya boys (like me) were, as we knew the country and how to work most effectively with the local communities. "Besides," he said, with a wink my way, "if I tick them off too severely they would just say bugger you and take off back to their thousands of acres."

After an excellent lunch the Colonel actually thanked me before being sent off by John in a new Land Rover to his next destination. The outcome of all this was that a new bunch of vehicles were supplied to the district and I received a new jeep just out, an Austin Champ. This vehicle was beautifully sprung and had a very lively engine that could drive really fast over rough ground. But the front suspension could not take this treatment and the front wheels would collapse and had to be modified and strengthened. The other redeeming feature was that the car had the same amount of gears and speed in reverse! This was soon put to the test by an exceptionally spirited DOKG, one Willy Young. Willy's camp was on the top of a very steep ridge with a long and very winding track with many hair bends to get to it. On Sundays he would hold 'The Muraranjis Hill Climb.' It had to be done on a time basis and in reverse. All the DO's would be invited and of course the Austin Champs always won, and always with Willy at the wheel. However, after some bad spills and bent vehicles that could only be straightened in the District HQ workshop, John Pinney put a stop to the race!

Willy had a contingent of the British Black Watch Regiment stationed in his Location and was always setting up pranks against some of these somewhat 'green' youths. Once he set a charge in one of their 'Long Drop' loos, and one afternoon as a soldier ventured into it, he lit the fuse whilst hiding in a nearby bush. It fizzled away until there was a mighty bang and the poor soldier, who'd been sitting on the seat came flying through the door, grabbing his pants. He took off at the double believing he had been attacked by a gang.

On another occasion, while the Command were in a large marquee tent bending over a table poring over a map, Willy took someone on a bet that he could shoot an arrow over the tent and cause an alarm. Unfortunately for him the arrow did not make it, but instead it went through the tent landing in one of their buttocks! He certainly won his bet that it would "cause an alarm." I never heard the end of the story and to this day I have never met up with Willy again since the end of the Emergency. I did hear though that he calmed down considerably after he wrapped his car around a pylon killing his girlfriend.

For years one of the top Mau Mau leaders, General Kago, was active in the Fort Hall area. Kago had had military training during the war in which he had been a successful soldier. He was very brave, utterly ruthless and good at tactics.

I was motoring back one day from Embu when I noticed a plane dive bombing over an area south of Embu known as the Mwea plains. It turned out to be Punch Bearcroft, In Charge Police Air Wing, who had spotted Kago's gang on the open plains. He had run out of hand grenades and was attempting to knock out gang members with his wheels. The Police Air wing flew four-seater Piper Tri-Pacers at that time. With all passenger seats removed, Punch would fill the aircraft with grenades until the front wheel came off the ground, then he would remove one or two until the wheel was back on the ground, then he would be ready to go. Punch had lost his right hand as a boy in a motorbike accident so he would tie a piece of car inner tube around the stump, which he in turn tied to the 'joy stick.' He had a tube constructed on his left side with a stick clipped to it, which was easily removed. When flying over a gang like this he would pull the pin with his teeth and drop the grenade down the tube with his left hand. If by chance it got stuck, he would poke it on its way with the stick. I never learnt how successful his grenade drops were, but they certainly gave the people on the ground a hell of a fright! Anyway, on this occasion he had finished all the grenades.

Watching this episode I, with my two askaris, made for the scene of action across country. The Mwea was north of the Tana River. I reached the river on the south bank to see scores of terrorists making for the river with their hands clutching the top of their heads as the plane dive-bombed them. As the three of us lined up and lay low above the river bank we watched the fleeing Mau Mau dive into the water and stay submerged with bits of hollow bamboo up each nostril protruding above the water as a breathing aid. The river water was chocolate brown so we could not see their bodies. Besides, shooting into the water was like shooting into a brick wall! Having expended most of our ammunition, we saw a line of the military in the distance making their way down to the river opposite us. When their bullets came whizzing in our direction we crawled back to our vehicle and made haste back to Fort Hall.

On the way I met John Pinney the DC who asked what in the hell was going on. I explained the situation and he said we better make it back to HQ to find out more. The battle was in Embu District and we needed to know what help was required on our side of Fort Hall. The gang never came over and scattered on the Embu side. The night before they had raided a shopping centre, just South of Embu, killing the inhabitants and making off with all the food. They were being followed by the military who, like us, were making for the dive bombing plane. It was lucky that none of their firepower hit any of us three or my hidden vehicle!

General Kago was eventually killed by a Home Guard during a huge sweep combining all the Home Guards, the Army and Police, when Kago's gang of some 300 were caught in daylight in a valley not far north of Fort Hall Boma. General Kago's men were well armed from an attack made on Naivasha Police Station in March 1953 when they released prisoners and carried away the whole armoury. In the sweep when General Kago was killed, many of his men were also taken and many of the arms retrieved.

After the demise of Kago and his gang, we only had some minor activity locating the remaining supporters. In late 1956 the Emergency was officially declared over, I was demobilised and ready to return home after being given some overseas leave. Arnold Hoff and some others remained on as permanent administrators, while others returned to their farms or previous jobs.

When Jomo Kenyatta eventually came out from prison and was elected in 1963 as Kenya's first President, he called a meeting in Nakuru to which most European landowners were asked to attend. Kenyatta stated, "Let bygones be bygones, all land titles will be honoured, and in the spirit of 'Harambee' (pulling together) lets continue to build this country together." This spirit lifted the hearts of the Europeans, and to some extent stopped the flow of farmers leaving the country. It was said that he asked a prominent member of one of the earliest settler families, Richard Wilson, to help him prepare this speech. Nevertheless it was realised that with the issue of land hunger, a settlement scheme had to be initiated whereby farmers could sell their properties and emigrate with their capital. However, it was on a willing seller, willing buyer basis. Few wished to remain in an island of smallholders, as land was sold in blocks. Thus, most of the high production land that could be split into smallholdings was sold off. These were mainly smaller farms that had been settled after the last war, while the larger ranching land was retained and the majority of these European owners elected to become Kenyan citizens.

Book Three

1932 - Present

Michael Prettejohn - My Story

Chapter Twenty One

MY EARLY DAYS AND SCHOOL

I was born, as previously mentioned in this book, in the Nakuru Hospital under a Dr Tennant on the 8th September 1932. At that time we lived in the Naishi House built by my father who worked for his parents on Larmudiac, Njoro. Although we were less than 15 miles out of Nakuru the roads were appalling and impassable during the rains. Neither my mother nor grandmother drove. With my father and Jock out on the estate all day, mother left for Nakuru a week or so before my expected arrival. Grandmother travelled everywhere in her ox drawn buggy pulled by two beautiful well-trained white oxen, and I believe mother travelled in this to stay with Dr Tennant's nurse, to be on site when the event happened. After my arrival, father collected us in our Durant box body, and drove us back to our Naishi House. The house by now was a collection of four rondavels made of mud and wattle with thatched roofs and joined up by covered passages. One of these was designated to be my room. As our family departed for a new job at Naro Moru in 1937 when I was five years old, I remember little of Naishi, bar a few incidents that have always stuck in my mind.

The first, I suppose, happened when I was about two. Sitting between father and mother in the Durant, I suddenly developed a piercing headache. In the centre of the steering wheel was a great black knob of a horn that protruded out. As my headache increased and a fever started, this knob appeared to wobble and jump around as I became delirious. Tick fever was diagnosed and I spent weeks in bed. We didn't have the antibiotics we have today for a quick cure. The house had a lawn in front, but the only flowers were in beds by the wall, otherwise the bushbuck ate them all. The rest was forest. Today the house stands derelict with all the forest cut down, and hundreds of small holder *shambas*. Father had built a large dam and the house looked down onto it. Father had left little islands in the dam where there were clumps of trees.

We had a pack of Alsatian dogs and one day I was throwing sticks into the water that the dogs would chase after and retrieve. But one stick was a bit large, and when I tried to throw it in, I went in with it! It must have been quite deep because I remember sinking and wondering if there were any toys at the bottom to play with. I began to splutter and looked up to see a mirage of my father who plunged in to pull me out.

The next episode I remember was one day while standing on the lawn a pack of wild dogs came rushing through after a bushbuck. Father had just imported a black Alsatian from England named Courier, who joined the pack of wild dogs and ran away with them. He was spotted from time to time by our Maasai cattle herders, but had gone completely wild. We had a young Maasai dog carer who used to brush the dogs regularly, picking off the ticks and putting them in a tin of paraffin as there was no chemical dog wash at the time. He was sent off to follow Courier. He came back with the dog weeks later. We welcomed Courier back, as did the rest of the Alsatian pack – as if he had never left!

Finally, I remember a large train of *siafu* ants invading the house. They started climbing up the wall in a column, devouring a bird in its nest on the way, leaving nothing but a skeleton and feathers of mother and her chicks. Father called in his Maasai witch doctor, 'medicine man,' who waved his wand, while chanting specific Maasai songs. As we watched, the column of ants turned and moved out and away!

At the age of five, as explained in an earlier chapter, we boarded the Durant box body, together with the dogs and all our paraphernalia, and set off on the hundred mile journey to Naro Moru. Many of father's Maasai dogs followed the car. Somehow they must have been collected later. The roads were but tracks, and crossing the black cotton soil of the Laikipia Plains meant putting chains on the back wheels when wet. Invariably a chain would come off, wrapping itself around the axle, forcing one to lie in the mud to remove and replace it!

After a year at Naro Moru, at the age of six, I was sent off as a weekly boarder to Mrs Steptoe's school, St Christopher's, at Nanyuki some 14 miles away. This was a traumatic experience at this early age and I loathed it. My first day there, I was too frightened to ask where the loo was, with horrible consequences. Mrs Steptoe beat me on the hand with a ruler. Those weeks seemed like months or even years. I drive past there often today, some 70 years later, and peer with bygone thoughts at the same old wooden buildings with a sign on the driveway, 'New St Christopher's School.'

I don't remember many specifics of those days, but one incident sticks in my mind. One day a very fast open Ford Tourer drove with speed up to our house. It was Arthur Cole, brother of David whose family owned Solio where father worked. He asked if anyone would like a lift to Nanyuki? Father was too busy. David Sheldrick, later to become the famous Warden of Tsavo National Park, elected to go. They obviously had a good lunch at the Nanyuki Sports Club, and on the way back, Arthur misjudged the sharp bend over the bridge to the Burgeret River, and plunged into the water, then a fast flowing clear pebbly stream. No one was hurt but word got out of their dilemma and father went to retrieve them, sending a tractor to tow the bent sports car out of the river. We always named the spot 'Arthur Cole's Corner.'

Today there is a grand tarmac road over a muddy stream with little water. The bend in the road was straightened out with the new road, but the old one can still be seen. Nobody knows what I am talking about when I mention Arthur Cole's Corner. I suppose in those days such accidents were rare occurrences whilst today there are upside down vehicles on the roads every day!

In 1939 war with Germany was declared. As Nanyuki would be first in line should the Italians advance into Kenya from Italian Somaliland

and Abyssinia, the school was evacuated to South Kinangop, below the southern Aberdare Mountains. To my utter horror this meant three months per term away from home. I remember little of this period except for the evacuation safari. Three or four tourer or box body cars were hired, from Younghusband's garage in Nanyuki for the 100-mile trip. It must have been during the rainy season. In the tourer I travelled in, I was against a huge bulge of water collecting on the canvas hood. I put my foot against it from inside and a cascade of water came rushing in from the side soaking us all. It was very cold crossing the Aberdares at over 8000 feet. We soon got warm as we pushed the cars out of the mud, or assisted in putting chains to the back wheels and collecting scrub bushes to fill the ruts in the road. We ended up covered from head to foot in mud.

Father left for Nairobi to join the Regiment and mother soon followed. They lived in a cottage rented at Muthaiga in Nairobi by some of the Officers. Thus, I was sent for a short while to stay with my grandparents at Njoro where I attended Mrs Dudgeon's kindergarten. The teacher I remembered was in fact Sarah Seth-Smith's mother, whose husband was the first Kenyan casualty during the war. She later married Fielden, Sarah's father. I remember little of this period except that all of us developed mumps and whooping cough at the same time, which was most painful.

By 1941, as described in the chapter on the war, father had moved back home to look after all the farms in the area where the owners had mostly gone up north to fight the Italians. He was placed in charge of the Kenya Defence Force, made up of the older members of the community. They manned and guarded strategic bridges or specific places that could be infiltrated by the enemy, and gathered information for the higher command. I, too, returned home and was sent as a boarder to Pembroke House, a prep school at Gilgil. This was a boy's school of some 60 pupils, where boys were basically prepared for Public Schools in England.

Pembroke was a very expensive school at the time at some £60 per term. My parents were unable to afford it, so my grandmother paid for me. Although there was still rationing, grandmother and Jock owned several shops in Nakuru. I was sent with a huge reinforced heavy wooden box with metal joints and hinges about 3 feet x 2 feet, full of 'tuck.' It was locked and I was given the key attached to my school belt. This belt was of the school colours – two blue lines with red in the middle. The uniform consisted of a large grey felt hat with the

The Prettejohn brothers:
Left to right, Richard, Timothy and Michael

same coloured ribbon as the belt, a khaki tunic, and shorts together with knee high grey stockings, again the school colours around the top. The hat had to have a red lining against the sun's dangerous rays. To be out in the midday sun without it was an offence, commanding three strokes with the Headmaster's cane if caught more than three times without it on.

Although, I guarded that key, it was confiscated on arrival together with the whole box. In fact all tuck was held and pooled. We were given two sweets apiece after lunch before going to afternoon rest. I think that box supplied the whole school throughout the term and probably the teachers too!

It may have been because of the war, but we were restricted to only the circle of lawn in front of the school on week days. I remember one day we went on strike and agreed not to go into class when the bell rang. The Latin teacher for the next class, Basil Chard, was a great burly man. He appeared on the veranda with a menacing look as we all chanted, "We are on strike." Basil came down the steps, and when the first boys in front received massive clouts from those bear like hands, we all scuttled back to our desks! Thus ended our strike.

With little to do at break and in such small vicinity, we collected 'rose beetles' which abounded in the hedge surrounding the lawn. We went into class with tunic pockets full of beetles. We glued a long thread of cotton to each beetle. One by one we let them loose in class. Basil had a shiny bald patch at the back of his head, and the beetles would make straight for that as he was writing on the blackboard. However, on impact we would pull them back ready for the next opportunity. That opportunity seldom came, as Basil would soon spot a culprit, and give him a hefty clout on the ear. I sat next to one Gordon-Fenzi, and noticing out of the corner of my eye that Basil was making for him, I gave him a nudge. Just as that great hand came down, Gordon-Fenzi lifted his arm holding his pen nib up, which went straight into Basil's palm. This made matters worse as pulling the pen away, Basil almost knocked him out with a left and a right!

We had a long weekend at half term when we could go home or away with a pal. One time I went out with a Leslie-Melville and we spent the weekend at the home of their family friend, Lady Idina Sackville. She had a house called 'Clouds,' which was well known for wild parties among the Happy Valley crowd. Little did I know then of the goings on in this house, but I did wonder why there was a mirror on the ceiling over the bed.

Besides half-term there were several Sundays, when we could go away for the day. One such Sunday I was to go out with Grandmother and Jock. I had arranged for a couple of pals to come out with me. We waited in front of the school, expecting them to park off to the side of the road circling the lawn. However, Jock and Grandma arrived in their box body Ford V8, jumped the step onto the lawn and parked in the middle of it. I rushed forward to greet them, and as Jock stepped out of the car and I turned to introduce my two friends, they were gone! One look at Black Harries was enough to scare any young boy! However, they soon came out of hiding and we set off for a picnic lunch to 'Duffer's Pool' on the Malewa River. We had a great day using dinner plates as paddles, boating around the pool on fallen logs. Grandma brought enough food to feed an army, which helped us through the next week or so, with bits and pieces we had hid around the hedge back at school.

Duffer's Pool on the Malewa River.

The food at school was probably not too bad but we still complained bitterly. There was one rice pudding with raisins that came up once a week. We called it 'Spotted Dog,' while another meat plate was 'Dead Donkey.' One week, a boy who detested spotted dog smashed the whole pudding up with his spoon. Not only did he get three strokes with the cane, but was made to eat the remains for every meal until it was finished! This was an Irish boy, called O'Neil, and as he was always in trouble, he came back one term with leather patches sewn into his shorts. Unfortunately for him, they were removed after the first 'Dhobi.' Six was the maximum number of strokes with the cane. After one beating of six, he turned to 'Tunk' the Headmaster and said, "Please sir may I go now and put my buttocks in cold water?" He was given one more stroke, earning the maximum ever of seven.

Only the Headmaster, Turner, gave the cane and only on Fridays in his office. The culprits for the week were all lined up outside the office door. If you were caught doing some offence on Saturday you had a whole week to mull over the situation. It kept me awake at night wondering if I would get three or six strokes! Also you hoped to be last in line, by which time perhaps Tunk was getting tired. The next in line would have his ear to the door and with fingers indicate to all how many strokes had been given to the culprit inside. As you went into the office, you had to stand in front of the desk to receive a lecture while Tunk was seated flexing the cane. At the end of the lecture you were led by the scruff of your neck to the spot for beating, a worn out patch on the carpet and told to bend over and touch your toes. You tried to have a long tunic, hoping the flap would give some protection, but, alas, this was pulled up over your head. Great welts of black and yellow came up on your bottom, and if you had had a caning the previous week these welts would start to bleed and were mighty painful! One strapping lad, Laurie Sutcliffe, always received very weak strokes. His mother Ethel had given a warning to the Headmaster that her one and only son had a very weak disposition and was not to be beaten. When no culprit would own up over some demeanour, Laurie was told to go and say he did it!

I suppose being so restricted some students were always planning to run away from school. There were two serious attempts while I was there. The first was George McCall. He hid food, an axe, a sheath knife and other paraphernalia in the hedge. George snuck out a window in his dormitory after lights out and before the prefect came to bed. We placed pillows in his bed to make it look as if he was fast asleep. Alas, some four hours later all hell broke loose and we were awoken by George's return. He had got as far as the Gilgil railway station and had purchased a ticket for the train to Endebess where he lived. The station master had telephoned the headmaster to say, "I think one of your boys is asleep on the waiting room table!"

The second attempt was made by Peter Fenwick who lived in Kiambu. Peter left in daylight, skiving off from a Saturday afternoon walk. He stopped a car, and with a clever cock and bull story got a lift all the way home. His father was delighted at his success, and rang the headmaster to say Peter had come home and brought him back to school a couple of days later. The headmaster was not so delighted and promptly gave him six on the behind. Other excitement at Pembroke included 'The Day of the Locusts.' A cloud of locusts arrived and darkened the sky so that the lighting engine had to be turned on at 4 pm. Everyone raced around with sticks and empty cans to move the insects on, and to stop them from landing. Branches broke and fell from the trees with the weight of these pests. When they did move on, it looked like an atomic bomb had exploded. Nothing was left but skeleton trees and bare ground. Cars skidded on the roads as the squashed insects made the surface like driving on ice.

I spent most of my holidays at home hunting and fishing. The Naro Moru River ran below the house only a mile away and had been well stocked with rainbow trout. We had picnic lunches on the riverbank, often having to move in a hurry when disturbed by elephant or an angry rhino.

I was made to learn the game of bridge, and once a week mother and I were invited for a game with the Baines, who lived north of the Naro Moru River, but required a drive of some ten miles. We had to dress properly, so I had to wear grey flannel trousers, a tie and my school blazer. The only reason I agreed to go was because we were given a scrumptious tea and I was allowed to drive the Hudson. Mother seldom drove; she was such a timid driver she almost came to a complete stop before a corner and dismounted to have a look around first to see if there was another car approaching.

One time on the way home after it had been raining and the roads were slippery, I was driving a little too fast. When my mother ordered me to slow down, it only made me drive faster. I was in complete control of the large Hudson, or so I thought. Suddenly we glided sideways and before I could stop we shot off the road, nose diving into the ditch with the back wheels in the air! We always had strict instructions to be home before dark because of wildlife crossing the road. When we did not appear, father came in the farm truck to look for us. He was not amused and that was the end of my driving for that hols. The Hudson had to be pulled out by the farm tractor the following day.

Both my parents were avid bridge players and must have played at least three times a week. Only the other day I found a letter from Rene Gascoigne asking mother to spend the weekend with her in Nanyuki for bridge. The letter was undated, but must have been sometime around 1945. The Gascoignes were among the first settlers in Nanyuki. They built the first shop, manned a post office and had a team of Sikh builders to build new settler homesteads. My house today was built by them on contract in 1928. But at the time of this story Major Gascoigne had passed on and Rene was alone. I remember her being a very elegant lady. She dyed her hair blue and had a wonderful blue Hudson straight-eight with spare wheels placed in metal casing slotted into the front mudguards on either side. She was a very careful old bird, and when mother went to stay with her she took her own firewood as it got pretty chilly playing bridge all night and Rene only used one small log for the whole evening. At dinner one night mother forgot herself and took two potatoes. The waiter immediately picked up a fork, stabbed one potato saying, "*Rudisha moja.*" There was only one potato per person.

I was given a .22 rifle by Chico, a neighbour down the road. Father gave me instructions on handling, cleaning and how to shoot straight. Removing the bolt, I lay on the lawn aiming at a small hole in a metal disc. Father peeped behind the metal disc to check that I had the rifle sights pointing correctly. If I had the rifle in the house without the bolt open, or if ever the rifle pointed at somebody, father confiscated it for a week. I was only allowed to shoot pigeons, mouse birds, and hares, and small animals, but nothing bigger than a steinbuck. So I was extremely careful as I did not want to be a day without my rifle! I treasured that rifle although it had been well used and was somewhat tatty. I became very jealous one day when the Henleys came to stay and their son Tony not only had a far superior .22 but a .410 shotgun too!

Tony was five years or more older than me so we hardly talked until many years later when we ended up in the same profession and his son Henry married my daughter Jessica. Tony had also been at Pembroke House, but he left the term I started. It was said he gave Turner a new cane as a parting present. If so, it was the one used many times on my behind, but I never checked on this and now it is too late!

One holiday I was given a treat by my father to join him and our neighbour, Chico Basto, on a bird shoot to the NFD (Northern Frontier District). I think it was for my 12th birthday, just after the end of the war. This was my first viewing of that wonderful wild bit of country that stretches for many miles right up to the Somali and Ethiopian borders.

The family on a bird shoot, NFD.
Back: Father, Herbert Raynor, Michael.
Front: Timothy and Richard.

It is thorn tree country abounding in wildlife wherever water was to be found. We had no tent, but slept by the vehicle on camp beds. The first night we drove a mile or so off the main road north of the Uaso Nyiro River, just driving through the bush to the edge of the water, for there were no tracks at that time, and no people. At that time there was a mile or so of heavily forested thorn and doum palms bordering each bank. We had little sleep that night for there was a constant stream of elephant and a persistent rhino that came down to drink. I think father and Chico must have spent most of their cartridges in banging away to stop the animals from trampling us. So for the rest of the week's safari we were careful where we placed ourselves for the night.

I don't remember exactly where we went, but father and Chico shot sand grouse in the morning and walked up yellow neck francolin and guinea fowl in the afternoon. In the daytime we drove around watching animals. We drove up hills looking down on waterholes and through binoculars watched elephant and once a pride of lion. They only shot sufficient for the pot each day to feed the staff and ourselves, while I rushed around picking up the birds. On the last day we had a big shoot in the morning as on the way home we dropped off birds with friends along the way. At home we had no freezing devices or even a fridge, but kept provisions in a wire netting enclosure filled

Swimming in Buffalo Springs.

with charcoal and dripping water. With the wind passing through, it kept everything amazingly cool.

On that last morning I was allowed to use father's 12-bore shot gun. I hid myself lying in a clump of bushes and fired at a mob of sand grouse flying towards me. I collected about 15 birds besides getting a much bruised collar bone from shooting in such a prone position. I was scolded for this, as the sport was to pick out only lone fast flying birds. We used the farm International pick up, the three of us in the front seat with staff on a makeshift seat in the back with the kit and all the birds behind.

Four families in our district had boys at Pembroke and the fathers took it in turn to drive us all to Thomson's Falls where we would board the train to Gilgil for Pembroke at the beginning and end of terms. We were particular good friends with the Boyds who had 10,000 acres of ranching land outside Nanyuki. Their son Robin was at school with me and if his father Roddy drove us to school, I sometimes stayed a few days with them before leaving.

Robin missed a couple of terms once when he found a left over bomb from the war on the farm. As he tried to budge it with his foot, it exploded damaging both of his legs. He however had no disabilities in the end, but was left with horrific scars. Their farm abounded with Thomson's gazelle and I took my .22 with me so we could shoot a Tommy or two for the pot. The Boyds were one up on us for they had a newer model Hudson. They also had two elder beautiful daughters, Peggy and Jane. I fell madly in love with the elder, Peggy, who kissed me good night one night. I was over the moon and on getting to school I wrote a letter to her at Limuru Girl's School asking for a photograph. On return I received a rather blurred photo of a little girl in gumboots with a felt hat that covered most of her face. But before I knew it she became married to a handsome man, Rogue. Rogue has now passed on but Peggy and Jane remain in Nanyuki with Peggy the oldest born '*mzungu*' resident of the district.

The greatest benefit for me attending Pembroke House was not the formal education I received – I only did enough to pass the exams – but in the long term friends I made. A number of these came on to public school with me and even took up the same profession, remaining close friends right to this day, some 65 years on! Probably my longest friendship has been with Tony Archer, who has written the preface for this book.

Tony and his elder brother David were known as Nandi Ma and Nandi Mi because their father was the first white man to see the mysterious Nandi Bear. To this day no specimen of this creature has ever been taken, though every forest tribe has a name for it. The general opinion is that the Nandi Bear is probably a form of brown hyena.

By 1945 when we were due to move on from Pembroke House, the war was barely over and travel still difficult, so it wasn't possible for my parents to send me back to England. Instead, we took our exams to enter the Prince of Wales School in Nairobi. Tony passed with flying colours. I failed and was forced to catch up the following year, after being pressed to work somewhat harder!

I joined Tony for my secondary education at the Prince of Wales School in Nairobi. The Archer family lived close to the Prince of

Wales, and their home became a second home for me. Tony's mother and father passed on much sound advice. At school I did little studying, but we played hard and had a good education in other fields. Tony was in Nicholson House while I was in Rhodes House. They were sister Houses, which shared a dining room, so we saw a lot of each other and spent much time in planning safaris for the holidays. We were allowed bicycles and during the long weekends I cycled around the country. Tony was not one for bicycles, so most of my companions on these trips were the other boys from Rhodes House.

Rhodes Boys were mostly those who would have gone to a Public School in England. I had a place at Wellington where generations of Prettejohns have been educated for mainly military careers, but due to the war I stayed in Kenya, which I have never regretted.

Chapter Twenty Two

BREAKING BOUNDS - SAFARIS BY BICYCLE
AND
FURTHER SCHOOL HOLIDAY ADVENTURES

L ongonot is the English derivative of the Maasai name L'engelat meaning 'of the clothes' for the formation of gullies and ridges that appear like the folds in the leather skirts worn by Maasai women. Inside, Longonot's walled crater has steep vertical sides that can only be broached by using ropes.

At the Prince of Wales school in 1948 some friends and I planned to climb the mountain and to be the first, so we believed, to get to the bottom of the crater. On a Saturday night, after lights out, we stole out of school on our bicycles thinking we could travel the 66-mile distance there, climb the mountain, drop down to the base of the crater, and bicycle back to school to arrive there by Sunday evening of the following day. It was an ambitious expedition that turned into a nightmare.

Pedalling up to the top of the escarpment, which we reached at around midnight, proved a long haul. Although freewheeling down was less exhausting, the chill from the freezing night air forced us to stop at the small roadside church built by Italian prisoners of war in memory of those that had died while building the main Nakuru to Nairobi road. We huddled around a meagre fire and tried to get some sleep warming ourselves by putting hot stones inside our sweaters. Hugh Rutherfurd, nicknamed Puffin, woke up with a headache when the heated stone he had been resting on cracked open with a bang when it cooled.

Longonot Crater.

As soon as it got light we started off again and reached the base of Longonot just after sunrise. Two of the boys stayed behind to look after the bicycles while the rest climbed to the rim of the crater.

From there three of us elected to make the descent somewhere about 9.30 am. Puffin chose to go one way, and Alan Johnson, alias Cactus, and I chose another. Cactus and I soon found our route too difficult, so we called out to Puffin to tell him we would join him.

"Don't bother!" Puffin shouted back. "It's too steep here. I'm coming back." However, at that moment we heard a crash. Thinking the others at the top were throwing stones down at us, we yelled at them to stop. When they denied throwing stones, we wondered if Puffin had fallen. We called out to him. There was complete silence. Climbing further down, Cactus spotted Puffin's hat about two hundred feet below! Puffin must have fallen!

We thought the only thing to do was to go down to find him, so we lowered ourselves down the bad place which had turned us back earlier. It wasn't too easy, but we helped each other and managed somehow. We had no ropes but tied our two belts together to help each other down. One of us would be anchor while the other inched his way down and so on. It would have been very easy for one or both of us to have slipped.

We came to another bad place that seemed impassable, but we knew we had to find our way to the bottom of the crater to help Puffin. Johnson managed somehow to climb down this second steep bit. I went back to tell the others waiting on the crater rim that Puffin and fallen and to get some water because if Puffin was still alive he'd need water. George Bumpus brought a water bottle and he and I went back down the crater wall, just managing to get down the second precipitous bit of rock face. Later Nicholas joined us.

We found Puffin lying on his back with his head wedged between two rocks. He was fearfully bruised and in great pain. He moved in and out of consciousness and complained of the cold. We took off all our clothing except for our shorts and wrapped him up against the cold and padded him to make him comfortable.

In the meantime a group of 40 Ramblers from Nairobi led by A M Champion had arrived to climb Longonot and heard that a schoolboy had fallen into the crater. One of the Ramblers, Mr Bowles, hurried down with Durand, one of the Prince of Wales schoolboys, to drive to the Longonot Railway Station to call for help from the Naivasha police.

Champion asked Corporal Spencer-Jones of the Royal Corps of Signals, who had a bit of mountaineering experience, to climb down into the crater to look for the boy. This was about midday.

Spencer-Jones recalled his descent. "I started down with David Willis, who is in the Royal Engineers, and we both made several attempts to get down, but he was finally defeated and had to go back. I then went down alone, as I have done a certain amount of climbing in the Peak District in England and am fairly expert, but I confess that I found it an extremely difficult matter to make a safe descent into the crater. There is a lot of loose screes which is mixed up with large and small rocks, some of them loose, some of them fixed, and it took me an hour to get down to where the young Rutherfurd was lying, something like 300 feet from the lip of the crater. The last 50 feet above where Rutherfurd was lying was very steep and crumbly and the slope was almost precipitous, and it was a very difficult job indeed to get down it in safety.

"Rutherfurd appeared to be unconscious. He was terribly battered and bruised, particularly on his face, and practically all his clothes had been torn off him. There were two schoolboys with him, whom I later found to be Prettejohn and Johnson, and they had wrapped Rutherfurd up in their coats to keep him warm. They had also given him water."

Spencer-Jones climbed back up to the crater rim to report he had found the boy at the bottom. He said other boys were with him, who had wrapped their clothes around him. Rutherfurd's heart was beating but he was seriously bruised and unconscious.

Later Police-Inspector Steenkampf and seven African policemen arrived from Naivasha with 25 feet of rope. Steenkampf went down on a rope with a stretcher in its rigid form. Corporal Spencer-Jones climbed down with the rescue party.

Spencer-Jones wrote about the behaviour of the boys at the bottom. "Rutherfurd from time to time regained consciousness, and I was tremendously impressed by the way Prettejohn and Johnson talked to him, keeping his spirits up, telling him he would soon be all right and in my view keeping him alive. He was in great pain."

The rescue party couldn't get the stretcher up in its rigid state, so they bundled Rutherfurd in it. As they pulled him up, the ropes drew tight and Rutherfurd screamed in agony, restoring him to consciousness. With great difficulty they finally got the badly injured Rutherfurd up to the crater rim at 7 pm as darkness closed in.

Spencer-Jones said this about the climb out: "The two boys, Prettejohn and Johnson, were suffering from cold, as it was a very cold evening, and I had to help them considerably on the way up. It was obvious that they were not experienced climbers in any sense, and I consider it was extremely plucky of them to have gone down after Rutherfurd as they did."

A medical officer from Nakuru had been summoned and met the rescue party on the rim. Rutherfurd was rushed to hospital where, apart from other injuries, he was found to have a double fracture of the skull. We were told our actions almost certainly saved Puffin's life. However, when we got back to Prince of Wales School, the

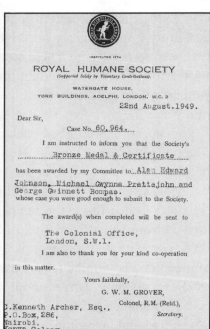

ROYAL HUMANE SOCIETY
(Supported Solely by Voluntary Contributions).

WATERGATE HOUSE,
YORK BUILDINGS, ADELPHI, LONDON, W.C. 2

22nd August.1949.

Dear Sir,

Case No. 60,964.

I am instructed to inform you that the Society's

Bronze Medal & Certificate

has been awarded by my Committee to Alan Edward

Johnson, Michael Gwynne Prettejohn and
George Gwinnett Boumpas.
whose case you were good enough to submit to the Society.

The award(s) when completed will be sent to

The Colonial Office,
London, S.W.1.

I am also to thank you for your kind co-operation

in this matter.

Yours faithfully,

G. W. M. GROVER,

C.Kenneth Archer, Esq.,   Colonel, R.M. (Retd.),
P.O.Box, 286,   *Secretary.*
Nairobi,
Kenya Colony.

Governor Mitchell awarding the Bronze Medal
of the Royal Humane Society to the author.

Headmaster did not regard us as heroes. Instead, he gave us each six of the best since we had left school without permission!

Visiting a friend, Tony Archer, a few days after Puffin had been saved from his ordeal, Tony's father Kenneth Archer asked me to recount the entire episode. Mr Archer listened carefully and wrote a letter to the Headmaster, and later another letter recommending that we receive an official recognition by the Royal Humane Society for our actions on Longonot. (Kenneth Archer's letter can be found in the appendix of this book).

At the end of that school term Mike Younghusband, Ivor and Humphrey Clarke and I decided to cycle home via Nakuru to visit Puffin Rutherfurd in hospital.

We found Puffin in good form and recovering fast. In fact, due to this fall the doctors found a defect in his spine, which they rectified by putting him in plaster, albeit for many months. This would otherwise have affected him in later life.

Leaving Nakuru we set off up the escarpment to Thomson's Falls where Mike Younghusband lived and where we were due to spend the night. The distance is only 40 miles but with the dirt road climbing all the way up to over 8000 feet, the journey is very rough. On the way we ran into a heavy hailstorm and got sorely bruised from the stones! We passed only one car on the way, and this rushed past spraying us with even more hail! We cursed that driver and thought at least he could have slowed down or even stopped. So it was a great relief to arrive at the Younghusbands, where we were given a high tea laced with brandy, some dry clothes and thawed out by a huge cedar log fire.

The following day the Clarkes and I set off to Naro Moru where we all lived. The distance is some 60 miles, which we thought we could easily do in a day. However, it was wet and the road passed over a lot of 'black cotton' soil. We did not see a single car, and had to push the bikes most of the way across these black cotton plains. The mud clung to the wheels so every hundred yards or so we had to stop to remove the mud with a knife or stick. Come nightfall we were still on the plains. We thought we would have to spend a cold and wet night without any food, blankets or shelter, when suddenly we saw the driveway to a cattle ranch owned by a famous bachelor Boran cattle breeder, Brian Curry. None of us knew Brian except by name, but my father knew him well, so Curry welcomed us and gave us the same treatment we'd received from the Younghusbands. We went contentedly to warm beds with full bellies and slightly 'tiddled' after copious cups of tea laced with whisky.

Curry's ranch was about half way between The Falls and Naro Moru, so the next day we only had 30 miles to cover. Again we did not meet a single vehicle. It is strange to look back on when today some sixty years later the road is tarmac while busses, matatus and cars speed along almost head to tail. At the time those black cotton plains seemed endless, but that day it was drier and we made better progress. The wind whistled through the whistling thorn trees. These thorns have a bulging hollow base in which ants bore holes to nest in. The wind then causes a whistle as it blows through the bushes.

Besides the odd herd of cattle, the plains and gullies swarmed with game animals that grazed and browsed the roadside unconcerned at our passing. At the top of each rise as the plains rolled on, we gazed into the vast distance with zebra, giraffe, Grant's gazelle, impala and other animals as far as we could see.

On reaching Ngobit, the Clarkes continued on to their farm on the Eastern slopes of the Aberdares, alongside the forest edge. It was called Charity Farm. Their father, Paul Clarke, had been allotted a farm further south which turned out to be Kikuyu-owned land, and so he had to forfeit it. The Government had then offered him another piece of land of his choice, which he found on the edge of the Aberdares in 'No Man's Land.' Their mother had died during childbirth and their father had very little time for his children. Subsequently, the two boys were more or less brought up by an elder sister who never went to school, so they lived a pretty rough existence. Paul Clarke was somewhat of a recluse.

I continued on my own for the last 12 miles and I soon arrived home at Naro Moru to a well-earned rest and holiday. I didn't rest for long. My father had arranged a birthday trip for me to climb Mt Kenya. A mountaineer, Klarwell, had set up a camp at Naro Moru with mules, camping equipment and porters for a 14-day hike to the peaks. Unbeknown to me father invited Humphrey and Ivor Clarke to join us. We met at home and drove some six miles up to the forest edge where Klarwell had set up a base. Packing our gear on the mules we set off through the forest to a base camp Klarwell had set up at around 10,000 feet on the edge of the moorlands. We followed Klarwell along game trails. He insisted we set a pace that suited us all and to keep to that until he called for a rest. Buffalo, rhino and elephant swarmed all over the place and we had to keep up a chant to keep them off our path.

We arrived at the base camp at an altitude of 10,000 feet where he had more mules that had taken kit up a couple of days earlier. We found one of them dead, killed by a lion, which the porters chased away before he could eat it all. Klarwell insisted we remain a day here to acclimatise. So the following day we set off to his next camp, pup tents set up near the base of the peaks at around 13,000 feet. We crossed a section called the 'vertical bog.' It was tough going through wet, cold and tufted grass, where bits of ice brushed off against our bare legs and down into our boots. We all made it and gladly dried off and warmed up around a fire. It was a smoky fire made from fallen leaves and bits of fallen groundsel. This was our first view of the peaks, which we had not seen since leaving Naro Moru as the steep vertical bog obscured any other view. We camped in the Teleki Valley and we had to round the bend at the top of the valley to have a full view of the peaks, which come out of the middle of a crater with only two thirds in view from further down. Count Teleki was the first white man to visit the peaks, making a diversion from his and Von Hoenell's epic safari in the late 1800s, from the coast to the discovery of Lake Rudolf in Northern Kenya, now called Lake Turkana.

Klarwell had been asked to map and name some of the unnamed tarns and if possible to measure their depths. For the first week we named some of the tarns, but today only Klarwell's name remains. Lake Hoenell is one of the larger tarns, and we had a go at finding its depth. Klarwell had brought up an inflatable dingy in which we placed some sacks to keep warm. With a ball of twine, marked with a knot at every foot, and a stone tied on the end, we paddled out to the middle of the lake and let the twine roll down. I think we got to 60 feet but ran out of twine. Since that time in 1948 there have been regular trips to the peaks and the paths are now well worn. All the larger tarns have been stocked with trout, which was done by helicopter, and wealthy clients can fly up by helicopter to fish them.

(In 2008, a helicopter taking off with four people from Lake Michaelson did not quite make it. The rotor blade tipped the water and in it went. The pilot and front passenger broke through the windscreen to get out. They rescued one passenger from the back, but the fourth went down with the machine, which lies on the bottom of the lake to this very day. The three survivors could not be rescued until the following day as the weather set in with low cloud and rain. Luckily, the survival pack in the helicopter was in a floatable box, which came to the surface, and the three retrieved it. They found a cave and lit a fire to dry out. After their rescue, expert naval divers came in to retrieve the body, a very tricky operation with the cold and 14,000 foot altitude and the depth of the lake, which I believe was around 60 feet, the same as Lake Hoenell, which we had measured.)

Back to our trip in 1948, it was not until the last few days that we were allowed to have a go at climbing the peaks. We were not equipped for rock climbing. I had a little experience as a member of the school Mountain Climbing Club. I had trained on a rock face at Athi River, but the Clarkes had no experience. In those days it was a serious climb to get to the top of Batian and Nelion at 17,040 feet. The climb is some 1200 feet and one had to be up and back in a day. We set out to climb the third highest peak, Point Lenana, at 16,400 feet. This is but a slog, walking up scree besides the Lewis Glacier. Every step up, one would slide two down. We all made it to the top and had a wonderful 360-degree view looking down on distant horizons through a blanket of cloud. On the way we passed what was called the 'Curling Pond', a frozen ice cave with icicles hanging from the rooftop and growing up from the floor. (The Lewis glacier has now receded to such an extent that the curling pond has disappeared and is only a bare rock cave. During January 2010, on a beautifully clear, calm early morning, I flew up with Halvor Astrup in his new helicopter. We hovered over the top of the main peaks descending to hover over Lenana. I looked at the stone I had sat on over 60 years earlier feeling sick and tired, and thought, "This is the way to climb the mountain.")

We had an easy scramble back down to camp after that first climb to Lenana. Klarwell had some sheets of corrugated iron in our camp, with which he was to build a hut by one of the tarns, now known as top hut. The next day we climbed Lenana again taking one of these sheets with us. Humphrey, Ivor and I thought it would be fun to sit on this and toboggan back down the Lewis glacier. We started out fine. As we had long trousers and leather gloves we thought we could use our hands to break the speed and somehow steer the course. On our way down a crevasse loomed up ahead and we were unable to stop quickly enough to avoid it, but fortunately we bounced over. We gathered speed and hit a soft patch of snow, skewering us to a stop the far side. All three of us shot off, with the iron sheet stuck behind in a near vertical position. Luckily the deep crevasse at this point was narrow. If we had fallen into it instead of jumping over, it would have been another story. We decided to go no further, making our way to the edge of the glacier on foot and arriving back in camp with a buckled sheet of *mabati*, much to Klarwell's annoyance!

The following day we returned back to base and reached home the same day. After a week or so of rest we returned back to school.

After this I did several trips to Lenana to assist Klarwell. During one holiday with another neighbour and schoolmate, David Allen, we decided to take another route to Mt Kenya made by Raymond Hook, but not used for many years. This went up from the Burguret River further to the north of the Teleki valley. Two girls elected to go with us, June Fenwick and Cathy Hook. Cathy was a niece of Raymond Hook who had bred some sturdy animals for mountain climbs. These were called zebroids, a mule crossed by a Grevy zebra stallion, on a horse. We borrowed the zebroids and their handlers who had much experience of Mt Kenya and the surrounding forests. The tents were very basic and heavy, but the strong animals carried them to the base of the peaks. On the second night of the journey the girl's tent collapsed and had to be abandoned and retrieved on our return. The sleeping bags were very thin and in order to keep moderately warm the four of us huddled together in the one tent.

This route is longer than going up the Teleki Valley but the joy of seeing the peaks getting nearer and nearer, enticed us to keep going. We visited several tarns before making the climb to Lenana. We all made the climb and although we did not try tobogganing on the Lewis, we had fun skating about on the Curling Pond and going deep into the caves behind. The safari went well without a mishap, but we were boxed in for a couple of days with a heavy snowfall before returning. The delay caused anxiety to our parents who had observed the excessive snowfall on the peaks and mountainside from home. My father consulted with Bunny Allen, David's father, and suggested sending up a rescue party Bunny was less concerned and said with two girls in tow we were bound to be a week or so late!

Having taken June Fenwick up the mountain, her brother Hugh Anthony, one of my best mates at Pembroke House Preparatory School, decided to make the climb too. This time we went back to the Teleki route as I had borrowed equipment and porters from Klarwell. There were only the two of us and a couple of porters as Klarwell had left kit for us in the two camps. We reached the first camp without incident, as usual singing to scatter the buffalo, rhino and elephant. On day two we continued up to the base camp, but while climbing the vertical bog Hugh suddenly felt violently sick. The two porters went on ahead to dump their loads with instructions to return to help, if necessary. Hugh and I struggled on but after every hundred yards or so Hugh would be sick again. We both carried small packs. It was too late to return to base camp, but we had only half-an-hour to reach top camp. Hugh was suffering greatly from mountain sickness. I suggested he rest where he was and I would take his pack up to the camp and come down with the two porters, to assist him into camp. I found the two porters on their way down, so I sent one back up with our packs while the two of us returned to help Hugh up to the camp. But, horror of horrors, the mist came down and completely blanketed everything; we could not see a yard ahead. I began to panic. If Hugh was lost and left out for the night he would be an icicle by the morning. We inched our way down whistling and calling, but when we stopped to listen for a reply, there was utter silence. Calling against the mist was like calling against a blank wall; our voices just seemed to bounce back! It was getting late and we were very tired ourselves. The silence became terrifying, and with the visibility at zero we had a good chance of missing Hugh if he was lying in the tufted grass. To our great relief, out of the mist appeared a sad figure hobbling along on a bamboo stick, retching all the way. Slowly we climbed up to camp. We got Hugh into his sleeping bag, forced down a hot cup of sweet tea, and he was out for the count. He had the most miserable night and did not even want to look at the peaks in the morning. We knew we had to get him down to a lower altitude as quickly as possible. On reaching the camp at the bottom of the moorlands at 10,000 feet, Hugh felt fine. We stayed an extra day at this location before returning home for Hugh to rest. At the end of another term at Prince of Wales, the Clarke brothers, Mike Younghusband and I decided to cycle the long way home by going east of the mountain via Embu and Meru.

At that time the road from Embu to Meru was a winding muddy road passing through many miles of beautiful forest with the trees overhanging on both sides. We soon ran out of food but managed to buy bananas along the way to keep us going. It rained every day, but we begged the odd meal and a bed at the occasional mission station. At one of these I managed to have the front fork of my bike repaired; one fork had broken in two.

One night we slept in a disused Kikuyu hut by a banana shamba. Little did we know it, but on returning home, we discovered loads of jigger fleas burrowing themselves into our toes causing terrible itching. Jiggers were common amongst the Kikuyu then, and one often saw Kikuyu women carrying great bundles of firewood, having virtually no toes; they'd been eaten away by these wretched insects. At home the 'kitchen toto' was an expert at removing them. He would carefully dig away around the sac with a needle, avoiding pricking the hundreds of babies, which could get left behind to continue feeding on the toes. A gaping hole would be left which was filled with a green

Fixing the first puncture near Thika.

Wibo and Donald during a spill.

antiseptic paste called 'Zambuk.' But with the advent of shoes worn now by all, the jigger flea appears to have disappeared.

We had planned for our safari to take four days or so, but by the fourth day we were still only midway between Embu and Meru. The bike wheels became so clogged with mud that we had to push them down the hills and almost carry them up the other side.

The whole route now was up and down and at the bottom of each valley was a river. Reaching a river we slung the bikes into the water until all the mud had washed off; we washed ourselves too. Starting up the other side was fine, but it did not take long before the wheels became jammed with mud once again. Once through Meru the route was dry and we soon reached home again to anxiously waiting parents. We had no mobile phones then and the landlines didn't work. The copper telephone wires were much sought after for making bangles to wear around the arms, ankles and even the necks of pretty damsels.

Once back at school we took weekend cycle trips to the Kedong Valley behind the Ngong Hills, or to Lake Naivasha. I had a friend, Cyril Mayers, who owned a ranch at the base of the escarpment of the

Mending blowouts on the Magadi road.

Rift Valley. We could cycle to the Mayers on a Sunday in time for breakfast; it was an uphill slog of some fifteen to twenty miles. Cyril would loan us a rifle and an old Ford truck, to get some meat – an impala or kongoni. Hundreds of wild animals roamed the plains at the bottom of the escarpment. If we were too late getting back, Cyril bundled us and the bikes into his pickup and rushed us back to school, where we were supposed to be before dark. If it was too late Cyril made the necessary excuses for us to our House Master, Pansy James.

At the end of another term Tony Archer and I were to be dropped off at the southern end of the Aberdares. We planned to climb the 'Elephant Peak' and from there hike across the top of the Aberdares, and arranged to be collected above Ngobit at the northern end. Unfortunately, Tony's brother David became seriously ill with rheumatic fever, so the trip was postponed. In fact it never happened and probably just as well. With experiences later of hunting and tracking during the Mau Mau uprising, this would have been a mega safari and we had no idea of the difficult terrain. However, Tony visited me at home that holiday and we made several memorable shooting trips. One was a 16-mile bike ride to Dudu O'Hagen's ranch. He was nicknamed Dudu by the Africans because he had a head like a locust grasshopper. Dudu's ranch reached from the edge of the Thego Forest on the slopes of Mount Kenya going down to Sangare Hill, part of which now borders our Sangare Conservancy. The area was abundant with wildlife. Dudu gave us his game scout Kariuki. We tracked animals with him for many miles down to the Rongai River by the hill. We shot a large eland bull. As Tony and I did the skinning,

Kariuki walked back to collect the ox cart to ferry the trophy and meat. By now the Rongai River was swollen and the oxen and cart could not cross it, so we had to carry the carcass and trophy to the other side in butchered parts. But the water had become too deep for Tony and me. Kariuki carried us both across the swollen and rushing waters. He was a huge and very strong man, and it was befitting that years later Tony would save his life during the Mau Mau uprising.

Kariuki also became a tracker with us in the safari business in later years, and his life story follows in a later chapter. Dudu lived alone in a wooden house so covered in flowering plants and creepers that it was like walking into a large bush. We returned late that night expecting a sumptuous dinner before going to a much-wanted bed. Before doing anything, the rifles had to be cleaned and oiled. Dudu made us open them up, and while dinner was served on a trolley tray by an immaculately dressed servant, the rifles were placed by a huge cedar wood fire. The warmth helped to sweat out the powder fouling in the barrel. They were not to be replaced in the cabinet until Dudu had inspected them himself, satisfied that the inner barrels shone like silver.

On another occasion Tony and I did a shooting walk on Impala Farm ranch, north west of Nanyuki. This is dry thorn bush country so we did not bother with a tent or camp beds, but planned to sleep on the ground in the open, digging a hole in the ground for our hips. We had a single porter-cum tracker, who carried some basic food provisions and one blanket apiece. We thought we could survive with some tea, posho (maize meal) and the meat we shot. We bagged a nice trophy bushbuck, while we trekked to the junction of the Narok River where it joined the larger Uaso Nyiro. We found a water bailiff's camp, but the bailiff was not there. On his table we found an open can of sweetened condensed milk which we could not resist sucking dry. We did at least leave him a note saying we would replace it for him when we got back to Nanyuki. But we never met or heard anything from him.

We were out this time for five days, returning to the ranch house with our bushbuck and a gerenuk trophy, together with some guinea

Family picture, Naro Moru. Michael, Mother, Father, Richard and Timothy

fowl. We had hoped to bag a buffalo, but although we tracked them up, we never got a shot. They disappeared into the thick, *girigiri* – wait-a-bit cover. This was a devilish thorn that took forever to disentangle from our clothes and skin, once we followed buffalo into it.

Back at home we went night shooting for reedbuck, which abounded in the growing wheat fields. We never had a very strong torch and only open sights on the Mannlichner .256 that my father had. But by combining the torch with 'firefly' juice, obtained by squashing the insects to keep the light going and painting that on both the fore sight and V back sight, we had some success.

While on the Impala Farm safari, we learnt there were greater kudu in the Mukogodo Hills, home of the Ndorobo tribe. This was a much sought after trophy, so on another holiday we planned a safari to this area to try and bag one. The general game licence, which we each held, allowed us one kudu apiece. Arriving at the Mukogodo Hills we discovered an old, willing man who agreed to take us into the area. We knew it would take a lot of walking and climbing over the hills and valleys, so we said we would like a younger man. "Really?" he asked. "Follow me first for I saw a big male while herding my goats only yesterday." We set off and

Walking safari on Impala Farm, Laikipia.

neither of us could keep up with him, much to our indignation! We said nothing more! I don't remember if we ever saw a kudu, but we certainly never got a shot. We had great sport in seeing new country, trekking for miles up and down those hills.

There was never enough time during the holidays, so as we were both about to leave school, we decided that before doing anything else, we would plan some longer safaris to explore and hunt new country.

Surprisingly, we both passed our school certificate

Author with young bushbuck.

exams and I received a very positive letter from the Headmaster Fletcher on leaving school. Tony never divulged his report, but I think it must have been an improvement on mine? We made a couple of safaris after school, but events cut these short. Our parents had other plans for us.

Chapter 23

LEAVING SCHOOL, EARLY SAFARIS
AND
MY DEPARTURE TO ENGLAND

On leaving school Tony Archer and I thought we would either join the Game Department or one of the Professional Hunting firms. But our parents thought otherwise. Tony's father said he should first have some Military or Police training, while my father wanted me to become a farmer and land owner after some agricultural education abroad.

For generations, especially on his mother's side, we were so called 'landed gentry' going back to 400 AD. But until a placing at college and a berth on the boat had been booked, Tony and I thought we would fill the gap organising our own safaris. We purchased a 1932 Chevrolet converted into a pickup, for £25. With full game licenses purchased and the minimum of equipment stashed in the back of the car we set off to the Northern Frontier District to do some hunting and explore new country.

I had made a few safaris to this wonderful wild country with my parents and friends on bird shooting safaris, but this trip we were

Archer and Prettejohn setting out for the NFD in their 1932 Chevy

217

on our own. We hoped to bag a lion apiece, two of which were included on the licence.

After coordinating our food provisions and water, a couple of camp beds and folding chairs, we set off for the border town of Isiolo. It is quite a climb up to the escarpment at Timau at 8000 feet and the Chevrolet boiled all the way up in spite of the

Bogged down in a swamp while lion hunting in Ngare Mara, NFD.

car having great silver air flaps to open on each side of the bonnet to cool it down. At Timau we replenished our water supplies, cleared the radiator blockage and glided down to Isiolo without any further problems. Once at Isiolo we had to get a District Commissioner's permit to enter the Northern Frontier

Camp on the Ngare Mara, NFD.

District, which took much explaining and time. After getting some additional water cans, and filling up with petrol at the vast price of some three shillings per gallon, we set off towards the Uaso Nyiro River.

Tony had just acquired a Rigby double .450 rifle and father had lent me his Mannlicher .256 and a 12-bore shotgun, so we were well armed for all events.

On the journey north we came across large herds of Grevy's zebra, Grant's gazelle, impala, and oryx, and even a small group of elephant resting under a large umbrella thorn tree. We did not have an elephant licence but thought it would be fun to stalk up on them to see how close we could get. Loading the rifles, we left the vehicle on

Tony Archer checking his .450.

Anthony Fenwick and author with buffalo head on the Ewaso Nyiro.

the side of the road and set off on foot to have a closer look, testing the wind direction as we went. We stalked carefully and noiselessly trying not to step on any dried twigs and hiding behind bushes. We reached within fifty yards while the great pachyderms stood cooling themselves with their great flapping ears. Remaining still we tried to assess the weight of the tusks on the biggest bull. We estimated about 50 pounds each. Quietly, lifting the .450, we set the sights on the heart area, and then for a side brain shot. After, this we quietly retreated back to the vehicle pleased with ourselves that we had been completely undetected and had left the elephant in peace.

Moving on we found some Meru cattle herders by a small stream called the Ngare Mara. We asked if there were any lion in the vicinity. "*Mingi sana,*" they said, pointing their spears towards the east where the stream runs into a large swamp. They were delighted to show us, as they were always losing stock to lion. We only had room for one man, who perched himself on top of the baggage, while we set off across the country. Every now and then he had to disembark, and trotting along in front of the vehicle, guided us through the tufted grass with endless lava boulders. After several miles we came to his *manyatta* where he said we could not motor any further, suggesting we leave the car here and set off on foot. "*Hapana mbali,*" he said (not far), but we knew otherwise. As it was getting late we decided to camp the night and set off on foot in the morning.

The next morning after having a swill of sour milk from a gourd washed clean with cow urine, we checked the rifles and set forth on foot. We had in mind to shoot a zebra and tie it to a tree for bait. Our guide said this would not be necessary as we could easily stalk up on them. Getting close to the swamp it was surrounded by thick low-lying wait-a–bit thorn bushes. The lion could lie up in this for the day. We hoped to catch them before they went into this thick bush as the hooked thorns stuck onto one's clothes and skin making it impossible to move. Soon we were tracking the lion's spoor, which we followed slowly, with the help of our newfound Meru herdsman. We were tense with excitement. The Meru took off his shuka and wrapped it around his left wrist. This, he explained, was necessary if the lion charged.

He could push his wrapped left hand down the lion's open mouth and into its throat, letting him bite on the shuka while spearing him with the right hand.

Scrambling through shortish reeds and tufts of grass, we knew we were getting close when biting lion flies descended on us. These blighters have hard skins and are impossible to swat or squash. You have to pull them off and grind them under foot, but there was no time for this. The Meru suddenly stopped dead and pointed at a clump of reeds with his spear. Tony and I moved to the front, rifles at the ready. We could see nothing until a lion's head popped up. We both let off a shot and the head disappeared. A second later it popped up again and we fired again. Once more it surfaced and we fired a third time. There was much growling and some fifteen lions sprang up and, luckily for us, bounded away into the thicket.

We wanted to rush forward but the Meru held us back saying, "*Ngoja kidogo,*" (wait a minute). We waited probably ten minutes shaking with excitement. Then slowly, inch by inch, we moved forward. All went quiet with the anticipation. Was the lion ready, waiting to pounce? However, arriving at the scene we found the bodies of three dead lionesses. We inspected them carefully in case any were pregnant or had cubs, but all three were without. Making sure none of the other lion were close by, we set to work, skinning them. With the skins removed we carried them wrapped to a pole back to camp, while the Meru collected some of the much-prized fat. Back at camp we lay the skins out in the shade, removing any particles of fat left on them and

The end of a lion chase on Ngare Mara.

covered them with salt. We only had some cattle salt so the sooner we could get some fine salt the better. It also dawned on us that we had taken three lion, but only had licenses for two. As soon as we could we had to make a report to George Adamson, the Game Warden in Isiolo. We knew he had lookout scouts all over the country.

Lion cubs on the Ngare Mara.

On our way, to the manyatta the day before, we had seen a very good trophy gerenuk. We had decided not to stalk it at that time for fear of disturbing any lion. So the next day, before leaving for Isiolo with our lion skins, we thought we would track the antelope as it is only found in this low thorn bush country. We soon came upon a small group with a very impressive male, which we bagged giving us an excellent trophy with 16-inch horns. As we returned to camp with the

Delivering lion cubs to George Adamson, game warden Isiolo

gerenuk, we came across two lone lion cubs, which ran towards us.

Before picking her up, we made sure no lioness was lurking nearby. The cubs had not eaten for several days and on taking them back to the manyatta they gorged themselves from an improvised teat on a bottle. The Meru wanted to kill them, but we thought it best to hand them over to George Adamson, the district Game Warden. It was too late to find our way back to the main road so we held them overnight whilst they slept peacefully with us on our camp beds, to the horror of the Meru.

With trepidation we drove up to George Adamson's house the next morning giving him details of our hunt, and handed over the two lion cubs. They were immediately taken into the care of his wife, Joy, who seemed to know exactly how to care for them. This was long before the famous Elsa, now a world-renowned lioness. I believe they were sent overseas to a park or zoo. Wherever they went, Joy would make sure they had a good home, as she had an amazing reputation of bringing up lion. George was little concerned that we had shot an extra lion. He had already heard about us and said he was forever being called out to deal with that particular group. With much relief we bade George and Joy farewell and continued on our journey home up the escarpment, while the Chevrolet boiled all the way.

On reaching home, father explained that he had secured me a place at Shuttleworth Agricultural College. The new term did not start for almost a year. It was difficult to book a berth on a boat to England, after the end of the war. In the meantime, he had arranged for me to do an Artificial Insemination Course with a Dr Anderson at the Government Experimental Farm in Naivasha. So to Naivasha I went. Unfortunately Dr Anderson was called away overseas as I arrived. I boarded with the manager, Mr Swan, and his wife. There was little to do except to control the hippo that raided the Lucerne shamba nightly. I soon bored with this and returned home to help father on the home farm, for it turned out that Dr Anderson would not be returning for several months.

Once settled back at home I met up with the man who was to shape a great part of my life for the future. This was Eric Rundgren. Eric had been the Game Control Officer for the Game Department for many years. He had now retired, and with his wife Pat, had bought a farm north of the Naro Moru River on the forest edge of Mt Kenya.

Most of this control had been on all the Laikipia ranches, where he had rid them of some 400 lion, over 500 buffalo and countless elephant and rhino. It is horrific to think of this happening and in such huge numbers, in this day and age, but at the time it was thought to be necessary to make room for imported stock and the growing of wheat and barley. Eric Rundgren was no farmer. He employed a Danish manager to grow wheat while he would be on call to control the wildlife on neighbouring farms. There were many new settlers in our area after the war, mainly Danes who ploughed up all the open glades along the forest edge to plant wheat.

I joined Eric in this work, and together we tracked up herds of buffalo that came down from the forest and by dawn had retreated miles back into the forest. At one time Eric had a pack of some 150 dogs as well as a pet lioness that joined in the hunt. By having the lioness in the pack, the dogs, who were usually petrified to follow lion, became used to the lion smell and although some dogs would get killed by lions, they did not mind following them up. Latterly, with fewer than 15 dogs, we followed up the marauding buffalo herds. It was energetic and very exciting tracking. The dogs would bay

*Tony Archer and author were attacked by a rhino
while hunting buffalo on Mt. Kenya*

them up, several at a time, while the rest of the herd scattered in all directions. Sometimes the buffalo would come head on at us through the bushes and forest. This needed accurate shooting and often a very quick dodge. There may be half a dozen dead buffalo at the end of the foray, but Eric ensured no wounded beast got away. There were no tracks or road nearby, so the meat had to be taken out on poles by the trackers. Meat was also packed tightly around the dogs' necks – sufficiently tight so they could not turn their heads to eat it before they carried it out to a waiting truck on the edge of the forest.

All the time I was with Eric he used a Rigby's .416 magazine rifle, while I borrowed Tony Archer's .450 double.

(Later when I went to England, the first thing I did was to visit Rigby's to get a .416. Eric said to make sure I bought a 'long action.' The new models had a medium action, which was prone to jamming. But Rigby's knew of none for sale. Then one day I got a call from them to say that in 1925 they had made a special lightweight model for the Prince of Wales to use on his safari to Kenya. Only a few of these models had been made. Luckily, they found one unused, the owner having died before getting to Africa, and it was lying in some

Author's first buffalo hunt with David Allen in Bunny Allen's Model 'B' Ford.

old lady's attic. They retrieved this rifle, and after lengthening the stock to fit me, I purchased it. I later drove with it back to Kenya in 1953. I used it throughout my hunting days and have now passed it on to my son Giles.)

Eric had the instincts of an animal, was a crack shot, completely fearless but sensible. By instinct he knew how to protect himself being very quick witted and fleet of foot. He had more experience than anyone past or present, so both Tony and I could not have wished for a better tutor.

With time before my departure to England, two safaris materialised. Tony called one day suggesting we try hunting for the rare bongo antelope. He had a cousin Tim Barnley who had a farm on the edge of the Cherengani Hills in Western Kenya, where bongo abounded. We thought the old Chevrolet was not up to making such a safari, so Tony's father let us use his 1938 Ford box body.

Loading up with food, water and a minimum of equipment we set off to stay with the Barnleys. There we hired a pigmy of a man, a wild Maragoli. He had a pack of 'shenzi' dogs, but we said we were not allowed to hunt with them; we just wanted to track them up and choose a good trophy. We must have spent a week to ten days tracking these animals through thick wet forest but never came up on one. Today this part of the mountain is bare of forest, and settled with farmers. On this mountain today, even the small area left with forest on the higher peaks, does not have a single bongo remaining.

After the unsuccessful bongo hunt, rather than driving back on the main road we decided to take a detour going via the Tot escarpment round to Lake Baringo and on to the Northern Frontier District, crossing the Uaso Nyiro and so back through Isiolo. This took a good deal longer than anticipated as the roads in places were almost non-existent. With so many steep and stony hills, we had to take everything out of the vehicle. We could then progress, with the support of local tribesmen pushing behind, and carrying our kit to the top. The road down the Tot escarpment drops some 3000 feet almost sheer and gives one of the most stunning views of the country below, stretching out to the horizon. This is a great expanse of thorn bush intercepted with streams and *luggas* bordered by huge shady umbrella thorn trees. The track is cut into the side of the escarpment descending through thousands of hairpin bends.

We would look at a track a few yards below, but it took twenty minutes to reach there. The tribesmen here were utterly wild, with huts perched on a pinnacle with thousands of feet falling away below. It was said they perched themselves here to avoid 'hut tax' which had recently been imposed. It was first gear all the way and we must have burnt out much of the brake linings before reaching the plains below.

We saw little game here for the area was heavily populated. Hundreds of streams come down off the escarpment and water is fed to countless shambas through bamboo troughs from the forest above. We never knew it at the time, but all these streams bear alluvial gold, which we returned to prospect many years later. As we proceeded west it became drier and drier and really rough going through miles of lava rock.

Passing through Kapedo we came onto a crystal clear stream. In fact, it was so hot that one could boil an egg in it! With this soaring heat below us and the harsh sun above it must be one of the hottest places on earth. Cooler water was obtained from wells in otherwise dry luggas. Camping by one of these we had a lucky escape when pouring petrol into the car from jerry cans. A spark from the campfire some distance away ignited the fumes. I opened it and dropped the can. Instantly flames shot into the air. The can and petrol was lost, burning me slightly

Crossing the Wei Wei river near the Cherenganis.

Staying at the DC's banda in Baringo.

on my arm. The vehicle, however, and Tony were unscathed. We had no other source of petrol, but as luck would have it, we passed a government surveyor's camp by the road the next day. There was nobody there, but we found petrol and filled up. Tony's father later contacted the survey headquarters in Nairobi and explained the situation and reimbursed them with the fuel.

From here we proceeded without event reaching Lake Baringo, where we stayed in the District Commissioner's banda, having a good wash and swim in the lake.

Today, Baringo is a tourist resort with lodges and camps galore, but at this time the only building was this particular banda and only other presence were fishermen on reed canoes who paddled way out into the lake, disregarding the hippo and crocodiles that abounded. The lake was so full of fish, they did not bother people. Having said that, many years later a good lady friend who swam daily amongst the crocodiles was taken by one she knew, but she survived after a terrible mauling. It turned out, however, that the beast had received a spear wound in its back.

On leaving Baringo, Tony and I headed into the Northern Frontier District camping on the Uaso Nyiro River where we crossed the river at the Barsalinga Ford. The water was deeper than expected and the Ford vehicle sank in the middle with the water almost going into the back, but luckily the front part of the car was higher so the water did not cover the engine. I think we removed the fan belt so the water did not spray over the spark plugs in order to keep the engine running. It took a full day to get out but we managed to surmount the opposite

Author visiting his grandmother and Jock at Solai.

The Solai house.

bank, camping there to let everything dry out. We were getting a little hungry by then, and managed to shoot a crocodile, the tail of which Tony had understood was good for eating. We buried it in the sand and lit a big fire on top and had a look after some six hours. I thought it tasted quite disgusting but we had little else.

With no communications we thought we had best make for home as our families may be wondering where we were. They most certainly were! As was the District Commissioner and George Adamson the Game Warden. When we arrived at Isiolo, they asked why we had no entry permit. We explained we had approached from the north east where there was no post. They were happy to see us go through on our journey home.

On the way we met up with the Allens. Bunny, then a professional hunter, had recently returned from safari and had two elephant licences spare. We both said we really wanted to bag an elephant with good ivory. If we bought these licences, perhaps we could join him on a hunting trip. With just sufficient time to spare before going overseas, we hastily organised a safari to the Tana River.

Once back at home, I put the proposal to father. His main concern was how I was going to fund the cost of the licence, which was now £25 on top of the general licence. Also my grandmother and Jock had requested that I stay with them to learn more about farming. My grandmother said, "Unless you show some interest, and if I die before Jock, it is likely that you will lose your inheritance to the Solai Ranch of some 15,000 acres." This is exactly what happened.

Tony had money to buy his licence and his father lent me the cash to purchase mine. We set off to the Tana River by Land Rover, a new four by four box on wheels, a sort of copy of the war time Willy's Jeep. Bunny had borrowed the Land Rover from his friend, Buster Cook, who suggested Bunny try it out. This was to be a proper safari with a lorry carrying a full range of camp equipment, servants, trackers, and skinners and just about everything else. This set up was a sharp contrast to the safaris of Prettejohn & Archer! We made camp around Ijara on the Tana River, setting up tables and chairs, with the waiters wearing smart *kanzus*. We even had table cloths and cutlery. Bunny explained that we would take four elephant, pooling the ivory to cover the costs and share the balance. In the end there was no balance, but enough to cover all the costs including returning my £25 to Tony's father.

It was a fabulous experience. Bunny's second son Anton came along too. We trekked up and down the river tracking many elephant, stalking up on them to assess the weight of their ivory while Bunny explained where to make the vital shot in order to make a good clean kill, and how to avoid being charged. We spun a coin to see which one of us would make the first shot. He explained, when tracking, to follow large footprints. The big 'tuskers' have big feet but not all big feet have big tusks, so careful reckoning is required when stalking. We had three weeks for the whole safari. In that time we must have tracked up and seen over fifty bulls before bagging our four. With Bunny's tuition I am glad to say we three made perfect shots, each dropping our elephant on the spot. It is so exciting to level one's rifle

Camping with Bunny Allen on the Tana River.

Tony Archer and author with our first elephant, Koro Koro, Tana River.

231

bead at these majestic monsters, slowly taking time to squeeze the trigger.

Bunny explained, "You must wait until your heart stops pounding, and only then pull that trigger." As the heavy rifle booms, it is a very tense time, as the quarry could either drop or come charging at you. There is little chance of escape should this happen at such a short distance. One is so elated with the excitement of the stalk and the delivery of a good shot. However, at the same time I always felt sad at seeing such a great beast lying dead and gone. I suppose it is little different to breeding steers to slaughter. An elephant feeds many people and taken on a sustainable, well thought out policy, as was the Game Department's measure in those days, the money went towards their ultimate protection.

From this safari we ended up with our four elephant, the largest having ivory of 75 pounds aside. These, when sold, covered all our expenses.

One day while in camp a truck pulled in with two sets of enormous ivory tied to the sides; one pair of over 130 pounds per side and the other 112 pounds. These had been taken by American clients, Mr and Mrs Ralph Hammer from Redlands, California. Little did I know at the time, but Ralph and Ethie were to be my very first clients when I started Professional Hunting myself some six years later in 1957, when they came to Kenya to try for the rare bongo and greater kudu. They had taken these elephant at distant waterholes from the river. Tony and I were sure that if we had hunted inland, we would similarly have secured heavier ivory ourselves. If we had been hunting with Eric Rundgren, he would have taken us inland, whatever the difficulties and discomforts. Eric had a no "holds barred" approach for nosing out good trophies, for which he became renowned. Bunny's prime interest was for a good time and a good hunt. He had such charm that he could convince clients that they may not have a record trophy, but it was still a good trophy and wonderful hunt, which was the prime reason for their safari. For our safari his primary consideration was for the well-being of three young lads and to return them home in one piece!

Besides elephant we hunted for camp meat, securing good trophies at the same time of lesser kudu, gerenuk, and hirola (today the hirola is critically endangered). All too soon the three weeks came to an end and we had to return back home.

I discovered my berth had been booked on a Dutch boat leaving for England in a couple of weeks' time. The journey would take three weeks, and I was to be met by a cousin and looked after by an aunt, who would ensure my delivery to Shuttleworth College. Tony also discovered that he had been booked into the Police Training School, at Kiganjo, so our 'fun time' had come to an abrupt end! The fun for me certainly continued on the boat trip where I met two lovely Australian girls who were on a world tour, hitch hiking their way around. They suggested I join with them instead of going to college. I was all for a new adventure, but it was not to be. I loathed returning to school, though, and vowed I would find a way back to Kenya as soon as possible!

Chapter 24

THE LONG WAY HOME
Trans Saharan Drive

I had been barely a year at College when I received news that a 'state of emergency' had been declared in Kenya. This was the Mau Mau uprising. Tony Archer had completed his Police training and was later seconded to 'Special Branch.' He was stationed at Naro Moru where he worked closely with my father and David Cole before the Emergency was declared on the 20th October 1952. I wrote home, expressing my keen interest to return, but father insisted I should complete the course as this was to be a long war, and there would be plenty to do when I got back. I thought otherwise and with Brian Macintosh and Gordon Herbert, who wanted to immigrate to Kenya, we made a plan to return. I decided to purchase a vehicle and drive back home. This amazing journey took us five-and-a-half months.

We purchased an old army 1941 Dodge Power wagon ambulance from a farmer for sixty pounds and did it up ready for the journey. We then had to find the money for the trip. A farmer gave us a patch of forest to clear, saying we could have the timber in exchange. We borrowed axes and saws, a tractor and saw bench. By camping in the forest we saved on living expenses. There were no straight trees to cut for timber, so we cut the wood into logs for fireplaces. The logs we sawed were too big to sell for the English fireplaces, so we had to cut them again into smaller pieces. With insufficient profit from this project, we had to secure jobs on farms, milking cows, feeding pigs and swilling out the dairy and pigsties. By October 1952 we thought we had made sufficient cash to make a start.

As a boy in the mid-1940s, I had always had a strong desire to follow in the footsteps of Colonel Ewart Grogan who had walked from Cape to Cairo at the beginning of the century. Grogan had his chair and table in the Muthaiga Club, which no one else could use if he was in residence. He often sat there alone and my mother would drop by for a chat enjoying his great wit and unequalled command of the English language. One day, with Grogan's book in hand, she took me across to his table to have it signed. After his signature, he added a little drawing of a rhino. From that time thereafter, I tried to sit by him whenever I could, absolutely spellbound by his stories.

It was far too late to do such a walk, as Grogan had once done, but I did have the luck and opportunity to drive from north to south, and later as a pilot with my own plane, to fly it too. By fitting extra fuel and water tanks, and strapping them on the sides and roof of the Dodge, we set about getting new tyres. Dunlop gave us a set for

Leaving London for Kenya in a Dodge Power Wagon 2nd World War ambulance.
Michael Prettejohn, Brian Macintosh and Gordon Herbert.

the advertisement (and I must say these did over 9000 miles without even a single puncture). With a coat of paint we were ready to go by the 19th October 1953. It had all been somewhat of a rush and we soon discovered the Dodge had not been thoroughly checked out. However, we had to leave because of the timing of bookings and transit visas.

We left Uxbridge, outside of London, where my fellow traveller Brian Macintosh lived, and set out for Dover that night. We arrived at 1:45 am leaving time for a short sleep, camping in a bombed out building, before sorting the vehicle and filling up with as much fuel as we thought we could smuggle over. (There was still rationing from the war at that time.) The next morning after a light breakfast we set out to refuel and fill up spare tanks. We had used 15 gallons in the main tank and filled two spare tanks with another 15 gallons apiece, only to discover that both of these leaked like a sieve. The boat was due to leave in 20 minutes, and we just had time to decant the fuel into jerry cans and hide these amongst our kit, leaving the balance in one dripping tank. We passed through customs, and onto the ferry smelling of leaking petrol. They gave us ample room and placed us apart from other vehicles on the ferry, with a basin of sand to collect the drips! We lost four gallons of petrol.

Customs at Boulogne in France didn't care about the spare fuel tanks, but asked about all the rifles and ammunition. All three of us had taken our rifles with us. I had been corresponding with the Chief Game Warden in French Equatorial Africa where I particularly wanted to hunt for a giant eland. He had sent me a letter to get a hunting permit at the border. We told the customs officials of this hunting opportunity and how later we'd have to defend ourselves against the Mau Mau, in Kenya. This finally satisfied the authorities. They initially removed our ammunition. However, with another precious packet of cigarettes they let us proceed.

About 100 miles after leaving Boulogne we stopped to repair leaking tanks, tape shorting wires and tighten various loose bolts. We camped by the roadside en route to Paris and the next morning Gordon Herbert, my second companion, set out with his .22 to poach a rabbit or a partridge, but found neither. So, after a bowl of oat porridge (our staple diet), we were on our way. Driving through Paris we became slightly lost and drove round the Arc De Triomph several times before finding somewhere to park. At one point we almost ran over a priest on a bicycle, but luckily he decided at the last moment that we were larger than he was. After spending the afternoon mailing post cards and purchasing some more rations, we set off for Poitiers, camping on the roadside some 22 miles along the way.

Going through Poitiers, Gordon noticed a gun shop and bought a dozen rounds of ammunition for his .635 automatic pistol, for which no permit or explanation was required. We had now driven 500 miles from our starting point at Uxbridge. We filled up with petrol and worked out that the Dodge was barely doing 10 miles to the gallon. With some 7000 miles ahead of us, we were going to need an awful lot of petrol. Even at three shillings equivalent per gallon that was still a lot of money for fuel.

We camped in the open countryside three miles before Bordeaux. During the night it became bitterly cold and started raining at about 4 am. We hurriedly spread a tarpaulin over our camp beds, and unfortunately for Gordon and Mac this covering filled with water. As they tried to empty it, water poured into both their beds. We folded away the wet bedding and continued on our way. The rain followed us most of the way to Bordeaux. We passed many flourishing farms where they still cultivated in the traditional way using horses, mules or oxen; we did not see a single tractor. Passing through Bordeaux we headed for the Spanish border passing through acres of Corsican Pines. These plantations were used to tap a resin. The following day we arrived at the Spanish border in the late afternoon, with beautiful views of the Pyrenees. We had no problems passing through. The French were pleased to see us go while the Spaniards took one pound (125 pts) for the vehicle tax and 15 pts stamp tax for the firearms licences. An hour later we drove into the beautiful sea resort of San Sebastian.

There were very few vehicles and crowds of people thronged the streets in complete awe at this strange beast arriving in their midst.

We could hardly move and could not understand a word anyone said. We were negotiating our way through a narrow street when disaster befell us. With people milling around and trying to touch the vehicle, an old man tripped and fell, hitting the left hand side of the Dodge. He was bruised, but not badly hurt. Luckily, a person out of the crowd came forward indicating we should take the man to hospital for a check-up. He helped get the old man into the car and showed us the way to the nearest hospital. There the old man was treated and released, but the police arrived wanting statements, but no one could speak English or French. However, statements were written with sign language and while our passenger indicated it was not our fault, we all signed the documents, together with the old man. However, this was not the end. The police brought a woman from a nearby hotel who could speak English and further statements were made. They told us we had to leave the vehicle at the police station until someone from the British Consulate could be found. A woman from the Consulate was very helpful but the police insisted we had to go to prison to await a hearing at Court on Monday morning.

With the help from the woman from the Consulate, the authorities agreed that if we handed over our passports and left the vehicle at the station we could stay in a hotel. The good lady took us to a small and very cheap boarding house saying she would come to take us to court on Monday morning, and to enjoy our stay. This cost us 40 pts for 24 hours with all the food we desired. We met Mary, a Scottish girl who spoke Spanish. We subsequently met lots of locals and had a great weekend. On the Saturday night we bought a couple of bottles of wine and had a merry sing song with Mac coming out with many Scottish songs, before staggering back to our cosy house in the early hours. On Monday morning the court cleared us, but said we had to stay until the old man's bruises had completely healed. We explained we had to leave because we only had transit visas. They arranged for us to leave a deposit of 400 pts (about £4 at the time), which we could get back through the Consulate if the man survived. As far as we know the man survived but we never got our money back. We bid farewell to the Consulate lady, Mary and our nice boarding house family and left for Madrid in the early afternoon.

From San Sebastian we climbed up and over the Pyrenees with

glorious views of hilly wooded country with mule and oxen used for farming; again we did not see a single tractor. Sheep dotted the hills with shepherds in blankets and sheepskin leggings, while women strode beside with children strapped to their backs. We wound through the worsening roads down valleys and through little towns with narrow streets, trying to avoid running over any other people! We arrived in Madrid on the afternoon of Wednesday 28th and headed for the Spanish Consulate for Gordon to get his Spanish-Moroccan visa. They said this was not available for at least 24 hours, so we carried on without the visa. Gordon had the gift of the gab so he thought he could talk his way through. Leaving Madrid through grape and olive growing country we headed for Granada.

Come dusk and before camping we asked a young lad where we could find some water. He led us up to his home in the hills where we filled our container from a well with water drawn up by bucket. The family looked so poor we offered to pay for the water, but they wouldn't take anything. It was a cold and frosty night but at least dry. In Granada we replenished supplies with some very cheap wonderful grapes and custard apples before setting out for Malaga. After two miles, we had our first sighting of the Mediterranean, thousands of feet below. Across the bay a mountain range stuck out above the clouds as we wound our way down to the sea through hundreds of hair pin bends that taxed the old Dodge's none-too-good brakes. On the way we had to stop and move a heavily laden cart drawn by a poor mule that had dropped dead in its tracks.

Reaching the sea we made a dash for the water, little realising it was bitterly cold. Nevertheless it was good to cleanse our sweaty bodies! After another night camping in the rain, we drove on to Alqecivas, arriving in the late afternoon just too late to catch the boat across to Ceuta. We collected some mail at the post office before camping by some pools a few miles out of town. We enjoyed reading the letters by the campfire. We also recorded at this point that we had motored some 1,551 miles from London.

On Sunday the 1st November we returned to the docks to book our tickets while Gordon went to see if he could get his visas for French and Spanish Morocco. They told him visas were only available in Tangiers or Gibraltar. We pushed on without Gordon's visas. They stamped our passports before boarding the ferry for Ceuta at 4 pm that afternoon. It was a smooth and uneventful crossing taking just one hour. We drove on into Ceuta where the banks were closed, but we managed to cash some cheques with an Indian trader getting 90 pts to the pound. We were seven miles from the customs barrier and there was no way Gordon could talk his way through without a visa. We camped by the roadside for the night.

The Moroccans at this time were rebelling against the colonial powers and the British Consul told us the following morning that 26 bodies had so far been counted. The Moroccan authorities looked on us with suspicion and the many gendarmes watched our movements keenly. Most carrying ancient firearms dated 1907 and their ammunition looked even older! They all had the rifle muzzles blocked with plugs of cloth and we wondered how many would forget to remove these obstacles before firing, should they have to do so in a hurry.

The following day turned out to be a holiday so we spent an extra day in camp. With the holiday over we discovered a Spanish Moroccan visa could not be obtained until a French Moroccan visa had been acquired first in Teuten. The Consul offered to take Gordon on Wednesday.

On Wednesday, Gordon managed to get his French visa. He waited until the following day to get the Spanish visa. After successfully dealing with Gordon's visa issues we proceeded south, but on reaching customs they told Brian and I that we did not have the appropriate French Moroccan visas, even though the deposits had been paid in London. We'd have to go to Tangiers to sort it out. Then the authorities decided Gordon could not now return to Spanish Morocco! So we left Gordon with the car while Brian and I hitch hiked to Tangiers, some 150 miles there and back. Luckily we got a lift all the way there and obtained the forms, but we had to find somewhere to get passport photographs and these could not be processed until 7 pm that evening. With the weekend approaching nothing could be done until Monday.

With limited funds we found the cheapest accommodation we could in the Kasbah, a room with two beds for 40 pts. The only way in to the adjoining room was through ours and we were rudely awakened well after midnight by a drunk barging and gurgling his way through. However, that Sunday we had a most interesting day looking around the area including the Sultan's Palace full of the most beautiful carpets and Venetian glass. We relished the food, though surroundings were rather dirty, but enjoyed a glass of wine thrown in at the equivalent of only two Kenya shillings! A snake charmer sat outside making a cobra rise out of a pot by blowing on a handful of dry grass that would go up in flames, while at the same time playing music on a kind of flute.

Rest stop in Morocco.

We met two charming Australian girls who were hitchhiking around the world on a shoestring. They had run out of money and were looking for work. One wanted to join us to Kenya but had no visas and we decided this was not a good idea. Nevertheless, we enjoyed their company and together probed the Kasbah through all sorts of narrow streets with amazing shops and strange beings.

Eventually on Tuesday the 10th November, our visas were ready and after buying some provisions that we were unlikely to find for some time, such as oat porridge and All Bran, we set off to join Gordon and our Dodge truck. But the hitch back was not as easy. After walking for many miles we thumbed a lift on a lorry. After passing through Spanish customs we picked up many women loaded with sugar, soap and much other contraband, each paying 5 pts to the driver. We also picked up two German student hikers. We had not gone far when police stopped the lorry. Bedlam ensued; the women tried to hide the stuff amongst their clothes and gave us some to hoard for them. The police started to throw stuff off, kicking one woman badly in the stomach. A fight ensued and all the women ganged together threatening the two policemen. We were left to carry on, but the women lost all except what we had hidden for them. A battle then ensued amongst them as to who owned the stuff we held. All we could do was to put it in a pile and let them fight it out amongst themselves.

We were dropped off a few miles short of Larache and walked into town without any further lifts. It was getting late and we thought we might have to find somewhere for the night, when we found a car going our way and thumbed a lift. After a couple of miles we discovered we were in a taxi and the man wanted 300 pts to take us on to our destination. This we did not have, so we quickly disembarked and started hiking again. We walked until 9 pm when we were given a lift by an army captain who first scrutinised our passports. Back on the road there was nothing for it but to continue walking. We walked and walked until we thought we were losing the soles of our feet. We soon saw the lights of Ceuta some 12 miles on, but they never seemed to get any closer. Another lorry advanced us some three miles and we eventually staggered into camp at 2:30 in the morning to find Gordon asleep in my bed (his being completely broken) and Francis, a hitch hiking American, fast asleep in Brian's. We soon dislodged them, and after cooking some food, and taking a cup of hot tea we climbed into bed at 3:30 am, with Gordon and Francis sleeping on the ground. At dawn the police woke us and told us to move on, as the King of Libya was about to pass through. We moved off the roadside and waited for him and his cavalcade to pass, eventually getting on the road again, heading for Algiers.

By Wednesday 11th November we were getting rather short of cash having spent so much more time en route than anticipated. Francis, who continued with us, suggested that once in French Morocco we could get temporary jobs at one of the U.S. military bases to augment funds. We passed through customs without any problems at all, not even with all our firearms, and diverted to Port Lyankting to call in at some of these military bases. However, being British, we had no hope of work, as the French would not allow a work permit.

We continued the journey to Algiers joining the main road at Petit Jean and hoped for the best. The road climbed back up 2000 feet and ran along the Chaine Du Riff, a vast and eroded country of desert, sandy hills and gullies. It was occupied by Riff Arabs living in mud and dung huts surrounded by cactuses. They herded sheep, cattle and goats, while cultivating small patches of ground in the gullies worked by oxen. We arrived in Fez in the late afternoon to find everything shut, so we camped a few miles out. We entered Fez early the next morning, which consisted of a new French town where everything was rather expensive, and an old Arab town, which had again a most interesting Kasbah with wonderful carpets and collectors' items, if we had had the money and space to carry. There was an interesting museum, which contained a showcase of clay models of pairs of fornicating men and women in every conceivable position. But we could not afford to linger here too long, so set forth on the road to Taza in the early afternoon. The road wound through rough and rocky hills with little water. Before reaching Taza we diverted across country to camp for the night on a precipice overlooking a tributary of the O. Sebou. It was a stunning view, but during the night the wind got up and we nearly lost everything over the precipice. Early the following morning we walked down to the river for a much overdue wash and clean up of not only ourselves but our utensils. We then made a steep climb through shale and rock to the top of Dj Tazekka at about 6000 feet and scouted around with our field glasses for any signs of wildlife, a Barbary sheep or Dorcas gazelle, but we saw neither, only some partridges that were too quick for our .22 rifle.

Passing through Taza, where we filled up with petrol at 2/6 a gallon, we headed for El Aioun across a vast open plain scattered with small bushes. Upon reaching the Za River the country became more hilly and populated. Here little donkeys carried Arabs with feet almost touching the ground and loaded with baggage. Large areas were now under cultivation making it difficult to find anywhere to camp. Camping between fields we were molested by a dog that tried to get at our food and we had to fire a shot to scare it off. Thinking this might alert the police we packed up and left very early in the morning; stopping in Mascara for Francis to have an aching tooth looked at. He found a French woman dentist who did a filling for the equivalent of 12 shillings, but the filling fell out after the next meal.

With the country becoming more and more populated as we proceeded, we arrived in Algiers in the afternoon of Wednesday the 18th of November. We found a woman who could speak some English. She told us of a small park on the edge of town where she thought we could camp. We had travelled 2,556 miles and the old Dodge needed quite a lot of attention before crossing the Sahara, so we envisaged a few days stay. Here our troubles and delays really started. The next day was yet another holiday so we spent the time servicing the Dodge, fixing a leaking sump gasket and changing broken springs. We met a Frenchman who had come in via the Gao route in a Dodge like ours. He said in the heavy sand he was only doing about one mile per gallon and when he could get petrol it cost about 16/- a gallon. Thus, we decided to make minor adjustments to our vehicle by putting on a Chevrolet carburettor and removing the pump within. This reduced acceleration, but was to give us more miles to the gallon.

After the holiday we approached the Consulate to see about the possibility of work, but once again this was not allowed. We also discovered that the Tamanrasset route across the desert, which we wanted to take, was closed, while the Gao route was easier but was 800 miles longer. We also discovered that whichever route we took we had to leave a substantial deposit, which we were unable to do and have enough money to buy the petrol, we needed. We discussed selling the car and hitch hiking or even taking a camel caravan. But we couldn't sell the car without first paying a 43% duty on their valuation. What if we just dumped the vehicle in the sea? "Then," they said, "we will pull it up and you will still have to pay the duty!"

Another problem was that Brian had a job waiting for him in Kenya, which he would lose if he did not get there in time. So when the possibility arose of a lift on a transport lorry via the Gao route to Kano in Nigeria, Brian, Francis and another British hiker took it. With the departure of Brian and Francis, we had more flexibility to look for a paying traveller.

In the meantime the only solution for cash was for me to cable my grandfather in Kenya and ask for a loan of £100. This was organised through the Consul. I loathed doing it, but £50 arrived and a rude note saying I should be back working in Kenya, rather than playing around in the desert! In fact, grandfather was against me going to England in the first place, saying I should be working on the estate in preparation to take over, one day in the future. But he died before I reached home, and I lost a 15,000-acre ranch in the Solai valley, which went to the manager. I had to return the £50 loan to my Uncle Dick, who decided to let me keep it.

With some money available, all we needed was a fare-paying passenger. Our luck turned with the meeting of Ben Thomas, an American university geography lecturer, who was studying some of the more remote Arab settlements in the Sahara. Ben said if we could wait until January 1st, and take the Tamanrasset route, he would pay the deposit and some £35 plus food to travel across to Kano in Nigeria. In the meantime, Ben offered Gordon a job drawing maps while I looked after the camp and prepared for the trip. I visited Shell and Esso to see if we could get any fuel on an advertising stunt. Both companies liked the idea but they had no budgets for such a thing and it entailed permission from London. It also transpired that we could purchase fuel in drums sealed by customs to be opened only on passing into the Sahara, where there was no duty. With the help of Ben's finances we purchased two sealed drums holding 200 litres each. At the same time Ben offered to hire us to do a 500-mile round trip back to Algiers visiting seven holy cities, where normally aliens were forbidden entry.

Ben acquired all the research he needed over a period of a month and we headed back to Laghouat. After Christmas, having restocked with rations and filled all the water and petrol tanks, we loaded our two sealed drums and set off to cross the Sahara via Tamanrasset

Stuck in the sand at the start of the Sahara Desert.

Tuareg people with their camels.

to Kano. Our rations consisted principally of oatmeal porridge, powdered milk, tea and dates. I also remember purchasing a 50-pound sack of spaghetti! Passing once again through Laghouat we headed for Ghardaia some 100 miles south. Here Ben left the deposit for the Saharan crossing while our sealed duty-free petrol unit was opened. The route across the desert was only marked by a line of cairns. Sometimes we had to divert for miles on either side because of the heavy sand. We became bogged down many times but with the aid of our metal sand mats and shovels, we managed to dig our way out. We carried a large ship's compass to steer a course back to the line of cairns, making sure we knew on which side of the line we were, for there were few land marks other than the dunes.

Twice we ran into huge dust storms and had to stop. We closed everything while we sat out the storm in the car. Sand covered everything, even our food. Eating our morning porridge was crunchy, like having an overkill of sugar. The engine, too, was caked in sand; everything had to be cleaned and brushed before we could continue. Somehow the sand even got inside our sleeping bags, which had to be turned inside out. Even so the particles still remained.

Leaving Ghardaia we headed for El Golea, 195 miles on. It was such a picturesque country of dunes and rocky outcrops with the odd clumps of dry grasses and shrubs. We saw no other vehicles, only the odd camel train with weather beaten Arabs and an occasional Dorcas gazelle. In El Golea we filled up at the oasis, taking water from deep wells by donkeys that walked around the well, attached to a pole with palm rope that wound up skin buckets of the precious liquid. Dates were the only other commodity to add to the larder. As we proceeded further into the desert it became more flat with empty rolling dunes. There were no visible signs of any animals or any grasses, only pure sand. We continued to get bogged down in the sand.

Fort Miribel, large and white, appeared on the horizon, perched on top of the largest dune. It was a reasonably sized settlement standing above the oasis. The French Foreign Legion manned the Fort. Convicts sentenced to the gallows or life imprisonment could alternatively join the Legion. Many were German but a number spoke

English. All their vehicles were Dodge Power wagons. By spending a few days with them we replaced some spares such as broken springs. They invited us to join them for meals. A metal bathtub full of goat's stew was placed on a table. We scooped some stew out with a mug onto a tin plate.

One evening Gordon and I went with three of them down to the Kasbah to replenish some rations, mostly dates, the staple diet, covered in flies. As we walked through a dark alley, I noticed three rather fearsome looking Arabs following us. "Don't look back," said one of our Legionnaires, as they led us even further into an even narrower alley. I could hear them getting closer and closer. I could feel the hair on the back of my neck rising as I anticipated trouble. I looked across at Gordon who said not a word, but was clenching his fist. The Legionnaire turned around and with a flash of his knife an Arab fell to the ground gurgling, as the other two hurriedly retreated. Not a word was said as we increased our pace while the Legionnaire wiped his knife on his trousers and without concern put the knife

Ben Thomas looks on while we dig the Dodge out of the sand.

back in its hidden sheath. Back at the fort, Gordon and I decided to sleep the night within the fort itself, and made a hasty departure in the early morning. We said nothing to Ben until we were well on our journey. He calmly said this sort of thing probably happened all the time. These men ruled the area, and it was just as well we did not fall out with any of them ourselves!

Feeling somewhat shaken, we put as much distance as we could between ourselves and the fort, travelling all day and most of the night before we dared stop. For several days we saw no one at all. We approached our next port of call In Salah, 200 miles from the fort. On leaving Fort Miribel we crossed what is known as the Tademait Plateau, 200 miles of flat pebbly sand. The surface was reasonably hard, but as soon as speed was reduced or we stopped, we sank.

But as usual we moved on with the aide of sand mats, a process of digging and jumping on board with the mats without stopping again until our camp. The country was so flat; it was difficult to take a constitutional walk. Ben was hopeless at directions so we had to keep

Crossing the Tademait Plateau.

a watch on him to check that he did not take off in the opposite direction on returning. Luckily he always wore bright green underpants, which showed up for miles so that he could be spotted! We did not wish to leave more skeletons in the desert. We had come across many bones from luckless camel treks, likely from lack of water.

We passed through In Salah without meeting any officialdom, and again filled up with water and more dates. We continued forward to Fort Laperine, some 450 miles ahead. Here we ran along the edge of the Ahaggar Mountains, which rise to a peak of 9,500 feet. These spectacular and rugged peaks were once forested but today are bare rock. We tried to avoid heavy patches of sand by driving east or west of the beaconed track. We travelled in four-wheel drive, in a low gear. We were lucky to cover a 100 miles in a day. It was four days before we reached the oases and fort. We avoided the fort itself and again met with no officialdom, just bought more dates and filled the water tanks. We travelled another two days and some 225 miles in the same conditions and terrain until we reached the larger oasis at In Guezzan.

Without any mention of the Fort Miribel incident here, we rested for a couple of days on the outskirts to attend to little jobs on the Dodge. Our own bodies were in dire need of a good wash. The nights were freezing, and in the morning the tarpaulin, which we stretched over our beds, was like a piece of cardboard. We could not fold it up until it thawed out. Any water left on our tin plates would also be covered with a layer of ice. We had a paraffin cooker and ate either spaghetti or oatmeal porridge, mixed up with dates. Departing from In Guezzan, the next stop was Agades, a further 225 miles south. Here we crossed many luggas, all tributaries of the main Assakarai River. From this point we began to see some scrub and the odd camel, but no sign of any wildlife.

Once we found some water in one of the luggas, so we made our camp by this. At Agades we stopped again for an extra day to prepare ourselves and the vehicle for the next 400 miles to Maradi the border oasis of Nigeria. The further south we travelled, vegetation appeared and luggas were more plentiful and had water. We saw camel herds with Arab keepers and large flocks of helmeted guinea fowl that were exceedingly tame. Ben suggested they must have belonged to someone and was apprehensive of us shooting any. We assured him they were wild and we took enough with our .22 rifle each day for the pot. We roasted or boiled the birds and ate them with relish mixed with spaghetti.

There was little at the border oasis of Maradi, but we could not escape officialdom. However, our papers and visas were all in order. They welcomed us into Nigeria, with no concern about our firearms. We headed for Kano, capital of the north some 150 miles on. We now came out of the desert and into country very similar to Kenya's Northern Frontier District. I felt very excited to be back in my Africa. The climate became warmer and we saw more and more black Africans herding camels and goats. Great flocks of guinea fowl kept our larder full.

It was great to arrive in Kano where English was spoken. We found a good workshop where we camped and did much of the work needed on the Dodge. We also purchased plenty of fruit, eggs and other provisions for the next part of the journey. It was good to have a varied diet again. In Kano we met the manager of Shell who had at one time worked in Kenya. The only fuel he could offer was two drums of old aviation fuel of which the octane content had fallen too low for aviation, but was just perfect for our vehicle. With the two drums loaded on board he arranged a sale for the two empty drums, which surprisingly fetched more than the price of the duty free petrol within them.

At Kano we said our farewells to Ben who had arranged a flight back to Algiers. We were so grateful for the help he had been to us. We heard no further news from him until we received a letter once back in Kenya. All was well with him and he had had his deposit refunded.

We continued driving some 100 miles south and then turned east travelling through the north of Nigeria towards Fort Lamy in Chad. Our next destination was Potiscom, some 490 miles on. The road was but a rough track running parallel to the Komadugu Gana River,

Making repairs to the Dodge in Kano, Northern Nigeria.

which ends up in Lake Chad. There was plenty of water in the luggas; after heavy rains they flowed into the river, and still held puddles and wells. The area was fairly well populated with nomads herding camels and flocks of sheep and goats, and still plenty of guinea fowl for the pot. Not much happened at Potiskum, which we passed through with another 150 miles to Maiduguri. We were still covering only 100 miles a day, and as there was only another 150 miles to Fort Lamy and the Chad border, we pressed on through Maiduguri as well.

At Fort Lamy there was a reasonable workshop where we spent two days tightening loose bolts and working on the springs, which had broken under the heavy load of extra fuel and water, on the rough tracks. After fitting one complete spare spring, changing leaves in others and stocking up with eggs and mangoes, we continued south. It was 350 miles to Fort Archambault in what was then French Equatorial Africa, now the Central African Republic. Our journey here was easier with plenty of water, and scrub forest providing lots of 'kuni' or firewood for campfires. It was welcoming to have a fire to cook on and we enjoyed copious mugs of tea and coffee. Although we did not see much in the way of game, we saw signs of animals including elephant and stalked many guinea fowl for the pot.

There were a number of nomad homes along the route; besides sheep and goats, cattle replaced the camels. All the men carried spears and hunted wildlife.

Before leaving London I had visited the British Natural History Museum where I was given equipment to collect moths and butterflies along the way. While camping at night we put out a sheet with a blue light attracting thousands of moths. In the morning we placed them in packets and labelled them to send back at the end of the safari. We continued with moth collecting during the night's camping throughout our journey in Central Africa and Uganda and filled all the containers. The museum particularly wanted specimens from the Central Regions. The Dodge had started to have an ominous knocking sound in the engine, which sounded like big end bearings. In Fort Archambault we found a good workshop as part of a cotton estate and they helped us open up the engine. The cotton company also ran Dodge Power wagons so they had a good stock of spares, including a set of big end bearings and plenty of springs. It really needed to have the crankshaft reground, but with new bearings they suggested it should be good for another 5000 miles or so, which would see us back to Kenya. Their prediction was precise, and on reaching home the Dodge started to knock again. I had the crankshaft reground before I sold it on to Chief Erastus in Fort Hall.

In Fort Archambault I produced a letter from the Chief Game Warden of Equatoria, and they gave me a licence to hunt for the pot and specifically for a giant eland. Back on the road with new springs and bearings, full tanks and provisions, we moved on to Bangui at the border with Congo, almost 400 miles away. We had to report midway at Fort Crampel. Luckily, the locals knew a few words of Swahili and we gathered information along the way on where to find giant eland. The road ran parallel to the Shari River, which although miles away, had many swamps and streams that ran into it. Stopping by a homestead, a man nearly seven feet tall appeared, wearing nothing but a loincloth.

He volunteered to lead us to eland, as long as we shot a buffalo for the community on the way. He informed us buffalo were everywhere but the eland would be a three-day walk for there were no roads, only game paths. We had no locking devices on the car anymore and worried about leaving it on the roadside. He assured us nothing would be touched. If anyone was found stealing, he informed us, they would get their hand cut off, so the vehicle will be safe.

With the offer of porters we took our food, water containers and a couple of blankets together with our rifles. We abandoned the Dodge and set off on foot with the

The warrior who led the author and his friends on their search for giant eland in French Equatorial.

tall man leading in the front, followed by Gordon and myself and then the porters. The tall man said we must pick up his dogs, as they would bay up the buffalo. We tried to explain that we were only sport hunting and not officially allowed dogs. He was most unhappy with the situation but we made it clear we did not want dogs with us. We soon picked up buffalo tracks from a nearby swamp. The tall man confirmed the buffalo would be at the next swamp area, not far. After four hours we reached the next swamp, but the buffalo had moved on. He suggested they would be in the next swampy area where there was better cover. We surmised they'd be bedded down by the time we caught up, and difficult to approach. However, we proceeded seeing the tracks of other animals, as well. We abandoned the buffalo and stalked up on a waterbuck male, which I suggested Gordon take, as he had never hunted large game before. Gordon dropped the beast with a single shot, which gave him an excellent trophy and meat for the local people. We made a camp by a puddle of water. The tall man sent a representative back to his home for the men to come and collect the meat. We set up camp under a large tree and brewed some tea, then scouted the surrounding area. We soon found tracks of our main quarry, the giant eland, but they were not fresh enough to follow, so we returned to camp, bagging a couple of guinea fowl on the way to eat ourselves. The waterbuck meat was not that good to eat.

Luckily, we had brought mosquito nets as the whine of these insects started soon after dark and they were hungry for a meal. The chaps kept a smoky fire going all night and slept by that. At first light the next morning we were out again after a mug of tea and bowl of porridge. One of Gordon's arms was covered with mosquito bite welts, as he must have slept with an arm out of the net. I noticed my net was full of bloated mosquitoes as the nets were just hung from the tree branch and tucked around our bodies as we only slept with a blanket on the ground. I also found that moths or some 'dudu' had chewed the odd hole, which the mosquitoes soon detected.

We soon found some eland tracks, which we followed for many hours, until we heard a crashing in the bush ahead and the stampeding of hooves. The eland must have got our wind and were off. We followed for many hours without getting in sight of them until it was time to return to camp before dark. It was a long and thirsty trek back; I couldn't believe how far we had gone as we wearily walked into our camp at nightfall. The next day we tried our luck again but saw no new tracks. On the way back to camp we came onto some roan, which we carefully stalked. Hiding behind an anthill, I picked out a good male and dropped it with a single shot with my newly acquired .416. This was a new trophy for me and we had some good camp meat with enough to send back to the community. We had been away for four days, so we returned to the truck with our trophies. Nothing had been touched. They were more than happy with the meat for their families.

The following day we continued on our journey as we had been out of touch with everyone for weeks. We reported at Fort Crampel that we were still in existence and doing well. We continued on the next 200 miles to Bangui on the Congo Border. Here we had a contact there who invited us to stay a few days. We enjoyed the luxury of a warm shower and replenished our larder with fruit and eggs. We still had some spaghetti and dried meat from the roan so we were well stocked up with provisions. Our acquaintance had a pet baboon who insisted on going through my matted hair and the beard, which I had grown, looking for lice. Luckily the baboon was disappointed!

Leaving Bangui we headed west. Our landscape dramatically changed from desert and dry bush to thick forest. After travelling for miles without seeing water, it was now everywhere. We travelled all along the north of the Congo, where many of the river tributaries lead into the Oubangui Shari or River Congo. One day we made eleven river crossings, all on makeshift rafts built on canoes paddled across the rivers.

The roads were fair as we passed through Banzyville, Buta and Watsa to the border of Congo and Uganda at Aru. On the way we stopped at Putman's Camp where they had some okapi in large forested bomas. I had never seen these magnificent rare forest animals before, so this was most exciting. I wish we had spent more time in these forested areas, but having already been some five months on the road, we were anxious to get home.

The ramp onto one of the ferries.

The ferry platform sat on canoes which rowed the Dodge across the river.

We crossed the border from Aru to Arua in Uganda. We took the road from Arua to Gulu, stopping for a couple of days in Uganda at Murchison Falls, where they were building a footbridge across the Albert Nile overlooking the falls. The thousands of elephant in the area often held us up. We left Uganda at Tororo and entered Kenya, hurriedly making our return via Eldoret and Nakuru, to an overwhelming welcome home party at Naro Moru, some 1,575 miles from Bangui. We had travelled over 9000 miles during this amazing trip.

Unfortunately, our welcome home party was brief, as Gordon had a job waiting for him and I had to report to the Kenya Regiment. For the next three years we were tied down in the administration, with the Mau Mau uprising. I did however get the extensive collection of moths back to the British Museum who were most thankful and believed many could be new species. I did not make contact with the British Museum for a further six years. When I did visit the museum, I could not find any details of the collection.

A brief safari to complete the drive from the North to the South of Africa.

In December of 1955 I was given three weeks leave over Christmas while working with the Administration in Fort Hall during the Mau Mau Emergency. Together with Jock Rutherfurd, my future brother-in-law, another District Officer, a school friend Ulrick Middleboe, and Gordon Eccles, the owner of a transport business and workshop in Rongai, we decided to spend our Christmas leave on a drive south to Angola at Lobito Bay. Gordon had an ex-army Dodge Power Wagon command car. Unlike my Dodge, this particular vehicle was open with a canvas roof and slips on the side windows. It was in excellent mechanical condition as he owned a large workshop. Jock and Ulrick had driven from England to Kenya in one of these, two years before my journey, after leaving military training at Sandhurst. They had driven down alongside the Nile through Egypt rather than crossing the Sahara.

(My own son Giles made this drive, too, in 1980, after leaving Cirencester College but in a Mercedes Unimog. I remember flying up to Lokichoggio on the Kenya-Sudan border to meet him and his party, taking up some delicacies. One of our house staff came along with us, and as he thought Giles and his party looked so starved he offered them his loaf of bread!)

Back to our own trip to Angola. After loading provisions and the minimum of equipment we set off through Tanganyika checking in at Tabora. From here we crossed the southern end of Lake Tanganyika and on into Northern Rhodesia. As we only had three weeks for the whole trip and the road was in reasonable condition we did not linger. We made good time through Ndola and headed for Dilolo in Portuguese Angola.

It was the rainy season and the roads near the Congo River became almost impassable. At one point we met a family of Portuguese completely bogged down in the middle of the road. The land on either side of the raised road was awash with standing water, so there was no room to pass. The family had been there for days, but in the back of their truck they had a supply of chickens and pigs, which they steadily ate, waiting for help or drier times!

Portuguese truck stuck in the mud on the way to Lobito Bay.

Reloading after winching a lorry out of a ditch in Congo.

The only hope was to push them aside into the ditch and pass. With the Dodge in front we could then winch them back onto the road and get them turned around. We suggested they follow us to Dilolo. However, with only two-wheel drive they did not get far, and we had to pull them out again. As our time was limited we left them to their own devices and continued on as best we could.

Our next challenge was a very rickety bridge across a flooded river. This needed some extra heavy tree branches, which we cut and roped to the bridge. By anchoring the vehicle to a sturdy tree on the far side, we gingerly winched and drove our way across, the bridge literally groaning.

We slowly made our way into Dilolo where we put the Dodge and ourselves onto an open bogie on the next train to Lobito. Here we stayed in a cheap hotel celebrating Christmas on suckling pig, which still had all the hair on its skin, swilling it down with copious glasses of wine that we bought in gallon flasks. The following morning we did not feel too well, and I had a fearful headache. I don't think I have ever been so ill with vomiting either before or after. On the other hand Jock, with his capacity for alcohol, was none the worse for wear.

After Christmas we put the Dodge back on the train to Dilolo where we disembarked, returning via the Congo by road. It was tough going travelling along roads that were like small rivers from the constant rain. We made for Bukama, Kamina and on to Bukavu. From Bukavu we made for Mwanza, crossing into Uganda and across the Nile at Owen Falls, arriving back in Kenya via Kisumu and back to Fort Hall. I was three days late but with sufficient excuses to explain things to John Pinney our District Commissioner. Although this was a rushed trip without time to keep a diary, I felt it had sort of completed my wish to drive the length of Africa. At this time Grogan was no longer with us so I never had a chance to compare notes with him!

Chapter 25

TO RANCHING AND PROFESSIONAL HUNTING

During the Emergency I lived for a while in the same house with Jock Rutherfurd in Fort Hall. I met his sister Gillian who would come up to stay at weekends while working in Nairobi. We fell in love and Jock persuaded us to get married since we came from the same sort of background and enjoyed the same lifestyle! Thus on 26th November 1955 we married in Nakuru with a reception in Aunt Rutherfurd's delightful garden in Solai, not far from where my grandparents, the Harries used to live, as well as the Rutherfurd home where Jock, Gillian, and Hugh (Puffin) were brought up.

Mike Prettejohn and Gillian Rutherfurd's wedding in Nakuru.

At the end of the Emergency I returned home to Naro Moru and started to look for a farm to purchase. I had my new wife Gill, to consider and my father was determined that I settle down with my own farm, to purchase as I had lost my inheritance of the 15,000 acres at Solai. He was prepared to give me some initial support with £3000 from a family trust. I could become 'An Assisted Owner' under the 'European Agricultural Settlement Trust' of which he was then the Chairman.

In the meantime I assisted Eric Rundgren with animal control work around Mt Kenya. The glades along the forest edge where I used to hunt buffalo were now all taken up with new European settlers growing wheat and barley. Buffalo and elephant continually raided these crops. One of these new farmers was Mary Grosvenor. Besides having a large farm in South Africa, the Westminster family owned some 60,000 acres in Scotland on the Laxford River. Mary invited Gill and I, to stay at her home, Kylstrome Lodge, in Scotland, as we had one month of leave before returning home after the Mau Mau Emergency. We drove up to Scotland and instead of buffalo hunting, I had the opportunity to go deer stalking accompanied by the estate's gillies. In place of trout fishing on the Naro Moru, there were three miles of private salmon fishing on the Laxford River. In one morning's fishing we caught five salmon and six sea trout. I thought life in the Isles was perhaps not as grim as I thought it was while attending College! It was not the season for deer stalking as the antlers were still covered in velvet, but Mary said take a 'switch,' which was one that had antlers like an impala horn. Thus with a very fine old gillie, a VC veteran from the First World war, we set out to Glencoul to hunt the Reay Forest, which in fact was completely treeless! As Mary and Gill watched with telescopes from the Lodge, we slid along on our stomachs as we stalked a herd of deer with a 'switch' buck. I now knew what it is like to be a client with 'buck fever' for on positioning for a shot the so-called experienced hunter from Africa fired a shot, missing completely. I knew everyone would be watching from the Lodge, and after a second stalk, I took careful aim and squeezed the trigger, dropping the stag with a single shot. As the antlers were not worth keeping, the gillies prepared a front foot as a paperweight with a silver plaque attached giving the location and date, 4th August 1956.

From Scotland we drove across to Ireland, firstly to Gill's family estate, which was located on the Blackwater River. Then we moved on to a delightful fishing hut, based on Lake Connemara. We went salmon fishing on the river and fished for trout on the lake. On the Naro Moru River one of the best fishing flies to use was a Coachman. This had never been used on Lake Connemara. I happened to have one with me, which I used with great success. We spent a couple of days staying at the hut on the lake, which was covered with beautiful rhododendrons. We had to get there by rowing boat, and we fished from the boat as well.

In Kenya, Eric Rundgren grew wheat on his farm, but this was not his focus. He recruited a Danish manager to do the growing, while he concentrated on game control work. We took out special forest elephant licences, which allowed us to hunt four elephant per annum together with one rhino. We combined cropping with hunting these trophies. We would be lucky to collect any elephant with ivory over 50lbs a side in the forest. The sale of the ivory covered our living and travel expenses. I collected a rhino on my licence which had a 36 inch horn, and took another on control on Gustav Blixen's farm (a nephew of the famous hunter Bror Blixen), which would have had an even longer horn, had the tip not been broken off.

Eric's rhino licence was about to expire so he suggested we go back to the area where I had shot these two with exceptionally long horns, as he said the rhino in this area must carry these particular genes. We camped in a disused forester's hut so we could make an early start into the forest. We entered the forest at dawn. We walked all morning until reaching the moorlands. Buffalo and elephant were everywhere but we hadn't found any rhino tracks.

We wearily made our way down out of the forest before nightfall. To our surprise halfway down we saw rhino tracks crossing our path. It was not a very large track but Eric decided we should follow it anyway. Testing for the wind we quietly followed until we could hear the beast munching away. We made a slight detour, checking the wind so it could not get our scent. We suddenly came across its backside protruding from a bush. We carefully inched our way forward. Eric whispered, "At least it's a male," and when he got a glimpse of the tip of its horn showing over its back he decided to take it. On firing, the rhino swung around and we saw the biggest horn ever. In a flash his second shot dropped it. He had managed to collect a 45-inch horn, the biggest male rhino horn ever shot. I believe this still stands as a world record for male black rhino, the overall record being a female with a 52-inch horn. Hurriedly, we took the horn and head skin off, and the trackers carried it down tied to a pole. We made our way back to the hut arriving just after dark.

We were no longer tired, and after a well-earned meal we sat for hours around the campfire, reminiscing on our hunting times while the trackers chewed on buffalo tripe warmed by the fire. Eric relished this delicacy too. Tripe at the best of times was not to my taste. This tripe was intestine that had been cut open, its contents scraped off with a knife, before wrapping it around a stick and warming it over the fire until it was crispy and blackened before eating! I have to say

Eric Rundgren with his record male black rhino – 45.1 inches.

the effects were most telling. Marching behind Eric was like walking behind a horse passing wind. The trackers and I never said a word; just turned our heads with a big smile!

From the proceeds of an excellent wheat crop, Eric bought a plot on the Kenya south coast. He stayed down there for weeks at a time. He bought a fishing boat and spent days out at sea catching sailfish and marlin during the season. He suggested Gill and I join him in this sport before we got involved in farming. Even after being occupied on my own farm, I continued to hunt and fish with Eric until he sold his farm in 1963 and took up full time professional hunting, mostly in Tanganyika and finally in Botswana. His boat was no luxury fishing vessel but completely open with a minimum amount of canopy cover to protect one from the sun, with only bench seats. It had an on board diesel engine with an uncovered exhaust pipe that came out of the side. At least he had some belts to hold the butt of the rod while fighting a large fish. If a sailfish or whatever was caught from under the boat and came flying out of the water, one had to dash around the boat trying to avoid the red hot exhaust pipe, but inevitably got scalded on the way. One could always tell if someone had been fishing with Eric; indeed he himself had bits of plaster stuck all over his legs.

He had no fancy equipment or sensors to guide him to the underwater banks the fish favoured, but Eric had the same instinct as when hunting on land; he seemed to always sense where to go. We would set out before dawn and fish till mid-morning. Then he would drop anchor and while bobbing around on the rough sea, we would do bottom fishing to get fish for the table. If his guests were not feeling sick by then, the bottom fishing, together with the diesel fumes did the trick.

Myles and Kay Turner stayed with Eric while on their honeymoon. Myles had a small farm near us at Nanyuki and had joined a safari firm as a professional hunter. If he was not working he sometimes joined Eric and I on buffalo control work in the forest.

Myles joined Eric and I fishing for a day, after being bullied into it by Eric. Myles was inclined to seasickness and I watched him go quite green. I thought it quite mean of Eric to suggest we stop for some 'bottom fishing' But this he did, and enjoyed the spectacle of poor Myles being really ill with his head hanging over the side of the boat. Thereafter, he teased the poor man unmercifully.

Eric was then asked to do some elephant control work on the African shambas further down the coast at a place called Vanga near the Tanganyika border. We set out in Eric's old Land Rover pick up. We arrived at Vanga and found not only the marauding elephant were coming into the shambas nightly to feed on the maize and millet, but there was a man-eating lion at large. The lion had taken two people from the village. They asked us to deal with the lion first.

Eric located where the lion was coming from, tracking the spoor a short distance from the village. He placed the vehicle in a hidden position, covering it with brushwood, so we could ambush the beast on its way into the village. At dusk we were in position with Eric in the driving seat. Gill was squashed up in the middle seat and I on the outer seat, holding the spotlight with my rifle at my side for back up, if necessary. We removed the doors and rolled back the canopy on the roof and waited. After a sandwich and coffee from the thermos, we sat in silence, waiting. All was quiet as the night drew on. We each took our turn on duty watch and Eric promptly started to snore rolling his great bulk onto Gill in the middle seat. By midnight we hadn't heard a sound. I was stiff from sitting in an upright position, so I got out of the car and stretched out on the ground for my nap. I had hardly closed my eyes when I heard the familiar grunting of a distant lion. I thought it was coming closer, so lost no time in scrambling back into the vehicle so I would not be its next victim. The lion did not appear and I was blamed for scaring it away with my snoring!

We tried for several nights without success, but as Eric had limited time we had to focus on the elephant problem. If the lion continued to harass the village, Eric would organise another date. (In fact, later he returned on his own, tracking up and killing the lion, which had a porcupine quill stuck through its mouth, preventing it from hunting successfully.)

We made a rough camp a short distance away, sleeping on the ground in blankets under a tarpaulin stretched from the Land Rover, while Gill cooked up some food on the campfire. We kept our rifles at the ready by our side. Before dawn we drove quietly to the shambas. Arriving at first light we could just make out the backs of the elephant as they started to return to the forest. Alighting from the vehicle, Eric told Gill to stay put, as we would have to move fast to catch up on them, but we would not be long. We certainly moved fast, for the elephant knew they had to move faster still to be out of harm's way. We walked and walked until the sun rose and it became hotter and hotter. We had not even brought any water. It must have been nearly mid-morning when we caught up with the marauders. Even then they were not resting, but taking a bit of forage along the way. We had to shoot six elephant before they moved out of the area completely. Making sure all six were dead, and the rest of the elephant had departed, we left the trackers to remove the ivory, while hordes of people descended with the vultures to collect the meat. With just a couple of gun bearers, we made our way back to the Land Rover and to Gill who was waiting.

I was really worried for poor Gill but at least there were water charguls hanging on the car and she had a book. A chargul is a canvas bag holding a gallon or so of water that either had a 'tie up' mouth or screw top like a bottle that one could drink from directly. We always used these on safari tied outside the hunting car on the wing mirror or such like. The water seeped through the canvas and with the wind and evaporation kept the water delightfully cool

Eric Rundgren with ivory weighing around 120 pounds per tusk.

and the perfect temperature for drinking. After a long walk in the boiling sun, I had no problem downing a full chargul at a go directly off the side of the vehicle. The dust would collect on the outside, which turned muddy and made sure the water did not seep out too fast. It looked somewhat unsavoury, but the water inside would remain crystal clear. Some clients thought it looked so disgusting they refused to drink it. But usually after a hot trek and without any other source of water, they soon got used to it and thoroughly enjoyed a thirst quench.

"Leave the explaining to me," said Eric as we arrived back at the car at 3 pm. My mouth was so dry that all I could think of was taking a gallon water chargul from the car and drinking the lot in one go. I was sorry to have left Gill for so long and sad for the poor elephant. Nevertheless, these people were starving. Soon game reserves and national parks were to be established with the objective of protecting the wildlife within them for eternity (or so we thought).

Leaving the men to take care of the ivory until Eric could collect it, we drove back to Eric's house that evening. Gill and I made the long return drive to Naro Moru the following day. Back home the Settlement Trust had several farms for sale on their books for us to inspect, but although all these were economically viable for farming, I wanted to ranch and have wildlife. To my father's dismay I turned them all down. Of more interest to me was the 15,000 acres of Cyril Mayer's ranching land in the Kedong where we used to go shooting at school. My capital together with a maximum loan from the Trust could not make the purchase price, so I suggested that perhaps Tony Archer would like to form a partnership. Both fathers thought it would not be a viable proposition, and certainly not for two families.

Gill on the farm at Mweiga.

Then one day I went to visit my old school and family friend Dave Allen, who was managing a farm at Mweiga for a retired

Provincial Commissioner, Jack Pease. Jack farmed for pleasure after retiring and not to make money. He had a few paddocks around his house and a small herd of Ayrshire purebreds for milk. Otherwise the 3000-acre stretch was wild bushland of steep gullies, with lots of wildlife and two rivers stocked with trout. The house itself was built of beautiful cedar with panelled rooms and had a vast veranda looking across to the forest of Mt Kenya to the east, and the Aberdare range to the west. The farm bordered with the Cole's 64,000 acres to the north and the Nyeri forest to the south. The area teemed with wildlife. I was really keen to have this property. David said the Peases might consider selling as they were talking about retiring to their estate in Scotland. Father said he did not know the farm but would talk to a neighbour who knew it well, another retired administrator, Gerald Hopkins.

Gerald said, "I will tell Jack he must sell or recommend he considers further development. As a distant relative of the Prettejohns I am sure he would be happy to sell to you. Anyway I will tell him to do so." This is how it all began. The price was £9000 and I could become an assisted owner with a loan of £6000 to pay back at a peppercorn rate of interest over 20 years. Further agricultural loans could be had to cover the purchasing of more cattle and approved developments.

Father and another member of the Trust Board came with me to look the place over and work out the economics. I was most excited, but both of them looked glum. In unison their first words could be paraphrased as follows: "You can't live off a view. This grand house is going to take a lot of maintenance, and you'll have five miles of private road, all on black cotton soil, to maintain. The place is full of buffalo carrying East Coast fever, a deadly disease for cattle which means you will have to dip twice a week if you are to graze through the bush land." However, I was insistent, knowing I could supplement funds through safaris with hunting guests. This factor had not come into their calculations. With the price being below value, at least it would be possible to sell and get back what I had paid for it if things didn't work out. It was agreed to let me have a try. Thus, in 1957 I became the owner of Laburra, as the farm was called.

Eric put me forward for membership of the Professional Hunter's Association, and with further recommendations from Bunny Allen and Sid Downey, I obtained an 'Unrestricted Licence' which covered me to assist in the hunting of all big game. I put a one-inch advertisement in a US hunting magazine, *Outdoor Life*, offering hunting from a family home on a ranch, covering the forests of the Aberdares and Mt Kenya. This small advertisement brought me my first clients. Thereafter, I was fortunate enough to get future clients through word of mouth.

Now established on Laburra, we set about acquiring some Boran cattle, a hardier breed with more resistance to diseases. We crossed the Borana with the Ayrshires. I also started a flock of dual purpose Corriedale sheep and some large white pigs to produce baconers. Continuing with the dairy, I arranged with a Mr Trikam to come and buy the milk wholesale, paying cash for what he took. Mr Trikam was a tricky fellow. After a while he asked if he could pay me by the week instead of by the day. Then I got a call from a neighbour also farming on the Aberdares, Robin Camm. Robin said, "Now that you

Harry Barton with trophies outside Prettejohn's Laburra house in Mweiga.

are selling milk to Trikam, he has stopped paying me!" That morning Robin had hit Trikam over the head with a torch, so that he got paid instead of me. Thus this source of income came to a very abrupt end. Instead, we separated the milk, giving the skim to the staff and to feed the pigs. I kept the cream in a cold room, driving it into Mweiga, twice a week where it was collected by the KCC (Kenya Cooperative Creameries) who paid a monthly cheque. The visit to Mweiga was quite a social event as all neighbours met up here when delivering. Thus dinner parties and 'bridge sessions' were arranged.

Although we had a telephone it was not too reliable and very public. One wound a handle to ring the exchange and the girl would then connect you to whomever. The exchange would often say, "You will have to ring Smith, for Charles is having dinner with him tonight." Immediate neighbours could be contacted by short and long rings. There was one old girl who had nothing better to do than to listen in to every conversation.

One day Robin gave me a call telling me a most disgusting joke. I asked him, who told him. "Old Mrs so & so," he said, whereupon a woman's voice chirped in, "I certainly did not!"

Chris Luies was my neighbour at Mweiga. Chris's father, Lion Luies, a South African, gained Atlas distinction when it was reputed he lifted a D4 Caterpillar tractor clean out of the mud literally by putting his back to it. Chris had a massive build like his father. Chris's much older wife, however, matched them both. She was known as Mama Kali Wellmans. She took off in a temper one day to return a few days later while Chris was away. To get back at him for some perceived peccadillo, she removed the wheels from his prize lorry. Chris returned home aghast and remonstrated with his workers demanding to know why they had given her the spanner. "No, we did not!" they insisted. "She used her bare hands."

I always smiled at the sight of one neighbour, a Lieutenant Colonel AW (Arthur) Sutcliffe (known as the Animated Prawn) who delivered his milk in his Rolls Royce. This machine was built to be chauffer driven, so Colonel Sutcliffe would be hunched over the steering wheel with his employees in luxury in the back, hanging onto the straps as the cream cans bounced around between them. The Sutcliffes owned Monte Carlo Ranch, which was situated opposite us, south of the Amboni River on our common boundary. The previous owners had broken the bank gambling at Monte Carlo and had built a huge mansion with a museum attached. On moving in Colonel Sutcliffe was asked what he was going to do with the museum. He replied, "Put Ethel, (my wife) in it of course."

Robin Camm had invested in an expensive automatic milking machine, as he could not sell whole milk. To cover the expense he thought the selling of cream would be an option. I suggested if I sold him some pig breeding stock they could use the skim.

Robin came down to select the pigs and I offered to deliver them to him. He gave us an invitation to dinner at the same time. A roast chicken was on the sideboard, which Robin started to carve, but in doing so it slipped off the carving board straight into the mouth of a waiting hound, which promptly made for the door with it. Robin turned around and said, "Colonel (a term of endearment for his dear wife Nancy), scrambled eggs!" The Camms were forever having guests who never seemed to depart. Robin enjoyed his drink, and he thought the milking machine could be put to far better and more economical use as a distillery. This of course was quite illegal so it was well hidden. It produced a fearfully powerful gin and to show its pureness Robin would light his breath to make a pure blue flame! In later years their house burnt to the ground, and all that was left was the distillery for which he had some explaining to do to the police.

The Camms' farm was situated on the forest edge, a ridge across from Eric Sherbrooke Walker's famous Tree Tops Hotel. This is where Princess Elizabeth became Queen of England in 1952. At that time Robin was asked to guard the route where the Royal couple would walk to keep them safe from wildlife. It was arranged that he would be introduced to Prince Philip and Princess Elizabeth when they walked by. The wait took so long that Robin just had to have 'a leak.' He had barely unzipped his pants when suddenly the Royal party appeared! He had no time to zip up, so had to hold his pants with one hand, while shaking the Royals' hands with the other.

When the Camm house burnt down, Robin told Sherbrooke Walker he would put up a big sign overlooking Tree Tops, saying, "Site of new Camm House" and hope Sherbrooke would pay for him not to build there. This Sherbrooke never did, so it was cheapest to rebuild on the old site.

At the same time the local duka wallah in Mweiga was concerned that with Robin building a new house, Robin may never get his grocery account paid. Robin had worked out that by having an account he was paying some 30% over the top. "Give me 30% off and I will pay you cash," said Robin.

"Please, please Sahib, don't do that." So the account stood, but the duka wallah was now wondering whether he had made the right decision.

Robin and Nancy Camm became our dearest friends. On one occasion I lent Robin my old John Deere model D Tractor. This was a great hulk of a machine with two pistons and a great flywheel that one swung to start the engine after putting a few drops of water into a brass cup, which protruded out of the side of the cylinders. After a week to ten days I called Robin to say I needed it back as soon as possible. He would return the tractor next day after doing a repair. After three days without another word from Robin I thought I had better go and investigate. There it was in a million pieces spread over his front lawn with Robin covered from head to foot in dirty old oil. The tractor would not start and unfortunately on investigating a spanner had dropped to the bottom of the bulge and Robin had to dismantle the complete engine to get it out! It must have been a week before it came trundling down the drive.

I had bought two of these tractors from our friends Jens and Tutti Hessel who had been leasing land on the forest edge to grow wheat, and where I used to help control the marauding buffalo and elephant. They had now bought their own farm, also helped by my father and the Trust. These machines were surplus to their requirements, being somewhat outdated. However, they suited me well to grow some barley on one of the glades to feed the pigs. The pigs had cooked barley together with some buffalo meat from a shoot once a week or so, or when one was taken for a trophy by a hunting client. I built small movable pig houses that could be moved around the paddocks towed by the old John Deeres. This also improved the pasture with the pig manure. With the diseases that pig contract from wart hog and other wild pig, and possibly pass on to humans, the pigs had to be kept either in a properly built pigsty, or enclosed with fencing. Thus, I had moveable electric wiring around each pig house. In those days the electrics were not too hot in the dry weather and the pigs often received a shock from the wire as they scratched their backs on it.

The pigs bred like flies and I took some every Friday to Naro Moru to put on the railway to the Uplands Bacon Factory. I had bought a Morris 30cwt truck for this and farm use, and often met with friends also loading pigs. Sometimes a baconer would get loose. The Station Master (the Babu) would go mad while everyone gathered to catch the culprit running loose around his station, delaying the train's departure. Then the Uplands Bacon Factory went belly up and instead of the monthly cheque, I received useless shares instead! To add to this problem, a pig inspector arrived at the farm one day and was not pleased to see pigs running wild over the farm, so this business, like the whole milk sales, came to a grinding halt and I sold the lot. I concentrated on beef, mutton and wool, but as predicted by the Trust, I lost many animals from mainly East Coast fever in the cattle, Blue tongue and foot rot in the sheep, besides having degraded wool full of burrs (grass seeds).

Besides constant dipping (and there were not the good dip wash ingredients that there are today) the best I could do was check the calves regularly by temperature taking. As soon as the temperature was above normal with no outward signs of illness, the animal could sometimes be saved with high doses of injectable antibiotics. Now I began to see the woes predicted by my superiors, who had warned me not to buy this farm. And my five miles of private road! During the rains this became impassable and many a day I had to abandon the vehicle and walk home. The following day the old John Deere would chug along with a tow bar to pull the vehicle out, making the road even worse. Each time this operation occurred the tractor carried along a load of stone in a trailer to fill the ruts.

I was indeed financially strained, but the problem was saved when hunting clients arrived giving me some additional income. I could hunt from home where I made an estimate of our wildlife population, taking off trophy males on a sustainable basis. On the farm I could offer clients excellent buffalo with more than a 46" horn spread, very good trophies of rhino, leopard, bushbuck, eland, waterbuck and other animals. These could also be supplemented by hunting in the nearby forests where all these animals abounded, as well as the rare and much sought after bongo.

Then one day a film crew arrived. They wanted to use the house and farm to film the story of June Carberry. The Carberrys were involved in the 'Happy Valley' set, a film that was made later. Soon after this another film crew arrived to film 'West with the Night.' This was the story of Beryl Markham, who flew the original professional hunters such as Bror Blixen and Denys Finch Hatton around the country looking for large elephant trophies. She also became renowned later for being the first women to fly the Atlantic alone in a single engine aircraft. I knew Beryl when she settled at Naro Moru and lived with us while building her own house, but strangely, she never talked of her flying experiences. Nor did she mention any stories of a son she had with the Prince of Wales whilst he was out on a safari. It was said, in order to keep the matter quiet, she was paid a monthly sum by the 'Royal House' for the rest of her life.

I realised I had asked for far too little for the first film, so I upped the price considerably for the Markham film. We now had two small children, Jessica and Giles and I had their future education to consider. Our offer was accepted. We had a huge camp to house and feed. The movie set, together with a mobile kitchen, was established in the paddock behind the house, while we all had to move to our guest cottage. The house was refurbished as the Clutterbuck's (Beryl's family) final home. They built a shack by the Amboni River to represent their original home and their arrival was depicted with a hired wagon, pulled by a team of sixteen oxen. A safari camp with the original old International hunting car was set up in the fever trees along our Sangare Lake for the safari with the Prince of Wales, and we all took part in the set with Beryl being acted by the well known Stephanie Powers.

I don't remember how long the film took to complete, but at the end of it all, I had enough money to pay off my loan on the farm in full. However, father said that as the loan was such cheap money, it would be better to keep the loan and invest the money to pay the interest, when it became due. I think I actually invested in a new old car, and a double Rigby .470 with spare .458 barrels. Never again was there any argument about purchasing a dud farm or living on a wonderful view.

In 1960 I had the Anderson family out for a month's safari. Marty, Ille and their daughter Christine came from Honolulu where Marty was a partner in the law firm of Anderson, Wrenn & Jenks. After that they came out every year.

After 1962 Marty offered to join in partnership with me purchasing more land adjacent to Laburra. He purchased a 2000-acre block on our western boundary. This area was flatter and more open, and we increased our cattle and sheep. We also put some 500 acres into wheat and barley. I did this in partnership with a young Danish couple using the two old John Deere tractors. We leased another 1000 acres off a farmer in Kiganjo to the east towards Mt Kenya. However, the rainfall was marginal, and although we harvested several reasonable crops, it was hardly enough to support the two families, and the Danes, through the Settlement Trust again, purchased their own farm at Njoro on the Mau.

At that time one could get a GMR, (Guaranteed Minimum Return) on which an advance was available to purchase seed, fuel and weed killers etc., if approved through the local farmer's District Agricultural Committee. My father was chairman, but of course he could not make the decision on his own, and eventually they decided we qualified as marginal land for crop growing. Then one day in early 1963 father came over to have a serious discussion. He had been called to London to a conference at Lancaster House to discuss Kenya's independence and a proposed million-acre settlement scheme for Africans in the 'White Highlands' at Independence, which would potentially be declared by the end of the year. This was a tremendous shock. He thought it might be very difficult for us to stay on in Kenya. He was not prepared to be ruled by an African majority and had already made plans with a South African group who said they would make land available for any settlers wanting to immigrate.

Father had held talks with all the Naro Moru farmers who had mixed farms suitable for a settlement, and they all agreed to have their land valued en block and they were about to prepare for it. He said we could include Laburra if Gill and I so wished. Although it was marginal land and may not be approved by government, an agent would come round to value each farm before inclusion. This was a terrible decision to have to make, and I had to consult Martin Anderson first. Marty said he would go along with whatever decision Gill and I made, but the information he got from the American government was that they, together with the British, were determined to see that an independent government could be successful and they would both make plans for substantial financing towards that cause. The USA encouraged private investment and were planning an insurance scheme to protect the capital if need be. Any dollar investment could be registered with the Kenya government so that capital in dollars and any potential profits would be reinvested. I discussed the issue with Tony Archer and other colleagues, and we thought that our generation who were born here had a better understanding of Africans, especially after having close contacts with men living and working together in the forest and reserve during the Mau Mau uprising. We felt we should support them in making a new country, so we decided to stay. Gill, who had been born and brought up in Kenya like myself, was all for staying.

We arranged for Jessica and Giles to attend a weekly boarding school for primary education in Nyeri some 20 miles away. When viewing the school, Giles took one look at the large dormitory with rows of beds and decided it was not for him. On the day we were to take them to school, Giles was nowhere to be found. Eventually, he was discovered at the top of the tallest tree in the garden. He had to be coaxed down by a young member of our staff.

Both Jessica and Giles only survived a couple of terms. Gill decided she would teach them at home through a correspondence course until they were nine years old. After this they attended as full time boarders, Jessica to Greensteds Girls School and Giles to my old prep school at Pembroke House for boys. In later years both these schools took both girls and boys. All my grandchildren subsequently went to Pembroke.

Marty was pleased with our decision to stay in Kenya. He was sure there would be good opportunities to buy more adjacent land for a good price with many settlers wanting to leave. This is exactly what happened. In 1963 the 3000-acre Sutcliffe land, which joined with Laburra east of the Rongai River, came up for sale. There was no house on the land but it included a 20-acre lake and swamp surrounded by yellow thorn. The lake was slightly brackish with soda, but had a couple of fresh water springs, and fantastic bird life. The rest of the

Jessica and Giles with a leopard trophy shot on safari in the eastern Aberdares.

land consisted of open grass glades surrounded by olive forest rising to the top of Sangare Hill. It was a block of land as God had made it, teeming with buffalo, rhino, eland, leopard and migrating elephant between the Aberdares and Mt Kenya, as well as smaller game. This would be a perfect addition to Laburra for home-based safaris. It gave us a river through the middle of the property, and a mile or two extension of the Amboni River on the southern boundary. The price was £3000 (at this time there were about 17 Kshs to £1, while today there are some 140 Ksh to £1). I did not have £3000 but Marty was keen to purchase and amalgamate all three properties. Once the repayments were made, 50% of the land would be mine.

Hence, the land was bought and all three properties were put into a single company, Sangare Ranch Ltd. It was a smart deal for Marty, but I probably would have done better myself by borrowing from the bank. (By this time the Settlement Trust was not purchasing more land for Europeans, but only catering for existing clients). Des Bloxum, the manager of the Standard Bank of South Africa, often came around suggesting money loans, but the interest was high. Marty gave me no time limit or interest for repayment. As it happened I bought a mob of 300 steers, at a really reasonable price from someone selling up just outside Nairobi. We railed the cattle to Kiganjo station and walked them a further five miles onto Sangare. All survived and were sold within a year with a £3000 profit, which I used to pay off Marty.

In order to make more grazing land available I brought in contractors to clear the bush on Sangare Hill, letting them have the charcoal. To replace stock after the sale of steers, I went into a grazing partnership with an old school mate, Peter Becker, who was still farming on the lower land of the Aberdares by Ngobit. Peter found a cheap buy of 1000 Merino sheep from Molo, and as all his land was under wheat we decided to graze them on Sangare. These sheep were in terrible condition. We dosed them for worms and inoculated them against all diseases. They still died like flies. I used the carcasses to bait leopard for clients. In the end we made some income by selling poor wool full of burrs, then we sold them off for mutton. We only covered costs. My parents by this time had moved to South Africa where together with my brother Richard they returned to farming. My brother Tim became a Settlement Officer carving up the Naro Moru farms for the new African settlers. When that job was completed, he too moved to South Africa where our Uncle Dick had purchased a farm. He managed this while Dick remained on the Njoro Larmudiac farm where he died in 1972, leaving the South African farm to Tim.

With all the changes we looked around in 1964 at properties for sale in case Kenya went belly up. We found nothing either pricewise or attractive that could compare with Sangare. There was cheap land around Palabora, South Africa that I thought was wild bush country that could be developed into something. In fact, they later found this land to be very valuable for minerals and a mining company bought it. If I had decided to buy then, I could have sold for a huge profit.

During 1964, soon after independence, I received a registered letter from the Minister of Lands. This letter had a sealed letter inside stating that he had a group wishing to purchase Sangare. I replied that it was not for sale, whereupon I was ordered to attend a meeting with him in Nairobi. I attended together with our lawyer. At the meeting the Minister asked why I was not considering selling Sangare. I said that all my employees had shares, and they were more interested in land than money. To this he said it would be no problem, and he would see my employees were sufficiently compensated. He then said, "Perhaps you are not aware of the present policy?"

I replied, "I thought the policy was based on willing seller, willing buyer?"

"We are now into Africanisation," he said.

I replied that I was a Kenya Citizen, and that my skin is so sunburnt that it is almost black. Besides, I said I had an American partner with a dollar investment approval and he didn't wish to sell.

He said I'd better ask my American partner and come back to him soon. On leaving the meeting my lawyer said he thought I'd be forced to sell whatever, but I could ask for a price over the top. I never got back to the Minister of Lands, and he never asked me again. I believe the dollar investment probably saved the situation. However, Marty suggested we should take on an African partner because our ranch was in overcrowded Kikuyu land. Marty also thought we should make adjustments and look for a larger ranch up north.

At independence my lawyer had suggested giving our employees some redeemable preference shares, which was organised. The employees later announced they did not want shares and would prefer the land. So we took on an African shareholder who was happy to purchase a third of the Sangare shares. He was a good friend and quite wealthy. We set about putting all the land into a settlement scheme, which gave us freehold titles. At the same time we sold the 2000 acres Marty had first purchased to President Kenyatta's son Peter, who divided it into small portions for settlement. On this we kept enough land for our employees to have their plots in place of their redeemable preference shares. They could then move from their shambas along the river on Sangare, and have their own land or property.

Sometime later our shareholder became ill with cancer, so we divided our land again giving him his own piece equivalent to his shares. When he died, he left the land to his wife and children. She in turn divided the land into plots and started to sell. As we did not care for settlement within our boundaries, we bought most of the land back from her. By then there were some eleven children involved, which took a lot of dealings with a good African lady lawyer who knew the family well, and somehow eventually got them all to agree on a price and to sell, as the offer was conditional on them all selling.

We started to look around for a larger property to the north. My immediate neighbour on our northern boundary, David Cole, had died leaving all to his American wife. She in turn put the 64,000 acres of Solio up for sale together with 6000 head of cattle for £100,000. Unfortunately, this was just too much for Marty and the property was bought by an American, Court Parfet, who had made millions out of the sale of chewing gum. Court Parfet imported a Charolais stud from France and put 20,000 acres aside for a rhino sanctuary, which today holds more rhino than anywhere else in the world on one single property.

There was then an opportunity to purchase Pat Ayre's property of 20,000 acres on the Loldaika Hills, north of Nanyuki for £36,000, and in hindsight this would have been the ideal property to buy. Instead we bought a very wild 40,000 acres in the very north, Louniek, with 1,800 head of cattle for £40,000.

My school friend Humphrey Clarke had sold his Charity Farm on the Aberdares for settlement and being a confirmed bachelor and somewhat of a recluse, Louniek was the perfect place for him to manage. He also had capital from the sale of Charity to invest and so he became a partner. With the addition of Louniek, the scope for ranch safaris increased and gave us some other animal species such as lion, gerenuk and Grant's gazelle, that are not found on Sangare and the forests. Profits from these safaris augmented the income from our ranches and helped with running expenses and also had to cover school fees as Jessica and Giles set off to boarding schools. At this time Gill and I had a third child, Vivien, always known as Bim as she could never pronounce the V.

Louniek was 100 miles from anywhere, but by this time I had learnt to fly and had bought one of the Tri-Pacers used by the Police Airwing during the Emergency. In this we could just squeeze the family of five, and it took barely 45 minutes to fly from Laburra to Louniek. One day we had some friends over for a picnic lunch on Louniek. As Vivien was then only at the crawling stage we left her at the main house with an ayah (a nanny) while we were picnicking some five miles away. Suddenly a runner appeared in a real state to say that Bim had drunk a bottle of paraffin and was dying! The cook kept a bottle of the spirit in the kitchen to light the fires and Bim, crawling around the kitchen floor, had picked it up and before the ayah could stop her and had taken a great gulp. We drove back to the house in a fearful rush, collected Bim, who was in a coma, and rushed by plane to the hospital in Nanyuki. The Doctor said paraffin was not a poison but a very unclean purgative. So with some stomach pumping and careful nursing, Bim came round and all was well with no after effects.

On the new ranch, besides working out a sustainable takeoff of animals for clients, we put aside one area as a sanctuary. There was little water on the property so we relied on dams built by a previous

A large maneless lion in Lorien swamp, northern Kenya.

owner, which we renovated while building more. There was one permanent spring where we made a waterhole and built a small tree house within this sanctuary. Here one night we had such a chorus of lion calls that I decided to tape them. Marty had left me a pocket dictating machine that had a removable tape that fitted an airmail envelope which I posted off to Marty every month with our news. I filled the tape with talking lion and posted it for the month's news.

We had few rhino at Louniek, unlike Sangare where rhino often stirred up excitement while hunting the forests. We were hunting buffalo on Sangare one afternoon, when suddenly out of the bush a few yards away charged this huffing and puffing steamroller. Directing the gun bearer to take the client to a nearby tree, I tried to make the rhino change its course. But this was not going to happen. I probably left it too late to move myself for as I turned towards the next nearest tree, the rhino veered around. As I saw the horn about to go up my pants, I dropped the poor animal, shooting it in the head, by firing the heavy rifle, an old .600 I had inherited from Jock Harries. The kick from the rifle almost broke my hand. We reported the incident and Rodney Elliot, Game Warden of the area, who was a stickler for

A good rhino trophy on Mount Kenya.

the rule of law, hurried over to take a statement and verify my report. Measuring the angle of shot with a stick thrust into the bullet hole, he concurred I had had no other option, but he confiscated the trophy.

Rodney came to Kenya after the war. He had been left for dead on the beaches of Dunkirk, when a faithful friend nudged him with his boot and finding him still alive, though full of shrapnel, dragged him to safety. Soon after arriving in Kenya he joined the Game Department and was placed as warden in one of the hunting blocks in northern Kenya at Maralal. He would put his askaris as spies with binoculars to watch the goings on of hunting parties. My friend Eric Rundgren was hunting there one time and asked Rodney to dinner. Rodney gorged himself with the guinea fowl offered him, after which he asked Eric, how come he had been shooting guinea fowl when bird shooting was closed. Eric answered it was not guinea fowl he was eating but a vulture that had gorged itself to death. Eric thought it would be a special treat for Rodney!

Soon after this event, I too fell foul of Rodney while hunting in his domain. My client was taking aim at a large buffalo male and just as he squeezed the trigger, the head of a cow buffalo popped out of the bush and collected the bullet instead of the bull. It dropped dead instantly. The shooting of females is prohibited, so I had to make the necessary report to Rodney. We were moving camp that day and I had to send our vehicle and the camp lorry on ahead to the next destination to be sure they got there before us, while we followed by plane, the Piper Pacer, parked on a bush strip nearby. Rodney's HQ was in the opposite direction to where we were going, so I wrote a note on a piece of toilet paper, the only thing I had to write on at the time. I said we had shot a cow buffalo by mistake and I would write a full report of the circumstances at the end of the safari. I put this missive in a 'drop' sack and dropped it on his office out of the plane window as we flew off. It was not long before I received a threatening letter from the Game Department HQ in Nairobi stating there were special forms and a correct procedure for making such reports.

Another time on Sangare we were just driving around looking at wildlife with a good hunting friend, Tony Seth-Smith, his wife Sarah and small daughter Tana. At the time I had a double-cab Land Cruiser, and Tana was riding in the open-sided back. As we drove through the bush on a very narrow track, a rhino was upon us, and before I could accelerate forward the beast slammed into the side of the truck right at the point where Tana was peering out. Luckily she was not touched but the crash jolted her to the other side of the vehicle, while the rhino veered away, disappearing into the bushes on the far side.

Even when not hunting, I always carried a rifle when walking the ranch. Once, however, I was walking without one, when I walked straight into a sleeping rhino. Turning sharply I tried to make for a big enough tree to hide behind, for there was no time to climb up one. I tripped on a root while watching the rhino and fell flat on my face.

Author hunting bongo in the Aberdares.

There was nothing for it but to sham dead, holding my breath as the animal ambled towards me. It came right up, gave a fearful snort and thankfully crashed off into the bushes without even a gentle prod with its horn, on which it could have easily carried me off.

There were two further rhino incidents, which became good laughing points when we met up at Mweiga on milk delivery days. One early morning I got an urgent call to help a neighbour, Barry Thatcher, who with his wife and small daughter were returning home from a bridge night with another neighbour. They were driving home late at night in their smart new Mercedes through the Nyeri Forest when two rhino came at them from the side, one bashing the front of the car, pushing the fan into the radiator, while the second bashed into the boot, puncturing a tyre. Luckily none of them were hurt and another car following took them home. In the morning I went to help Barry retrieve the wreck and tow it back to their coffee farm.

The second incident happened to an old Colonel Jarman who daily motored from his home in Mweiga to the Outspan in Nyeri where he acted as 'Hunter' accompanying parties nightly up to Tree Tops. He drove a little underpowered Fordson van. One early morning driving home he heard what he thought was another vehicle coming up behind him. He pulled aside waving his arm out of the window for it to pass as he was slowly climbing the hill through the forest. He heard a mighty thump at the back of the van, pushing him against the steering wheel. As Colonel Jarman veered forward at speed, he turned around to find a rhino in the back with him! He stopped the car and reports differ whether he shot the rhino in the back of his van or if the beast ejected itself and careered off into the forest.

As many clients came back to hunt in the following years they inevitably wanted to hunt elephant. Heavy ivory trophies were not available in the forests or on Luoniek. This meant that I had either to hire camping equipment, or purchase my own. I invested in a Dodge five-ton lorry, all the necessary camping equipment and extra staff to hunt further afield while Gill stayed at home to run the ranch.

In the late 1960s during one particular year of a severe drought, political overtones developed in Luoniek with the Samburu, who

90 pound ivory tusks hunted on a family safari in Mbere country on the Tana River near Embu.

bordered to the north. They wanted more grazing and the Pokot to our west demanded access to the water on our springs. The smallest excuse started warring and cattle raids between these two tribes. After one of these wars, one of our cattle herders was murdered. The Kenya government suggested they should buy us out. At the same time the government was offering private enterprise to take over the 1.5 million acres of the Galana elephant cropping scheme some 90 miles inland from Malindi on the north coast, to develop further for game and cattle ranching over a 40-year lease. If we were interested in this, we could apply in part exchange for Louniek. We applied and won the contract to develop this immense area, but lost Louniek. The 1,800 head of cattle were not included in the deal, so we sent them by rail to Voi and walked them to Galana as a nucleus breeding herd to start the Galana Game & Ranching scheme. Marty Anderson has published the history of this scheme. My personal involvement comes in a later chapter together with some experiences from the many young men that were employed there from time to time over the years.

Chapter Twenty Six

THE MAKING OF A HUNTER
AND OTHER STORIES

My First Buffalo

Brought up on a farm on the foothills of Mount Kenya that bordered the forest edge where game abounded, I started hunting at the early age of six. At nine years old, I received my first rifle, a .22. Aged 14, I shot my first buffalo, by default.

A school friend, David Allen, whose parents were either away or certainly unaware of his intended antics, invited me to join him on a buffalo hunt. He said he'd shot one the day before, and added, "There's really nothing to it!" While our parents allowed us to hunt small game, larger game, especially buffalo, was considered highly dangerous and inappropriate for fledglings like us to hunt on our own. However, this was far too good an opportunity to miss so I made plausible excuses to my parents. It was a hunt I shall never forget.

In those pre-Mau Mau emergency days our parents didn't keep guns and cars under lock – indeed daughters alone were sacred!

We set off at dawn the next day in an old "borrowed" Ford 'B' Model box-body car, with David's father's .375 and .303 rifles and an African tracker and a pack of ridgeback dogs. Negotiating some rough and hilly tracks, irresponsibly mindless of the welfare of the car, we soon came onto fresh buffalo spoor. Leaving the car, we followed on foot with the dogs racing on ahead. I knotted up our small reserve of ammunition in a handkerchief so it would not jingle in my pocket as we hunted.

We had barely gone an hour when we heard barking about a half-mile ahead. As we approached, hearts racing, bushes erupted and buffalo crashed and careered in every direction. We dived to the ground or made for the nearest tree for protection, having to strategically place a foot to fend off a young animal. The dogs soon singled out and bayed up an angry cow. I managed to drop her with the .375, which took some manoeuvring so as not to shoot a dog as well. Once down the dogs left to chase up another. I had shot the buffalo in the lung and she was lying upright on her belly. David called out not to waste more .375 ammunition; he would finish her off with the .303. This smaller rifle had little effect. The buffalo struggled to her feet and charged. David made for the nearest tree, with the buffalo close behind. In the excitement I had a hard time undoing the knotted handkerchief with the spare ammunition. Scrabbling with the knot, I finally freed a spare bullet and hurriedly placed myself in the line to fire at the charging buffalo, without hitting David. At that moment, David tripped and fell. I fired and dropped the buffalo with a lucky shot just before she hooked a swipe at the seat of David's pants!

Returning home with pride and a tremendous sense of achievement, we learnt our first lesson. We needed to give total respect for buffalo, an aggressive animal that had its wits about him. We even conceded that parental advice might be worth something. We realised how close we'd been to disaster. David had to explain to his father, Bunny Allen, why the Ford had a hole in its sump and had lost all its engine oil! David must have made up a good story for Bunny had no idea what we'd been up to, and remained mystified by the holed sump.

Big Elephants and Mbala Mbala Island

In this day and age it is difficult to perceive the excitement and toil of collecting an elephant carrying 100 to 120 pounds of ivory on each side. The biggest elephant ever was reputed to live on Mbala Mbala, an island in the middle of the Tana River whose waters come from the Aberdare Moutains, flowing into the Indian Ocean, at the coast north of Malindi. Mbala Mbala island has extremely thick vegetation and hunters had to get so close to an elephant to judge its tusks that many times the elephant charged and the hunter had no option but to shoot, regardless of the size of the tusks. I would tell clients that if they wanted a hundred pounder they could expect to walk 100 miles in searching and tracking in hot and waterless country with the possibility of sleeping out on mother earth, on the tracks. Eric Rundgren tried several times to find this monster elephant on Mbala Mbala, reputed to be carrying at least 250 pounds of ivory on each side, but he never saw it. He had however collected a number over 100 pounds, I think the heaviest being 140 pounds. Rundgren heard that a South African hunter had winged the Mbala Mbala monster and it had disappeared into Somalia.

Two tusks believed to be the heaviest ever known, and certainly the heaviest ever recorded, were sold in Zanzibar during 1898. Both are now in the collection of the British Natural History Museum. It is said they came from an elephant killed near Kilimanjaro by an Arab hunter after he had been trailing it for several weeks. The heaviest tusk weighs 226.5 pounds and is 10 feet 2.5 inches in length while the second weighs 214 pounds and has a length of 10 feet 5.5 inches. Girth measurements are 24.25 inches and 23.5 inches respectively. The longest ivory on record is in the United States, National Collection and these have a length of 11 feet 5.5 inches and 11 feet, but with a girth of only 18.5 inches, the tusks only weigh on average 146 pounds each.

One afternoon in the late 1960s Ray Ryan and a friend known as the 'Little Bull of Texas' drove up to our home on Sangare in a handsome Rolls Royce. I noticed a trail of oil down the road from our gate, stopping under the Rolls. On inspection it had hit a rock in the road and the aluminium sump had a crack. We patched it up with soap, which got its occupants back to Nanyuki. Ray Ryan had just bought the Old Mawingo Hotel with two companions; Hirshman, a Swiss banker, and William Holden, the famous actor. The hotel is now known as The Mount Kenya Safari Club. Ray had asked me to take him on a safari to look for a 'big elephant' and had come to tea to plan the trip. Ray and the Little Bull of Texas wanted a luxury safari as their two girl friends were flying in. Although the girls would remain in camp, the two men wanted a hunter each. I contacted my school friend Peter Becker, a hunter with Ker & Downey Safaris, to hunt with the Little Bull.

Ray had been a bell boy at a hotel and had purchased a plot of land in Texas. He dug a hole in his garden to plant a carrot when oil squirted out. Oil made his fortune, so money was no object, but in the end he lost everything, including his life when his car was blown up by the Mafia.

Peter Becker and I decided to use Ker & Downey equipment, and they too would supply the luxury food and quantities of booze required. At tea we discussed the plan. I suggested we safari and set camp on the Tana River and hunt Mbala Mbala island opposite, if they wanted to look for real 'Big Ones.' Peter and I would go ahead by road and set up camp and Ray and his group would fly to a nearby bush airstrip on the banks of the Tana for us to collect them.

Peter and I set out in our two hunting cars, following a heavily laden truck with all the staff and provisions. We found a beautiful campsite under the vast acacias growing along the bank of the river and waited for a radio call with details of Ray's arrival by air. I seem to remember that in those days we did not, as later, have HF radios, but received a message broadcast after the 7 o'clock news in the mornings and evenings from the Kenya Broadcasting Station in Nairobi. And so the world knew exactly who was going on safaris and what was going on. For days we waited with no news. When news did come with their expected ETA (estimated time of arrival), we discovered that the Little Bull's girlfriend had cabled to say, "Pussy cat stuck in Rome without dough." Thus a cable and $1000 was sent from "Cheesy cat." A return cable said poor pussy cat had not received, so a further $1000 was sent. When eventually they did arrive, they rolled off the plane with bottles of booze sticking out of their pockets, and it was quite obvious that Pussy cat had had a whale of a time in Rome. They arrived in camp in the late afternoon and disappeared to their respective tents till sundowner time. Ray was quite sober, but the others were not. I was more than happy that I was to hunt with Ray. At sundowner time the Little Bull said, "Let me give you a tot." I decided on a whisky and water, but on taking a huge gulp to wish them happy hunting, discovered that the water was in fact pure gin! I certainly declined a second, but the one was enough to encourage some exciting hunting yarns around the campfire until late into the evening.

In spite of the overdose of alcohol I was ready to go first light, as was Ray. We decided to make directly for the island, crossing by canoe. Peter and his client would hunt inland from the camp. Peter knew his client would unlikely be ready to go for some time. We had a great day creeping up and looking over a number of bulls, but the biggest had only some 60 pounds of ivory. The wind was basically from one direction but with the heat of the day it could suddenly switch. The head tracker held a little bag of ash which he would tap from time to time to make sure of the direction. It was so thick that one had to squat low to look at the tusks from less than 50 metres. We would then wait for what seemed hours, keeping dead quiet until one was sure both tusks were there and we could estimate the weight. We would pull out after deciding the trophy was not large enough, hoping we would not be detected. Ray was brave to the point of being almost reckless, and I had to prevent him getting even closer unless we had decided to take the animal. Even at 50 metres if a serious charge was made one would have to take it, and be sure to stop the elephant in its tracks with a brain shot.

We had taken a sandwich and charguls of water, so we were ready for a stiff drink and relax by the fire when we returned just before dark. Back in camp we met a disgruntled Peter. He and his client had not left until about eleven o'clock. They found an elephant, but Peter said the tusks were too small, probably only 55 pounds. "I will take it," said the Little Bull, firing before Peter was prepared. The Little Bull had only winged the elephant and they had to follow it. After a few hours of tracking the animal was still going, but at least he was on his own, making away from the main herd. The Little Bull was unable to keep the pace, so Peter left the trackers to continue, having them place cut branches along the way so he could follow later. Peter returned to camp with the client, and then went back with extra rations and water for his men to keep on the trail of the wounded elephant. Peter arrived back at camp when we did.

We had a discussion and agreed that on the following day Ray and his friend were happy to remain in camp, and Peter and I would follow up the wounded elephant together. It was a long trek, and although we returned to the camp in the evening, it took us two further days to track and shoot the animal. The Little Bull was quite happy, he had got his elephant and was happy to make short walks around the camp and shoot some guineafowl for the pot. Ray and I returned to the island and had great sport looking at and dodging charging elephant. On the fourth day we came up on a large bull with tusks of 75 to 80 lbs. We were so close, less than 20 metres, that Ray decided to take it. The next couple of days, the clients relaxed and shot a few birds, while the tusks were removed and the ears and feet skinned and salted. We all set off back to the Mount Kenya Safari Club, leaving the truck and staff to follow a day later.

I used to take my own elephant licences each year and make a family hunting safari. Usually we went to an area on the Tana River below Embu. It was close for us to drive there and a fairly unknown area of thick bush, with ravines running down to the river, and only accessible by foot. It was a remote corner where big bull elephant could be found and it was full of buffalo and rhino. Not a hunt went by when we were not 'treed' by these animals. Gill, Jessica and Giles would stay in camp while I went hunting. It was the home area of most of my safari men, Ngengi, Njui, Thauthi and others. They were delightful people and would sit in camp telling stories to Gill and the children while some of the others went out hunting with me.

Thauthi had one bent leg, but it did not stop him walking for miles in the bush. Apparently one day he was trying to dig a warthog out of its hole when the animal came out at speed hitting and tusking his leg, which broke the bone. It took months to heal because it was never properly set. Subsequently, it was permanently bent. Jessica and Giles had their own small tent and were initiated into safari life which they thoroughly enjoyed until they were bitten by ants, stung by a bee, or a scorpion. The African men on our safari always had a remedy and they were soon cured. Thauthi would show them how to use a bow and arrow. They would try their luck shooting at francolin or guineafowl. Giles had an air gun and would shoot the odd bird for the pot. So they were well occupied while I was in the bush.

The area was full of snakes, which was a worry with the children being only six and eight and who would always be picking up sticks and stones. I told them always to keep a watch and use a stick when moving stones and bits of wood to make sure there was not a scorpion or snake lying underneath. At night they were zipped into their tent to make sure no creepy crawlies could enter.

The biggest elephant ivory I collected was of 98 pounds. I shot several in the 90s but never topped 100. I saw one that must have been 120 pounds, but it got our wind and though I followed it for days I never saw it again. We would come across old sculls with gaping tusk holes that must have carried ivory of over 120 pounds. Each time Ngengi would say it had been shot by a certain Dutchman, Martinus Nell. Eric Rundgren as a game warden was often after Martinus who was known to have taken many elephant with ivory over 120 pounds,

but he never caught up with him. Martinus would safari with the whole family of aunts and grandmothers and have all of them take out elephant licences for him.

I only took clients to this area who really enjoyed walking. A Hollander, Otto Shoemaker, came to me every year. We hunted this area, camping with porters by a rather murky waterhole. Otto

Author with symmetrical ivory of 105 pounds shot in the Lorien swamp on safari with a client.

complained of showering in baboon piss, so I suggested that a drop of Dettol disinfectant be added to the shower bucket. I was sitting around the campfire smoking a pipe and enjoying a whisky, when I heard screams coming out of the shower tent and out popped Otto in the nude holding his testicles. Unbeknown to me the shower man had put not a drop, but half the bottle of Dettol into the bucket. Otto said his privates felt like boiled potatoes, the skin all wrinkly and peeling. I was amused and I'm afraid to say I had a good laugh. I gave him a soothing sunburn cream, which seemed to do the trick. It certainly did not prevent him climbing a tree the following day. We were tracking an elephant when Otto said, "I have had enough."

"Wait with Njui under this tree," I suggested, leaving him with some water while Ngengi and I went on to have a look at two elephant not far ahead. Neither had big ivory and we turned back a few hours later. On approaching the area where we left Otto, we noticed him up the tree with a rhino below. Njui was assisting by shouting and throwing sticks from another tree. A couple of shots over the rhino's head sent it on its way.

I only managed to get one client an elephant with tusks over 100 pounds aside. This was a Danish hunter, Jens Weddell-Neerburg, who also had the luck of collecting a record bongo, a huge forest leopard, and an exceptional buffalo trophy with horns of a 48-inch spread, huge boss and beautiful curve. For the elephant we hunted the Lorien Swamp, a huge swamp area north of Wajir towards Somaliland, where the Uaso Nyiro River from the Aberdares and Mount Kenya deposits all its water, never reaching the sea. Unfortunately, the swamp today is no more for the Uaso dries up many miles back. However, at that time it was an area of tall reeds and only the backs of the elephant could be seen. It was therefore very exciting to part the reeds and see before us this monster elephant at point blank range. It had a beautifully matched pair of ivory with one tusk of 105 pounds and the other exactly 100 pounds.

Jens took the elephant and later we had an exciting follow up with a huge male lion feeding on the carcass. The lion had one of the biggest bodies I have ever seen, but as is usual in that hot dry bush country, the lion did not have much of a mane. All the record Northern Grants gazelle were taken in this area. Jens bagged one of these with a 27-inch set of horns.

On a safari with another returning client and good hunter, Buddy Schoelcoff, we should have collected an elephant with huge tusks that could have been around 120 pounds. We were hunting in heavy bush around Kibwezi near Tsavo National Park and we spotted a bunch of eight bulls with the huge tusker in the middle. We had a good view from a distant tree, and as it was in the middle of the

The author with 90 pound ivory on safari in Mbere country.

day they would not be moving for several hours. We decided to wait until they started feeding and fanned out. As soon as they started to move we gingerly made our way forward, but from the ground could see nothing. We managed to get really close to one that we thought was him, but it wasn't. It was however spooked, so we made a dash into the middle of them as they started moving at speed, but the big one was now ahead and we never caught up with him. We spent several days thereafter searching but we never saw him again. Such is the luck in hunting.

I could write a separate book on hunts and clients, so I have decided to just recall the exceptional incidents here. However, I should relate the most difficult hunting of all, is the hunt for the rare and elusive bongo. I took my friend Martin Anderson on a bongo hunt in 1963 and the bongo trophy he collected won him The Shaw & Hunter Award for the best trophy of the year. He wrote the story for *Karatasi Yenye Habari*, the magazine of the Shikar Safari Club in America. The story is reprinted here:

BONGO ON A FAMILY SAFARI

"It's your bongo," Mike whispered. Mike Prettejohn, our white hunter, confirmed the fact that the dark chocolate chestnut brown form slowly emerging through the early dawn mist was in fact a bongo, one of Africa's most coveted trophies.

An early morning breeze had sprung up at the first light of day, about 5.45 am, to clear away a web of mist that had been clinging to the floor of a narrow forest valley. There, exposed, was a magnificent forest antelope with lyre shaped horns.

Our family safari had travelled half way round the world from Hawaii to the Aberdare Forests of Kenya for this opportunity. Up to that moment, we had not really dared hope that the safari would produce more than an interesting search for the elusive phantom of the forests. A few tracks, the noise of breaking bamboo stalks, or perhaps a fleeing glance of our wary quarry in the dense forest high country was the most we'd really expected. To see a splendid bongo bull fast taking shape out of the mist in one of the infrequent forest glades was dreamlike – beyond reality.

Thinking back now, we should have appreciated that the planning and preparation of Mike Prettejohn had reduced substantially the heavy odds facing a hunter for bongo. From the time we'd coveted this antelope trophy mounted in the Nairobi Museum of Natural History two years earlier on our first safari in 1960, Mike started turning over ideas for a hunt.

It would have been difficult to place the problem of a bongo safari in the hands of a better man. Mike was born 29 years ago in Kenya, raised on a ranch in the White Highlands near Mount Kenya and the Aberdares Range – the heart of bongo country. He has hunted Africa's big game since his early teens and has been conducting safaris successfully since his retirement from the Government's Security Forces after the Mau Mau Emergency.

There had been more to do than just the usual safari preparations

The author with Marty Anderson's record bongo taken in the eastern Aberdares.

of booking hunting blocks and gathering provisions and equipment. A year earlier my wife Ille and my 12-year-old daughter Christen and I had finalized our plans for a 1962 family safari for bongo with the Prettejohns. Mike, in the meantime, had selected areas on the slopes of Mount Kenya (elevation 17,040 ft.) and the adjacent Aberdare range (elevation 13,104 feet) for special scouting assignments for bongo spoor.

Mike gave us several preliminary reports on bongo activity in the months prior to our departure from Hawaii. His letters were encouraging. Bongo definitely had been on the increase. Eighteen months earlier the Mount Kenya herds had been hard hit by rinderpest, but that scourge of the hoofed animals of East Africa had not reached some fifty miles across the intervening saddle of land to the Aberdare Range.

By the time we arrived in Nairobi July 22, 1962, Mike and the African trackers had zeroed in on several areas in the Aberdares where bongo bulls were active and frequent visitors.

Now it's a big decision to carve ten or fifteen days out of a thirty-five day safari to concentrate on just one animal, especially when that animal is a bongo; and the chance of success is so small. It means foregoing a stalk or two a day for the abundant assortment of Kenya game and being prepared to spend days on end following spoor where the quarry has the advantage of terrain, heavy forest growth, bamboo thickets and only an occasional clearing along the deeply worn game trails.

The decision to follow bongo wasn't made easier by the statistics given to us by Mr Sanderman of the Kenya Game Department:

	1960	**1961**	**½ Year to July 1962**
Bongo shot	2	5	2
Bongo licenses issued to visitors and residents	30	41	20

It should be pointed out that relatively few safaris have been willing to devote time to the bongo. On the average there have been 200 non-resident full licenses issued each year and approximately 500 resident licenses. It was interesting to hear that in 1958 a substantial number of the licenses issued were in fact by professional white hunters – on a busman's holiday it seems.

Since this was to be a family affair, we decide to spend the first one-third of the safari in elephant and rhino country bordering the Tsavo National Park, near Kibwezi, the next third in the Masai area near Narok for lion, buffalo, Grant and other animal; and the remaining time on the Prettejohn ranch near Mweiga from which we'd concentrate on bongo. That would balance our time and interest – my wife Ille would have plenty of opportunity to fill up her sketch book with wildlife and camp sketches and my daughter Christie and her friend Carolyn Camm from Kenya would have close contact with the tribal life of the colourful Masai people. Mike's wife Gill and his two children, Giles and Jessica, would join the camp to round off a real family safari.

The accomplishments of the first two-thirds of the safari – the trophies, pictures and good family adventure – are another tale. It is sufficient to say that we had arrived at the Prettejohn ranch with ten days left and the safari already a success.

A day of rest and then Mike and I with a couple of superb African trackers headed into the Aberdares to survey the areas in which Mike previously had noted bongo. The weather had been cold for Kenya. Nairobi recorded a record temperature drop and rain had fallen in the Aberdares, generally – a touch unseasonal for mid-August. The Aberdare range with its blunt nose summit ridges stuck into the heavens had been soaked. Mike grinned happily as we swung along a slippery, dark, red clay game trail.

"Actually, this rain is a blessing," Mike had said. "The bongo should be dropping down out of the high forest bamboo to dry off a bit."

This first day was strictly devoted to a reconnaissance of the areas Mike had been checking out for some months.

The sun was brightly shining, though the ground was slippery and wet. Immediately we had run into fresh, deep tracks of buffalo and rhino on the trails. We were walking through an umbrella of thin tall trees that were all but blanked out by the sky. Passage would have been difficult, but for the well-travelled, criss-crossed game trails. About ten minutes after we'd left the Land Rover, we struck tracks that should have alerted me to the fact that this bongo hunt had more than a chance for success. I saw the head tracker stoop and, parting the grass, point to a fresh bongo track. "Mguu Dongoro," he said in Swahili. Again and again, the damp clay soil betrayed the bongo. There was no real thought of following that particular bull now. Our strategy was to select an area well frequented by a bongo bull and camp the night nearby. We would then move with the first light of day and hope to catch a bull as he started to move back into the heavy growth from his night's grazing.

The bongo is largely a nocturnal feeder that comes out of the high bamboo forests to graze in the lower open glades during night and return. To attempt to track the animal in the heavy growth is nearly impossible. The bongo is intelligent, very timid with extremely good sense of hearing, sight and smell. There are some who have been successfully hunted by backtracking on two-day-old spoor on the theory that bongo often travel an elliptical path of two days duration. By back tracking, one hopes to meet the bongo on his next time around. Usually one tries to be moving down ridge when the bongo is heading up. The risk of noise and changing winds is still great however. We felt if we could be in the more or less open, lower glade areas at the first morning light, we would be able to see and stalk from a greater distance.

For the rest of that first day, we continued following the old game trail looking for the big tracks betraying a favourite haunt of a lone bull.

Then the bongo hunt was interrupted for a short time. About 9.15 am we heard the unmistakable "crunch, crunch" of a rhino grinding up the last of his late morning snack. A big grey shape moved ahead up wind. The rhino wasn't 20 yards away, but the dense foliage wouldn't permit a clear picture of the big animal. I wanted a good close-up colour slide of "Kifaru," and while Mike covered, I tried to angle around the foliage to where the 35mm. telephoto lens would pick up this throw back to prehistoric times. No use. While the wind was steady, it wasn't safe to get closer for a clear picture without risking a charge and the necessity of shooting. I backed down the path and conferred in whispers with Mike as to how we might get a picture. "We'll get Ngeni to call him," Mike said, and whispered a few words in Swahili to get the head tracker. "First, we'll get up a tree and you'll get some fine pictures."

I saw a broad grin spread over Ngengi's face as Mike explained the plan. The rest of the trackers quickly backed down the trail. "Crunch, crunch," the big rhino was grazing noisily 30 yards away upwind. I'd slung my camera over my shoulder, leaned my rifle against the crotch of a tree and prepared to start up a promising looking sapling. Long before a leisurely climb would have put us at a safe, comfortable height in the trees, Ngengi let out the nicker and snort of a baby rhino. The reassuring "crunch, crunch" of a contented feeding rhino stopped abruptly. The big beast whirled and froze facing the sound except for the twitching of its ears. If movement and sound stopped in the rhino area, the situation was far different where Mike and I had been standing – we shot up our respective trees and both let out bellows to Ngengi to stop his all too plaintive and effective call. As I gained a safe position in the lower branches of the tree with a speed envied by a Colobus monkey, I caught a glimpse of Ngengi smiling impishly below from behind the safety of a fallen tree. The rhino trotted towards us a few yards and then moved off with dignity. When we'd caught our breath, we had a good laugh all round.

We gathered the boys together after that and followed bongo tracks the rest of the day into the bamboo forest belt. Towards the end of the day, we felt we knew the latest pattern of the bongo in the area. We had noticed a fresh set of heavy tracks apart from the numerous signs of cows and calves. At first the tracks were hard to read on the downhill lay of the land where the animal had slid in the soft earth. Mike was sure it was a big bongo bull, but the sign was so much larger than other tracks we'd seen I'd wondered if we weren't looking at a young buffalo's sign – there were buffalo tracks everywhere.

Satisfied that we had located an area for concentrated effort, we turned back toward the ranch. We spent the next day preparing a leopard blind. The day thereafter, we returned late in the afternoon, prepared to spend the night. Just after we left the Land Rover and some way from the bongo area, a great black giant forest hog crossed the trail in front of us. He turned and faced us in an ill-tempered manner. I was first in line on the trail, fortunately and so close to the boar that I wasn't conscious of having to aim at the large target presented.

I shot, and down the big boar fell. We left a skinner to care for the trophy and pushed on to a spot downwind, just a few minutes from the area where we had noticed the bongo bull had been feeding two days before.

That evening had been quite an experience in itself. The forest was crowded with Cape buffalo that moved noisily about, commencing just after dark. A group of three giant forest hogs put in an appearance.

Their great black bodies moved slowly down the game trail a few feet away from our bed rolls. Somewhere not too far off a bush buck loudly barked warning of the presence of a stalking leopard. The night air was pierced again and again with the calls of night birds, and the odd noises that marked the comings and goings of the forest game population.

Sometime after midnight I dropped off to sleep. A mist settled down during the night and obscured what little visibility the bright African stars had earlier provided. We arose just before dawn. The night noises had stopped now. It was as though the forest wildlife had never been out. Only a soft fresh morning breeze stirred the silence and swirled the mist higher onto the treetops. There was just enough light filtering through the trees and mist to see the game trail leading up the narrow valley walled on the sides with thick lush green bush and trees.

We followed the game trail and approached the spot where we had seen the bongo tracks two days earlier. Suddenly the tracker froze ahead of us on the trail peering at the ground – fresh bongo tracks, really fresh! A big bull was headed up the narrow valley towards a clearing. The wind was right and the heavy dew muffled our steps as we followed.

We slowed our pace and in a few minutes cautiously approached the clearing. As we parted the bush, I saw a shape materialize to our left. The scene was detached from reality in the early morning hours, a soft white mist, swirled within the walls of deep green forest in the background and the lyre shaped horns majestically carried by the animal 75 yards away, all combined into a dream in which I seemed to have no part.

Mike whispered, "It's your bongo!" Even his words didn't break the spell. Mechanically the 30-0.6 went to my shoulder, the cross hairs of the scope lined up on the thick heavy neck and 58 grains of 4350 powder in the expanded Ackley modified case sent the 180 grain nosler bullet home. Absent was the pulse throb that had required 15 to 20 seconds to calm before I'd been able to hold steady on the lion in the Masai area a week earlier. But, as the bongo fell shot, we all snapped back to reality and exploded with excitement and back pounding. The horns that day measured 34 inches in length, 12 ½ inches in circumference at the base with a 17-inch spread.

This was a truly magnificent trophy and a credit to the skill and preparation of the white hunter, who had made this possible.

The bongo appears to be on the increase and there is not much hunter pressure except for the ever present "poacher" problem. It does seem to be an opportune time to try your hand for the bongo. It is important to select a white hunter with special experience in such hunting. In addition to Mike Prettejohn, Kerr & Downey, also have been successful of late in bagging bongo. I am happy to report also that while England is soon to grant independence to Kenya, my wife and I saw no indicators that the political situation should discourage anyone from safari.

With a farewell to our Kenya friends at the Nairobi Airport, I bundled Christen and Ille aboard the big jet and we started our swift passage home to the other side of the globe. In a few minutes we winged over the Aberdare Forest, and I reflected on the fact that the real satisfaction from this family safari came from sharing a wonderful adventure with two young ladies at my side.

My Rhino Hunting Tale

Having thus far remained unscathed on my hunting trips, the law of averages had to dictate sooner or later a downward trend on the scale of mishaps. The first of these occurred with a rhino. It was reported that a large bull rhino had been harassing cattle grazing along the edge of the Aberdare forest. The herder, who no longer dared risk his cattle, explained that the rhino was always to be found in a particular patch of semi-isolated forest nearby and seldom moved far. This seemed simple enough. My brother was getting married in the afternoon. Why not kill two birds with one stone; claim a trophy for a client and rid the area of nuisance in the morning, while attending a family wedding in the afternoon? However, events proved otherwise.

The tracks were easily picked up by seven in the morning. The 'rogue' was much nearer than I anticipated. We hadn't been tracking for more than half an hour when there was a loud snort and crashing of departing feet. The rhino had got our wind and we didn't even get a glimpse of him. It must have been another half hour tracking before the rhino slackened his pace, but his tracks headed in a determined direction towards thicker bush. Towards mid-morning, just as it occurred to me that I might miss the wedding, we heard another loud crash. I hastily encouraging the client forward to get a glimpse before the rhino again disappeared. To my surprise the rhino was heading towards us snorting like a steam engine. I was carrying a magazine rifle with a throw-over safety catch. Before I could release it, the rifle was thrown from my hands and the wind expelled from my lungs as the horn struck me and threw me into the air. A split second later I landed on my back breathless and shaken. I was alive! The rhino gone! I couldn't believe it! The client looked down at me in awe. Events had happened so fast he had had no time to shoot.

Fortunately, the rhino's long, back-curving horn hadn't penetrated. I must have been caught squarely by the rhino's nose and lifted skywards. My tracker appeared, as I was fighting for breath, with a broad grin from ear to ear. The grin was one of relief rather than derision for at the point of impact he had dived into the bushes dragging the client with him, while the rhino had passed within inches of them both. Besides a fair amount of bruising, I had nothing worse than a cracked rib. The client was a doctor and fed me enough sedatives to see us through the wedding. He didn't get his trophy, but a good story instead, the telling of which improved remarkably with each glass of champagne!

A week later, with the wedding behind us, we made another attempt. This time round, we were more alert. The horn measured 32 inches.

The Buffalo Incident

The second incident happened a few years later with an old lone bull buffalo whose cantankerous reputation was well known. He had recently killed a woman fetching water, and had previously claimed others. We tracked him into a heavily wooded 'donga' where he was resting up for the afternoon. The client wounded him and I was unable to get off a second shot before the buffalo disappeared. We followed him and put him up three times that day without ever seeing him. Unable to continue tracking at nightfall we returned to camp. The following morning, picking up spoor again, we found where he had lain up for the night before moving on. While debating our next move, the nearest bushes exploded. I hastily moved into position to shoot before he disappeared again. Flight was not his intention. With that momentary sinking feeling of 'déjà vu,' I was confronted head on with a speeding black charging mass, nose pointed forward and horns locked back. I loosed off a shot instinctively, but to no avail. Before I could get off another shot, the buffalo was on me, knocking me backwards and, without trampling me, passed right over the top of me.

There was hardly time to be grateful for the end of this bout when he wheeled round and came for me again, head lowered. Luckily, he was an old bull with a heavy head and stub-ended horns, which made it difficult for him to hook into me. I clung onto his head and horns anchoring my legs around his neck, and hoped to God that the client or my gun bearer would hurry up and get it over with. The buffalo, realising he could not hook me, dragged me along the ground before kneeling on me to knead and pummel my chest into the ground with his boss. Thinking I was 'a gonner,' I heard a loud report. My ears rang. Although the pressure on my chest was released instantly, I found myself unable to move, pinned under the dead weight of the buffalo. It took six men to roll him off me. Surprisingly, I had no broken bones; just severe bruising, punctures, grazes and cuts. Suffice it to say it was all extremely painful but nothing compared to the lavish infusion of iodine that followed. I ran a high temperature that first night back in camp and was given a shot of penicillin in the buttock by a safari crew member accustomed to taking on an odd variety of chores in the bush. Later I discovered the fever was probably caused by lead poisoning, but I had no idea at the time.

For months my right leg gave me a lot of pain and at times I was unable to use it at all. Eventually, simultaneously with the development of a large bruise on my behind, the pain subsided. The doctor suggested this highly coloured lump was due to internal bruising and fat solidification and gave me medicine to rub on with a special finger pad. The more I rubbed, the larger the bruise appeared until

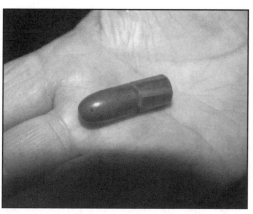

The bullet that spent a year in the author's backside.

finally a solid, but movable lump appeared. I no longer felt any pain, simply the feeling of a heavy extraneous object bumping and jostling as I ran.

While on safari with a doctor from Denmark, he proposed, in the course of sewing up a deep razor-like cut on my cheek, and without means of administering anaesthetic, to remove the offending object. I declined. The cut on my cheek was the result of a very close shave from a bullet fired from behind while hunting an elephant what we had encountered at close quarters. It must have been a piece of cartridge wadding. Whatever, half an inch to the left and that would have been final.

On my return from safari, my own doctor admitted there was indeed something more than a bruise and said he'd operate under local anaesthetic. As he peered into the hole with his tweezers poised, he commented that the object appeared to be gold plated. With more determined probing, he produced a perfect .458 bullet! This was exactly one year after the buffalo incident. On reconstructing the events of that day, my gun bearer's shot had raked the buffalo from behind, travelled on through its neck, and lodged itself in my leg, which was at the time wrapped firmly around it. By the time the bullet's trajectory had reached me it was luckily well spent and eventually worked its way out, via the sciatic nerve, which accounted for the terrible pain.

Michael Prettejohn

These are the risks of course in the life of a professional, but there is a very real dread that it can happen to a client as well. Here's a story of a client who found himself pinned down by a rhino in heavy bush while we were hunting elephant.

Client Incident with Rhino

We had a long and hot walk following bull elephant adjacent to Tsavo West in the late 1960s. When we came to an inviting shady tree where we stopped for a drink of water. We sat down and rested our rifles against the trunk while the trackers moved to a higher point of overhanging rock on a hill some half mile distant to scout ahead for the elephant. On the way there they inadvertently aroused two sleeping rhinos who thundered back in our direction.

The trackers shouted a warning and we were on our feet, rifles ready. I told the client to stick tight against the tree while I made for another to his right. As the trees were sparse and slender, I thought it best we had our own cover. Before I reached mine, the rhino spotted the movement and changed direction toward me. I raised my rifle but found, to my horror that the client was directly in the firing line. Deciding my tree was more secure than his, he had come to join me!

Half-way he tripped and fell. I watched as he appeared ready, from a seated position, to drop the rhino now almost upon him. No shot rang out. Instead, there was a swirl of dust out of which a figure landed prone at my feet. Once the dust had settled I watched, with immense relief, as the rhino's two backsides headed towards the bush. The groaning figure at my feet roused himself, uttering unmentionable expletives in Dutch. One hand was clutched tightly to the seat of his pants holding the flow of blood, which jetted out in spurts.

The car was at least 12 miles away, but we did carry the minimum first aid with us. Trousers were downed for a closer examination. It did not cross my mind at this point that had anybody happened to appear around the corner, their immediate reaction might have been one best not imagined and the thought amused me. Once the flow of blood was staunched, the damage didn't look so bad. There was a bruising and a gash three inches long just off centre. With the support of a couple of trackers and the wound buried under antiseptic pads and Elastoplast, we slowly made it back to the car. From there we headed to the local dispensary to get a shot of tetanus.

To stitch the wound, the African dresser produced a needle, the size of which remains unknown outside veterinary circles. My client reluctantly agreed to undergo the operation providing I remained in attendance to ensure the right hole was sewn up. The dispensary itself was a mud hut with an earth-beaten floor and no windows, only a large gap between the top of the wall and the roof. As the client lay on a makeshift bed in the middle of the hut, a row of smiling black faces peered through the gap above. The dresser performed a miracle nonetheless and, in gratitude, the client, owner of a large pharmaceutical company, sent out equipment and drugs which I was delegated to give the dresser on my return to the area. Luckily, the client and I had hunted together on several occasions. We were good friends and could laugh the whole matter off. Two people hunting together over long periods share a lot in common and often friendships are made for life.

Zebroid Safaris

In the 1920s an early settler in the Nanyuki area of Kenya, Raymond Hook, successfully crossed Somali ponies with a Grevy zebra stallion to produce large sturdy mules called zebroids. These animals looked like a horse with various stripe patterns and made excellent pack animals for safaris. They were very sturdy and able to endure long treks without water. When Raymond died, the zebroids were taken over by his daughter Amber. When their farm was taken over for african settlement, she had nowhere to graze the animals.

My wife Gillian had died of a heart attack around 1972. I had been seeing a lot of a neighbour, Jane Hook, who was interested in learning to fly and I had been giving her some unofficial lessons and flying experiences. With Gill's death this developed into more than flying lessons, and Jane, the same age as I, decided to part with her much older husband and come and live with me to help look after

Zebroid safari in the Hagenia forest of Aberdares.

the children. We were married a year later when her husband Hilary consented to giving her a divorce.

Since Jane had been married into the Hook family and enjoyed horses and riding, Amber was happy to pass the zebroids on to our family in the 1970s. As most of the animals were by then getting on in age we decided to breed some more, borrowing a Grevy stallion from Andrew Holmberg, one of the early well-known Professional Hunters. After breeding another six zebroids the stallion unfortunately broke a leg and had to be put down. Once old enough to be trained as pack animals we set about doing some safaris with them ourselves, together with some mules we had bought in Ethiopia. We used them on trips to Mount Kenya, the Aberdares, and would truck them to the North for safaris around the hills and mountains there.

One such trip with zebroids was with Tony Seth-Smith and some clients. We had taken a safari to the head of the Kipsing Lugga. It was a dry year and there was little water to be found anywhere. After making camp by a well in the lugga, where we could dig for a little of the precious liquid, Tony and I set off on foot to see if we could find a better source. We headed in the direction of the top of the lugga, which was surrounded by high rock cliffs. There we did find a larger though very murky and stagnant pool but with difficult access for the animals. As we made our way down we noticed hordes of baboons screaming at us from the cliffs above. On reaching the water we endeavoured to move rocks and make a pathway for the animals. Suddenly a huge boulder tumbled down, just missing us. We looked up and could see the baboons had obviously rolled this boulder onto us. Was it a distinct warning to keep off their water supply? Neither of us had ever heard of baboon doing this before or indeed have never heard or experienced it again since.

On some of these zebroid safaris we were often accompanied by a special friend Sandy Field, who was a great entertainer for the clients. Sandy was a retired Provincial Administrator from years of service in Uganda. As a Senior Warden of the Serengeti National Park in Tanzania he had many stories to relate. He hated riding and was scared of horses, therefore he and I always walked with the pack animals while the others rode. He and I considered them dangerous at both ends and uncomfortable in the middle. One day camped below 'Uaraguss' the highest mountain of the Northern Frontier District, rising to over 9000 feet, we decided to move across to the table mountain of 'Ololokwe' which was a full day's trek.

Jane with zebroid bred on Laburra.

The Samburu informed us there was a good spring located half way up the western side of this mountain where we could camp. We spent two days climbing to the top of the mountain. It was a longer trek than anticipated, and on reaching the spring at dusk, with very thirsty animals, we discovered to our horror the spring was almost dry. It took half an hour to get but a cupful of water! There was nothing for it but to move on to a borehole further south in the desert, another three-hour trek. Sandy said he had had enough and was not prepared to move another inch, to hell with the horses. I had to admit Sandy was some 15 years our senior. Jane said we had no option and proposed putting Sandy on a horse. Jane instructed Sandy on how to put his foot in the stirrup and throw the other leg over until seated in the saddle. But, each time he tried he ended up the wrong way round, facing the back of the horse. This at least caused much amusement to us all. After some three tries he was righted and riding like a sack of potatoes and we headed on our way. We reached the water at 9 o'clock that night. There was no grass for the animals so the following day we had no choice but to safari back to the waiting vehicles.

We did a few trips into the Aberdares but these could often be somewhat alarming, especially while walking along narrow paths through the bamboo. An elephant could easily come the opposite way towards us. On one such trip three zebroids bolted on confronting an elephant, thus leaving all our pots and pans strewn around the forest. Luckily, the elephant was even more surprised and bolted in the opposite direction. It took us two days to gather all the animals and equipment before advancing through the bamboo onto the moorlands. Once there, it was a delight to be in new country far off any road or track. The trout fishing on the moorlands was superb, as the streams had never been fished before. We would catch enough to feed the whole camp each day. As usual Sandy would be with us. He could not travel anywhere without his canvas folding bath and his 'man' to look after him. We spied him one evening. He thought he was hidden behind a large hagenia tree. He was sitting in his steaming bath tub whilst his man was scrubbing his back.

Sandy had a small house on the outskirts of Nanyuki town, and the local business people and especially the local provision store were happy to see Sandy go off on safaris. He was a very 'timely' customer. He would spend his day chatting up people who were busy trying to get on with their daily chores. He had a curtain ring the same size as his egg cup. He would while away the day going through every egg in the egg trays of Settler's Store, in order to purchase his two eggs of the right size for his breakfast of boiled eggs for the following day.

Alas, Sandy is with us no more. We had a particular bad spell of weather one June, when Sandy just had to get to Nairobi to change his book at the Muthaiga Club library. He never drove, but kept a small plane on the Nanyuki airstrip for trips around the country. He had lunch with us at Sangare on his way and reached Nairobi that afternoon. The following day the weather worsened and he was told at Wilson airport that he should not fly. But Sandy had a mission and he did not want to stay longer in Nairobi. He persuaded all to let him go.

It took several days before it was noticed that he had not reached home, nor had he returned to Nairobi. Ground and air recces were mounted with every private aerocraft. Hundreds of hours were flown but to no avail. It must have been a year or more later that his plane and body were found by honey hunters in the bamboo forest of eastern Mount Kenya.

Galana Lion Story

In 1968, together with two friends, one a former client, the other, the son of early settlers, we won a government tender to develop 1.5 million acres of cattle ranching and game utilisation over a period of 45 years. The development of this area is told in another chapter. Suffice it to say here that by 1976 when the hunting ban was declared, we had put some 500 kilometres of road, 50 airstrips and a network of piping and dams to water 30,000 head of stock. At this time there were over 6000 elephant (30,000 then in the ecological area) and some 350 rhino besides a myriad of other game. We built permanent camps and took off trophy animals on a sustained yield basis. Our elephant trophies averaged around 80 pounds a side and in time, with special selection, we were hoping to offer 100 pounders. The largest tusker was 116 pounds although we found old tusks of up to 150 pounds.

After 1976, with organised hunting closed and an end to all game utilisation, the poaching started in earnest. The poaching was beyond our control, organised as it was by people in important positions or carried out with a ruthlessness that frightened off the anti-poaching units.

Our resident game manager was shot dead in the course of attempting to fight against poaching on the ranch. The elephant population dwindled to a mere 50. The rhino population was obliterated. With the realisation of the dangers to ourselves, the lack of support in the anti-poaching field, and in spite of the fact that the cattle operation was doing well, we were bid to move out after 20 years, just at the point when the ranch was nearly fully developed. While the pressure to leave was brought about by the government, it did honour its word and compensate reasonably.

Besides trophy hunting, we periodically had to do some game control, specifically on lion when they became ardent cattle killers. We lost, on average, an animal a day, 365 head a year. However, we only shot a lion after it had killed cattle twice before.

One night, sitting in a hide rigged over a stud bull that had been killed, there appeared on the kill two male lion, both large animals. One had a good mane so I decided to leave him for a client and took the other lion, a maneless one. I had borrowed a rifle for the occasion and the ammunition was old. Subsequently, what I believed should have been a fatal shot only wounded the animal. I saw him disappear before keeling over so thought it best to leave him for a while and let him stiffen before taking the car up to him. As I approached I could see he was still breathing. Getting slowly out of the car I walked behind him to give the final 'Coup de Grace.' Just as I reached him he turned a backward somersault propelled by his tail and came down on top of me like a bolt of lightning. I got off one shot and broke a leg, but before I could get in a second, I was on my back under a growling angry mass of lion. I instinctively put up my arm to ward off any blow to my face and got my thumb chewed. I then tried to lever him off with a leg and foot only to have him sink his teeth into my calf.

Lion mauling author on Galana.

There were no other weapons to hand and my mind signalled a depressing finality. My stepson, ironically a professional cinematographer, had an automatic flash camera which he wielded with deadly effect. The flash miraculously drove the lion off. The lion was found dead the following morning, not far away. At the time, however, my only concern was to stem the flow of blood and get back to ranch headquarters as quickly as possible. With luck my partner was there with his aeroplane and after initial administration of veterinary antibiotics, we flew on a rising moon into Mombasa. By midnight I was on the operating table with a blood transfusion and all the necessary medication. Fortunately, this was a time before AIDS awareness and with modern therapy I was out in 15 days, not much worse for wear.

My good fortune was brought home to me by a visit while in hospital by an old timer who, in 1904, hunting with a friend, had a similar experience. However, in those days it took him a week by ox wagon to reach hospital and, without antibiotics, he had had his leg strung to the ceiling to drain for another month after which they amputated it anyway!

Before my luck runs out completely I thought I should not chance it anymore and have retired to ranching, leaving my son to do any hunting control. However, 'Old Hunters never Die.' Hunting has always been in my blood, not least because of the wilds that it takes me to, and the special bush friends that accompany me. I still take to the bush occasionally on the odd buffalo hunt to keep my wits active and prove to myself that I can still shoot straight. But more and more I hate the actual killing!

Chapter 27

Hunting Companions and African Friends

No book on Africa can be complete without mention of those local bush men who made it all possible. These men have shown great character and I've built memorable friendships with them across the years. The following stories are the history of some of the men who have been involved with us for many years, starting with Ali.

Ali bin Mohammed Kariuki - Ali, was a warrior gentleman, born on Sangare in 1912. It is fitting that he is buried on the same ground having died in June 2004, at a ripe old age of 92. His mother was a Maasai from Narok and his father a 'Burji' Ethiopian from Marsabit. Being born and raised in a Kikuyu area he was called Kariuki in his younger days.

Sangare in 1912 was no man's land used as a buffer to stop the wars between the Maasai and Kikuyu. It was occupied by a South African whom the Africans called 'Wanyongu.' Wanyongu did all the district's transport using large wagons with a team of sixteen oxen. He left in about 1922 when Ali and his family moved towards Mount Kenya to work on the farm of Captain O'Hagen.

O'Hagen was known to everyone as 'Dudu.' I don't know why, but I suspect it was because he had an unusually large dome at the back of his head akin to that of a grasshopper. He also had a large wart on his cheek from which protruded a long whisker, giving the appearance of an antennae. O'Hagen's farm was on the edge of the Thego Forest. The house was built of cedar off cuts, the whole construction being covered with golden shower and other creepers, giving one the feeling of creeping under a large bush. From the veranda, which looked onto the majestic peaks of Mount Kenya, one could look across to the forest glades where elephant, rhino and buffalo grazed in tranquillity. The inside of the house was dark and panelled and the O'Hagens had it fitted out with superb old English furniture and silver while many fine trophy heads adorned the walls.

Ali Kariuki

Kariuki (the Ali came in later) at about 10 years old was given the job of looking after the house milking cows, which consisted of four special pedigree Friesians. These he took out to graze in the forest glades shared by the bushbuck and eland in which he took such an interest. Dudu asked Kariuki if he would like to learn to shoot. Kariuki was beside himself with enthusiasm. He was given an airgun and instructed in the art of rifle shooting and the proper handling of firearms for his own safety and others. His job was to shoot mouse birds and bulbuls in the vegetable shamba but nothing else. No bird was to be left wounded. If stuck high up in a tree he had to climb up and get it. Again he so excelled at this that it was not long before he graduated to a .22 rifle and was allowed to shoot small buck such as suni, duiker and steinbuck. Again nothing was to be left wounded and he should shoot only males. Also he was only allowed to shoot the animal in the head or neck. His first trophy was a duiker shot with a single shot in the neck. This gave meat for all the household and the many dogs and cats.

He also learnt the art of stalking as no animal was to be shot at at over 50 yards. He learnt to shoot straight, for if an animal was wounded he was not allowed back or given a meal until it was retrieved. If he entered the house with a loaded gun, even in the magazine, or was seen with the rifle pointed in the direction of anybody, then it was confiscated for ten days or more and his wage cut. In about 1928 Dudu thought Kariuki was wasted on the farm and suggested he should send him to Rumuruti to be trained as a Game Scout under the tuition of Jack Bonham, Alex Seaton and J A Hunter. Kariuki walked the sixty miles to be enrolled at 'Kampi ya Simba.' Kariuki remembers being whipped hard until he could hit the bull's eye at 300 yards with a .303. This he did and passed with flying colours. His first assignment was to control wild dog and hyena on Solio Ranch.

Solio was a 68,000-acre spread owned by the Enniskillen family, running beef cattle and a large flock of merino sheep. David Cole, the eldest son, had just arrived from Ireland to manage Solio. These predators were taking many animals, so Kariuki applied for the position as Game Scout to help with control work. Kariuki walked the 60 miles back, for Solio was next door to the O'Hagens, armed with a .303 and several hundred rounds of ammunition. On arrival it took him a week to assess the situation and work out a plan. He soon found the exact location where the wild dog (now a much endangered species) were living and he chose a spot where he could target them all in one go.

He waited several days before he saw a pack of dogs single out and surround an impala, driving it into the water hole where he had chosen to make an ambush. Kariuki waited until the dogs had downed the animal and were wading in. He dropped several, whereupon the bewildered dogs started to kill each other. Kariuki then waded in himself and accounted for 15 animals before the rest took off over the hilltop. David was so impressed that he gave Kariuki a sheep and 100/- to augment his wage of 36/- per month.

For the hyena, Kariuki worked out another plan. He asked David if he could visit the Singh family who had a stone quarry at Kiganjo and bring back some ballast, gelignite and a fuse. David could not imagine what Kariuki was up to, but after his success over the wild dogs, he did not query. In due course, the material arrived and with Kariuki's instructions the load was placed under a large acacia tree. He set up the charge and led the fuse to another tree some way off. There Kariuki set up his hide with camp bed and blanket. One afternoon he shot a zebra and had it dragged to the charged tree where he firmly hung and tied up the carcass. That night soon after dark he heard the whooping of hyena, getting louder and louder as they came nearer.

He waited until there was a mass of them all tearing at the carcass, whooping and laughing as they do. Then he got well behind his tree and lit the fuse. The spark raced along the charge unnoticed by the mob of hyena. Soon there was a mighty bang while debris and bits of carcass were flung about the countryside. Then dead silence for the rest of the night. David, having heard the explosion appeared at dawn. He and Kariuki sorted the carnage and estimated some sixty or so hyena had been accounted for. This was the end of David's stock losses for a long time. He was so pleased that he gave Kariuki another sheep and 1000/- this time. This was a lot of money in those days.

In 1930 Kariuki was posted to Kitui to keep elephant out of the shambas. Alas, I have no stories from that time. Soon after the start of the Second World War with many Italian prisoners of war encamped around Nanyuki, Kariuki was employed to shoot zebra as meat for the prisoners. At this time he was based for most of the time again with the O'Hagens where he helped out shooting meat once again for the household, staff and many dogs. It was during this period that I met Kariuki. My family lived some 16 miles north at Naro Moru.

During the school holidays a school friend, usually Tony Archer, and I would bicycle across to spend several nights with Dudu and go off at dawn with Kariuki. We would be out all day, usually around Kariuki's old haunts around Sangare Hill, which was at the western side of Dudu's land. I remember Kariuki being a tall and very powerful man. If we shot an impala he would disembowel the animal and carry the carcass home single-handed. Once we had to cross the swollen and fast running Rongai River (now no more than a trickle at best). Kariuki lifted Tony and I under each arm and together with rifles lifted us across.

Sometimes we would shoot a big bull eland. Then Tony and I would lie up nearby, while Kariuki sprinted home, some five miles, soon to return with spanned ox cart. We would arrive back late and very tired but before anything else Dudu insisted that the rifles were properly cleaned. After being oiled and wiped, boiling water was poured down the barrel to remove the fouling and then the rifles were placed by the fire to let them sweat. At this point we could take a drink, usually a cup of tea, before going for a wash and change before dinner. But before eating, we oiled and cleaned the rifles again, and Dudu inspected them before putting them in the gun-racked cupboard in the office. Nothing was locked up in those days. Only then could we relax, but not before being thoroughly questioned on the days hunt. What did we see, birds and plants besides other animals? How did we make the stalk, how close were we to the animal when we shot it? Where exactly did we shoot the game? How many shots? Dudu would soon know if we had lied. We knew that if we had not acted as proper sportsmen we would not be invited again or until such time as we had received further schooling from him.

Eric Rundgren or 'Muchungi' as the Africans called him, was the District Game Department Control Officer at the time. Muchungi, 'the man who was always on the move,' had recently retired and became Kerr & Downey's ace white hunter. He also bought a farm at Naro Moru bordering the forest of Mount Kenya. Here he grew wheat with a Danish manager. He employed Kariuki to keep the elephant and buffalo out of the wheat. At this time the Mau Mau rebellion broke out. Kariuki did not like the situation and as much as possible kept to himself hiding and sleeping by day in the field or forest, while protecting the crops by night. Eric was away on safaris most of the time, so Kariuki had no one to confide in. Little did he know that his wife Wangui, together with one of his own brothers, were strong Mau Mau supporters. They reported that Kariuki had not taken a single oath. Though not actually a Kikuyu himself, Kariuki spoke Kikuyu fluently and had married a Kikuyu wife. So they arranged that when Kariuki returned for a night to his hut the local Mau Mau gang would be waiting. Kariuki could not understand why a goat had been slaughtered and a huge meal set out. Soon after dark the hut was surrounded and Kariuki could not escape. His option was to take the oath or be killed. Having taken the oath, he became a very worried man for he was now compelled to do what the Mau Mau instructed him to do or be killed. On the other hand, if the security forces discovered his activities, he also faced death or at least being interned.

Luckily, the Police Officer based at Naro Moru was none other than my friend Tony Archer. Tony soon grasped the situation. He had Kariuki interned and gave him a new identity and sent him out of harm's way.

Hence, Kariuki became Ali Mohamed. Ali's brother worked next door with Jens and Tutti Hessel. They thought Ali's brother was completely loyal until Tony divulged the situation. Thereafter Ali's brother broke away from the Mau Mau and became a loyal gun bearer to Jens for over 30 years. Ali was also employed by Jens and spent 10 years or more running the day-to-day chores of all his safaris. Tutti today has many fond memories of Ali taking special care of her when she joined any safari. "Ali did absolutely everything, from driver to gun bearer to cook to doctor." He protected her when they were too close to dangerous animals, always saw to her personal comforts, and was a protector when Tutti received the wrath of Jens for some demeanour.

After the Emergency Tony Archer joined Kerr & Downey safaris and brought Ali with him. They did many safaris all over Africa. Ali turned his hand to everything from game scout to driver, to skinner, to tracker, to camp staff and protector of clients. When in the late 1970s the hunting ban was imposed, Tony retired from safaris and got Ali a job with Lonhro. He had the mundane job of driver and protector of clients for the Mount Kenya Safari Club and later at the Ark.

By this time I had purchased and now lived on Ali's old Sangare haunts. He was retired from Lonhro on account of age. I managed to get him a job as watchman for Sangare Camp that was leased by Savannah Camps and Lodges. For some years I employed Ali's son, Ndururi. When I sold a section of land after independence, I gave all my old employees a plot of land on this and Ndururi was one of them. He and Ali, however, never saw eye to eye, so in the meantime Tony negotiated for Ali to get ten acres of his own adjacent to me. On this land Ali built his retirement home and grazed a few sheep, which he herded personally almost to the day he died. It was so fitting that Ali was buried almost on the spot where he was born.

Elijah Kagiri Wangai.

Elijah Kagiri Wangai - When I purchased Laburra Farm at Mweiga off 'Posho'and Segrid Pease in 1957, Kagiri already had the position of Headman. Posho was an ex-administrator and a gentleman farmer. Segrid did all the farming and was well loved by her labour. She was very strict but fair, and was known as 'The Bwana Memsahib.' Both Kagiri and his brother Kamau helped Segrid run the farm through the Mau Mau Emergency. It was said they were both awarded 'Loyalist Certificates' for never having taken a single oath. At the time this was an extreme act of bravery and put them and their family in the limelight for horrible and cruel retributions. Segrid was very watchful and careful that this did not happen.

Kagiri had come from another well-known farmer on the Kinangop, Johnny Nimmo. Johnny ruled with an iron hand, but again was fair. My father, who knew Johnny Nimmo well, said he was almost illiterate but an excellent farmer and staunch supporter of the old European Agricultural Settlement Trust for which he was on the board with my father.

So there I was a young man with Kagiri, an experienced cattle man and labour administrator. I must say Kagiri and his brother Kamau taught me an awful lot. I trusted both explicitly. They were very loyal employees for over 20 years. At this time I had a heavy mortgage on the farm and augmented the farm income with some professional hunting.

I would be away for many weeks at a time, but knew that my wife and children were safe and assured that everything on the farm would run without any problems. I am sure Kagiri had Maasai blood, for he looked after the cattle like his children and could see instantly if an animal was sick. He was very strict with the herders. He stood no nonsense with all the workers, but he would never ask anyone to do something that he could not do himself - and he could usually do it a lot better.

I remember once Kagiri caught a herder twisting a cow's tail to get it into the dip. This always annoyed him intensely. He said the chap could bite the tail but not twist and possibly break it. When the herder did just that, the cow gave him a swift kick under the chin and knocked him out. Everyone laughed and no one twisted a cow's tail in Kagiri's presence again! Kagiri passed away in his 90's, a great patriarch of the old school and sadly missed. I attended his funeral and was happy to see how many of his children were leading successful lives. We all missed him and were sad to see him go. They all agreed he had taught them well how to lead their lives.

Ngenge Nginga Ngengi was my head tracker as he had an uncanny, almost instinctual way of understanding animals. If an animal on safari was wounded he would track it to the end without consideration of his own safety. Tracking a wounded lion, leopard or buffalo into thick cover needs extreme caution and observation. He was also quick to be out of the way when something came at us, giving me time to drop the animal before it dropped us. One client, who returned many times, got very annoyed when each time he made a lousy shot and Ngengi gave a disgusted, "Tut tut tut." I suggested Ngengi take the next shot. When he made a clean miss, as happened, we all went, "Tut tut tut." Ngengi did not do it again.

I remember once sitting

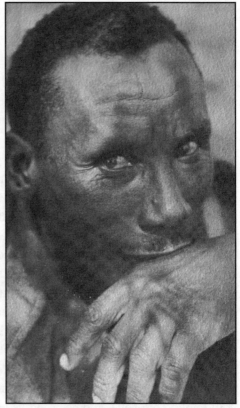

Ngenge Ngengi

in a leopard blind, hardly daring to breathe. An annoying bird kept making a disconcerting regular chirp. Ngengi looked at me fingering his nose each time the bird chirped and we all got the giggles. Then turning to peep through the hole in the bush blind, we found the leopard staring at us through the hole from the opposite side, less than six feet away! The giggles stopped immediately and we all froze waiting to see if it would jump in with us or move away. Luckily it moved away.

I used to make a bet with Ngengi to see if he could creep up to an elephant and stick a stamp onto its bum. Many times he almost made it, but always at the last moment the elephant became aware. In a flash Ngengi disappeared like greased lightning. When the American astronauts were walking on the moon, we happened to be hunting elephant in a very remote corner of Galana. It was a beautiful balmy clear night with a full moon shining bright. I gave Ngenge my field glasses and said, "Look, there are some people walking on that moon."

Adjusting his eyes to looking through the binoculars, he said, "I don't know about anyone walking up there, but I can't see any trees, bushes or elephants, so why bother to be there, let alone looking for them – they must be idiots!"

At home when not on safari he spent his time collecting honey from his many bee hives. When he retired I gave him twenty improved hives and agreed, every few months, to purchase the honey from him. On the first safari to buy his honey I had difficulty in finding him. When I did he was legless. He had made all the honey into pombe (a lethal beer). With a big smile he said he had kept some for me, producing several fermenting 'debes' (containers) to which he had added filthy water with many dead and swimming bees. That is the way it went until his dying day. I still employ several of his sons, but none are quite like Ngengi. All delight in his pombe to this day.

Njui Muchoria - Njui came from the Mbere tribe of lower Embu on the Tana River, the same as Ngengi. He was a meticulous skinner, and would spend hours skinning out trophies, especially 'head skins' for mounting, where the ears, lips, noses and ears had to be turned inside out and every bit of fat removed and then salted. If a client had to be left in the bush for several hours I could rely on Njui more than anyone else to protect them. Many years later a close relation of Njui, who was an eye surgeon, saved my sight in one eye.

I was walking the dogs one evening in 2007 on Sangare when our Labrador ran full tilt into the back of my knees while chasing a hare. I was crossing a valley with thick dry bush and I went headfirst, face down into the bushes. When I recovered and crawled out, I realised one eye was looking up to the sky and the other at my feet.

I realised a stick had pierced the corner of my eye and broken off inside. With one hand over the eye I made for the car and drove home. My third wife Diane was in the UK, so I called my daughter Jessica who lives about 4 kilometres away to come and help extract the stick. When Jessica arrived, we found some tweezers but she said although she could see that there was something, the whole eyeball had swivelled around and there was nothing protruding to grab with the tweezers. So instead she drove me to a doctor in Nyeri who took one look and immediately sent me straight to a surgeon in Nairobi.

The Nyeri doctor said it was just as well Jessica had not tried to pull the stick out as the whole eyeball might have come out with it! It was now dark and they put me in an ambulance for an extremely

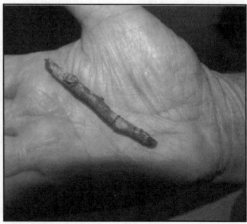

The author in hospital after eye operation to remove stick by Dr Nyaga.

uncomfortable drive to Nairobi. It was midnight before we reached the hospital. Dr Nyagga was in attendance. I was immediately put under a scan and Dr Nyagga took one look and decided to operate. Discovering he was a relative of my Njui, I knew I could not be in better hands.

Gideon Arap Tonui

The theatre was not available till 3 am, but as I was heavily sedated, I knew nothing until dawn. When awake I saw Dr Nyagga looking down upon me. "So what are you going to do?" I asked.

"It's already done," he said. He produced a plastic bottle with the stick inside nearly as thick as a pencil and four inches long. He said he had to remove the eyeball to take out the stick, then replace the eyeball and sew it all up. By extreme luck, neither the eyeball nor any of the tubes that are attached to it, had been pierced or broken. It was two weeks before both eyes settled and began looking at the same place, and today the eye is perfect with not even a scar to show! The surgery was truly amazing.

There are so many more stories of my African companions, but I can only record a few here.

There was Mungai the cook who joined me when I was a DO in Fort Hall in 1953 and remained with me to his dying day in the 1980s. Kipkrui, my house servant and cook, came to me in 1960. He was retired in the 1990s, but he became bored sitting at home so continues to help to this day. Last but not least, my present Headman on the Ranch, Gideon Arap Tonui. He has been with us for 46 years and remains ever loyal.

Chapter 28

FLYING SAFARIS
FRIGHTS AND FLIGHTS

In 1963 I decided to learn to fly. Over the years that followed and over 9000 hours of flying time, I have flown the length and breadth of Africa, and a little bit beyond.

After eight hours of instruction in Nairobi's Wilson Airport, where I learnt to fly in a tail wheel Piper Cub, VP-KFZ, I was ready to purchase my own aeroplane. I found one of the old Piper Pacers, 5Y-KKX, that had been used by the Police Airwing during the Mau Mau Emergency. It had had an engine overhaul and had been refabricated and painted. It cost all of £800 and aviation fuel at that time cost little over 3/- per gallon.

There was no radio at the time; we just flew wherever we wished, but coming into Wilson the instruction was by lights. Green was acceptable to land, red to go round and white just get the hell out of it! My instructor, Bosky, who was flying for Keith Campling's firm at the time, gave me permission to take my plane home and come back for a test when I had completed 40 hours. I had managed to level a piece of ground at Laburra near the house to use as a landing strip. I practised 'circuits and bumps'- landings and take offs. All the farm children including my own, Jessica and Giles, would line up along the fence at the end of the strip to watch this performance.

One day I came in a bit too high and a little too fast. Instead of pulling back on the stick to lose height and speed, I pushed it forward making the craft go faster, although descending. So I hit the ground half way down the strip and at speed. Seeing the fence fast approaching, I pulled hard on the brake. This was a hand brake rather than pedal brakes on each wheel. Unfortunately, the braking system failed. There was nothing for it but to steer between two fence posts and hope for the best. I have never seen the children scatter so rapidly! Breaking through five strands of wire certainly slowed the craft, but unfortunately the left wing strut just tipped a post, which skewed the plane to one side, making us head for the cattle dip. Luckily, before plunging in, the front wheel caught the edge of the dip and we came to a halt! Except for a slight bend of the strut no further harm was done.

It was a day or two before I made contact with Bosky. Bosky had been a Spitfire pilot during the Battle of Britain, and was one of the few who survived a bail out after being shot down. So a minor bend was of little concern to him. If the wing was still firmly attached, then it would be alright to fly and bring the plane down and have the strut replaced. "What about the brakes" I asked.

"When you land just steer towards the hangar, but switch off and stop the engine in good time and we will just hold you back and place a chock on the front wheel." It transpired the brake line had been rubbing against the fuselage, and the extra pressure of a hard pull had caused the fluid to break through and it had all squirted out.

Our good friends and neighbours, Jens and Tutti Hessel, had also learnt to fly at the same time. They, too, had a sister Tri-Pacer 5Y-KMH. Their daughter Josephine was a boarder with Jessica at Greensteds School for girls at Nakuru, on the other side of the Aberdare Mountains, to us. Giles was also a boarder at Pembroke House School for boys at Gilgil, some 25 miles from Nakuru. Returning to school at the end of one holiday, we decided Jens would fly the girls back to school while I flew Giles to Pembroke. Jens took off first. Just after take off we heard a bang and a change of engine noise in Jen's plane, but it carried on and disappeared out of sight, so we thought no more about it. After I took off with Giles, I turned towards the Aberdares and noticed a plane on the ground just below the Aberdare Country Club. "Funny," I thought, "I never knew there was a landing strip there." On a closer look I saw to my dismay that it was Jens! As I flew over them the girls waved at us. It transpired that the bang we had heard was a blown engine plug that had taken out the complete hellier coil! The plane kept flying but with considerable loss of power. Jens, being a very capable pilot, had somehow held the plane aloft before plunging into the Amboni River gorge, and made a perfect, though rough, landing in a field on the far side.

The blown engine plug was fixed in no time, and after making a rough strip at the site, Jens flew out alone. This meant an extra night at home so the girls were quite happy. The following day, flying Giles over the Aberdares, we noticed a glade with some thirty bongo out in the open. This indeed was a rare sighting of these elusive antelopes, and it would become even rarer in the future. To capture this sight, we turned and made a rush for home, picking up my 8 mm cine camera, informing Bill Woodley, the Warden of the Aberdare Park. Luckily the bongo were still in this location and we took lots of footage. Bill said if the parks put up another 'Tree House' this is where he would recommend it to be. In due course the Ark Lodge was established on this site.

On another occasion after dropping Giles off at Pembroke House School, he found he'd forgotten his Bible. He knew he'd get in trouble from the school for not having his Bible, so I got a frantic message to bring his Bible. I put the Bible in a plastic bag and flew back to Pembroke, dropping the bagged Bible onto the playing field and headed home, mission accomplished. I only heard much later that the Bible had exploded into a flurry of pages on impact and Giles and school friends like Nigel Carnelly had to desperately dive all over the school compound to gather the pages and piece the Bible back together. And Giles still got in trouble for having a few missing pages!

The Tri-Pacer aeroplane was a fun and very forgiving little four-seater. With the birth of Vivien, our family of five could just squeeze in. We spent many weekends flying away to camps and lodges all over the country. When we acquired Luoniek Ranch it took us only 45 minutes to fly there while it was half a day's journey by road.

Sometimes on a safari I sent the vehicles ahead to make a camp and a rough airstrip on site. We could have a couple of extra days hunting on Sangare before flying the client to camp. When Luoniek Ranch was later replaced by Galana Ranch near the coast, Marty Anderson suggested we get a larger and more powerful plane.

I found a Cessna 180 tail dragger 5Y- TCL, the perfect bush plane. It was still only a four-seater, but it could fly with whatever one could put in it. This plane too was ex-Police Airwing, but it had been completely overhauled. I was lucky to purchase it from the bank for a reduced price of £1,200 after a default in payment from its previous owner. Meanwhile the Tri-Pacer was passed on to the manager of Galana Ranch. The Cessna 180 was a very spirited aircraft with so much power it could land and take off on rough ground and short strips. I used it extensively on safaris, and for the opening up of Galana, to fight fires, site new roads and dams and for regular game counts. I never made it spin, but delighted in stalling, turning passengers green with fright, dive bombing friends and pulling up steeply to near stall. Today I am more mindful of the saying: "There are lots of old pilots and lots of bold pilots, but no old bold pilots."

After Gill my first wife died in late 1973 I married Jane in 1975. She had a great interest in flying, too, and later took her own pilot's license. We flew ourselves all over Africa and made one flight to England. Our good friend Eric Rundgren, whom Jane had also known since childhood, had retired on a large game ranch in South Africa. We flew down to visit him regularly. This was very much an Afrikaans area and Eric, now alone after his second wife had returned to the USA, was somewhat lonely. We had great times together driving and flying all over that country, until Eric emigrated to northern Australia where he died and I never saw him again.

Fishing on Lake Turkana

It was a very busy time of life in the mid-1970s. Jane enjoyed entertaining and our house on Sangare was forever full of guests. Jane ran several tourists shops around the country. We made many flights with the family during the children's school holidays, including interesting flights to the 'Jade Sea' (Lake Turkana) in the very north of Kenya to catch giant Nile perch. We would fly in several aircraft and land on South Island. There was no real airstrip; we just landed in a sand lugga, landing up hill, using the heavy sand to create an immediate stop. For take off we taxied with full power to the top of the hill, then rushed downhill, getting up speed before hitting the water, and away we went – hopefully. We caught perch using live bait, usually tilapia, which we cast out as far as possible standing on rocks at the water's edge, aided by balloons tied to the line. At the time this part of the lake was rarely fished, so practically every cast brought in a perch. We carried beer and drinks in cold boxes filled with dry ice and as we drank the contents we filled the cold boxes with Nile perch fillets to take home.

Once when fishing with Tony Seth-Smith I was reeling in a perch and just as I was about to land it, a monster perch took the fish on my line. I yelled to Tony to come and help gaffe the monster. Tony took a swipe with the gaffe (a hook on an extended rod), but slipped on the rocks and went in himself. He tried to catch the fish by putting his hand through the gills, whereupon both Tony and the monster perch shot out to sea, diving to the bottom. It seemed ages before Tony came gasping to the surface, sadly without the fish.

On most of these trips Punch Bearcroft would fly up in a second aeroplane. One time Punch suggested we find a landing spot in a gorge at the south end, where no one had ever fished before. Punch had a small but powerful Reims Rocket, so we went together in this for a first landing. On the ground we marked out the spot between two thorn trees where we should touch down, then removed some boulders and filled up some wash outs over a 400-yard strip so we could bring in the Cessna 206.

Punch had a son the same age as Giles, so together we made many trips into this area. There is a strong, continuous howling wind on this side of Lake Turkana, but our gorge was mostly sheltered from it. Unfortunately, by being out of the wind mosquitoes plagued us at night. On our first night, we had no mosquito nets, so in order to have any sleep we had to move our camp beds up onto the ridge. This was quite a haul but good practice for the boys, especially after we erected the first camp bed and the wind blew it straight back to the bottom again. To avoid this situation repeating, once we had erected the light 'Hounsfield' camp beds we loaded them down with lava rocks, which were only removed when replaced by a body. It was vital to ensure the rocks were replaced if one wanted to return to a bed after getting up in the middle of the night!

Punch only had one hand, so when fishing he often got tangled up with the fishing line, when both he and the fish would plunge back into the lake. One of us always had a rifle on standby to ward off any approaching crocodile.

One could fish any time during the day or evening, so in the early mornings we would fly off to South Horr in the Chalbi desert where thousands of sand grouse would come in to drink at precisely 8 o'clock in the morning at the water hole there. With four guns we would soon have enough birds for a change in our diet of fish. We added any leftover birds to the fish in the cold boxes to take home. Once we finished the beer and filled the boxes full of fish and sand grouse we flew home to await a return when the home larders were empty.

Flying for Gold

One day in late 1979 Tony Seth-Smith asked if I would be interested in going into partnership with him on a gold mining project on the Turkwell River in western Kenya. He had been approached by an Australian geologist called Campbell Bridges who had a concession in the area and needed help with the ground operations. The idea was that Tony and I, under Campbell's instruction and using his mining equipment, would get the operation in the field underway then fly the gold as procured, if any, back to Nairobi. Jack Block would organise sale permits and do the selling and sharing of the proceeds after costs.

The Turkwell River came off the northern end of the Cherengani Mountains eventually flowing into Lake Turkana in northern Kenya. It was a very remote and inaccessible area with spectacular scenery.

Author and Tony Seth-Smith flying into the gold operation in Turkana.

The Cherengani escarpment descends some 3000 feet into the Kerio valley via Tot and the Turkwell gorge.

Tony arranged the initial transport, camping equipment and provisions. We were to be based at a farm owned by the Barnleys, between Kitale and Kapenguria, which had a small airstrip. Tony, Campbell and I flew in establishing a camp halfway down the escarpment on the edge of the Turkwell.

Small riverbeds, usually dry, ran into the Turkwell River, which always had flowing water. Campbell said all of them bore pure alluvial gold. He claimed the bulk of the gold had probably settled some 30 feet down at the bottom of the riverbeds in a 'golden pool' of pure solid gold. However, to get at it would take a huge effort and require some very expensive equipment. Transporting such equipment into the area would be beyond our means. Therefore, we decided to just work near the surface to see what percentage of gold we could procured from panned soil. Campbell had brought along some plastic 'panning' pans, and a machine onto which we poured liquid sand.

This was powered by a portable petrol engine, which shook the contents, dispersing the soil and leaving the heavier gold to be collected on the bottom.

Establishing camp, we set about panning and shaking the sands, but no gold appeared. Campbell became frustrated and said we were just a bunch of morons and we had not a clue what we were doing. Tony nicknamed him 'Afrogas' (waka mara moja) meaning Swahili for a gas that lights immediately. On the third day of our pathetic gold mining shamble, we noticed a bare-bottomed Turkana standing on one foot and leaning on his spear with a big grin on his face.

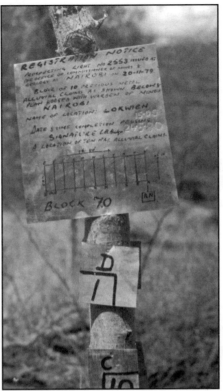

Turkwell gold mining claim.

"You people haven't a clue how to find gold," he said.

"Well, how do we go about it then?"

"Bring me a *karai* (a traditional African cooking bowl)."

"Try this special panning tool," we suggested.

"That's no good, just give me a karai." We gave him a karai and he disappeared, returning to our camp in the evening. Out of his hair he produced a porcupine quill with a wooden plug. He removed the plug and poured a few grains of gold onto the palm of his hand. "If you get me many karais, I will bring all my people here and you can buy the gold we collect."

At last we had made some progress and purchased his gold. We said we would return the next week. Tony suggested he return to Kitale and buy up all the karais and fill his lorry with posho to feed the Turkana, while I flew Campbell back to Nairobi with his kit and to test the gold.

To our delight and amazement the gold turned out to be some 20 karats! We purchased six sets of gold weighing scales and flew back to the Barnleys to meet up with Tony who had bought out Kitale's stock of 300 karais. With a lorry full of posho we returned to the Turkwell. At the same time we collected a friend, Van Someren, who had sold his farm at Mweiga and was now living with his Kikuyu wife on a small property in Kitale and who desperately needed a job. Van jumped at the idea. He was to manage the camp, collect and store the gold, while Tony and I would fly in with the money to purchase it and take the 'pots of gold' back to Nairobi. He would also prepare some rough airstrips on the site so I could get the Cess 180 in and out to bring in the rations. We set up six weighing stations along the river. Records were taken of what was owed to each person, and a price set per gram to pay the Turkana. Van stored the gold, burying this in his loo, which he thought may be the safest place. We also set up an HF radio so we could keep in contact. We needed to know what had been collected and how much money would be required to purchase the gold. All payments were in 50 cent pieces!

For three months the process worked like a dream, then more and more Turkana came in. This meant more and more food had to be purchased and even more money brought in to purchase the actual gold. Women and children appeared too, and we had to keep medicines to dress the sick and wounded. We had several airstrips but all of these were at the absolute minimum in smoothness and length. With either Campbell or Tony to operate the hand-lever wing flaps, we had to gather enough speed to take off. I would call out two or three notches, whichever I figured would be required to jump the trees at the end of the strip, before we were away. It was not easy!

Panning for gold in the Turkwell.

On flying in we would be sitting ducks for any bandits. Each time we used a different pre-arranged strip and had a good scout around before landing. A Kikuyu group soon appeared in competition, but they did not last long. One night their camp was raided by the Turkana with the leader being bound while they castrated him and sewed his testicles into his mouth. We then had to employ armed guards, as ours was the only legitimate licenced operation.

When digging down for gold there is a formula on how wide to dig the top according to how deep the hole will be. The Turkana dug down like beavers until one of the women was drowned by a fall coming in on top of her. Then when cholera broke out the administration said we had to have a dispensary and school for the young instead of using underage workers. All this was not feasible in such a remote area and the gold was not sufficient to cover this type of expense. So, we continued with a fixed labour force. We then purchased a tractor and some implements. The first was an ox plough operated with a man behind and drawn by the tractor. My ex-safari man Ngengi was the first to try to operate this, but in the wet sand by the river the plough went in too deep. The handle shot up and knocked him out with a blow under the chin. We all laughed at the sight, but Ngengi did not think it so funny.

We added a Greek to our team who knew all about mining and brought in a special dredging and panning machine. He chose a site to cross the Turkwell River and drove the tractor himself deeper and

deeper until all went underwater. Nothing could be seen but the Greek's broad brimmed hat floating on the top. They emerged on the far side, but everything was choked in sand. Both the Greek and tractor had to be overhauled before further use. Even after

Left to Right: Rene Babault, Mike Prettejohn and Tony Seth-Smith.

337

this trial no gold could be procured. So we went back to Turkana manpower.

Van had to return home and his place was taken over by my ex-brother-in-law, Jock Rutherfurd, whose farm at Soy had recently been purchased. Jock was an excellent administrator and had good control over the Turkana. He kept a tight control of the gold and held enough cash to pay on a daily basis. He kept the gold in film canisters hidden in the loo, as before. A prominent politician came into the area to compete with our gold operation. He had a European manager we called Red Head, but we had never met. Soon after this rival operation started there was a raid one night on Jock's camp. Jock resisted and the raiders shot him in the chest with a pistol. There was no vehicle in camp at the time, as Jock had sent it to Kitale for rations. The nearest neighbour was a mission station some sixty miles away. Camp staff sent runners and messages and before dawn Jock was taken to the station for treatment. By early morning a message was sent to Nairobi and the Flying Doctors came in to take him to the Nairobi Hospital where doctors removed the bullet. Thankfully, it had done no internal damage. However, we agreed after that incident to end our gold mining episode! I sold my share of the gold to an ex-Danish client Peter Didrichsen and bought a new Toyota Land Cruiser with the cash proceeds.

The Little Bit Beyond

In September 1979 Jane and I decided to fly our Cessna 206, 5Y-AUN to England and back. My youngest daughter Vivien and her great school friend Lucy Wood had passed into a 6th Form College in Oxford to do their International Baccaloria. We thought this would be a fun and interesting way of getting them there. Also my eldest daughter Jessica was about to get married and we had to collect a wedding dress. It took awhile to make a flight plan, secure all the maps and obtain the necessary permits to land or to overfly. We had a minimum of instrumentation in the plane and sorely missed having a transponder (an instrument to indicate exactly where you are in relation to other flying aircraft). In those days we didn't yet have a GPS (global positioning system). We decided I would do all the flying and Jane would navigate. The two girls in the back seats would act as hostesses keeping us with food and drinks. (Not too much to drink, as we knew there would be long flights with no toilet facilities.) They were seated in the rear as we removed the two middle seats to fit a drum with 200 extra litres of fuel and an electrical pump to top up the left wing tank giving us a good 10 hours non-stop flying if necessary.

We were also advised it would be of great assistance in dealing with airport officials if we wore captain's stripes. This indeed proved to be the case, and we borrowed a couple of pairs from pilots at Wilson. Navigation had to be precise. Jane would hold the current map of 1: 1000,000 and with a ruler and flying tools give us a precise location every half hour or so, or when over a prominent position. Without a spot beam location we aimed at a position some five miles either left or right of a target. On reaching that point we knew we were left or right, as the case may be, of our destination. Also, we were used to flying around the equator where one's variation was very slight. As we moved north this increased and unless we synchronised the gyro compass while on the ground, the regular compass would swing

Daughter Vivien and Lucy Wood, 'air hostesses' on our flight to UK.

so drastically that it was impossible to follow accurately and one could get hopelessly lost. Also without a GPS to home in to the point of intended landing, if avoiding a storm or some other diversion, one had to be precise on the angle and time off course. We would then need to work out how to regain that route. Luckily, we never did get lost! However, on one flight with Sandy Field, a friend and fellow aviator who was doing the navigating, I told him we were way off course. He got in such a fluster that

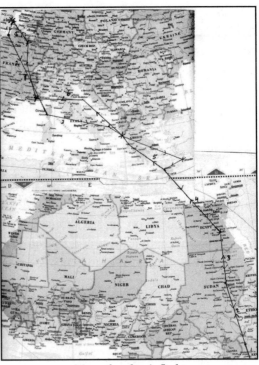

Map of author's flight, Nairobi-London Sept. 1979.

his knees wobbled while ruler, gadgets and map fell to the floor and rolled under his seat.

By September 7th 1979, the day before my birthday, we were ready to set off from Nairobi Wilson Airport for Lodwar in northwest Kenya. Arriving at Lodwar, where we arranged to refuel at the local mission station, a ragged *toto* rolled a fuel drum up to the aircraft, which we filled up from with a small hand pump and filter we always carried. Nothing is more disconcerting than a spluttering engine with water or dirty fuel. Clearing customs, we flew on to Ferguson's Gulf on Lake Turkana for the night in a comfortable camp.

September 8th 1979 saw us up bright and early for the long non-stop flight to Khartoum in the Sudan. The route took us over very wild and interesting country, little occupied except by bandits. On leaving the northwest Kenya border we first flew over Ethiopia where the little known but greatest of all animal migrations known takes place. Thousands upon thousands of white-eared kob leave the highlands for the Sudd. Flying on from Ethiopia we entered the Sudan flying space over the Sudd and continued down the Nile to Khartoum, arriving some six hours and 25 minutes later. It was gratifying to be able to keep the fuel tanks full, although our own tanks sorely needed a 'refill' but we dared not drink much during the flight. With no reason to prolong a stay in Khartoum, where officialdom took hours, we continue our flight the next day.

We departed early on the 9th September 1979 and set off up the Nile for Luxor. The authorities advised us to keep away from the Nile, especially over the Aswan Dam, which they feared we might bomb! We did fly over Abu Simbel and on to Luxor where our stripes led them to greet us as 'El Captain.' We had lots of chat without too much red tape. In Luxor we stayed in a very comfortable hotel overlooking the Nile and that evening went to a wonderful 'Son et Lumiere' narrated by Laurene Olivier at the Karnac Temple. Before dark we walked the souk and talked to some of the desert Arabs. Jane had lived a while in the Sudan and spoke Arabic well and we conversed with these interesting wild people. They were fascinated with Lucy's long blond hair and could not help stroking it. Someone made an offer to buy her for 20 camels. We said that as she came from a very distinguished family (her uncle was knighted for his part in creating the 'Flying Doctor Service') she was worth at least 50! We had to tell them in the end that her father Chris would not part with her for any amount of camels.

On September 10th we set off for Heraklion on the island of Crete, a very long flight of six hours and 15 minutes over desert and then over the Mediterranean. We were ordered to avoid the Nile and route via 'the Green Valley' maintaining 20,000 feet. The so-called Green Valley meant retracing our course so we cut a corner and kept to our normal 1000 feet or so above ground. We did not discover why it was called the Green Valley; it was just mile upon mile of desert and endless sands. It was a pleasure to reach the Mediterranean Sea, although a forced landing on sand would have been preferable to water and rough waves. We were given certain points to communicate our position. These were just points on the map to us, as nothing was visible except sand or water. Only carrying a VHF radio we were soon out of touch with anybody. However, reporting our position blind over the Mediterranean a Pan Am aircraft forwarded our message for us. They also said, "What fun piloting your own small craft."

"Fun, yes indeed," we replied, "but somewhat lonely at this point."

"Not to worry," they replied. "You have the world's largest fleet under you, the Russians!" Despite this fact, we only saw one ferry the whole way across the Mediterranean.

Eventually Crete came into sight. We dived towards the airport holding our thighs tight in desperate need of the loo. But alas the air controllers on the island directed us miles back out to sea to join the correct flight path in. What a relief to be able to dash for a pee on landing. All the officials wanted to do was chat. They told us we could remove our stripes, as we were no longer in Egypt.

After two long flights, we needed a bit of rest, so the next day the 11th of September we flew from Heraklion over the sea to the Greek island of Kefallonia, a mere two-and-a-half-hour flight. This was the original home of Jane's greatest friends the Contomichalas. Kefallonia was a very attractive island but we found it too full of British tourists. We stayed in a horrid hotel with bad food and wondered why we had chosen such a place to spend our extra day, but we needed some rest!

On the 13th September we headed for Cannes stopping off in Corfu at Kerkyra to clear customs before continuing up the east coast of Italy over the Adriatic. We had wonderful views of the fierce looking Albania Coast and mountains before crossing over the top of Italy. We did not realise how high the Alps were at this point until we came too close to some high peaks and had to climb up through cloud to get over them. Climbing through cloud seemed endless especially as we should have only been flying visual. Jane kept her eyes glued to the artificial horizon, the speedometer and the compass direction. We were taught that without instrument rating one had two minutes before the fateful dive. Breaking cloud we were not quite level but quickly righted our position. Arriving in Cannes we had a great epicurean evening feasting on oysters and moules much to the horror of Vivien and Lucy. What a pleasant change to eat French after Greek food while sitting outside colourful cafés watching the passersby.

We had a leisurely start on September 14th 1979 and flew the length of France stopping en-route at Dijon (of mustard fame) and landed just on the border of Belgium at a small airport called Sedan where we were met by Michel de Mervious and taken to their delightful home and estate La Forge, in the Ardennes. Michel and Francoise were Belgians who had to flee the Congo after independence. They had happened to be staying next door to us at Mweiga and we found them one day wandering over the farm looking at birds. With this meeting we formed a lasting friendship making several safaris with them taking horses and zebroids up Mount Kenya and another with camels to the Northern Frontier. It was wonderful to now experience 'their' home. Michel would not have anything mechanical on the farm so everything was done by horses. It was a beautiful setting and Vivien often visited them while schooling in England and also learnt to speak French at the same time.

We made a short flight of just under two hours to England on 15th

Arrival at Southend, Oct. 2nd 1979.

September landing at Southend. The train on to London took us two-and-a-half hours. The whole flight from Kenya to England took us 28 hours and 10 minutes, over nine days.

Having deposited Vivien and Lucy safely in Oxford and collected Jessica's wedding dress, we set off for Southend on October 2nd 1979 staying in a small bed and breakfast with plans to fly out on the 3rd. We had left the aircraft to have a service and inspection. We found it all ready for us to go. The service, however, had been done by a Piper Agency and they set the front wheel too extended. We got the impression we were in a tail wheel craft. Used to flying tail wheels I did not worry and as the weather was deteriorating we decided not to waste time rectifying the oleo but to get going.

We had planned only to fly across the channel landing at Dieppe to stay with Kenya friends, Alan and Shirley Douglas Du Fresne. Alan had inherited a beautiful and famous Manoir Grauchet, but had no capital to run it. Life was a constant challenge as the place needed many repairs. Alan had to live there ten years before he could sell it on. The weather turned very cold and misty and flying the English Channel the sea soon merged with the sky! Dieppe was closed for visual aircraft but we were let in on a 'special VFR.' The mist was on the ground and all we could make out were the lights of the landing strip. It was a tough landing with our hard and extended oleo.

Before going on to Alan's we adjusted it ourselves letting out air and oil to get the right pressure. Alan and Shirley lived by an Aga stove in the kitchen. All but two of the many bedrooms were closed. The only bathroom was served for hot water by having to take up a lump of firewood before bathing and stoke up the boiler in the bathroom itself. The boiler too had to be filled with water first by manipulating a chain downstairs that also indicated the water level. A real 'Heath Robinson' contraption, which obviously gave Alan ideas for developments when he eventually returned to Kenya! There was no central heating or any other form of heating. I remember being as cold at night as camping in the snow on Mount Kenya. This cold must have been very difficult for Alan and Shirley as they were used to living at Baringo in Kenya with no shirts or shoes.

The Manoir had been used as a hospital for French troops during the First World War and Madam Grauchet was one of the few French ladies who did such nursing work. Women from England helped her. Jane found a photograph of her aunt who had been one of those English VADs as the helpers were called. In spite of the weather we enjoyed our stay in such good company, spending two nights before the weather cleared for us to continue.

We were slightly nervous of going back over Egypt, as they would not reply to our requests to land and overfly. They told us if we went without permission we would be liable to be shot down. So on the 5th October we took off from Dieppe heading for Ajaccio in Corsica. The flight path took us over Lyon where we had to maintain a certain height. We told them we were in cloud at this level and requested visual. "Too bad," they replied. "Stay at your given level." We broke cloud and had a near miss with a passing Cess 210! With a transponder this would not have happened. It is now a mandatory piece of equipment. Beaming in to Ajaccio airport it appeared we would hit this huge rock. It did not bother us, but we wondered how the airliners coped.

On 6th October 1979 we had planned to fly over Italy, but with bad weather and even airlines being diverted, we set forth for Brindisi down the west coast. We were most pleasantly welcomed and enjoyed our stay with different but enjoyable food and met many interesting 'yachties.' Again without a transponder and flying past the flight path into Rome, we were made to keep only 50 feet above the water and six miles out to sea all the way down the coast.

Before leaving we had to report to the police but were told they did not function before 9 am. We arrived soon after 9 am but it appeared they were still not functioning, as the guard was asleep with his rifle resting against the gate. I gave the butt a push with my shoe making the rifle fall across him and so waking him up. This worked a treat and he staggered to his feet with much saluting and many apologies. All paperwork appeared in order to continue the flight. Alas, there was one problem. Did we have a dinghy for the sea crossing, and could they see it. No, we had no dinghy; but managed to purchase an inflatable child's duck, which did the trick and was passed without inflating for the required piece of equipment.

On the 7th October we departed for Kekira on the island of Corfu. A beautiful isle and we did not mind staying two nights while still waiting for our Egyptian clearance. On the 9th October we planned to fly on to Heraklion. The weather deteriorated and we found ourselves over a sea of endless cloud. So instead we got permission to land on Rhodes where they assured us the weather was clear. A hole in the clouds appeared and much to our relief we saw Rhodes. We had an enjoyable stay.

On the 10th October we flew on to Heraklion where our clearance for Egypt had arrived. Despite our earlier fears, when we arrived in Egypt the authorities asked, "Why are you late, we have been waiting for you for days." We retraced our steps to Luxor, Khartoum and Lodwar. Not much was visible on the flight back as there were many sand storms called 'haboobs' where the sand filled the air up to 9000 feet. We flew high over this as any sand intake into the engine would have acted like sand paper in the cylinders.

The stay in Khartoum was memorable for partying with many old friends who we had not seen in a long time. Pat Neylan, a Kenya friend, was there in a quandary. He was ferrying out a new crop-spraying plane and had filled the spray tanks with extra fuel. On landing he discovered these tanks were leaking and a huge puddle of petrol formed around his craft. He was made to push it way off the edge of the airport until it was fixed. How he did this and how long it took I forgot to ask when next I met him in Kenya. But at least he had made the journey somehow. We arrived back at Wilson Airport in Nairobi and to our own home on the 15th October. The flight back had taken 39 hours and 50 minutes over 10 days. We were glad to be home safe and sound and with Jessica's wedding dress intact. I think we donated the inflatable rubber duck to some children's party. I rather wished we had kept it as a souvenir. We both felt pleased with our achievement and shared an experience of a lifetime.

Flights to Collect Butterflies

Once the hunting ban had been imposed in 1976 I had no more excuses not to visit out of the way places. Inspired by Steve Collins, the world-renowned authority on African butterflies, I once more became interested in butterfly collecting. This hobby took me to outlandish places. Together we flew to all corners of Africa in this pursuit, mostly to the jungles of West Africa. One such flight was to Kinshasa in the Congo. This flight took us over a sea of jungle for mile upon mile. With no mod cons such as GPS we tried to follow roads and tracks where possible. Many of these were not visible from the air except by lines of mango trees where pits had been discarded by ground travellers and trees had grown.

Steve at the time worked for Monsanto, the large US chemical firm and was in charge of their African operation. So he had arranged for an ENRA vehicle from Robert Ducarme to be available for us at Kinshasa airport. Once flying over the airport, I could get no wireless communication so I made several circuits before landing. There were several aircraft strewn around the airport with engines and pieces falling out of them, and also a large military presence. On landing, several armoured cars dashed towards us, surrounded the plane and indicated we follow them to the parking lot. There they wanted to know why we had not announced our presence on radio. I replied I had tried without response. It transpired they had changed frequency the day before. Having said we were on ENRA business and that our

Ch. prettejohni ♀ f. dweitzi-like ʀ

Charaxes Prettejohni from Rubondo Island in Lake Victoria was named after the author on Steve Collins' recommendation for his help on many butterfly safaris.

vehicle was waiting for us (it was the only vehicle at the airport), they led us to immigration and customs. We spent the rest of the morning in negotiations and had to part with hundreds of dollars. We thought we were ready to depart when a man in a much-stained white coat claimed he was the health officer. He insisted we show him all our inoculation papers. We dispensed a few more dollars until finally we were ready to set out.

Jumping into the Land Rover at last, with Steve at the wheel and all our kit in the back, we were ready to go, with Peter, Steve's main collector man. Just as we drove out of the airport, a policeman blew his whistle holding up his hand to bar further progress. Apparently, we had driven out of an 'in' sign. So we handed out yet another dollar bill.

Besides procuring new butterfly specimens, the main object of this trip was to look for a female *Charaxe Thysi*. Although there were some males in collections, only one female had ever been collected and that was in the 1930s. To get to the main forest we had to drive through much secondary forest. There were many abandoned and burnt out buildings, including a church where all the missionaries had been locked in and burnt alive years earlier during the Simba Rebellion.

On reaching the main forest we set up camp, Steve and I sharing a small pup tent. Early on that first night a tropical storm hit us – a huge electrical storm with much thunder and forked lightning. Dead trees crashed to the ground and we soon realised we'd set up out tent underneath a large tree. If it had fallen on us, we would have been obliterated. The following day after moving the tent we set about putting up butterfly traps with banana bait and while driving down an old forest track we suddenly drove through a strip of grass that had been set across the track with a man frantically waving us down. Thinking he was merely trying to catch a lift we drove on. The back of the Land Rover had a metal cover, and just as we passed through the barrier there was a deafening crash on the back of the car as a giant tree hurtled down on top of us, damaging the back metal cover. Milliseconds earlier it would have landed on the cab with us inside. There were two men cutting down the tree and one of the biggest branches had hit us. It took some time in cutting this up to extricate us, and with the aid of a big jack and hammers we managed to straighten out the back.

We ambushed our morning deposits (our own dung!) as bait, excellent for male *Charaxes* butterflies. Steve managed to catch a very rare specimen of the *Charaxe Superbus* on his. We collected six specimens of the *Charaxe Thysi,* but they were all males. When our time was up, Steve arranged to leave his man Peter with the locals for an extra month to try for the female. When Peter eventually found his way home to Kenya, he looked drawn and thin. Peter said, "Don't you realise those people were cannibals. If you ate too well you would potentially find yourself in a cooking pot!" Peter had only managed to find one wing of a female *Thysi*.

We flew back clearing at the border with Uganda. There they made us empty the plane of all baggage while leading us to the office to have our passports stamped before we could reload. Steve had left in a hurry with the wages for his people back home hidden in the plane. When we got home he found this had been discovered and stolen while we were doing our paperwork.

On another trip we flew into Brazzaville to stay with a French collector there in the Moyen Congo or Congo Republic. He had arranged for us to stay in a French camp based at Ouesso some 800 kilometres to the north, where the French were building a new road through solid jungle to connect the two places. A commercial flight flew provisions once a week into Ouesso on which we could get seats. Steve spoke French as a Frenchman, but all I had was a few words remembered from French at school. Steve boarded the aircraft ahead of me while I was stopped on entering by a hostess enquiring what I was carrying. I had my nets and a bottle of fermenting banana on which many flies were gathering. All I could muster were the words, "Bananes malade (sick bananas)." She thought this so funny that I was let on board without further questioning.

At Ouesso the French had a huge camp with tennis courts and several large generators that boomed away day and night. Each day we got dropped off on the edge of the pristine forest and caught a lift back in the evening. Thanks to the booming generators we could make for the road each evening without getting lost. It was a supreme opportunity to collect many new and exotic specimens. We had planned to be out a week but that week the aeroplane never came, so we spent two weeks in this amazing location.

On returning, we made for the airstrip, which had just been hacked out of the forest without any buildings or even a shade structure. On arrival we saw a great heap of luggage piled on the bare earth including parrots in cages and enough junk to fill two planes. So when the plane eventually

Author setting a trap for Charaxes butterflies.

arrived, a twin-engine islander, there was a rush to get on board. Armed gendarmes stopped this rush. They herded us to the edge of the strip to await a command to board. Storm clouds started to gather, but no move was made to board the craft.

Then a distant wailing was heard and a procession approached the plane, the people waving banana trees and bearing a coffin. Apparently an important commander had died several days before and his body was to be returned to Brazzaville. The coffin was oozing slightly to say the least and flies massed around it. It was loaded into the luggage department and all the baggage was literally thrown on top, which only made it leak further. Steve and I made sure our luggage was included, before it was piled to the top and the door slammed shut. Unfortunately, the coffin was too long to close the baggage cabin door, so it protruded into the passenger compartment. The mighty rush of passengers followed. Steve and I made sure of our seats. He pushed aside a big fat bottom that was about to sit on his lap. Eventually the stewards pushed the surplus passengers out and slammed the door, but two more were sitting on the loo and they had to be removed before we took off.

With sweating brows the two pilots just lifted the plane off the ground at the very last moment as we staggered away over the forest, solid trees as far as the eye could see. We had hardly been airborne when the storm broke. I noticed one pilot throttling back, but the other pilot thrust it forward again. As we battled the storm, the plane jolted around. The coffin started moving into the passengers leaving a trail of fluid as it jumped around. This mixed with vomiting passengers was most unpleasant and I thought this was no way to travel! Thankfully we arrived in Brazzaville in one piece only too happy to be on solid ground!

Yet another collecting flight took us to Rwanda. We landed at Kigali where a train of luggage carts was driven to the plane for us to unload. This cost an arm and a leg as Steve had to hire the whole contraption. They had no single carry cart for small planes. We collected many new specimens from Rwanda's remaining Nyungwe forest. From here we made our way on to the Congo planning to look over the forests around Lake Kivu and the volcanoes. It was a brilliant clear blue sky as we flew westward with a mass of billowing white clouds hovering over the hills in front. I made the mistake of going over the top, but as we continued the clouds moved upwards faster than we could climb until we were completely amassed in cotton wool. As the volcanoes stood at 16,000 feet I knew we still had to climb up. But at this height we were still engulfed in cloud. Then through a gap below we saw the glowing waters of Kivu. Spiralling down we made it below the clouds with plenty of room to spare to slowly descend in an orderly fashion. Returning by the same route we made sure to keep below the clouds, in spite of having to steer via lower ground, to land safely at Kigali.

Over the years Steve and I have collected all over Africa. Steve continues to have people on the ground in many countries sending in specimens. Samples of Steve's collection are housed in the Natural History Museum in London and other national institutions, while he keeps a large butterfly house in Nairobi. He keeps breeding specimens and growing their food plants around his home.

Steve tells about one collecting trip. "On another safari to the eastern Congo we were to land at Bunia, the initial port of entry, before proceeding. As we overflew, the ground controller came in with wavy French instructions. Mike asked me to talk to the controller (the universal language for air traffic control is English, but Swahili would have been better). The communication kept fading in and out and when we landed we remarked how difficult it was to sometimes hear and understand the instructions. When they showed us the air traffic control system it became very clear why. The power source was a dynamo of a pedal bicycle. The harder the operator pedalled the clearer the transmission!"

Baringo Rescue

I flew in to Baringo once to visit Betty Roberts with some friends. The Roberts were the first family to settle and develop this area where they collected birds for export. They had a daughter and five sons, all of whom were brought up by their mother when their father died at an early age. All these children are now grown with healthy businesses all over Kenya. When asked how she brought up such a successful family, Betty Roberts said, "All I did was to ensure they put on clothes for meals, brushed their hair, and were not allowed to swig beer out of the bottle!"

Soon after our arrival screams were heard from Willie, one of the sons. It appeared he had been igniting the powder from his father's shot gun shells and the flames had shot into his face burning and temporarily blinding him. Willie should have been at school, but Betty said she had given up sending him to school because somehow after driving him there, he would be home before she got back herself! A wireless message was now sent to Uncle Garth who ran a pharmacy in Nakuru. Willie was subsequently bundled into the aeroplane and I flew him to Nakuru to be met by Garth at the airstrip. We got him swiftly to hospital where they saved his sight. It was fortunate to be on call with an aeroplane for the roads were impassable when the luggas became flooded. Today whenever I meet Willie he thanks me for saving his sight, as he has had no after effects. Betty died a year ago and over 200 people descended on Baringo to pay their respects. There were 21 aeroplanes on that small strip, all landing and taking off at the same time, but with today's good wireless communications between pilots, there were no mishaps.

Goats from South Africa

In 1964 when I checked out land outside Kenya, I also looked at stock in South Africa and was very impressed by the Boer Goat. I thought this type of goat would do much better than sheep on Sangare. I also looked over a Sahiwal cattle stud and thought these would make a great cross with my Ayrshires.

Some time later flying south in our own plane, I purchased a liquid nitrogen container and filled it with Sahiwal bull semen straws and brought it home to do artificial insemination. This was quite successful and produced some excellent cross bred animals. I also arranged to purchase a stud flock of 50 young Boer Goats to share with three other Kenya ranchers. The problem was that anything from apartheid South Africa was banned importation into Kenya. My brother Tim arranged to move them to Swaziland, calling them Swaziland Red Heads. We obtained an import permit from Swaziland, hired an old Dakota DC3 aircraft that was used by Air Kenya for ferrying tourists around the parks, removed all the seats and flew down to Swaziland to collect them. I built wire cages in the plane so the animals would not all shift down to the tail end on take off. It did not quite work and they all slid back but righted themselves as we levelled out. We had to make a landing in Malawi for refuelling, so we adjusted the cages so that it did not happen a second time. It was about a ten-hour flight and the party of Boers seemed to enjoy it. I had cut a lot of bush so they could browse along the way, but in spite of this they chewed all the window curtains as well, which Air Kenya had not thought of removing with the seats.

Flying over Tanzania we discovered one engine was using too much fuel so had to shut it down, only starting it up again for landing

Loading Boer Goats onto the Dakota DC3 in Swaziland.

in Nairobi. It soon got dark and we ran into heavy rain but the old Dakota ploughed through it with water pouring into the cockpit so that we had to put on raincoats. Also the windscreen misted up so we had to keep wiping it with a cloth or loo paper to check that we were not flying straight into the great 19,000 foot Mount Kilimanjaro. We flew at around 9000 feet as we had no oxygen and only one engine. Landing at Nairobi's Wilson Airport at 9 pm we had to arrange for the tower to be operative with lights for a night landing.

On the ground Gilfrid Powys, one of the Boer Goat purchasers, met with us and stayed with the goats till morning, as we were surrounded by great numbers of people who thought the goats looked very tasty. Once the papers were checked they were offloaded the next morning and trucked by lorry to Sangare where we shared them out. Meanwhile the DC 3 stood airing out for days with all apertures open to remove the smell before being refurbished for carrying tourists. The South African Boer Goat farmers told me that if we wanted them to do well immediately, we had to slaughter a local goat, mix the stomach contents with some water and dose them. This I did and they have never looked back. They replaced all the sheep, and we continue to sell breeding Billies all over the country to cross with the local goats, occasionally importing the odd new Billy to improve the genes. When talking to our vet about dosing with the stomach contents of a local goat, he thought it could only give the animals a new disease, but the South Africans claimed this would give them the local flora to digest the new types of shrubs.

The Sahiwal cattle crosses produced good animals, but my son Giles, a Boran expert, thought they were too wild and rather 'slab sided' for good beef. In South Africa the animals do not have to be handled and dipped as often as in Kenya. But an asset of being wild was at weaning all you need do is to put the dam and its calf in an eight-foot high boma, fire a shot and the mothers take off, jumping the fence and leaving the calves behind. We never had very good breeding percentages with artificial insemination and so reverted to chosen bulls, putting a Boran bull on the straight backs and crossing back with a Red Poll.

We now concentrate on breeding with the one-year-old steers going to Giles on Ol Pejeta, where they fatten more quickly and get slaughtered in the Ol Pejeta slaughterhouse. From here they are packed and delivered to the butchers in Nairobi for the best price. On Ol Pejeta Giles, who runs their 8000 Boran Stud, started the collecting of embryos, which have been exported all over Africa and even to Australia. In South Africa they have bred up their own stud and a bull in August 2011 fetched R.100,000, some $155000. Unfortunately Kenya does not have these markets and Giles is lucky if he gets the equivalent of $2000!

A Continuation of Southern Flights

With relations in Swaziland and long time friends in Botswana, my third wife Diane and I have continued with flights to these countries. In 1993 Jane and I had begun to diverge in the things we liked to do. I began seeing, perhaps too often, Diane Wilson whose husband (then long deceased) had been both a hunting client and business associate of my great friend Peter Becker. Jane said she was not prepared to share a husband and said she would leave. Diane moved in with me in 1995 and we were married in 1995 after Jane had consented a divorce.

Some time later Diane and I made a flight south. We were late leaving Nairobi and delayed again on landing and clearing at Kasama in Zambia. The customs had to be collected from town some three kilometres away. The same procedure was also required for collecting a drum of aviation fuel. There was no transport unless we hired a taxi from town, but the telephones were not working, so a runner had to be hired. Luckily, the time here was one hour behind, so we had plenty of daylight to get to our planned night stop at a small camp named Shiwa Ngandu belonging to the Harvey family.

It is rather featureless country with miles and miles of *miombo* forest. By this time we had GPS navigation and so there was just enough time to reach the camp before dark once the fuel and customs had arrived and we were refuelled and cleared. We set off with an hour's light in hand for the 40-minute flight to Shiwa Ngandu. After 40 minutes flying we were still in the middle of nowhere and with a very swampy landscape below. We had stayed here five years before. We remembered there being a range of hills by the camp, but these were nowhere to be seen, just mile upon mile of water. Diane remarked she certainly could not remember all this water. I suggested it had been an exceptionally wet year. Then the horror dawned on me. I had marked a point on the GPS to avoid crossing the Benguella Swamp, but had not changed the name. So instead we were now over the deadly swamp, which we were told to avoid at all costs. It would be nearly impossible to find a downed aircraft in such an area. It was still another three hours flying time to our next destination and so there was no alternative but to return to Kasama.

It became darker and darker with no moon at all. There was an occasional small fire as we flew over some cattle boma. I was

Mike and Diane at Sangare

strained and tired having flown a good eight hours that day and was extremely happy when the lights of Kasama came into view. There was no response on radio from the tower, but luckily the controller was still around. On hearing the aircraft approaching he rushed up to his tower and started pedalling the generator for radio power. Thus we were at last in communication. He said we could not land as there were no night aids.

"I have to land" I replied. "Can you get some lights on the strip?" It was still completely invisible.

"We have no lights," he replied.

"Please, can you put the lights of a vehicle down the strip," I asked.

"There are no vehicles," the answer came back.

I remembered there was a road and power line along the south end of the strip while the northern end was open with just long grass and shrubs. I said, "I will land from the north end."

Seconds later the controller came back. "I have located the fire engine and its driver so he can put the lights of this down the strip."

"Great!" I replied. "Can you place him at the south end with the lights shining along the strip so that I can line up on him?" I could see the revolving blue light on top of the vehicle, and as he put his lights down the strip, I lined up on a final approach. The lights of the plane were of no use at all until almost on the ground. I had to just line up on the point where I could see the fire engine lights. It was a very narrow strip so I had to be as accurate as I could on my final approach. Just when I was fully committed to fly in, at the last moment the fire engine drove away thinking I would run into him. In fact he was a mile away. In the meantime many thoughts rushed through Diane's mind. Like what were the facilities if we were hurt? None, she thought.

I was so engrossed with the landing that I had no time for such thoughts. On with the lights and there in front was long grass and bushes with the dirt strip about five metres to our left. Mowing the grass and twanging a couple of bushes on the aircraft tail, I veered onto the strip and taxied up to the parking lot. By this time a number of vehicles had appeared, including a German missionary who had a small guesthouse only some four kilometres away. He welcomed us to stay, which was a great relief. In fact we could not have been in a more welcoming and comfortable place. Father Joseph was a delight to be with.

The next morning I had to return to the airport to file a report of a 'crashed landing.' The damage to the tail plane was minimal but the controller said I had to have it inspected before continuing. This meant getting an inspector from the civil aviation authorities and reapplying for onward permits. As telephones did not work, all communications were done by wire and telex. A wire was sent to Swaziland explaining our late arrival. In Mbabane there was a first rate aircraft maintenance outfit where we had a thorough check and service completed on the aeroplane before continuing the return journey.

On the return journey we were to visit friends in Botswana. One was a camp in the Okavanga swamps. We were told to just fly along the main river and we would see the camp. Unfortunately, the rains had started and on reaching the Okavanga, no river was to be seen; the whole area was just one immense swamp. After several attempts at landing on short and dicey strips we eventually found the correct place. From here we were to visit Jack's camp on the Makale Makale Pans. Here the strip was a sea of mud, and on stopping dead on landing we wondered how on earth we would ever get airborne again. The camp itself was a sea of water and freezing cold. I thought such temperatures were only to be found in Europe. It was so wet that the campfire had to be made in a wheelbarrow!

Here there was little to do or see, but we were persuaded to visit a 1000-year-old baobab tree where Livingstone had camped. We set out in an open sided Land Rover on the 20-kilometre journey. We had blankets to cover us for warmth, but the rain poured down and a great bulge of water collected on the roof canopy. I tried to dislodge this with my foot, only to be showered and soaked in icy water. The tree was an immense baobab but not really worth the 20-kilometre drive through mud and cold rain. We had to wait out the weather before we could continue our flight home.

Three days later with a break in the weather and a plane full of glass from my brother Richard, who had taken over the ownership of a most successful glass blowing factory in Mbabane in Swaziland, we decided to get airborne. Holding down until the last moment, we pulled away with the stall warning blaring. We gained enough height to put the aircraft nose down and gather enough speed to get away.

We stayed again with father Joseph in Zambia. He was a great beer drinker so we presented him with a large blown glass beer mug with three handles from my brother's glass-blowing factory. Father Joseph had preserved a beautiful bit of forest around the guest house. As our stay became longer than anticipated, we did some very useful butterfly collecting and found many new specimens for my collection.

When the weather cleared to the north, we flew off and were soon home in Kenya with yet another great flight to remember.

Chapter 29

GALANA GAME & TAITA RANCHES

Fifty years ago Martin Anderson, his wife Ille and daughter Christie came out to me for a month's hunting safari in Kenya, based on my Laburra Ranch. We became good friends and the family fell in love with the country. Marty and I became partners in the ranching and land development business. We expanded operations on Laburra and ventured to the far north purchasing a wild piece of land called Luoniek of some 40,000 acres for cattle and including a vast amount of wildlife – elephant, buffalo and lion and all the smaller animals. Like me, Marty loved to hunt. It was not the killing, but the hard stalks and exciting moments culminating in prize trophies.

Luoniek was bordered to the north by the Samburu tribe and on the west by the Pokot. By 1965 there was political unrest and the Samburu and the Pokot were at each other's throats, as they still are to this day. The previous owners had allowed the Pokot to use the Nyambya Springs in time of drought, but now they claimed it as their land and had to be evacuated by force. At the same time the government advertised 1.5 million acres (2300 square miles) of land adjacent to the Tsavo National Park inland from the east coast of Malindi to be taken over by private enterprise on a 45-year lease for the development of cattle and wildlife. It was known as the Galana Elephant Scheme, which hitherto had been an experiment in the cropping of elephant for the local Walungulu people.

Marty showed great interest. I said if we were to apply we should find a third person well versed in large-scale cattle ranching. We approached a neighbour and good friend, Gilfrid Powys. Gilfrid's father, Will, was an early settler who had started sheep farming on Solio for the Cole family. Will had then started his own cattle and sheep farm in Timau expanding to Rumuruti. My father then took over the Solio sheep in 1937 when we moved from Njoro. So we had long-standing family connections. We believed we could work well together. Gilfrid had spent some time after leaving school helping out on the Galana Elephant Scheme, so he was well acquainted with that area and knew what developments would be required to progress into cattle ranching.

From hunting with clients I had ideas on what we might achieve on the wildlife side. Gilfrid and I both owned light aircraft and so had a good idea from low flying sorties, of what we would be taking on. Gilfrid was very excited too at the prospect of developing this large piece of country. Hence, we all three decided to apply.

There were about eight applicants and many ideas put forward. Marty said we should apply on one page and present only a page of facts to ensure it would be read.

In the meantime, everything came to a head on Luoniek with a

Left to Right: Gilfrid Powys, Martin Anderson, Mike Prettejohn.

herder being killed. The administration suggested it would be best if the area were to be administered by the ADC (Agricultural Development Corporation). In fact, they suggested as we were applying for the Galana Scheme they would help with our application, providing we allowed the ADC to purchase and take over Luoniek for the locals. They offered a price and we accepted and we were able to start the Galana Game & Ranching Company. The proceeds went as our capital for the Galana Scheme. Having won the contract to develop this huge tract of land and make it into a viable business proposition with game and cattle ranching, we decided to start a breeding herd of cattle enterprise moving the 1,800 head of cattle down from Luoniek Ranch in northern Laikipia, some 500 miles away. We decided to trek the cattle to the railhead at Thomson's Falls some 50 to 60 miles south. We hired a whole train to take them to Maungu, beyond Voi on the Mombasa line, where we were to hold them on a property owned by Ray Mayers.

Gilfrid undertook to supervise the trek, which went without a hitch. However, the temptation was too much for the Samburu, who together with the Maasai believe all cattle belong to them anyway. They have a tradition of cattle rustling and they could not resist helping themselves to ten animals as they were being loaded. Gilfrid soon noticed their disappearance and with a few good trackers, followed the tracks to a market some 20 miles away. Gilfrid retrieved all ten, remarkably the same ten too, or so the story goes. Even more remarkable was that all the animals reached their destination!

On 3rd July 1967 we received a 'Letter of Acceptance' from the then Commissioner of Lands, J A O'Loughlin. It took weeks of negotiations and discussions with prominent ministers, government officials and the Game Department to produce and sign the lease as a 'Letter of Allotment.'

Martin Anderson has recently written a detailed account of the history of the project, so in this chapter I have focussed on my involvement and various interesting episodes that took place during those 20 years of a 45-year lease.

Being responsible for the development of wildlife at Galana,

Debasso, a guide for elephant hunting on Galana.

I put forward a proposal on how to develop and utilise this asset. Firstly, we had organised aerial and ground game counts to determine what animals and numbers were more or less resident in the area. We then had to negotiate with the Game Department on the 'take off.' (The 1968 quota for animals we could shoot on a sustainable level included 300 elephant, six rhino, six lion, 12 leopard and 50 buffalo, besides all the plains game. Later, we cut this yearly quota drastically, especially the elephant, after serious air and ground counts).

The most practical way to utilise the wildlife, giving the highest returns, would be from sport hunting. Clients were to purchase a general licence. They could take off from the quota what they wanted. Besides the hunting fee, a fee would be paid on each animal taken, part of which was paid to the government. Where possible the meat was consumed by the locals.

However, for long-term storage with extra revenue and improved utilisation, I negotiated with a Mr Behmler, the chief engineer of the Kenya Meat Commission (KMC), to develop a mobile processing plant mounted on a trailer and hauled by tractor. The plant was designed, a trailer was purchased and Hartz & Bell were commissioned to manufacture it.

Unfortunately, the hunting ban in 1976 put a stop to all wildlife utilisation. However, as the lease stipulated wildlife utilisation, we argued the point and eventually received government approval for the project on condition we could supply them with approved markets. But on planning to deal through the KMC, we were banned from any form of utilisation of game meat. The KMC fell apart and was taken over from the US bidders, to be locally run. So, the mobile plant and trailer was sold, there being no way to utilise and process game meat products.

But at the start, when hunting was still allowed in Kenya, we combined safaris with Laburra and later included Indian Ocean Lodge, a delightful lodge overlooking the sea at Malindi – on land purchased by Marty. By the middle 1970s we were getting so many hunting clients, that it was necessary to have a full time hunter/game manager.

The first was Barry Roberts who retired after being bogged down overnight with clients, sleeping on the roof of the car in order to get away from the mosquitoes! Then there was Mike Hissey, who was a good hunter but unfortunately liked a little moan or two.

Ken Clark later took the position. Ken, sadly, was tragically shot and killed while chasing Somali poachers who he came across in the act of killing rhino. He was standing in the back of the vehicle when a bullet from the bandit shifta went through the windscreen, hitting his metal belt buckle and was diverted straight into his heart killing him instantly.

Finally Henry and Jessica Henley, my daughter and son-in-law moved in and led the photographic safaris and the lodge activity.

An anti-poaching force was established from the beginning with 40 convictions recorded in one year. Later, with the serious shifta bandits poaching by well-armed gangs, the team was integrated with the GSU (General Service Unit) for whom we set up a camp and rifle range.

With wildlife utilisation we became involved with various scientists in a domestication programme. This was started by John King, known as King John, with Mark Stanley Price, Jeff Lewis and Chris Field. Brian Heath managed the programme before becoming the general manager of the whole ranch. A few semi-domestic buffalo from Daphne Sheldrick were tried, but the buffalo, not having been bred for meat production, were too temperamental and dangerous to handle.

Other animals experimented with for domestication were the oryx and eland. Oryx with their spiked horns were dangerous and had to have bits of hose attached to their horn ends. Herding the animals was a problem with eland, because once let loose they travelled far and wide to get the few edible leaves out of each bush. The herders could not keep up with them. The oryx were easier, but at the end when a number of males were sent for slaughter the meat on each one was condemned for being beyond the limit of measles cysts. Although this was of a

Henley family operating Galana safaris

type that would not affect humans, it looked so unappealing that the meat could not be marketed for human consumption.

The catching was done by driving the animals by vehicle or helicopter into an enclosure. Punch Bearcroft, the Head of the Police Airwing, flew the helicopter with great skill in spite of having only one hand. He merely tied the handless arm around the joystick with a bit of inner car tube.

The first overall ranch manager was Charles Moore, seconded from the National Parks. Charlie's father was one of a very few surviving VCs from the First World War. His mother wrote a charming book on the animals of the Serengeti, when his father was Warden there. Charlie had worked previously for the Powys's. Knowing that they started work at a very early hour, and that his first job was to dose a mob of sheep, he had to be sure of being present by dawn. He had no watch, but on hearing a vehicle pass by he jumped out of bed, raced to the sheep kraal, aroused all the herders and completed the dosing. As it was still dark, he then returned to bed. When aroused at dawn and almost sacked on the spot, he meekly announced that the job was already done. The passing vehicle had been a neighbour returning home at midnight after a party.

Charles learnt to fly, as an integral part of his job. On the radio test for his licence he was placed in a box to simulate a flight. On going through the Mayday procedure he called Mayday and could not think of what followed. The examiner put his head around the box and asked, "What was wrong?"

"I have crashed," said Charles.

"Well, get in another plane and start again," was the swift reply.

Charles took over my Tri-Pacer KKX and had the misfortune to experience an engine failure on the maiden flight to Galana from Nairobi. He managed to land safely on the road. The engine was a write-off with a valve breaking and going through the block, so we replaced it with a 'Caribbean' engine, which was 150 hp in place of the original 135 hp. Once installed, Charles sited a headquarters and built himself a house and office. He then set about developing watering points, crushes and a spray race ready for the Luoniek cattle now grazing on Ray Mayer's estate at Voi, some 60 miles to the south. His first water trough was built in steps; he had forgotten that water finds its own level! The only piece of machinery we inherited from the elephant scheme was a McCormic tractor grader, a wonderful machine that made many kilometres of roads and went on to Taita 20 years later.

We purchased a brand new 4x4 Fordson bulldozer to compliment the grader. Its first job was to cut a track to a magnificent waterhole we had found by air in a large open plain, called Bissenballa. We had no GPS in those days. We just took a rough bearing from the plane and with a compass mounted on the bulldozer cut a way in through the bush, more or less in a straight line, after direction corrections from the air, to the water hole. There was much joy on reaching the water. I remember Charles taking a running rush into it and promptly going in headfirst as he stepped into an elephant foot hole.

There were only a few tracks on the whole property to act as firebreaks, one of the earliest hazards being bush fires. I remember a raging fire one day that took all night to beat out. After returning for breakfast, we had not accounted for the smouldering elephant turds, which as soon as the wind started up after sunrise, were whisked up and deposited to start the burn again. By 10 am there was a 15 kilometre line of fire once more.

Terrence Adamson, brother of the famous Game Warden and known for his years of releasing lion to the wild, came to help Charles with various developments. He used to tell us he was so glad to get away from George and his lions, he was quite sure he would be eaten one day, as was their cook.

As mentioned earlier the 1,800 head of cattle from Luoniek had been walked and railed to Ray Mayer's Rukinga Ranch, east of Voi. Ray was a veteran of the World War Two campaign in Abyssinia. He was one of a family of twelve Australian sugar planters immigrating to Kenya in the 1920s. Each had been left £100,000, which was a huge amount of money in those days. Ray had spent all his inheritance before leaving Sandhurst where he had completed his military training.

Ray developed Rukinga in partnership with his brother Cyril who had kept his inheritance and in fact made it grow. Ray was in a wheel chair commanding operations from the end of a long table, often with a bottle of whisky by his side. I remember I would visit him to enquire about the cattle and to pay a grazing fee, when he would demand I be seated and take a whisky. On starting to help oneself to a tot he would announce, "No no, that's my bottle, your bottle is just coming."

Before business could be completed, there were many tales of the good old days discussed, well into the night. Ray's wife Helen was the sister of our first manager, Freddie Seed, on Luoniek. Helen had been bitten on the toe by a cobra while in bed, and although she had duly recovered, her early death was potentially down to the long-term effects of the bite.

I remember driving down with Marty and Ille to the Galana River to watch the cattle crossing. We went across by a ferry made by Charles and Terrence of empty fuel drums lashed together with rope and a platform built atop. The whole contraption was guided and pulled across the river by cable. This ferry could not withstand a fast flow when the rains caused the river to come down in spate, so a cable car was then constructed.

Later, Tony Dyer, Gilfrid's brother-in-law, being licenced to use explosives, built a concrete causeway to actually drive vehicles across. This had a dog's leg in order to keep to a solid foundation, but when our political problems came to a head twenty years later, it was said that the dog's leg was intended to make it difficult to drive across and give us time to escape when the CID came to arrest

us. Tony Dyer, then Chairman
of the Professional Hunter's
Association, had joined as a
director for further help and
advice on wildlife matters.

The start of the cattle
operation, purchase of store
steers, machinery, building of
roads, dams and airstrips can
be better told by Gilfrid and
Brian Heath. Suffice it to say
that after 20 years with some

*Longori speared this lion that
attacked a cattle boma in Galana.
Henry then shot and killed the lion.*

39.5 million shillings spent on developments of roads, airstrips and
water, with 24,000 head of cattle and 3000 sheep, plus 22 million
shillings in hand to increase to 30,000 head of cattle, we had more or
less completed the 45-year terms of the lease. Marty put off retirement
at the law firm in Hawaii in order to keep the ranch going through this
stage of development. Together with all income reinvested, we now
hoped for 20 years of profits to come. Unfortunately, the government
thought otherwise.

During the height of elephant and rhino poaching in the 1980s,
the European nations pointed fingers at the Kenya government. Not
only was there poaching, but light aircraft were ferrying arms to the
Sudan. A letter on the poaching situation written by Prince Philip on
behalf of WWF probably also aggravated the situation.

The senior officials responded by pointing a finger at Galana
Ranch. "How come an area, one-eighth of Kenya was still privately
owned by white Kenyans and managed without local Government
and African participation?" Thus their story evolved. We all flew
aircraft and we killed the wildlife and were selling ivory and rhino
horn. We were the ones flying out arms and in cahoots with the Somali
poachers, through our own Somali herders.

The directive came that all Galana's airstrips henceforth would
be closed, cattle sales stopped, the culprits arrested and charged for
being in possession of illegal firearms, illegally killing and selling

trophies and aiding the Shifta bandits. The lease for the ranch would be suspended forthwith, all loans repaid before the end of the week and all assets and movables frozen while the ranch was to be taken over by the Ministry of Agriculture.

It did not quite go the way they anticipated. Weeks of desperate meetings with government officials, embassies, lawyers and other prominent people ensued, culminating with the President himself. All permits and agreements were produced together with a précis on all inputs and developments. Brian Heath was charged in court for being in possession of illegal firearms (this in fact was a dart gun supplied by the Game Department). If convicted, Brian could have been sentenced to a minimum of seven years in jail. A top lawyer, Byron Georgiadas, was engaged to defend Brian and the lawyer told him to plead guilty. He said the case was to be a forgone conclusion and the best he could do was to ensure a fine rather than jail. The fine was put at 10,000/- equivalent of almost 40,000/- today.

The game management operations at Galana were saved from court proceedings by the help of Bill Woodley, the Tsavo warden at the time, and with all permits being up to date. The British High Commissioner said there was little he could do, as we were all Kenya citizens, but he obviously put in a word. The US Ambassador was of greatest assistance together with Marty's US government contacts. They suggested that unless a fair price was paid for all developments and the assets taken over, that all aid to Kenya from them would be stopped.

Peter Hewett of Daly & Figgis Advocates wrote very strong letters saying we would sue against any illegal action taken by the Kenya government. The final outcome conveyed was that the President had been misinformed. It was too late to reverse the decision and we should negotiate with the ADC (African Development Corporation) not the Ministry of Agriculture, for a smooth take over and payment for the company shares at an agreed valuation. I remember Peter Hewett handing over a cheque signed by the President himself.

It was a sad and emotional ending on what had been one of the most successful dry land developments in Kenya. It was commendable that a new emerging Kenya nation under President Kenyatta had sanctioned the Galana Scheme to private enterprise, after the experience of chaos in other African countries gaining independence. Admittedly, the chief players still in government at the time were ex-colonial government officials.

In case the government did not take on all the stock or machinery from Galana, we hurriedly negotiated with Taita Ranch (they were in trouble over payment of loans) to move the surplus, and to take on a 15-year lease. After 15 years of successfully developing Taita Ranch, our lease was not renewed and Taita Ranch went much the same way as Galana, being ruined by Somali insurgents with most of the game animals going for bush meat and the trees to charcoal. After our departure from Taita Ranch, up to 4000 bags of charcoal were going to Mombasa per month.

Personal Galana Reminiscences

Galana was almost a country of its own, and many young men and women, not to mention the dedicated local people, participated in its development. When Churchill was Secretary of State for the Colonies on a visit to Kenya, he announced that all the "settlers were politicians and each the leader of his own party." One could say much the same for Galana.

Marty and Ille remained utterly devoted and dedicated with constant support during the 20 years. Many of us with minds and hearts on wild places and wildlife often spent too much time away. This often created a huge disruption of family life and many differences in opinions. We all look back with nostalgia to a dedicated time and to wild experiences that we believed could only have been possible in the time of our grandfathers. We worked hard and played hard.

The Story of a Cattle Manager – told by Barney Gaston

The first time I went to Galana I flew with Gilfrid. We started a little late and had a hot and bumpy landing at Danissa. Gilfrid had old, clipped sheepskin covers on the seats of his plane, a deep russet brown where the wool had rubbed off, made by Rose at her tannery at Ngare Ndare. The cabin of the plane had that peculiar warm smell that strikes one whenever a lift is in the offing. The faded green Land Cruiser had to be fuelled and I hung around near the service bay in the workshop, feeling spare, with a smell of diesel in my head. I can see that first hot afternoon; the oil-stained sandy floor with a dirty drum of used blue filters in the corner, an agama lizard bobbing his head, bright black eye under a severe orange brow, vertical on the wall.

I met Brian, who looked at me with undisguised scepticism. He had neatly rolled up sleeves and wore uniform shorts and his shiny chupplies. He sort of turned away without saying anything, not quite sneering.

Jim Howard stood there in his huge brown boots and knee-length socks; his socks were always pale bird's egg blue. He sucked a horrible pipe. Gilfrid started the slightly clapped out Land Cruiser and drove out past his aeroplane, through grey spiky *commiphora* and on to a dusty road. He was a much better pilot than a driver. We went swinging along towards Maili Saba, abruptly off the grey-white dust and onto red. We turned right with Dakabuku dead ahead, blue on the horizon. The road turned to black clay with completely different vegetation. Finally, we turned left onto the Pipeline Road, stretching straight into the far distance, the afternoon sun in our eyes and Gilfrid waffling away on the car radio in commanding but very traditional up-country Swahili. I remember thinking: "What the hell is going on?"

We came to a boma close to the road, set off to the left in deep, beautiful green grass fifty yards from a ziwa, with a new thorn fence neatly enclosing some cattle.

Jomo was our cattle headman who got the nickname because some thought he looked like President Kenyatta. A Samburu, Jomo had been convicted of cattle rustling in his home area, so he had moved to Galana. Jomo now came to the car where Gilfrid had parked a discreet distance from the boma. Gilfrid had been talking to Jomo on the radio and now he said: "Hello Jomo. This is Barney. He is straight out of school. (I was not, by the way). He knows nothing. He will be with you." He had that sort of apologetic look on his face, his brow creased into lines up to his curly hairline. He almost said sorry to Jomo. Jomo looked at me with that one eye of his, up and down, and I looked at him.

Jomo said, "Mmm," and we shook hands. We set up a small tent where I lived for the next three months. I took a cardboard box of stuff from the back of the car and went through the pox box with Gilfrid. Then they got into Jomo's car and drove off into the rapidly approaching night.

When I met Jomo about twenty years later, he gave me that same appraising look and told me I was far too fat. But in those days I was cocky and thought myself very clever. He patiently and tactfully taught me all I ever learned about livestock in that wonderful place, without once revealing the exasperation he must have felt when I screwed up.

When I got to Galana, Jim Howard was the General Manager. He was out of his depth and was nagged endlessly by June his wife, who hated the place. Jim built the dullest houses imaginable at Maili Saba for Jack and later for Tim. They were concrete block 'Ministry of Works' rectangles, looking over the plain towards those timeless Lali Hills. The hills changed colour every hour of the day. Jim was a good vet and very generous with his knowledge. He was always happy to point out the finer manifestations of disease in the spilt coils of the entrails of a dead animal, swatting flies and dripping sweat, with one eye on the blue sky, to note the arrival of vultures.

Ian Parker told me once they would climb those Lali Hills and look for elephant heading for that middle road. They would dash back to the road to shoot them as they crossed because the bush was so thick they couldn't hunt any other way. He said there had been a fire in the 1960s that swept up from the river as far as Dakadima in the north that had completely changed the vegetation and had opened it all out. Lali was visible from Jack's place, and sometimes we would sit on his pokey little veranda with a beer and look across at those hills.

Brian was in charge of the cattle, (and us, too, quite soon after I got there). It must have been horrible for him. We called him the

Head Boy because he was just like a prefect at school. Since that was a fairly recent memory for Chris Flatt, Jack Fairhall, Tim Wascher and me, I think we got it about right. He was the 'perfect' prefect, neat and meticulous to the point of appearing fussy. He always got it right and we mostly got it wrong (and he let us know that depressing fact). He was always punctual and we were seldom anywhere on time. Brian soon took over from Jim, and our easy lives changed. We had to appear to be slightly more serious from then on. He heard everything on the ranch VHF radio, our only form of communication for most of the time. I think he took his radio to bed with him. We had codes we thought were unbreakable, spoken fast and late at night that meant we were going to meet for a beer and get plastered and Brian always knew about it. He told us rushing around the ranch at night was strictly not permitted.

Brian guarded shooting as his own preserve, especially shooting lion. Jack and I longed to do the actual shooting, rather than merely holding the spotlight for him. He would go home after sitting up in a hide, with the carcass of a dead lion hauled into the back of his immaculate pickup, silver in the moonlight. We thought that Brian vain and he relished that moment in the morning, as the red sun came over the doum palms by the river, when the small crowd of Taita from the workshop, the prime domestics, and the drivers all said, "Waa! Kubwa…" The poor old lion would flop onto the ground out of the back of the truck. Off went the truck to be washed, immediately and off came the lion's skin and all the fat scraped away (rendered for potent medicine), and the skull and the floating bones saved. The lion was skinned and stripped of all dignity, and taken to the river and fed to the crocodiles.

Brian had a satisfied look on his face all day. He was doing his job and he did it very well. He was a very good shot and was quick and steady as could be.

On two occasions Brian was really put out. Henry and I once shot six lions in a single night. It was a cold July night in a heifer boma (very excitable animals) and a big pride stampeded and killed five heifers, as we waited in the gloom. They came in from three sides at once. We rushed to the closest scene of the excitement and Henry shot two lions. Then we dashed across the boma where I had a go and shot two. Then a fly got into my ear and I thought I would go mad with this thing buzzing away inside my head. The terrified heifers were tearing about, running everywhere. Henry calmly took a syringe from the Pox Box and filled it with very cold water and told me to put my finger in the other ear, to stop the water coming through (I did not find this funny) and he squirted cold water right into my ear. The fly collapsed and came out. It was an immense relief, but we had not a moment to lose. The lions were murdering something else. Henry shot two more for a total of six.

We went back to Danissa feeling very smug. I stayed with Henry and Jessica, and in the early morning took a slow drive beside the heap of six dead lions. Brian glowered and refused to say, "Good morning." He didn't say any more to Henry or me than was strictly necessary for about a month.

The second time was less clever and very nearly ended in tears. Marsale called from Menjilla saying his trading stock was being killed by a very *kali* lion. Brian did not respond for two nights and I hatched a plot with Marsale to shoot that lion with a .22 I had kept under my bed. I went to Menjilla in the afternoon and we tied the carcass of a beautiful white Orma steer to the base of a tree. It was a *commiphora* tree, silver barked, shiny and full of long thorns, with no leaves. It stood there, about a kilometre from the boma, with a glade of golden grass about knee high in front of it, where the cattle had not trampled; a perfect amphitheatre. Marsale spoke very fast, and his eyes glittered. I liked him a lot, but he was suspicious of everyone because he had a very beautiful wife, who for some reason was allowed to live on the place when no other women were allowed closer than the river, about 90 kilometres away. Every man on Galana thought of Marsale's pretty wife. She was a flirt and although Marsale was absolutely in charge, he was very jealous of her. She smelled of frankincense. Marsale, always in a lungi with a Somali belt and a waistcoat, had a quick answer for everything and no one was quite sure if he was entirely on our side. We put a wooden door from my place at Tank E in the tree we intended to sit in, directly over the dead steer, which was tied to the base of the tree. We very carefully avoided those evil thorns, climbed onto the door and sat there waiting. Marsale had a two-cell torch made in China. I had a .22 Mauser that was strictly not allowed. The plan was to shoot the lion we expected to come in later, right in the head, from our perch directly above the dead steer. The sun turned golden, that magic moment "twixt dog and wolf," when it is neither night nor day. Then suddenly a huge lion was right in front of us, absolutely silent, looking through blazing eyes, directly at us. I could not resist and shot him between those eyes. Down he went without a grunt.

Marsale and I looked at one another. It was easy. We started to climb down the tree. Suddenly there was a roar and that huge lion leapt into the air, growling terribly, and then it was on the ground dashing round and round in a circle. We scurried back up on that platform ten feet above the lion. I tried to shoot it again in the lungs, and that tiny popgun seemed woefully small. Then it suddenly grew dark. There was complete silence. We were in a tree, the car was in the boma and I had wounded a lion.

Brian was tucked up in his bed and I would have to tell him about this unfortunate episode. We climbed down rather fearfully and scuttled to the car. When we got back to the dead steer we saw in the headlights four more lions feeding on it. We had given ourselves such a fright. Marsale was beside himself with excitement, and said, "Shoot them; shoot them!" I was not about to do that. I was thinking of Brian and that supercilious look he had for anyone who really screwed up. There was lots of blood all around, easily seen on the yellow grass in the headlights. We went round and round looking for the wounded lion but never found it. In the morning I looked again and was defeated. I had to own up to Brian, who rightly was not amused. About three weeks later Marsale came to my place at Tank E, with a lion skull and it had a perfect pencil line of lead along that fearsome ridge of bone they have on the tops of their heads where a tiny bullet had knocked it out. One of Marsale's herders had found it dead and smelling under a really thick bit of bush. No one was very happy with this, not least because my secret musket had been revealed, and of course I was a 'disappointment.'

Occasionally Gilfrid and Mike and Marty (when he was there) would have a crack at those lion. Mike famously was photographed being bitten by a monstrous lion.

I once waited for a lion with Gilfrid. Galana was normally quite hot, but in the middle of the year the nights were cold and lying in a hide with Gilfrid wrapped up in the only blanket we had, I was freezing. I finally had to wake him and tell him that a lion had come. It hadn't at all, but I managed to grab a bit of that blanket and I was more comfortable by the time he lay down again to wait.

The best lion story in my time at Galana belonged to a small, wiry man, an Ndorobo who had come with Gilfrid. I have forgotten his name, but he killed a lioness one night when it attacked the cattle he was guarding. He stabbed this huge animal with a short, sharp spear and killed it immediately, as if this sort of thing happened every night. I found that heroic, but all he got for his trouble was a curt reprimand.

I was Jomo's assistant helping with the breeding herds, which numbered about 6,000. I enjoyed that job. There was some routine, centred on the monthly cattle count, inoculations of Samorin and Berenil for trypanosomiasis, dipping, de-horning, castrating, branding, and weaning. Much of that work was strenuous and dusty and I enjoyed it a lot. It made one curiously appreciative of warm Fanta, taken as a sort of prize from Ibrahim's duka. (Sue had the horrible task of taking stock of all the bubble gum and sugar in the shop once a month and when she was on leave I had to do this job. I made such a mess of it I was never asked to do it again.)

There was a lot of time to visit the camps where all the cattle moved to in the wet season. I was expected to do this regularly, as much for morale and to re-supply basic foodstuff to the men in the bomas as for any useful purpose to do with the herds. It was the very pleasing habit of the boma heads to offer a cup of hot sweet milky tea to a visitor. Countless tin cups of tea were had under the shade of a thorn tree, seated on clean cow skins, flapping at hordes of flies. I liked those people, too. They were all polite and pleasant. I cannot remember one single labour dispute and the only time there were bad feelings in that place was when a very sick herdsman died of what turned out to be malaria while on duty. It was our fault entirely and he should have been taken to hospital. In retrospect these things are easy to see, but at the time he had been to the dispensary at Tank E. The hospital in Voi was a very long way away.

Once a year we had a rodeo at Galana. We had the rodeo during the day and a party that night and everyone drank too much. We usually roasted a steer and had a bit of a dance. We had teams and events. The management, (the real management, not us), made up one team. When the weaner throwing came along, Mike, Gilfrid, Brian and the directors' team lined up near the young steer in the crush. Someone touched the steer's bottom with the hot end of a cigarette and it shot out of the crush like a bullet to the astonishment of the directors. Jack was kicked in the chest at one of these lively rodeos and we really thought he had been killed. He was always enthusiastic and he had a steer by the tail, pulling hard, dust flying. The steer kicked him hard in the chest above his heart and he fell like a stone. He turned a sort of blue-grey, lying there on his back in the sun and the dust, twitching a little. We all rushed to him. The steer skulked at the other side of the ring, eyes rolling and tossing his silly head from side to side. Slowly Jack came to and fortunately did not spoil the day by dying, to the immense relief of the crowd.

One night, at about nine o'clock, when I had showered, had supper and was in bed, an aeroplane came roaring low over my house. I thought something dreadful had happened. I dashed down to the airstrip where the plane had landed and there were Gilfrid and Brian who said, "Come on. We're going to Malindi for a party." Off we went, in the bright moonlight. We wound up in the Driftwood Club, and danced and boozed until the sun came up. We caught a lift to the plane in a pick-up truck carrying milk and flew back to Galana.

Gilfrid flew. Brian was asleep in the back and Gilfrid fell asleep in the front. The plane went into a slow arc towards the ground and as I began to sweat, Gilfrid woke up and gently corrected it and we finally landed at Tank E. I had to make an undignified dash for my car, red-eyed and hung over and dressed in a kikoi, under the astonished gaze of about twenty Muslim herders and others who were on the airstrip to see what cooked at six in the morning in these unorthodox circumstances. Gilfrid and Brian didn't wait and took off for Danissa.

Chris Flatt was the administrator and he kept the books and fielded the nightly radio call from Angela, who was in Nairobi. Chris was a rock. He was dependable, honest, generous and a very good friend. He always had a beer and supper when either or both was needed. But over and above his administrative competence, he would arrange for our household supplies to be brought in from Malindi and sent up to us: me at Tank E; Jack at Maili Saba; Patrick at Konofoda. Chris was always keen for an adventure. Once when the river was very high and he had Geoff Burrell staying, we decided to shoot the rapids from Danissa to Kisiki cha Mzungu, where the pump for the pipeline was located.

Angela would always report on the rain in Nairobi, and so Chris knew when to expect a big flood in the river. This was important because the only way into the ranch apart from the plane was across the causeway. As he was closest, Chris inevitably had to assess the depth and violence of the river and advise anyone on the other side on the likelihood of being washed off the concrete Irish crossing and being swept down stream. Chris certainly knew that there would be plenty of water in the river for our rafting scheme.

We had an inflatable raft. Chris and Geoff were in the stern with a crate of beer and Jack and I were in the bows with paddles, trying to keep in midstream. The river was brown with huge ridges of screaming waves and whole trees being swept down towards Malindi at great speed and it roared by in front of Chris's house. We had plenty of time to get excited about our trip to Kisiki. Off we set, and we careered down the river Jack and I paddling and very nervous. Chris and Geoff sat in the stern laughing and drinking beer and yelling at us to paddle harder. From the bank of the river we saw what appeared to be a hippo coming directly across the flood towards us, thankfully on Jack's side, at right angles to the flood. We paddled harder. It was actually a monster of a crocodile, swimming on the surface, straight towards us. No doubt it took us for a dead animal being carried on the flood and it came at us without visible effort as we shot down the river on our raft. We only had a millimetre of fabric between our backsides and a set of teeth with about 50 metres between us and the bank. The singing in the stern of the boat stopped abruptly. The monster disappeared under water about fifteen metres from us, and all of us expected it to emerge under the boat. We all had that horrible feeling one has when anticipating a beating from the headmaster at school. We steered for the bank and soon the danger was behind us.

Eventually the tall tamarind trees at the pump house came into view and the car we had arranged was there with the driver watching the vervet monkeys in the afternoon sunshine. We told each other with relief what fun we had just had.

I do not ever remember feeling lonely in that fantastic place. I had visitors and I had the occasional time off the ranch, in Malindi or in Nairobi, the choice depending largely on the state of the hormones. There was a route to Malindi that took us below Dakabuku and that came out north of the Sabaki bridge and afforded a few exciting nights in that place. One had to be back before six in the morning to avoid being caught out by the radio and it took about three hours if the road was dry, so one had to get as much into a limited night as one possibly could.

I once had a long weekend in Nairobi, and left for Galana at three in the morning, starry eyed, and came through the Park at Voi at about five when it was still dark. Those gate people at Tsavo East were very understanding. I was getting late coming to Sala Gate and was going quite fast and there on the road as the sun was just getting up was a huge flock of vulturine guinea fowl. I hit that flock and killed 25. I had to stuff all 25 into the car behind the seat. I had to be back before six in the morning and I still had to get through the gate, say hello to my sleepy chums who manned it and make it across the causeway and on to Danissa. I just made it. Kalama, who worked for me at Tank E, skinned all those birds and I gave the salted capes to Douggie

Walker, who sponsored a fishing fly tying school for the disabled outside Nairobi. We all ate guinea fowl for weeks and weeks.

I had two very exciting leaves from Galana. Brian asked me to collect a new Toyota in Nairobi for the ranch and deliver it when I came back after my leave. I was very much in love with a girl from New Zealand and she and I wanted to go to Lake Turkana, to Ferguson's Gulf. I collected the car a week early and off we went and had a splendid time. On the way back to Galana on the Naivasha road in this gleaming car and with a lovely girl, I overtook a Land Rover going quite slowly and, to my horror, saw Gilfrid and Patricia. They both looked at me. I sped on, cringing. Gilfrid was kind enough not to do much more than to raise his bushy eyebrows. I know he knew that I should not have been where I was in that new car.

Chris and I had bought a new pickup together and I took it to Sudan to look for gold. I stayed with David Oughton in Kitale, and then went through Lokichoggio to Kapoeta and had a huge adventure for about two weeks. I found just enough gold there to have a pair of earrings and a little pendant made for Caroline, who I loved then. I shot a lesser kudu and camped around it for a few days with some wild Toposa men who all had automatic rifles and no care in the world. Then I came back to work in good time, very pleased with myself.

My pay was five thousand, five hundred shillings a month, and I once asked Brian for a pay rise. He referred me to Marty, who was there at the time. Marty said to me in a measured tone and an American accent, "You know Barney, there is only one thing worse than not having enough money, and that is having too much." That was the end of the conversation and I didn't believe him.

Gilfrid always said working at Galana was a privilege and I see now that he was exactly right. In reality, I had as much money as I needed and I lived very well. I had a lot of fun and very few worries that were not entirely of my own making. Galana was a marvellous three years of my life and I am grateful for the experience.

In a conversation recently, an older Kenyan man, who is an advisor and consultant to our MP was talking about the beef industry. He suggested that if the government of Kenya was serious about fixing the broken beef industry, Galana should be offered to the old shareholders of the place for a dollar. "Those people made that place the hub of the stock trade from the North. They created an industry from nothing, just bush, and they provided a stabilizing influence in a turbulent region. It has been abandoned and has withered now and it is a crying shame!" I think he was right. That place was a magnificent investment and a vision and it was truly a privilege to work there.

Some Incidents at Galana Game and Ranching

Before the days of our own causeway, Daudi set off to Voi one day as usual routing via the causeway joining Tsavo East and Tsavo West. This was during the rains so he had three or four days rations, as the river went up and down like a yoyo at those times. Daudi had no radio. After a week to ten days nothing was seen or heard of him so it was decided to send out a rescue team. On arrival at the causeway site there was Daudi all intact with a big grin on his face and lots of "Asante sanas." The river had been up for longer than average. Daudi was about to turn for home when a police plane spotted him. Thinking it was a group of tourists that had broken down in the park, they flew out and dropped rations and all sorts of goodies. Daudi experienced good tasting food of varieties he'd never seen before. So as long as this went on he thought he was meant to stay. We thought this a great joke until we received a huge bill from the police. I seem to remember we argued the point and didn't have to pay in the end.

We built a small permanent hunting camp on the eastern side of Daka Dima Hill in the far north of the ranch. There was an airstrip at this site that we renovated. Denys Finch Hatton, a renowned hunter of the 1920s, and boy friend of Karen Blixen and Beryl Markham, had originally built it. Beryl flew in supplies and spotted for Denys and Bror Blixen who hunted together.

Before using this camp we would send in supplies in a tractor and trailer as well as a water bowser. On one such trip while returning to base empty a rhino took a dislike to this strange apparition, which sounded like a steam engine. The rhino came pounding after it with its head lowered and horn poised. The driver was unaware of the rhino with the noise of the tractor and empty bowser bouncing along. The 'turn-boy' sitting in the empty trailer saw the charging rhino and feared for his life. He yelled at the top of his voice and with great presence of mind picked up an empty metal bucket, leaned over the back and placed it on the rhino's horn just before it hooked the back of the trailer. The infuriated beast swerved off into the bush smashing the bucket to shreds. The driver never stopped until the turn-boy climbed out of the trailer, over the bowser and tapped him on the head. The driver, not knowing what had hit him, swerved off the road and almost capsized the whole train. They had a good laugh but the bucket was never retrieved.

Once we were established with hunters and had a number of hunting camps, we employed a permanent white hunter and built him a small house downriver from the headquarters. The first hunter was Barry Roberts. Little did we know that we had built this house right in the middle of a rhino path heading down to a drinking site on the river. A few nights after Barry was installed he awoke from a peaceful slumber to a steady thumping noise against the wall. At first he thought it was an earth tremor for the whole house was shaking. Across one corner of the room he had placed a couple of poles to support a metal ammunition box to store valuables. The wall was only made of pressed dried mud and wattle and soon a rhino head appeared in Barry's bedroom! Luckily for him the jarring had unsettled the metal box and as the rhino's head pushed through the wall, the metal box crashed down on top of its head and horn. The rhino luckily removed itself in haste.

When we started hunting on the ranch there were some 6000 elephant and 300 rhino besides a multitude of other wildlife. We made aerial counts regularly in conjunction with the parks. It was suggested we utilise 300 elephant per annum. We

Elephants by Galana camp.

Big bull elephants.

were never sure this was the right thing to do or how best to utilise the carcases. But economically we knew that the animals would support their existence if we took off some 30 mature bulls past breeding age for a substantial hunter's fee of which part went to government as a licence fee. The animal did not have to be paid for until it had been shot, so it meant that if a worthwhile trophy was not found, the hunter did not feel compelled to take one. The hunter could take the trophy while we utilised the skin and meat, but we were still not content with just drying the meat for crude biltong. Unfortunately, the hunting ban came into effect before we could utilise this outlay.

One time we had a hunting client from Denmark named Peter Didrichsen who went out with Barry. Another client, Otto Shoemaker from Holland, came early so I brought Otto to the ranch a couple of days before Barry and Peter had completed their hunt. There was still plenty of room for two hunters, except that both were looking for big elephant. My client was always out to make deals and on this occasion he said to Peter, "How about we both go out tomorrow and the one who gets the smallest elephant pays the other a case of Dimple Haig. Peter did not care for the deal but nevertheless he went along with it. Barry and Peter set off the next morning before light to be ahead of the elephant that we knew would be grazing inland from the river.

I said to Otto, my client, "We will go a little later and intercept the bulls who usually follow some distance behind the main herd." This we did but could find nothing larger than a sixty-pounder.

Otto said, "I will take it," and did. We knew the others would have heard the shot. Otto said, "By collecting our elephant by 8 o'clock in the morning they will believe I have shot a monster and will run around all day and get nothing." This is exactly what happened. Peter and Barry arrived back shortly after dark with nothing to show for their efforts. They were dirty, tired and thirsty. Otto and I had showered and were into our second scotch, sitting with the ivory propped up against the wall. "Have a Dimple Haig on my account," said Otto.

Peter was not amused. He said the wager did not stipulate what size bottles. "I will give you a case of miniatures." They were even more disgusted when they saw the tusks. "Lord, we could have shot a bigger bull than that, but as you shot it so early, we thought you had a monster. Otto's remark about the offer of miniatures is unprintable.

When our cattle numbered 20,000 head and more we lost up to 300 head a year from lion attacks. One day a report came in that a prize bull had been taken 20 miles east of the ranch headquarters and most of the carcass was still intact. The herders had covered it with brush so the vultures could not get at it. I had not brought a rifle with me on this trip but Gilfrid had his .450 double that he said I could borrow. Gilfrid and Brian were busy and as I had my stepson Harry with me, who was a keen photographer, we decided to sit up for the lion over the carcass that night. We also brought a couple of herders with spears.

On arrival we found the carcass in the middle of a plain with little bush around. We could not build a 'blind' too close for fear of being detected. The lion would remember if there had been any cover nearby. By dusk we had constructed a good blind constructed some distance away. We removed the brush off the animal and we sat ready with rifle and spotlight. Normally we would try to save the lion for a client if it was a good trophy animal, but on this occasion we had no clients. At about 8 pm two huge lion appeared at the kill. I decided to take the one with the least mane but nevertheless a very large beast. It was pitch dark by this time and the moon had not risen yet. As we heard the munching and tearing of flesh, I whispered to Harry to switch on the light. The two magnificent beasts raised their heads and turned as if to go. With only open sights it was quite difficult, but I took a shoulder shot and heard the bullet slap home.

There was a mighty roar, the lion leaped five feet in the air and was gone. I believed he had a heart shot, but with cats especially, one tended to let them stiffen up before following up. We drank a cup of hot coffee before getting to the car to follow the spoor. We had no trouble in following and only a short distance away we could see the lion in the headlights. He was on his side but I could see his stomach heaving so I knew he was alive. This surprised me as I thought the shot better placed. I did not think he could move much. So I left the car with the headlights on him, crept out behind him with the intention of killing him with a shot in the back of the head. Before I had time to fire, he let out a terrific roar, did a backward somersault with his tail driving him like the propeller of a plane, and pounced on me! I fired once before he actually descended on top of me, but this shot only broke his foreleg and paw.

Like lightning the lion bowled me over. One paw almost ripped my left thumb off as I tried to hold him off my face and chest. I tried to shove him off with my left foot. I was now on my back while the lion took a huge bite into the calf area of my leg. The sensation was of having my leg tightened in a vice. This whole episode happened in seconds, and luckily for me Harry was taking pictures from the car with an automatic flash. The lion must have thought the flashes meant another shot was coming for it leaped away after the one bite (or was it the 'taste?'). I gathered myself together and hobbled back to the car. I worried about septicaemia, gangrene and loss of blood.

We used the herders' *shukas* to try to stop the flow of blood and Harry drove for base as quickly as possible. It was quite difficult in the pitch dark to find the way across country to the nearest road. There were several different opinions as to the right way. As it transpired Harry chose the right way and we arrived back at HQ within an hour. Once there Gilfrid and Brian administered first aid. First aid during my grandfather's time would have been a feather dipped in iodine and drawn through the wounds. We had the use of cattle antibiotics and proper dressings. However, I was still losing blood, and could no longer bend my leg. So Gilfrid decided we should fly to Mombasa, about a 40-minute flight in the dark. The moon was now up, so we removed the back and middle seats of the Cess 206, put down a mattress and arrived in Mombasa just before midnight. During the short flight Gilfrid arranged by radio for an ambulance. On arrival I was whisked to hospital and by midnight I was on the surgeon's table with blood transfusion and all the antibiotics required. It took ten days before I was released and much of that time I was suffering from 'kit-cat fever' in spite of all the antibiotics.

The airport would not let Gilfrid fly back that night but at dawn he took off and returned to the scene to finish off and collect the lion. While in hospital an old settler visited me and said I was lucky to have modern medicine. He recalled his early days on the farm when his mate had been chewed by a lion. It took three days by ox wagon to get the man to hospital in Nairobi. There he had his leg tied to the ceiling for a month while all the muck was drained and in the end the doctor still had to amputate his leg. I certainly appreciated the access to modern medicine. This saved my life.

When we were awarded the contract to develop and tame this huge tract of land, some 2,300 square miles or 1.5 million acres, Gilfrid and I could not believe we would ever have the luck to do just what our forebears had been able to do 50 years earlier. The difference being that we had modern machinery and aeroplanes and were able to travel in four-wheel-drive vehicles instead of ox wagons!

There were many obstacles and perhaps the two worst were snakes and malarial anopheles-bearing mosquitoes.

My daughter and son-in-law, the Henleys, managed the tourist enterprise as pointed out earlier. One day Henry took off to Nairobi to collect clients but went missing for two days. It transpired that on nearing Nairobi he became almost delirious with malaria and ran a temperature of 105 degrees. He just managed to drive himself into the Nairobi Hospital but it took two days before the news filtered down.

Henry came to me before they were married to shoot some elephant on Galana to gain experience for his Professional Hunter's licence. He dropped two elephant with single brain shots. Like his father, the longest ever operating Professional Hunter, he was an excellent shot. Unfortunately, by the time Henry had his licence the hunting ban was on and he had to revert to photographic safaris. Henry and Jessica built themselves a small house next to the hunting camp. They dug a well beside the river for clean fresh water. They had not dug too deep before the digger came up claiming that he had gone blind because of the confinement of the well. A second man was lowered then a third man, all coming up with the same complaint. Henry decided to investigate. A spitting cobra had taken up residence in the hole.

By then Jessica and Henry had two small children, Howard and Anikia. Anikia was named after a particularly attractive waterhole on Galana. The family had been away a couple of nights in Malindi. While away the house girl put all the bedding out to air on the lawn, but unbeknown to her a small spitting cobra took up residence in Howard's mattress cover. The first night back home Howard awoke in the middle of the night complaining that something had stung him on the head. Jessica went to look, the mosquito net was still well tucked in over him and there was nothing inside it. However, his complaints continued. Jessica could see no marks on his head but she got into bed with him to try and calm him. This did not work either, so he was removed to their bed.

Jessica and Henry became alarmed as Howard's pulse started to drop and his neck swelled. By now it was almost dawn and they still saw no marks on his head. Henry went to the bed and pulled it to pieces. The cobra dropped out of the lining. He killed it instantly then got onto the HF radio to the Flying Doctors in Nairobi. Within an hour-and-a-half, a plane arrived. Howard and his snake were flown to Gertrude's Garden Children's Hospital. They administered antibiotics saying it could not possibly have been the snake, as he would have died by this time. But three days later two little sceptic fang marks appeared on the top of Howard's head. With the pressure of Howard lying on the snake it must have struck him from outside the net, dispelling most of the venom onto the net.

One time we had John Russell doing a safari for us. He was in a fly camp and his people were sleeping on the ground, completely wrapped in blankets from tip of head to toes like cocoons. In the middle of the night one man felt a companion was joining him. He lifted his head, removed the blanket whereupon a cobra attached itself to his bottom lip. He grabbed the tail and pulled. His lip extended well beyond the norm, until the snake released itself and spat him in the eye. A friend administered urine, John dosed the eye with milk, and he was whisked away to hospital in Malindi where he quickly recovered.

Before the construction of the causeway we built a cable across the river and later a cable platform that could be drawn across with a tractor. Even when the causeway was built the cable car was useful if the river was too high. Terence Adamson, brother of the famous game warden George, was working with us. We had just erected the main steel cable. I was on the south bank of the river with a new tractor tyre that had to be hauled across to the north bank. The river was a raging torrent and unbeknown to me Terence hated water and could not swim. He must have been in his late sixties, but without a second thought he volunteered to walk the cable with his hands, bringing across the finer cable so we could attach it to the tyre. He hauled the tyre across running along pulley wheels attached to the main cable. He tied the cable to his waist then with a secure belt hooked himself onto a pulley wheel, giving instructions that if he could not make it the men were to haul him back.

He reached the centre of the river but the cable sagged more than he realised. He was unable to pull himself up the hill. He signalled to his men to pull him back. They pulled faster than his arms could move and he came unstuck from the pulley. He could hold himself no longer and crashed into the roaring torrent. I was actually filming the scene with an old 8mm camera. I dropped the camera instantly and ran along the bank as I saw his old hat rushing past me on top of the water. But there was no Terence underneath it. Luckily, he was still attached to the cable and he washed up on an island some 500 yards down stream. We organised a chain of people holding the cable that was now anchored to a tree on the bank, to get across to the island and bring him back to safety.

Thankfully, Terence didn't drown or get eaten by a crocodile. We lost both cattle and people to crocodiles. The Heath's cook one day decided to visit a friend on the south bank. He possibly had a drink or two that may have delayed his return, so he crossed after dark. He never made it. It took some three days to find him; he had been put under a bank by the crocodile. One arm was missing.

Terence was an interesting fellow. He came out to Kenya after the first war with his brother George. They came from India and both spent a lifetime in the bush. George of course is best known for his "Elsa – Born Free" lion story. However, Terence hated the lion and ended up being buried, next to Boy, the lion that had eaten their cook and nearly Terence on many occasions!

Terence may have visited Nairobi once or twice in his lifetime, but he never left the country. He had one suit, one tie and a 'best' pair of shoes. They were soldered up in an old four-gallon petrol tin and only came out for weddings and funerals. He hated bugs as well as lion. I remember he lived under a huge net which had to have an old tree stump in it too so he could scratch his back like an elephant. He would take on any job that was in the bush; surveying and cutting roads, even dowsing for water with a pendulum. If George could not find his lion, Terence would collect a piece of the lion's dung, place it on a map and use his pendulum to find the lion's location for George.

I remember a cattle manager asking for a budget to mend the roof of his house because it leaked. Gilfrid replied, "Why are you bothering about a few drops of water? When my father first came out here he lived under his wagon for months."

The manager answered, "Well, Gilfrid if you want to go back to the good old days, why don't you hitch up your wagon in Rumuruti to come down here instead of using that wretched aircraft?" I believe the manager got an allowance to mend his leaking roof.

When there was good rain and the waterholes were full we kept all the cattle in the north of the ranch. As the water dried up we would move them south to the permanent water and the river. One time the cattle were moving south and sleeping in makeshift bomas. One night Mohamed, one of the herders, awoke to strange sounds and a shadow over him. In a split second he realised a lion was standing over him and it had seized Abdi, who was lying next to him, by the throat. Mohamed managed to lunge at the animal, which released Abdi and actually took off. They contacted the cattle manager who called in the Flying Doctors and Abdi was flown to hospital in Nairobi. He recovered well and was about to be released from hospital when he suddenly died. It seems the minute he felt well, he took one look at his surroundings and just pined to death. He had never been without his cattle in the bush. An even sadder story followed. The next night the same lion returned. This time Mohamed lunged at it with his knife before it was on him. Unfortunately, his knife missed the lion and he pierced himself in the groin. He must have cut an artery for he bled to death in minutes. The lion was followed up and shot. It turned out to be a completely emaciated lioness with no teeth and the size of a large dog.

Sue Heath had been shooting birds in the vegetable garden one day and by mistake put the .22 rifle back in the safe loaded. When Brian next went to the safe he pulled the rifle out, the trigger caught on something and it went off shooting him through the chest. Martin Anderson was on the ranch at the time and flew him to hospital. Brian recovered as the small .22 bullet did not penetrate far and no vital organs were touched.

The Heath's gardener used to clean out and generally look after the swimming pool. One morning he was doing this work when a packet of cigarettes must have fallen out of his shirt pocket into the pool. As he stretched out to retrieve them he must have fallen in. No one else was around; he could not swim and drowned. Sometime later Jessica Henley went along for a swim in the pool and then went home. Nobody missed the gardener for some time until his body surfaced and was spotted by someone passing by. Brian contacted Jessica and asked her if she noticed anything strange whilst swimming? She said the water was rather murky and did notice a packet of cigarettes floating about but that was all.

Ken Sheldrick who worked for us at one time, had some guests staying one weekend. They were unaccustomed to the causeway which had a 'dog's leg' in the middle and the water was running quite high at the time, so they left their car on the south bank and Ken took them home. On the Sunday evening the water was too high over the causeway to drive across but Ken suggested they could walk over. This exercise was accomplished fairly easily with Ken leading the way. He chatted for a while until they departed. As he turned to recross, he noticed that the water was considerably higher and rising. However, he still believed he could make it so started crossing. On reaching the dog's leg he was feeling his way when he slipped and fell. Luckily, he managed to grab onto something solid but was unable

Huge ivory collected from dead & poached elephant on Tsavo & Galana by David Sheldrick

to get a foothold to stand up again. The current was far too strong to swim and it was all he could do to keep his head above water. He thought he was a goner when some workers walking past spotted him. They were carrying a rope they had been working with. None could get close enough to hand him the rope. They tried throwing an end across to him, but each time the current took it away. This continued for some time until Ken made a desperate last plunge at the disappearing rope end. By pure luck and brute strength he managed to get a hold while he was hauled to safety.

The waterhole at Dera

In the far eastern corner of the Ranch there was a very picturesque waterhole called Dera. It was very remote and difficult to get to. In fact, it was easier to approach off the Garsen road north of Malindi. Myles Burton lived and ran safaris out of Malindi so I suggested he might like to use it. This was agreed upon, but unfortunately Myles was killed shortly afterwards in a light aircraft crash. In the meantime we decided to put in an airstrip and build a small tree house. Elephant would come through in droves. I remember spending a night there. It was incredible, as herd after herd came to the water, all night long. The pure delight and noise of those elephant trumpeting continued for hours.

First we put in an airstrip but the bush was thick, the ground very uneven and it was very sandy. We decided it was only serviceable for a Super Cub or Cess 180. I remember it was Friday the 13th when I first flew in. I am not usually superstitious, but I thought of it that day when I landed and stopped dead. On trying to taxi or turn around the aircraft would not budge, even with full power. It was a stinking hot day and I was alone. I dug and dug. I cut and put down brush after jacking up each wheel in turn. By late afternoon I got the plane to the end of the strip and turned around. I gave it full power, but she would hardly move. I pushed the nose forward to get the tail wheel off and as she moved I pulled her off to much screaming of the stall warning. Once airborne I eased down with the nose to gain speed. I hit the ground probably twice before bouncing high enough to gain sufficient speed to clear the bushes and trees. But the 180 did it and I was away.

Building the tree house was a challenge. We managed to get all the materials on site but could find no builders who would stay there. They all claimed that the place was spooked. I brought down a dozen Kikuyu from upcountry, who were delighted to have the work. I got them all on site together with provisions to last at least three weeks and said I would be back within ten days. A week later I went back but there was nobody there. Not a sign. Neither the safari groups nor the cattle people had seen or heard from anyone. We put trackers onto their spoor and searched from the air. We also alerted all the cattle bomas and had them search for footprints while out with their cattle. Some days later two of these bomas came across six of them and a day later another boma found the others. All were in a bad state of dehydration but they survived. All they wanted was to get back home. They said the place was spooked and they could stand it no longer. They started to follow the road out and then half of them decided to take a short cut. They split up but both parties got lost. Luckily, they came onto fresh cattle tracks so realised there must be bomas nearby. By this time they could hardly walk another yard, so they were lucky to be found.

The 1,800 cattle that Gilfrid had brought down from Luoniek were a total herd of cows for ranch breeding with bulls and their progeny. But for a quicker return we decided to use part of the ranch for store steers and we arranged with the local livestock officer, Hector Douglas, for us to purchase a mob of Somali steers way up on the Tana River. Gilfrid went up to make the purchase and a price was agreed on some 2000 animals. The deal included trekking them down to Galana. However, once the purchase had been made, news reached Gilfrid that all the cattle were assembled on the north bank of the river awaiting collection. In a fury Gilfrid went up to find all the cattle settled with the Somalis sitting 'on their bums.' When Gilfrid insisted the deal included delivery to Galana, the Somalis said they would take them but they required a further 200/- each. Not to be outdone, Gilfrid said, "Stuff the extra money," and returned to Malindi. He gathered up some 30 Giriama people to take the cattle over and started the march to Galana.

The scene soon turned into pandemonium with not a single animal wanting to cross the river. The whole morning was used in chasing the animals hither and thither while the Somalis sat on their hunkers laughing their heads off. So Gilfrid had no option but to send the Giriama home and make a deal with the owners. The leader, Mohamed, single-handedly talked and sang to the cattle using their names and remarkably they all calmly crossed the river. Eventually, Mohamed became a permanent staff member and was the one who drove his own knife into his loin while being attacked by a lion in the story told previously.

Taita Ranch

When the government forced us to cease operations on Galana Ranch, we were not certain if we had received a fair price by the government from the proceeds of Galana. So we put aside a breeding herd and a few tractors and implements to Marty's and my account.

We had the opportunity to take over the lease of Taita Ranch, a 90-thousand-acre wild bit of land to the south almost reaching to the Tanzania border.

The Taita Ranch Company was made up of a group of Taita people under the chairmanship of Mr Musamuli. Musamuli gave himself the majority of shares, while the Agricultural Finance Corporation (AFC) loaned them a large sum of money for development and purchase of stock to be paid back over 20 years. After five years the company went broke and neither the interest or capital instalments had been paid. The shareholders were up in arms, Musamuli was sacked and the District Commissioner elected an interim Chairman, Mr Walele, to sort out the mess. They were given six months to do this before the AFC foreclosed and put the Taita Ranch up for auction. We negotiated with all these three factions. A legal document was drafted whereby we, as the Galana Cattle Company, would pay off the arrears and take on the 15 years remaining on the loan with a 15-year lease on the land. I insisted we would only do this if we could purchase over 25 % of the shares with a seat on the board. The company put a rule in place that any member could only have a maximum of 200 shares, so we had to find six Kenya citizens to be member shareholders. We did this so our share money together with a further loan from Galana Cattle paid off all the arrears owing to the AFC and we started out on our 15-year lease.

Terrence Hopkins, our Galana Cattle manager took on the management of Taita Ranch, while David Taylor made the water developments on contract. We relied entirely on dams and piped water from the Mzima Springs, the water pipe supplying Mombasa. Marty put up a loan to purchase some steers. Terrence and I made an epic purchase of 8000 steers from our Orma friends to the north of Galana, all of which eventually arrived on Taita. With a full stock we nearly came badly unstuck when we had a drought year and all the dams dried up. A break in the main pipeline meant we had three days to move 8000 head of cattle to water nearly 100 miles away or bring in water bowsers. Luckily, the heavens opened and we were saved.

Like Galana, Taita Ranch was overstocked with lion and we had many interesting hunts tracking down these cattle killers. Strong bush bomas were constructed and guarded at night to protect the cattle. The lion started ambushing cattle coming down to drink at the dams. One day a whole herd smelled the lion and took off, not stopping until they reached Tanzania. We followed them up by air directing Terence below, who followed the spoor by vehicle. As we realised he would be away for at least three days, we packed up some food in a sleeping bag and dropped the package out of the aircraft window for Terence to collect. We watched as he retrieved the bundle, but unbeknown to us all the tins burst in the sleeping bag on impact. However, he scooped the food out and had a sticky night's sleep in the bag.

When we first took over, poaching for bush meat was at its height and many bush lines full of snares had been constructed. Large gangs of poachers drove many animals into these hidden snares and hundred of animals were regularly butchered. At night poachers on bicycles with whistles and strong torches easily forced dikdik into the snares. One night I caught a culprit with 14 dikdik tied to the back of his bicycle. Besides the depletion of wildlife, lorry loads of charcoal were carried out every day – an estimated 4000 bags a month going to Mombasa from this area.

To counter this problem we set up a permanent and mobile team of anti-poaching askaris. This was aided by funds from the Eden Wildlife Trust and run on a voluntary basis by Marc Gross between his leaving school and going to university. Marc's father, Ted, managed the Eden Trust and when he died after being trodden on by an elephant during a darting operation, Marc came to me as an 'adopted grandson.' To begin with Marc joined our bongo surveillance teams to assess how many of this rare and critically endangered species remained in the Aberdare forest.

When we started managing Taita Ranch, Marc put the anti-poaching team together, camping, training and operating with them in the field. This was most successful and virtually put a stop to the poaching and charcoal burning. Within five or six years herds of elephant, buffalo, oryx, eland, lesser kudu and gerenuk made a come back, while hundreds of dikdik were seen daily.

We started off by paying some 3 shillings per cubic metre for the piped water, but when the price rose to 40 shillings and later 100 shillings, cattle ranching became no longer viable. We sold most of the cattle to repay Marty's loan and concentrated on building a tourist camp. We hired this out to a tourist company, Ornithological Safaris, who developed a three-year contract with Earthwatch. The Earthwatch participants carried out a continuous three-year study on one of the lion prides on Taita.

We had a small camp for ourselves, including Terrence's house, where we would stay on monthly visits. We constructed a permanent water hole just in front of this. After several years of strong anti-poaching measures, hundreds of elephant, buffalo and other wildlife came in droves to quench their thirst in the dry weather. They were completely oblivious to us watching this spectacle, sitting by a campfire barely 20 paces away. On one occasion when several hundred buffalo arrived at the waterhole, three lions made a spectacular kill 'on the spot.' The stampeding animals almost ran over us. Subsequently, we made a stone barrier to deter them from coming into the camp.

The British Army Engineers volunteered as part of their training and exercises to help with road building, airstrip construction, and the construction of school buildings. We just had to pay for the materials. They helped build a school on the Taita boundary. Much to our surprise the materials for the roof far exceeded any cost we had expected. We subsequently discovered the timber used on the roof was built to British Army standard – it could withhold ten tonnes of snow. As Taita is mainly a desert type terrain with minimum rainfall, it did not really seem significant but standards are standards!

Daphne Sheldrick gave us a small herd of semi-tame buffalo to look after. We kept them at a boma at the ranch headquarters

The camp on Taita Ranch.

and a herdsman led them around during the day. Soon herds of wild buffalo came in every day and we tried to integrate them. A few of our females bred with a wild buffalo, but they always returned to their paddock every evening and were religiously gated in. We insisted they should be left out, but this did not happen until one evening when a young male refused to be shut in. It battled and killed his herder. After that we left the buffalo to their own devices, but they all continued to live around the camp.

One day a male buffalo calf was brought in to join our little herd. He had been found when really young and brought up in the education centre on a neighbouring ranch, where he lived and slept in the tents with the young pupils. However, when he became somewhat larger, they decided he should live with our herd. But Tyson, as the young buffalo was called, didn't like the idea and decided to live in our camp. Terrence Hopkins, our manager, barred Tyson from entering the tents, but he still insisted on sleeping between the tents and bathrooms. Tyson grew larger and larger and had massive horns. We hoped he would go off with a wild herd, but he preferred our camp.

Sometimes he would come up to us wanting to play while we sat around the campfire. We would dart off to the mess tent while he picked up the chairs around the fire and bashed them to pieces. When these games became too consistent and guests and wives could not enter the bathroom, we decided we'd have to put Tyson down before someone else was killed. I was all prepared one day to put a bullet in his head. He wandered up and laid his head on the stone wall in front of the mess. I walked up to him, but I found I couldn't shoot him in cold blood. Instead I stroked his nose until he almost purred with delight.

The only solution was to have KWS dart and remove Tyson to Tsavo National Park in the north where there were no lodges. This was successfully accomplished, but Tyson was miserable. He slowly tried to make his way home and stopped at a tourist camp along the way. KWS darted him again, but this time he never came out of the anaesthetic.

At the ranch headquarters we had a large stone dam that we kept full as a reservoir. The baboons kept messing up this water so Terrence

Michael Prettejohn

decided to put in a couple of crocodile to keep the baboon away. He also thought this would be an attraction for the tourists and a place to dispose of dead calves and other animals, giving the crocs something to feed on.

One hot afternoon I was there taking a nap after lunch when a runner came into camp with the news that someone had been badly bitten by one of the crocodiles. An Italian visitor had been showing off to some pretty girls seeing how close he could get to the serpents. One of the crocodiles struck, thinking he was being fed, and held onto the man's foot. The girls grabbed him and pulled back. Others joined and pulled the man in and beat off the croc, but his foot was badly lacerated. I sent word to our doctor in Malindi and flew the man in. He had to be flown later to Europe where they amputated his toe. The man then had the cheek to sue us but without success.

When Marc moved on to university, our very able headman Makala, a local Taita, carried on overseeing the anti-poaching team as well as watching over the cattle under Terrence. The team was instructed never to patrol with less than four persons with two firearms. But one day two of the askaris patrolled with no weapons except for spears and pangas. These two came across a poacher's tracks following elephant spoor. In the sand they found hidden a series of poisoned arrowheads embedded in blocks of wood placed for the elephant to tread on them and suffer a long and painful death. Nobody knows the full details, but our two men went missing. They must have been ambushed by the poachers for both were found several days later having been killed by poisoned arrow wounds, with their bodies horribly mutilated and hidden under the bushes. Even with extensive investigations by the police and administration, the culprits were never caught.

After 12 years of managing Taita Ranch from 1990 to 2002

Second murdered ranger on Taita Ranch.

we had generated enough funds to pay off the AFC loan in full, but as the interest on the loan was most favourable, I suggested we keep the loan and make a payment to the shareholders. However, Musamuli and Walele thought otherwise and withdrew the funds to pay off the loan. Having done this and cleared the ranch's commitment to the AFC, they declared they wanted to take over the ranch themselves and we were no longer required! However, we had a valid lease for 15 years and we were determined to complete our term.

The tourist camp had now been taken over and completely renovated by Mike Kirkland of Southern Cross Safaris, who had a booming tourist trade operating from the coast and bringing in a lot of income. We completed the next three years to complete our 15-year lease. Then we put forward a plan for a further term lease involving Mike Kirkland's group with shares in the company.

In the meantime court cases raged between Musamuli and Walele. Musamuli claimed he, and not Walele, was the legal chairman and all our shares were null and void and his 50% shareholding stood. Walele won the case and returned all the money for our shares. He suggested we now reapply and include Southern Cross as a shareholder and to arrange a long-term lease on a new contract. However, when we were negotiating on this, Musamuli got the support and a great deal of money from a Somali group and the court nullified Walele's court decision in favour of Musamuli. Walele asked us for money to fight his case in court again, but with Somali threats to our livelihood and the influx of uncontrollable Somali cattle, we decided there was no point in continuing. With many Somali bomas springing up in the area, grass fires raged. We had to defend our headman Makala in court when the Somalis accused him of starting the fires when he had been the one trying to put them out. Kirkland received a threat and a demand for huge sums of money from Musamuli for building and operating his business without his permission.

We decided to bale out, as did Kirkland. The area reverted to charcoal burning and serious poaching, undoing all we had accomplished over 15 years. We salvaged some kit and equipment including pumps and engines, but much was lost. It was sad to see the same destruction as we'd seen after we'd been forced out of Galana. Once again a wonderful 15 years can be remembered, but it is now too horrific for words to witness the destruction of the habitat to charcoal and the mass killing of elephant and all the other animals for bush meat. We retired to base and hope the next generation and a new government will be able to revive both ranching schemes.

Chapter 30

RETURN TO CONSERVATION
AND TO CONSERVANCY

With our departure from Galana and Taita Ranches we decided it was time to settle down and consolidate at home on Sangare. This location continues to have the most beautiful views to be found anywhere in the world. It is a most tranquil setting with wild deep gorges and flowing, winding rivers. The lake attracts a numerous variety of birds, while on the plains and in the forests the wildlife is still plentiful. My greatest pleasure is to see from my home Mount Kenya to the east in all its glory, majestic and snow-capped. The Aberdares to the west, are continuously changing colours, first wrapped in a golden light and then shades of soft violet and pale rose, as the sun sets for another day.

Times have changed as Kenya's population has increased since independence by some 32 million people. Over the years the surrounding forests and wildlife have been decreasing at an alarming rate and with thousands of people short of work, it was time to make changes.

A life-changing situation occurred in 2004 that made us all take stock of our lives and our plans for the future.

Diane had just returned from England and that evening while sitting at home watching television and having supper on trays by the fire the cook Joseph appeared and said, "These people with me wish to talk with you."

I replied, "Tell them it is Sunday and we won't see them at this time of the evening." At that moment, I looked around to see four very rough, hard looking thugs, one with a knife to the cook's throat while the other three surrounded me with knives and pangas (long knives) demanding money and guns. Luckily, Diane had just disappeared into the bedroom, so I had only myself to defend. They pointed a pistol at my face to reinforce their demands. As I peered down the barrel I could see it was rusty, so I hoped the gun did not work or they had no ammunition. I thought as in a game of chess the best form of defence is to attack. So I jumped out of the chair with the supper tray in front of me and I shouted at the top of my voice, "Get the hell out of here," at the same time lunging at the fellow with the pistol. I thought if he actually fired it, the tray might just deflect the shot. No shot was fired, but the fellow didn't expect my plunge and jumped back. The fellow behind took a swipe at my head with a panga. As there was a table between him and my chair, it was a long reach and only the tip of the panga made a nasty cut across the back of my head, without breaking my skull. As I swung around to face this man, he grabbed the family sword from a shelf nearby and shoved it into my abdomen, just missing my heart and any other vital organs. The man with a knife at the cook's throat then tried to plunge his double-edged knife into me. Holding my sword wound with one hand, I grabbed his knife with the other, which nearly severed my thumb. Unfortunately, I had no help from the cook who stood there paralysed with fright. Diane in the next room heard the racket and thought a leopard had come in for the dogs (all of whom luckily had bolted into the garden).

On observing the chaos and me, covered in blood from head to foot, she told the men to go with her and she would give them all the money she had. In the meantime the night watchman had rushed down to Gideon the headman, telling him to come to the house as the bwana and memsahib were having a bitter row. Gideon gathered his men and came round to the back of the house and peeped through the window. He soon worked out what was going on. His first thought was to turn out all the lights to distract the intruders.

In the meantime Diane tried to buy time and said she had to find her keys for the money. They tried to stop me following, but I said she would need my help to find the keys. I told them I could not give them any firearms as I'd recently been in Nairobi to collect Diane, so I had deposited them in the Mweiga Police station. This was not true and I wanted to get to my gun safe while Diane was busy dishing out the money. Then the lights went out. The gangsters heard the voices of other people and realised we had support, but in the darkness with so much noise they could not judge how many people had come to help. They decided to 'hoof it' and took what they could fit in their pockets. This gave me time to open the gun safe to extract my revolver with the light of a torch. I tried to go after them, but with the loss of blood I could not make it and fell to the floor. Diane made radio contact with a neighbour to organise the doctor in Nyeri urgently.

Bundling me into the car with the support of our driver we drove straight for Nyeri. There the doctor saved my life and kept me awake until I had managed to recoup my blood count. He put me into the Outspan Hospital in Nyeri, where the surgeon opened me up to be sure there was no internal injury, and to sew up the wounds.

Back at home the staff set about following tracks while word was sent to my son Giles and Gilfrid, our Galana partner, who flew in tracker dogs at first light the following morning. Giles followed with the police and the dogs, retrieving bits and pieces along the way, some English money, watches and a knife. Reaching the village of Chaka, eleven kilometres away, the dogs pointed to a specific hut and although it was empty, the two culprits were later caught and convicted in due course. Over the next week the other two were tracked to their respective houses and the local chief caught them by sending a message to each to come to his office to collect some money deposited for them. Both fell for this and were interned. These two were identified by our staff as being the main culprits and after months of court proceedings they were jailed for life.

And so ended probably the worst drama of my life, but the outcome could never have been achieved without the loyal support of our staff and local community, hundreds of whom came to visit while I was ten days recuperating in the Nyeri Hospital.

Once I had recovered, I decided it was time to make a longer term plan. I was determined to keep this 'little corner' of Africa as pristine as God had made it. To do this we had to demonstrate that wild animals could be of commercial benefit and that not only the grass but also the bushes had to be a valuable food asset for browsers. The trees not only brought rain but protected the rivers and could be used on a sustainable basis for firewood.

We had to work out a plan for full utilisation while preserving the environment. Thus we had an environmental impact study made by government experts who produced a study document based on our development plans. Once accepted this gave us the right to form a legal conservancy, which we hope will last for eternity. This plan had to be accepted by prominent members of the community on our boundaries, together with various agencies such as the forest and wildlife departments of the government. For the latter to accept we had to produce a biomass study of domestic and wildlife sustainable numbers, listing all existing browsers and grazers, water availability and the names of indigenous trees and shrubs. It was an interesting exercise showing that the Sangare land actually supports over 300 types of birds, 49 different types of trees and shrubs and 43 mammalia. In order to utilise the wildlife we set up a tourist camp on a long lease with a monthly rent and with clients paying a conservancy fee. For a greater spread of ownership, for we could not perceive owning so much land in Kikuyu country where land is divided into half-acre plots, we have allotted a set number of five-acre house sites, built not to be intrusive and with purchasers having shares and traversal rights on the whole property. By preserving the environment we are able to demonstrate to the community and school wildlife clubs the benefits of this by having educational visits.

We hope as the Sangare Conservancy develops we can continue via the house sites and tourism to offer local employment and career opportunities, too. At the time of writing this book, we estimate at Sangare we are supporting over 400 local people and children. The tented camp at Sangare is attracting travellers from around the world. Even more important many local people are staying and enjoying the wildlife and peace the lake offers. A local company now runs this part of the project.

Another major project that consumes my life now and is my 'passion' is the conservation of the critically endangered antelope, the Kenyan mountain bongo. The animal is endemic to the mountains of Kenya with most of the few remaining bongo being not far from Sangare on both Mount Kenya and the Aberdares.

In 2003 John Mahanga, the senior Warden of the Aberdare National Park, asked me if I knew why the bongo of the Aberdares had become extinct because no sightings had been recorded since late 1988. There had been sightings during the 1970s and 1980s at the Ark Lodge, deep in the Aberdare forest. I suggested that perhaps it was due to excessive intrusion, the degradation of the forest, as well as the escalating poaching incidents with dogs that drive such animals as bongo into the more inaccessible areas of the forest and deep gorges. Once grazing of domestic stock was allowed in the forest, diseases such as rinderpest also spread to the cloven hoofed wild animals and no doubt this was a further cause of the bongo's disappearance.

"If we can find the finance, would you be prepared to probe such areas to ascertain if any bongo are actually remaining?" the warden asked me. I agreed, little realising it would turn into such a long-term commitment.

Most of my old trackers by this time had passed on, but I found one man, Peter Mwangi, who had made a contract with several animal capture units collecting for overseas zoos in the 1970s. In those days Peter had a gang of 60 men who built holding pens in the bamboo and dug hidden pits on the game paths to catch bongo who walked over them. Over a period of a year or so they captured about 50 bongo this way. Once they had been semi-tamed in the holding pens, they were led into boxes one at a time and carried out of the forest. There are no exact records, but probably only 50% of the bongo captured in this operation actually survived.

These animals were despatched to Europe and America in the 1970s and have been carefully bred with the aid of the bongo stud book to ensure genetic stability. The number in captivity is over 500,

but our research unfortunately shows that less than 100 of these fine animals survive in the wild. It is our long-term vision to return some of these captive bongo to the wild.

The Bongo Surveillance Project (BSP) was formed in 2004. Peter Mwangi engaged a number of tough men, poachers and honey hunters who know bongo and their habits, and over the last seven years they have probed all the known bongo haunts. With financing from various individuals and grants we set about purchasing forest clothing, light tents and equipment.

Here's a description of a typical surveillance trip. With an established team of some 15 - 20 men, we break up into groups of four to probe the various bongo areas. Four of us with pup tents, a change of warm clothing and dry shoes and with what rations we can carry, set off on foot into the forest following the game trails. Two of us carry rifles for protection against buffalo or elephant that may come towards us down the same trail. This often happens and usually we can divert to miss a collision. Very seldom, and usually in low thick bamboo when we disturb a sleeping bull buffalo, a shot may

Laban and Stanley with author at BSP base camp in the south west Mau Forest.

Bongo photographed by author's cousin, Rob Prettejohn, in the Aberdares from a camera hide maintained by the Bongo Surveillance Project.

have to be fired, but we have never yet had to kill an animal due to the sharp hearing and instincts of these trackers.

We proceed up and down the slippery trails, bending low through the bamboo, silent and utterly alert. Eyes are on the trail for bongo spoor, looking up occasionally to probe ahead. Often when doing this a whippy bamboo shoot slaps you across the face or you put a foot into an elephant footprint full of water - soaking your shoe or filling the gumboot, which the men usually wear. We stop for a while to take a drink and a bite of food.

By evening, or if it starts to rain, we set up our tents around a large cedar or podo tree for protection, gather some wood and light a fire by a large dead tree trunk that burns slowly all night giving out some warmth. Wet clothes and boots are placed on sticks to dry out. Cooking a meal with lots of sweet hot tea, yarns are told of near misses down the trail until, after much laughter over a member's mishap, it is time to crawl into your sleeping bag, hoping a tree doesn't fall on you or an elephant step on you while you sleep.

In the morning we pack up the kit and with haversacks full weighing some 40 pounds apiece we set off again deeper into the forest, making sure the campfire is completely extinguished before leaving. Soon we come across plants that have been browsed. The height of the browsing determines if it is bongo, not bushbuck. We scout around and sure enough there are bongo tracks. We confirm the tracks are probably two days old. We follow them down to a stream where we decide to make camp.

Leaving a member to guard and set up camp, three of us continue tracking. Soon we find last night's bongo dung. A finger prodded into the dung ascertains that it is cold and therefore more than six hours old. Samples of the mucus are taken carefully from untouched piles and placed in containers with absolute alcohol for future DNA testing. From this camp two to three days are spent scouting the area further. When we find an area where bongo are regularly crisscrossing, we set up a trap camera. Bongo move little during the day, moving and browsing late in the night to dawn. Coordinates are taken with a GPS of the samples and camera positions for future mapping and to return for monitoring in two week's time. If no bongo are captured on camera over three months, the camera (if it has not been destroyed by elephant) is moved to another site until such time as photos are taken of bongo on a regular basis. These cameras are set to take a picture every 30 seconds over the 24 hours. There may be some 1000 pictures taken over the two weeks, but these mostly of elephant, buffalo, bushbuck, giant forest hog, leopard and monkeys. There may be a dozen bongo photos showing up to five different individuals, which are kept for monitoring.

By now rations are getting low. We contact base by mobile phone (or satellite telephone if there is no signal) for further rations to be brought in to the coordinate position supplied. Other team members and porters bring in these rations as ordered. (Sometimes, if funds are available and a landing site can be found nearby, we can call in a helicopter to drop off rations and spare our personnel the long hike.) With rations now in place, the porters and surveillance members stay overnight before returning the following morning, while the team of four continue deeper into the forest. Sometimes a member or two is replaced if for some reason they are unfit to continue.

And so in this way we cover all the possible bongo areas of the Kenya mountains. Now after surveillance continuing over the last seven years we have a pretty good idea in which areas to keep constant monitoring.

At the early stage of our surveillance visible signs through browsing and spoor confirmed that bongo still existed in small pockets, deep in the Aberdare forests. However, it was not until the advent of trap cameras and the collection of the dung mucus from fresh dung that it was proved to be bongo by DNA processing and that it could be confirmed to the general public.

Slowly we gathered photographs from the trap cameras and managed to have some 300 dung samples processed at Cardiff University for DNA. Without specific bongo 'markers' the samples could only identify whether the dung came from bongo or some other animals. A good 90% of the samples proved to be bongo, but the total of individuals could not be determined as many samples could have come from the same animal. It was, however, found that all had generated from two female lines, so most of the remaining bongo in the Abderdares are likely to be somewhat inbred.

The bongo surveillance team acquired Global Monitoring Systems (the GPS) and we mapped each surveillance recce and can monitor exactly the areas where bongo live. The mountain bongo has only been known to exist in recent history on the mountains of Kenya, basically the Aberdares, Mount Kenya, the Mau, Londiani crater, Eburru, and the Cherenganis. The BSP has to date probed all these areas to find that there may be only 100 animals surviving in the wild and these in very small pockets on southwest Mount Kenya, Eburru, the southwest Mau Forest and in three locations spread across the Eastern Aberdares.

However, there are still areas where bongo could be brought in while existing herds must be increased if they are to survive in the long term. At present it is estimated by scientists that unless intervention occurs, bongo could be extinct in the wild in 20 years. To reintroduce bongo we have to be sure that compatible genetic animals are introduced, and this can only be done with a full understanding of the DNA using specific bongo markers. These have now been produced in the USA and various universities have agreed to undertake the work. Results should give us full details of individual animals in all the above-mentioned areas, as well as all of those in captivity. This information also will give more accurate density figures. As to exactly how we introduce new animals, this will have to be a long-term operation with consideration of disease immunity, besides ensuring the genetic variety.

At least the government is now aware of the bongo situation and a 50-year plan for its survival is in the process of being implemented, depending on the ongoing BSP findings. The IUCN have listed the mountain bongo as a critically endangered species and it has been included on their 'Red List.'

We soon realised that no recovery plan could be implemented without the support of the communities on the forest edge of existing and future bongo habitats. The BSP decided the best way to communicate and motivate these communities was through the school children. Thus, the Bongo Wildlife Clubs were formed and today 13 school clubs are registered with the BSP. The schools participating were all chosen due to their proximity to the remaining bongo groups. The pupils learn about the importance of saving the environment

Another photo of an elusive bongo.

under the flagship of the bongo. Our outreach over the last five years we estimate at 10,000 people. We have had some really interesting days, taking the pupils and teachers to the National Parks, Mount Kenya William Holden Education Centre and Sangare Conservancy. In many cases these communities have never had the opportunity to visit these locations or see wildlife before. Through new technology we have had the

Baby bongo photographed at the camera hide.

chance to offer solar lamps, improved cookers (jiko), sustainable wood collection, and water conservation. All these things help preserve the environment as well as giving an improved way of life.

My inspiration to continue this vital work, as long as we can secure funding, is the regular evidence of photographs by the camera traps of the existence of these beautiful antelopes. Also, I know that taking young students into National Parks for a day's outing and activities in the schools could potentially make a difference to the future of this country and to a critically endangered species.

I have been so fortunate to have enjoyed such a varied life and I hope to continue sharing good times and experiences. I am as motivated now to learn as I ever was – and I feel 45 years not 79 years. In fact, as I looked at the bright planet to the right of Mount Kenya's peak the other evening, I wondered what it would be like to explore these new horizons, beyond this world. I guess I am forever the adventurer and explorer!

Appendix

Prettejohn Family Tree and Family Properties in Wales

Beyond two, at the most three, proceeding generations, family trees become ever more convoluted. We have included a short version of our family tree in this book, but the real tree is much more involved. In Wales, particularly, where the same few family names keep cropping up and where county families tended to marry amongst each other within the short distances covered by carriage, it is difficult to keep track. This may be of little interest perhaps to anyone outside one's own family, but I mention it here by way of plaiting together the loose strands of an inheritance before these were severed by Jock and my grandmother and which affected my father and, to a lesser degree, my own generation.

Of the many Gwynne properties that came and went over the generations, the four that affected father were Llanelwedd Hall on the river Wye where he was born, Trewarren House, Heathfield, and 'the Bungalow'. To move her family closer to her mother in Pembrokeshire, my grandmother Gwen bought Heathfield in 1911. Heathfield was typical of the many large, rambling country houses with too many bedrooms and too few bathrooms. Dick and father spent many idyllic holidays there from Wellington hunting and shooting, and later expanding their sporting activities as teenagers over an adjoining estate, Jordanstan. Both estates were later sold to raise money for Jock and Larmudiac.

The Bungalow is the house I remember best for it is where Aunt G (Aunt Gwynedd) lived out her days, a spinster, and was my and my brothers' home abroad in the early 1950s whilst we were at college. Built of wood and stone, this large rambling house, whose veranda sat perched almost directly above the sea wall, was often the focal point for extended visits by family and friends and their children.

Llanelwedd came into the family at the turn of the 18th Century when a male Gwyn married an heiress, Mary Gwynne of Garth, from which time the Gwyn line added the 'ne'. This male line continued for the next hundred years or so through a series of elder sons named Marmaduke until the mid-1800s when the estate succeeded to a younger son, Howel Gwynne, whose older brother was deemed at the time an unworthy successor because he had an affair with the household cook with whom he sired illegitimate and only later legitimate children. The property was left to him entailed in the event that he had no children, which he did not, and therefore passed back on his death in 1907, through the Gwynne line, to the eldest male child of his sister, Anne. All that was not entailed, however, Howel left to his niece, Anne Jane Warren Davis, and her only daughter, my grandmother, in trust for her children: father, Uncle Dick and Aunt Gwynne.

It was with that sister's marriage from which my direct line on the female side descends. Anne Howel Gwynne married a surgeon with the 6th Dragoon Guards serving in India whose surname was Howell, with two 'l's'. Howel, with one 'l', had been a given Gwynne male name since the 1400s. It was their youngest son, Thomas, who also practised medicine in India, and who died there, who was my great grandfather. He married Anne Jane Warren Davis from the large Trewarren Estate at St Ishmaels.

At about the time that the Gwynne line veered off centre in the mid-1800s, three young women of property, the Warrens, married a Kensington, a Davis and a Harries, adding the Warren name to that of the last two. Kensington, a peer, remained Kensington. To add confusion, the now double names Warren Davis and Warren Harries would thereafter be both linked to the Gwynnes and to Jock. Coincidentally, the childless Howel Gwynne, the last of the Gwynnes to live at Llanelwedd Hall, married a Warren Harries. Now a grandson of that first Harries marriage to a propertied Warren lady, Sam Harries of Hilton, married Rose Warren Davis, my great grandmother's sister. Thus Jock, their son, had the dual role in my life of uncle and stepfather.

Prettejohn Family of Barbados

Catherine Worsham
b. 1717 d. August 25th 1769

m = The Hon Richard Worsham

Charlotte Worsham   m =   John Prettejohn
b. 1740 (?)   b. 29th October 1731
                 d. 29th June 1803

John Prettejohn
b. 1766(?)
m = 1803(?)
wife dies 12th November 1836

John William Frederick Prettejohn
b. 1804
Ensign
d. 13th or 30th May 1827 at Kilkenny
not married

Richard Buckley Prettejohn
b. 1811
Lieut. General
m = Bertha Amy Smith - 10.9.1873
at Bangalore
d. 4.1.1891 at Exmouth Devon

Charles Prettejohn
b. 1813
d. 1893
m = Mary Chadbolt of Tottenham
Constant Estate Barbados
Daughter who died a spinster

Charles Buckley Prettejohn
b. 6.10.1874
m = Helen C Warral 31.10.1899
no children

Richard Buckley Prettejohn
b. 6.5.1877 at Exmouth Devon
d. 1953 (?)
m = Gwendolin Alice Gwynne-Howell
1. m = Gwendolin Alice Gwynne-Howell
2. m = Margret Besages

Ernest Lydston Prettejohn
b. 17.9.1878
d. 6.5.1881

Hugh Edward Prettejohn
b. 7.10.1879 at Exmouth
m = Eudoxie
no children

Richard Hugh Gwynne Prettejohn
b. 1901
d. 1971 in Kenya
m = Vivienne LeSeuer Green 1923
d. 1960 in Kenya
no children

Howel Gwynne Prettejohn
b. 9.11.1903 at Llanellwydd Hall
Builth Wells
m = Constance Catherine Trevor
7.5.1930 in London

Gwynedd Eleanor G. Prettejohn
Birtha Gwynne d. 1912
twins born 1908
not married

Hugh Maitland Prettejohn
b. 10.2.1924
m = Birdie Seton Gordan 1945

Michael Gwynne Prettejohn
b. 8.9.1932
1. m = Gillian Rutherford 1955
d. 1973
2. m = Jane Hook (nee Budgeon) 1974
3. m = Diane Wilson

Richard Gwynne Prettejohn
b. 1.2.1935
m = Susan Alixanrine Anderson - 24.1.1959

Howel Timothy James Gwynne Prettejohn
b. 26.12.1941
m = Anne Ruth Wylde - 8.1.1966

Jessica Gwynne
b.

Giles Gwynne
b. 23.12.1957

Vivien Gwynne
b. 28.4.1963

Gerald Gwynne
b. 5.1.1960

Edward Gwynne
b. 13.8.1962

Charles Gwynne
b. 18.6.1964

Louise Vivienne Venn
b. 14.11.1967

Hugh Ronalde Gwynne
b. 22.7.1969

Sarah Anne Gwynne
b. 30.11.1973

VIRTUS
ASTRA
(coat of arms)